The BP Guide to
EXPLORING
BRITAIN'S
WILDLIFE

Walks Through The Best Wildlife Areas

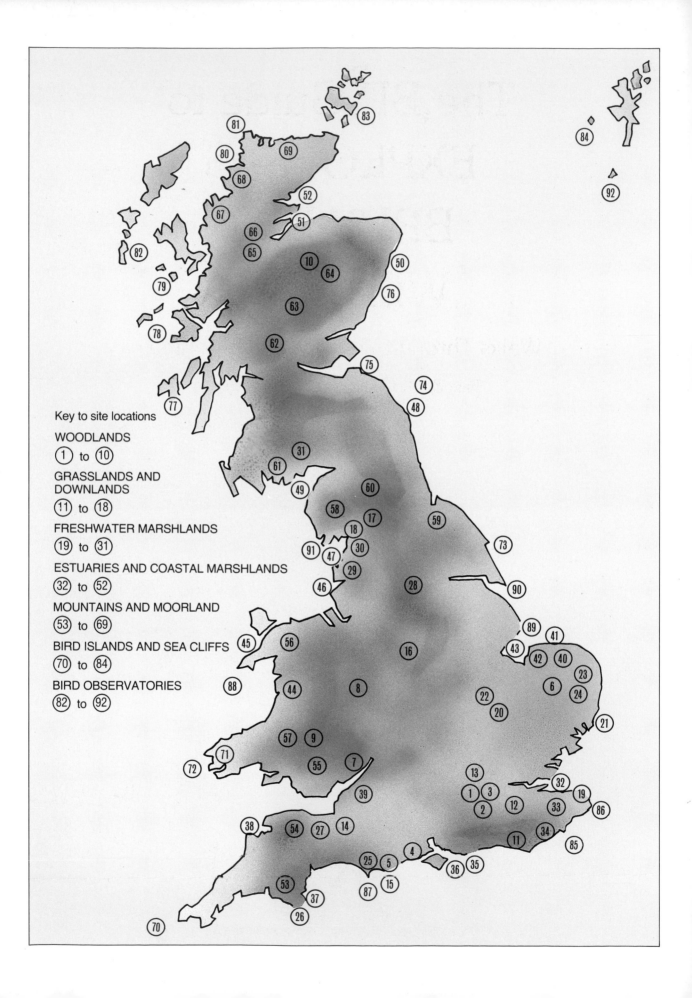

Key to site locations

WOODLANDS
① to ⑩

GRASSLANDS AND
DOWNLANDS
⑪ to ⑱

FRESHWATER MARSHLANDS
⑲ to ㉛

ESTUARIES AND COASTAL MARSHLANDS
㉜ to ㊿

MOUNTAINS AND MOORLAND
㊵ to ㊿

BIRD ISLANDS AND SEA CLIFFS
⑦⓪ to ⑧④

BIRD OBSERVATORIES
⑧② to ⑨②

The BP Guide to EXPLORING BRITAIN'S WILDLIFE

Walks Through The Best Wildlife Areas

Text & Photographs by Ian Beames

DAVID & CHARLES
Newton Abbot   London   North Pomfret (Vt)

ACKNOWLEDGEMENTS

Although I have travelled all the walks described in this book, some of them many times, it would have been quite impossible to gather all the information into any semblance of order without a lot of help. I am indebted to the wardens of the many national nature reserves, RSPB reserves and all others who provided time and information; also to Alan Vittery and Robin Fenton of NCC Headquarters who have helped organise so much concerning national nature reserves. Special thanks to Julia Gomm and David Mardon who helped with the botany.

Terry Smeeton provided detailed information about the Scilly Isles, finally persuading me to visit them, though at a time when there were more twitchers than birds, albeit the latter mostly American migrants! David Sewell provided freely of information, enabling me to see things I have missed in the past.

Thanks to Tracey May, my editor, and John Youé and his associates for their help and encouragement. Anthony Chapman of the RSPB kindly vetted all those sections dealing with RSPB reserves.

Kim Deane helped with typing part of the final manuscript. Lastly my wife, Joan, giving continual support, performed a singular feat of endurance in typing three-quarters of the manuscript for this book, despite a demanding career of her own and what is more, as a non-typist starting from scratch, first with two fingers and latterly using four or more.

British Library Cataloguing in Publication Data

Beames, Ian
  Exploring Britain's wildlife.
  1. Great Britain. Organisms. Observation.
  Sites. Visitor's guides
  I. Title
  574'.072041

  ISBN 0-7153-9177-1

© Ian Beames 1988

Typeset by Typesetters (Birmingham) Ltd
Smethwick West Midlands
and printed in Italy
by New Inter Litho, Milan
for David & Charles Publishers plc
Brunel House   Newton Abbot   Devon

Published in the United States of America
by David & Charles Inc
North Pomfret   Vermont 05053   USA

CONTENTS

INTRODUCTION

This book is intended for all those who are interested in wildlife, from beginner to expert, and sets out to describe the best wildlife areas in Britain so that a visit to any particular locality can be fully appreciated. A detailed tour, usually on foot, is given for each site together with a map showing the main features. For some large areas such as Shetland, two or three individual sites have been included. As well as the actual itineraries, each chapter mentions many other good localities and gives a brief résumé of each particular habitat – thus the best woodlands, estuaries, sea cliffs and so on, are described in turn.

Apart from trees, which most people seem to dismiss rather lightly, the most prominent of Britain's wildlife are birds and flowers; birds provoke most interest and are therefore dealt with most fully, but information is also provided for many mammals, butterflies and flowers where appropriate.

In the end the selection of a site is bound to be based on personal experience. I have visited every site and walked all the routes described myself, and most during the last two years. Even so places may change, fences appear overnight and stiles be moved. Fortunately this is unlikely and you should find the walks basically as described. By no means every route is mentioned: some are left for personal discovery. For example, the New Forest has hundreds of lovely walks and I have described only two. Even a restricted locality like Flamborough Head in Yorkshire has several alternative side paths to vary the route. All of these wild places may look very inhospitable in bad weather, and totally different on a lovely, sunny day.

I have made no attempt to give equal coverage throughout Britain, indeed there is a distinct bias towards Scotland and East Anglia because they are so good. Sites which are top grade but very difficult for the general public to reach, such as the far islands of St Kilda and North Rona, have been omitted, even though they no doubt merit full individual coverage.

If you manage to undertake all these walks you will have hiked over 1,000 miles (1,600km) and travelled a vast distance by road. You should also have seen nearly all of Britain's 280 regularly noted birds, most of its mammals and butterflies and many of its most beautiful flowers, besides many more not mentioned in the text for lack of space. You can accomplish this either with the minimum of equipment, or with a rucksack full of cameras, telescopes and so on. A pair of binoculars is an absolute essential – without them you will see little – and all the descriptions in this book assume that you are using a pair.

There is a brief section on equipment and also one on safety, as a number of these walks are in high, remote country. Such places can be hazardous for the unwary even in summer, and positively lethal for the unprepared in winter. Winter in Britain, in its wild places, can kill – the Cairngorms can be quite as severe as the Himalayas in a snow-storm. However, don't be put off! Winter also produces some of Britain's most magnificent wildlife sights.

Details of access for each site are given, and are up to date as at late 1987. However, the rules for visiting bird reserves change frequently and it is well worth checking information beforehand. Visiting most of these sites probably necessitates an Ordnance Survey map and presupposes the ability to read one. *The Ordnance Survey Outdoor Handbook* by Michael Allaby tells you all you need to know about maps and lots more besides, and most libraries will have this and other books available. In any case, maps are a great source of interest and information in themselves and provide a good souvenir of any area. Many of the best sites are RSPB or other nature reserves. Anyone who intends setting out on his own exploration of British wildlife should join the RSPB – the subscription is minimal for a lifetime's enjoyment and the RSPB has saved some of our most precious wild places from the rapacious hand of big business. For all coastal sites, advance knowledge of high tide times is essential; this is mentioned under 'Equipment' on p 8.

In the descriptions, details of common species have been omitted unless they are particularly notable. For example, the North Hide at Cley Bird Reserve in Norfolk is also a magnificent place to see rabbits which are thus included in the text, but clearly rabbits may be seen at many other sites. Similarly, the one pair of robins to be found round the warden's hut on the island of Handa are particularly mentioned since they are much rarer than puffins on Handa!

Clearly birds and animals may not appear where the descriptions say they should – it is obviously not possible to predict the movements of a fox or a golden eagle. Bird migrants in particular are entirely dependent upon the local weather conditions. Where unusual breeding birds are mentioned care has been taken only to disclose those areas already well-publicised in other books and leaflets. Definite localities for a few rare species are deliberately omitted to avoid undue disturbance. If you locate a rare breeding bird *please keep well clear*.

Nevertheless it is my firm belief that only with more public awareness, interest and access will our hard-pressed wildlife survive. It is no coincidence that the conservation movement and organisations like the RSPB have gathered momentum as wildlife has increasingly been given such wonderful publicity by so many TV programmes and books. Their growth is definitely not due to the secretive attitudes displayed by some organisations who see the public as an enemy rather than as an ally.

Unfortunately not everyone behaves well, and the 'twitching' section of the country's birders have come in for much criticism in the past. Obviously trampling a farmer's crops or climbing through private gardens will not do, and although most 'twitchers' behave very well indeed, the selfish few can sometimes ruin enjoyment and access for everyone else. Expert 'twitchers' are usually only too happy to help with field identification for beginners, and to identify distant birds at the flick of an eyelid is a skill and an education in itself.

Remember that you see most if you are quiet – talkative groups in bird hides please note! Also, please abide by the country code: it is set out on p 8. It should be emphasised that the country code is not a list of restrictions, but sound common sense and courtesy. Free access to Britain's countryside depends upon the co-operation of farmers and landowners who work and earn their living there. The least we can do is to respect this. It is thus quite unforgivable to leave sweet papers, polythene bags, cola cans or bottles lying about, or even to hide them under a convenient rock or in a ditch. Such rubbish poses a serious threat to livestock and to wildlife, and can be a source of fire. A single bottle can act as a death trap to perhaps twenty voles or shrews if left in a hedge.

Dogs are the greatest single cause of accidental death and injury to farm livestock. Damage blamed in the past on foxes has, on closer investigation, frequently been caused by dogs and a farmer has the legal right to shoot any dog caught worrying livestock. Fences and dry-stone walls cost time and money to repair – find a gate! Equally, it is unreasonable for a farmer or landowner to close a public right of way. Notify the Ramblers Association and your local council if you find a footpath blocked.

One of the problems of a guide such as this is that in encouraging even more visitors, the risk of overcrowding these precious and often quite small wild areas is increased – Minsmere RSPB reserve has recently started to restrict the daily influx of visitors. This clearly demonstrates the vital need to prevent any development of these remaining wild areas, not only to benefit the wildlife but for our own social and psychological good.

This book, despite its fairly prosaic descriptions, is about places that are wild and beautiful, sometimes easy to reach and sometimes hard. The hard ones such as Clo Mor, Torridon, Shetland, are full of personal adventure – I trust you will enjoy seeking this as much as I have done.

Ian Beames
Epsom, Surrey
1988

The magnificent limestone amphitheatre of Malham Cove high in the Yorkshire Dales

EQUIPMENT AND SAFETY

Clothing

The majority of the walks and tours described in this book are over easy ground and need little more than ordinary clothing and a modicum of common sense. For all the straightforward walks footwear is the main item for consideration. A lightweight pair of walking boots with a non-slip sole are a good idea – these will make even the nearly level walk along the Bempton or Fowlesheugh cliffs feel that much safer. However, many marsh, estuary and woodland sites need wellies in all but high summer.

Once you set off into the hills the equipment needed is much more specific. Even Lakeland hills can produce the most severe weather in any month of the year, conditions can deteriorate rapidly as one gains height, and a stiff breeze in the valley bottom can be a howling blizzard on the high tops. Wherever you go in the hills in Britain always carry a windproof anorak, a spare jumper, waterproofs and gloves. Shorts are quite unsuitable in Britain's hills and so are jeans, as they quickly become heavy and sodden in rain and could contribute to hypothermia.

Sturdy walking boots are essential for all the mountain and moorland walks described, and also for walks on many of the outer islands. These should fit snugly, using two pairs of socks to prevent blisters.

Rucksacks and Food

A small, lightweight rucksack may be very useful on any walk to carry sandwiches, a drink, and the inevitable waterproof anorak. Winter and hill walks demand more equipment and more food, so a larger one is probably needed. Heavy rucksacks make walking thoroughly unpleasant, especially when looking for wildlife, but a minimum amount of gear is required for safety. A five-mile (8km) estuary walk in winter may need only sandwiches, a small thermos of hot liquid and gloves jammed in the pockets of a good anorak, while a ten-mile (16km) summer hill walk in the Cairngorms will need a sack full of spare clothing and food. If venturing into wild country such as the Cairngorms, Torridon, Hermaness, always take sufficient food and eat frequently to avoid energy loss.

Other Equipment

Hill walks need a map and a compass and the knowledge to use both. Also carried should be a simple first-aid kit, a whistle and a small torch with spare battery. The international distress signal is six blasts on a whistle or six shouts or flashes of a torch, followed by a pause of a minute, then repeat the signal. The answer is three whistle blasts.

Route Finding

Most of the walks described follow footpaths and are quite straightforward. However, any path in the hills may be indistinct in places, and in mist or driving snow may be obliterated. It is important to realise that it can and does snow hard in the hills well into May and may even do so in July on a cold day. It is therefore essential to know how to use a compass, how to 'set' a map, and how to take a bearing with a compass and walk on it.

Up-to-date weather forecasts are essential, and a basic knowledge of weather conditions, especially how to recognise an approaching storm, is useful. Electrical storms occur on Britain's mountains, and if caught in one you should avoid summits and ridges.

River crossings can change dramatically after heavy rain, when a trickling stream can become a raging torrent in an hour. If you have to cross a stream which is flowing strongly, face upstream to avoid buckling of the knees from water pressure, use a stick for support and keep your walking boots on. There are several minor fords described in this book.

General

Advice for normal hill walking can be found in many books; visit your local library.

High tide times are published in many newspapers. It is also possible to obtain a booklet of Thames tide times from the Port of London Authority, Tilbury, Essex, and then apply the appropriate tide constant between your locality and London Bridge.

Walking in Snow-covered Hills

If you walk in the hills in April or May looking for birds there is bound to be a lot of snow, probably from 2,000 feet (609m) and upwards. You *must* carry an ice-axe if traversing high ridges and the tops. It is unlikely that you will find much wildlife up in the snow, but you must be aware of the precautions necessary should you attempt such walks. Once you undertake mountain walks in snow you need further advice and the following books are recommended: *Modern Snow and Ice Techniques* by Bill March (Cicerone Press), and *Climbing Ice* by Yvon Chovinard (Hodder and Stoughton).

Don't turn into a mountain rescue statistic.

THE COUNTRY CODE
1 Guard against all risks of fire
2 Fasten all gates
3 Keep dogs under proper control
4 Keep to paths across farmland
5 Avoid damage to fences, hedges and walls
6 Leave no litter
7 Safeguard all water supplies
8 Protect all wildlife, plants and trees
9 Go carefully on country roads
10 Respect the life of the countryside

OPTICAL EQUIPMENT

Binoculars

Binoculars are an essential item for watching wildlife, and this book assumes that anyone wishing to follow the walks described is equipped with a pair. For all general purposes the largest and heaviest binoculars are not recommended. Most books suggest a pair of lightweight 8×30, the 8 being the magnification and 30 the diameter of the front lens. My personal preference is for a 10×40 binocular, as this gives better magnification whilst still being light in weight. Prices range from £20 to £450 or more, the latter being superb glasses by Zeiss and Leitz from Germany; the £450 pair will last a lifetime, whereas the £20 pair may well be useless in a year or two. The quality of the optics is similarly dependent upon price. A good pair of quality binoculars will cost from £150 to £200.

Telescopes

The current image of the 'birder' shows a person with a telescope attached to a tripod carried perpetually over the shoulder. For studying birds and mammals from a distance, a telescope is extremely useful, but only once you are serious enough to envisage its regular use. Magnifications are much greater than those achieved with binoculars, and again quality depends upon price. A good telescope with magnification lenses, or a zoom facility from 20x to 60x may cost from £150 to £250. The wider angled lenses such as 20x and 40x, give much clearer images than a 60x magnification. The tripod on which to mount your telescope should be as light as possible – the alternative is to curl up on the floor with your head on your rucksack and a telescope propped on your knees. A monopod has some attractions as a telescope prop.

Cameras

Whole books have been written about camera equipment and its uses for wildlife photography. Photographing pretty girls may need only a simple camera, one lens and a light or two – but someone wishing to take wildlife pictures ranging from a close-up of butterflies to a distant shot of red deer may need all the equipment in the camera shop. In these days of superbly engineered automatic and electronic cameras it is tempting to assume that you only have to point the camera at the subject, press the button and obtain a picture. However, you *do* have to learn about light, perspective, angle and much more.

A 35mm single lens reflex camera is the best choice. 'Single lens reflex' means that the camera has an internal mirror set at 45° which passes light up to the eye-piece. As you press the shutter, the mirror flips up allowing the light to pass straight through to the film which is in the same plane as the eye-piece. The picture you see and focus in the eye-piece is therefore the picture you get on the film.

A camera system onto which you can add lenses, flashguns, close-up equipment and the like is essential. As with other optical equipment quality tends to depend upon price, although the top end of the market has become ridiculously expensive and now seems to be selling 'names' in the same way that Gucci sells shoes and handbags. Pentax, Minolta, Canon, Yashica and Nikon are all top-quality Japanese systems which have largely cornered the market. The German Leitz cameras are superb but are the most expensive of their kind.

Two zoom lenses, 28–70mm and 70–210mm, will provide everything from wide angle to moderate telephoto effects. Longer distance photography requires 300mm or 400mm lenses. 500mm light-weight mirror lenses are excellent to carry but the image is subject to camera movement, even of the 'flip-up' mirror. Such lenses need fast films and fast shutter speeds. Large lenses are very heavy and need sturdy tripods, so knowledge of your own carrying ability is paramount. A whole arsenal of flashguns can be used, from tiny flashes for close-up insect work to big professional 'hammer head' guns for photographing night-time badgers and foxes.

A good beginner's set would include one SLR body, two zoom lenses and a 2x converter to make the 200mm zoom a 400mm telephoto; a close-up lens would allow butterfly photography. Even at the lower end of the market this would cost £300–£400.

Finally a word of caution – you cannot walk up to most of Britain's wildlife and take a quick snap. You need to read avidly, develop patience to sit in hides or at least remain hidden, and above all you need to gain field experience. Wildlife photography can be a way of life.

WOODLANDS

Woodlands are a much-loved part of our heritage and still play an important rôle in the landscape – throughout history, forests have been allied with the changing fortunes of mankind. About 5,000 years ago tribal man began to clear the extensive British forests for pasture and cultivation, and by the Norman Conquest, most of our island's large forests had gone. Those which remained have been reduced still further for fuel, for furniture, for houses and for battleships. Now our precious trees are still being felled in favour of farmland or, which is more likely, property development. Today only 8% of Britain is woodland, most of it adapted or planted by man.

At their most extensive, woodlands covered some two-thirds of the whole country and so many of our native birds, plants and animals are woodland species, dependent upon trees to some extent. 60% of our breeding land birds, and more than half the butterflies and moths are found in woodlands; nearly 20% of plants are woodland species. Much of the forest cover in Britain now is 'new' woodland of the conifer plantation type, included in the overall total area of 8%. Little of our native wildlife can adapt to these substitute forests and so our native woods and trees are of tremendous importance for the conservation of wildlife in Britain.

Exploring British woodlands is more than biology: it entails learning about the changes in the country's climate and its underlying geological structure. As the last Ice Age retreated, woodland began to replace the arctic tundra vegetation of mosses, lichens and dwarf plants which covered much of the landscape. Arctic tundra survives in Britain today only on the highest tops – the Cairngorm plateau, Ben Lawers and the moors of Upper Teesdale are prime examples and are described on pages 128, 134 and 136. Some 15,000 years ago only the most hardy species could stand the bitter climate. The first woodland was almost entirely made up of birch with some willows, aspen and juniper. As conditions improved the Scots pine became the dominant tree, so that pine and birches grew together with here and there some rowan and hazel. Slowly the climate warmed. Broad-leaved trees advanced across the landscape of southern Britain. Deciduous summer forest established itself, dominating the landscape with elm, oak, alder, hazel and small-leaved lime.

Surviving examples of the first prehistoric forests of birch and pine are found only in northern Scotland. Strathfarrar National Nature Reserve, west of the Great Glen, and Rothiemurchus on Speyside are the two best known examples, but remnants of the ancient Forest of Caledon, with massive Scots pine, light birch woods, rowan and juniper, are found in a broad band across north-central Scotland. One good site is at Glen Tanar, a national nature reserve with access on paths only, near Braeoline on Deeside. Here, native Scots pine, rowan, juniper, birch and aspen provide a home for typical Caledonian forest animals and birds such as roe and red deer, red squirrel, wild cat, capercaillie and Scottish crossbill.

Another extensive tract lies along the shores of Loch Maree in Torridon and at Craigellachie on Speyside, which is a large remnant of ancient birch forest immediately above Aviemore. In summer, this open forest floor is clothed in flowers and filled with birdsong from a thousand willow warblers.

As the climate warmed and the pines retreated to the high ground of the north, so the beech, a species typical of warmer lands, occupied the southern counties. Beech grows better than oak on calcium-rich soil and so is found as climax forest on the chalk downs and limestone hills as far west as the Mendips and South Wales. Further north the oaks of the heavy clay soils give way to ash woods which grow on hillsides where the soil layer is too thin to support the 'upland' sessile oak. Ash also grows well on limestone and so becomes the dominant tree of many steepsided limestone valleys from the Derby Dales northwards.

Two species of oak are native to Britain: the sessile oak, found mainly in upland areas, and especially those of high rainfall down the west coast; and the pedunculate oak, the main tree of the drier lowlands.

Superb beech-woods are still found on the North and South Downs, in the Chilterns and the Mendips. Burnham Beeches in Buckinghamshire comprises 1,100 acres (445ha) on the western fringes of London, with good public access. Aston Rowant further west and north in Oxfordshire is a 350-acre (123-ha) national nature reserve of fine beech woodland, on the Chiltern escarpment. Between lie several Chiltern beech-woods, mostly new nature reserves. Kingley Vale in west Sussex is also a chalk down slope, but here the yew has become the dominant tree, making this the best yew-wood in Europe.

Good ash-woods are found at Eaves Wood near Arnside in Lancashire, and in neighbouring Yorkshire at Colt Park Wood, Ingleborough and Grass Wood in Wharfedale.

Good oak-woods in the lowlands include Cranborne Chase in Dorset; Savernake Forest in Wiltshire; Waterperry Wood, Oxford; Windsor Forest in Berkshire; Bedford Purlieus in Cambridge; and Charnwood Forest, Leicester. These woodlands house a rich lowland wildlife including roe and fallow deer, badger and fox; also woodpeckers and tits, common warblers and Purple Emperor and fritillary butterflies.

To the west and north there are notable sessile oak-woods: these are found in Borrowdale, Cumbria; at Coedydd Maentwrog, Gwynedd; Coed Rheidol; Dinas and Pengelli Forests, Dyfed; Yarner Wood, Devon; and Cannock Chase, Stafford. Very often they are found in steep-sided valleys, with pied flycatcher, redstart, wood warbler and buzzard as their most noticeable birds. Growing in a wetter climate, these woods have a fine 'atlantic' community of moisture-loving ferns, mosses, lichens and liverworts.

'New' forests are a different but important part of the woodland scene. Forestry in Britain has clothed many bare hillsides in dense stands of conifers – Norway spruce and European larch have been planted for some 400 years, usually in small copses by wealthy landowners, but the really extensive plantations were established when the Forestry Commission was formed in 1919. Lodgepole pine and Sitka spruce, both from west-coast America, thrive in our wet upland climate. Single-species forests are very unproductive from a wildlife point of view, and cause great controversy when their planting destroys precious natural habitat such as the Flow Country of northern Scotland. However, some of the oldest plantations are now mature, and have been much felled. The Forestry Commission provides access to all its woodlands and has developed vast areas for public amenity, with forest trails and picnic sites; this does not conflict with the basic requirement of economic forestry. Where these old plantations have been thinned or part felled, wildlife value is much improved with crossbill, siskin and sparrowhawk, wild cat, pine marten and roe deer, among others, all increasing in numbers.

Good conifer forests, now mature and open to the public exist at Thetford, Norfolk; Kielder Forest, Northumberland; Grizedale Forest, Cumbria; Clwyd Forest, Clwyd; Talybont Forest, Powys and Tummel Forest, Perth.

Woodlands, especially broad-leaved woodland, provide the widest range of plants and animals of any habitat in Britain. Exploring the woodlands described throughout this book will provide a constant source of pleasure at all seasons.

Scots pine and birch are typical of woodland on sandy soils. Native British woodlands such as these at East Wretham in Norfolk are precious remnants of our heritage, demanding conservation

Thursley Common
SURREY

1

Address of Site/Warden

Warden:
8 Homefield Cottages,
Highfield Lane, Thursley,
Godalming, Surrey

Highlights and Features

A mixture of wet and dry heath, woodland, and bog on sandy soil. Most is now a national nature reserve of 893 acres (361ha). Rare heathland birds, including one of the best sites for hobby and Dartford warbler. Superb range of bog flowers including orchids. One of the best sites for dragonflies in Britain.

Facilities

A small car-park at the Moat.

Photo Tips

Close-up lenses for bog flowers. An 80–210 zoom lens would be useful for insects, such as dragonflies and heathland butterflies. Use a small lightweight tripod.

The adder is the most widespread snake in Britain and is common on the sandy heathlands of the south

Surrey, although apparently a rural woodland county, is in truth largely urbanised. Away from the metropolitan fringes, however, this urbanisation takes the form of low-density residential areas with large wooded gardens. Apart from suburban gardens, Surrey's two prime habitats are thus the chalk of the North Downs (discussed on p 36) and its sandy heathlands on the west of the county.

The sands of the Surrey heaths, exposed by ancient forest clearance and subsequent leaching of the soils, are poor in nutrients. This habitat, fast becoming rare, is found only in the Dorset heaths and here in Surrey – all too often developers see it as wasteland when in fact it provides a unique community of plants, birds and animals. Thursley Common is the major example, recognised as such by being created a national nature reserve of 893 acres (361ha). Amazingly, in an area of such dense population, parts of the heath are still used for military training. One wildlife walk is described taking in all of the main habitat types. Do not touch any metal objects.

This heathland is a fragile environment, near to large areas of population and subject to considerable 'people pressure'. Keep to the paths and treat the area with care.

Wildlife Walk

The area is criss-crossed with paths and bridleways, allowing the visitor close views of all its wildlife. Best access point is the car-park at the Moat, one mile (1.6km) south of Elstead village.

The Moat is a shallow bog-lake of several acres surrounded by Scots pine and sallow scrub away from the car-park. Mallard and dabchick are the usual waterbird inhabitants; in summer dozens of dragonflies hawk and skim over its surface. Several paths lead onto the common from the Moat – the best to take is a path from its south-east corner opposite the car-park. This path leads through a narrow belt of mature Scots pine on a slight ridge of sand, and then runs east, raised perhaps a foot above the level of the surrounding peat bog.

All four seasons bring delights at Thursley and to really know the extent and diversity of its wildlife it needs several visits. In May and early June the bog, still very wet from winter rains, brings forth a multitude of early and southern marsh orchids. The path has been made into a raised wooden boardwalk in some places to allow close access to what is otherwise deep bog. However, any slight rise in the ground level changes the habitat dramatically, so that three feet (0.9m) above a bright green sphagnum bog can be a ridge of sand with sallow and birch scrub and tall Scots pine.

In May, the breeding birds characteristic of the area are all present, and Thursley is special in that they share the site with rare species. Out in the open boggy areas the most noticeable bird is the curlew. Several pairs breed, unusual in southern England, and their display flights and unforgettable calls can be savoured to perfection here. Later in summer when their chicks are on the move, they will fly in alarm over the bogs if disturbed by too many visitors.

From a vantage point on the edge of the heath the view is of a large, open wetland, bright green in places where fresh sphagnum moss denotes deep and dangerous bog. Considerable encroachment of birch and sallow scrub has taken place around its edges, and the higher and drier ground is dominated by Scots pine woodland. Tree pipit, grasshopper warbler, woodlark, stonechat and nightingale all breed in the scrub, and a broad range of commoner woodland species may be found, including all three woodpeckers, willow tit and several pairs of redstart.

Thursley is a noted site for birds of prey, with ten species on record. Prize bird of the boggy areas is the hobby: they arrive in May and breed in a number of the Scots pine woods in the surrounding district, and use the Thursley bogs to hunt dragonflies and also hirundines, which themselves are catching insects over the wetland. By mid-July they will have chicks to feed. Evening is the best time to see them, when four or five hobbies might provide an aerobatic display as they search for food. Find a Scots pine to lean against, avoid having your shape on the skyline, and bog-watch – you will be well rewarded. Sparrowhawk, kestrel and buzzard also breed here and are often seen.

In July the bog has more superb displays of flowers, with drifts of bog asphodel, sundews, bogbean and marsh St John's wort.

Thursley Bog is perhaps most important for its wonderful array of insects – nearly 10,000 species are present in the area as a whole. The most noticeable throughout the summer, and rising in numbers and variety, are the dragonflies. At least 26 species are known, more than at any other site in southern Britain; they start in May with Common Blue and Large Red damselfly; to June with the beautiful Emperor and Golden-ringed dragonflies; and culminate in July with many species and hundreds of insects flitting and twisting over the bog pools. Good populations of Silver-studded Blue and Grayling butterflies can be found among the heather. This area is noted for its reptiles: adders are frequent, while the very rare sand lizard and smooth snake have both been recorded.

The track across the wetlands rises eastwards onto higher, drier heath. It is possible simply to walk a complete circuit of the bog and return to the car park after a mile, but if you walk further east you will see in addition the woodland and dry heath species. The track (a bridleway) traverses some half-a-mile of birch, heather and bracken scrub, with gorse on the highest ridges, and emerges on the minor road near the junction with the main A3 east of Thursley village.

This dry heath scrub provides the other bird rarity of the area: the Dartford warbler breeds here. The numbers are often very low after a severe winter but build up slowly to eight or ten pairs, depending upon the run of the climate; one bad winter can all but wipe them out. You will see them best by staying on the track, being quiet and watching the tops of the bushes.

Hammer Pond and Warren Mere on the eastern side of the common near the A3 have more verdant streamside vegetation, with oak woodland. Kingfishers are occasionally seen on the stream here, and woodland birds are more in evidence, for example garden warbler, redpoll and bullfinch.

Winter brings total change to Thursley: gone are the bright bog flowers and summer birds, and winter birds appear in force with snipe on the bog, woodcock in the woods and – surprisingly perhaps, so close to suburbia – hunting hen harrier, with the occasional merlin and short-eared owl. The great grey shrike is a regular visitor, one or sometimes two usually arriving in November and staying until March.

From the eastern end of Thursley village it is a mile and a half back along the road through pine woodland to the Moat car-park.

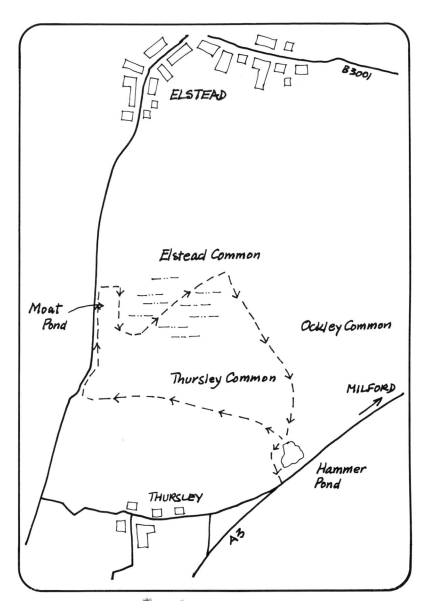

Bell heather is found on the higher, drier sands of Thursley

Chiddingfold Woods
SURREY

Address of Site/Warden

Forest office:
Chiddingfold Forest,
Chiddingfold,
Surrey

Highlights and Features

High forest with extensive
Forestry Commission
plantations. Many well
managed woodland rides.
Famous for its butterflies,
with one of the most diverse
species lists in Britain.
Stronghold of Purple
Emperor, Silver-washed
Fritillary and many more.
Good for woodland birds.

Facilities

Several small car-park areas
only.

Photo Tips

Close-up lenses for insects.
Some pictures may be taken
most easily with a longer
zoom lens. Woodland edges
may be dark so a small
flashgun will be useful.

*The familiar robin fills the
early spring woodlands
with wistful song*

A glance at the Ordnance Survey map will show a concentration of wooded areas between Haslemere and Cranleigh in Surrey: these are the wealden woods of Chiddingfold Forest. Much of the area is now Forestry Commission property but the plantations are carefully planned so as to conserve the richness of its wildlife. The whole area is surrounded by small farms interspersed with woodland glades. Most of the Surrey barn owls breed in this rural corner of the county and are often to be seen drifting along the hedgerows at dusk.

These are the 'butterfly woods' of Surrey, unsurpassed in Britain for their displays of large, rare and beautiful butterflies. Moreover the list of breeding birds is excellent, and reptiles and mammals are good too. Quite rightly, butterfly collecting is prohibited in all these heritage woodlands – the district is well wardened and often policed. Anyone found with a butterfly net is likely to see the inside of Cranleigh Police Station and earn a massive fine at Guildford Magistrates Court.

The circular wildlife walk described passes through some of the best woods and is accessible on public footpaths throughout. Kingspark Wood to the south is a well-protected conservation area with entry by permit only from the Forestry Commission. Visiting between May and July is best.

Wildlife Walk

One mile (1.6km) south of Dunsfold village take the right-hand lane signposted to Chiddingfold and Whitley; after two miles (3km) park near the Forestry Commission gate called 'Botany Bay'; enter here, keeping to the main ride. Plantations of Norway spruce grow tall on both sides; the ride is edged with sallow and tall marsh thistles, and honeysuckle grows everywhere. There are innumerable grey squirrels here with dreys in the conifers. Walk about three hundred yards (274m) and then stop at the end of the spruce plantation – this is an excellent place just to wait awhile.

In May the rare Wood White may be seen, flitting weakly from flower to flower. Grizzled, Dingy, small and large Skippers, Orange Tip, Brimstone, Peacock and Comma are all numerous; by June Pearl-bordered Fritillaries, followed two weeks later by Small Pearl-bordered Fritillaries

will be zipping along the rides at high speed. Late June and early July are the peak times. The large and dazzling orange Silver-washed Fritillaries search the flowers for nectar – in a good year these 'hand-sized' butterflies are often here in profusion, with ten or twenty to be seen on a single bramble bush. Two more special butterflies are found at this time of year: White Admirals, graceful and numerous, and Purple Emperors – here easier to see than anywhere else in Britain. Try wearing a pair of white trousers and see how a male Emperor dances along three feet behind you, distracted by the dazzle of white light. Hairstreaks abound: Green Hairstreaks along the rides in May, Purple Hairstreaks among the oaks in June and July, and the uncommon Brown Hairstreak in August and September; in July there may even be a few surviving White-letter Hairstreaks nearby, to complete the set. The butterfly list totals nearly forty species, making this the number one butterfly site in Britain.

The rides abound in flowers: primrose, violet, clover, woodruff and marsh thistle dominate, while the bramble blossom along the wood edge is irresistible to butterflies.

On warm days listen carefully at the scrub edge. These woods have many adders and grass snakes, and adders especially are often seen along the rides.

After only five hundred yards (457m) an S-bend in the ride dips to a bridge over a small brook. This is one of the secret streams of Surrey whose secret splendour is the kingfisher – in fact it is often seen on streams in the district. Many spotted orchids with some greater butterfly orchids grow in the grass verges near the bridge; here there are large clumps of tall hog-weed which attract dozens of butterflies.

To photograph these butterflies use a 200mm zoom lens on the camera, together with a close-up attachment. A monopod gives extra stability, and a small electronic flashgun will fill in the shadows and help stop wing movement in the photograph.

The birds which can be seen in this area are typical of a varied woodland with much scrub. Warblers are very numerous in summer, and include blackcap, garden warbler, whitethroat, lesser whitethroat, chiffchaff and willow warbler, the lovely downward drifting song of the last being the commonest sound. The greatest delight is the large number of nightingales, and there may be several dozen pairs present in summer. Goldcrests breed in the drooping branches of the spruce – ideally placed to hold their tiny nests. The rare and elusive firecrest breeds nearby and singing males have been noted along the paths here in June. Sparrowhawks are most prominent amongst the birds of prey, and there are nesting sites in several of the plantations. Buzzards may breed and even honey buzzards have been seen soaring over the woods in midsummer.

Three hundred yards (274m) beyond the bridge is a small triangle of paths resulting in a large open area which is full of flowers and bramble. This is the best butterfly spot with Emperors high above in the oaks. Following the path right at the triangle it is possible to continue for half-a-mile or so to join the road at Fisher Lane; turning left will take you a further half-a-mile to the southern end of the main ride, and by returning left along this, one rediscovers the triangle from the opposite direction.

Facing out over the open areas of low scrub near the triangle are three foresters' high seats, built into the wood edge and used for culling roe deer. These are excellent places for some quiet watching. Roe are frequent on the rides at dawn and dusk, and an early morning encounter with a badger is even possible, as there are two or three setts within the woodland. Whatever you see, the Chiddingfold Woods never fail to convey an air of serenity on any warm morning in high summer.

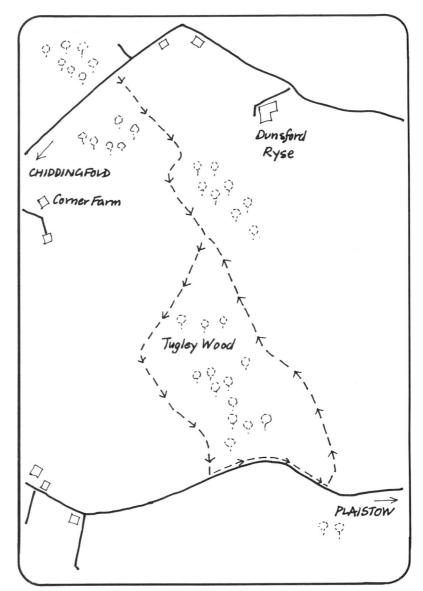

Chiddingfold Woods hold many families of young grey squirrels in late spring

Windsor Forest
BERKSHIRE

Address of Site/Warden

Information from:
Nature Conservancy Council,
Southern Region,
Foxhold House,
Thornford Road,
Crookham Common,
Newbury,
Berks

Highlights and Features

Ancient woodland, largely
oak with much mixed forest
from plantations, parkland.
Large lake which attracts
many waterbirds. Good for
woodland birds, insects,
fungi. Herd of red deer in
park.

Facilities

Various tourist facilities
nearby.

Photo Tips

Good place for some
waterbird pictures as birds
are accustomed to people.
Similarly good for grey
squirrels, magpies. Superb
array of fungi in autumn.
Birds and mammals need
long telephoto lens, while
fungi need wide-angle zoom
and low tripod.

*The false chanterelle, one
of the many fungi for which
Windsor Forest is famous*

Just twenty miles (32km) or so to the west of London, sandwiched between great arterial roads, lies Windsor Great Park and Windsor Forest. Norman kings set aside huge tracts of land for their personal use for hunting, and Windsor, like the New Forest, Epping Forest and the Forest of Dean, was one of them.

Still surviving the modern scourge of development are some 15,000 acres (6,070ha) of park and forest, making Windsor one of the most important ancient woodlands in the country. Near Forest Gate stands an oak tree reputed to be over 800 years old, so it was a well-grown tree when Richard I set off for the Crusades. Throughout these woodlands there are many oaks which are 500 years old or more; it is this continuity from ancient woodland which makes Windsor so precious as a wildlife reserve.

Windsor Castle, the sovereign's London country residence, looks down from the north over this lovely ancient park bequeathed by Crown to Country in 1760.

Wildlife Walk

The best time to visit is in the early morning, before too many people are about. Park in the large car-park just north of the Wheatsheaf Hotel on the A30 near the junction with the B369. Walk through the gates at the back of the car-park into a grove of fine old beech trees, with here and there a sweet chestnut. Grey squirrels are always active here, collecting nuts and scraps from the forest floor. Nuthatches and the occasional great spotted wood-pecker feed in the trees while magpies scavenge in the car-park edges for picnic scraps.

One hundred yards (91m) through the trees brings you to Virginia Water, a huge ornamental lake with a circumference of nearly five miles (8km). A large old tree on the far bank is used by cormorants as a perch – there are usually several present, and may often be seen fishing in the lake alongside numerous great crested grebes. The lake attracts many waterfowl, especi-ally in winter when rafts of pochard, tufted duck, teal, shoveler and wigeon may appear alongside the residents, which are mallard and mandarin duck. Windsor is famous for its mandarins, natives of the Far East, released here in the 1930s and now spread over several counties. A hundred or more can be seen on the lake at times, and in autumn they may be found feeding on the beechmast in the woodlands. They breed in tree-holes throughout the park in spring.

Follow the gravel track left-handed around the lake, using the occasional 'tree-trunk' seat to scan the water and its surrounding vegetation. After 400 yards (365m) a side-path on the left takes you down to a wooded dell and a 30-foot (9m) man-made waterfall. The noise from the A30 traffic nearly drowns that of the water, but there are always grey wagtails flitting about the rocks and the spot is especially good in winter when many woodland birds drink at the pools. Climb the rather muddy path up the left side of the lake – in summer the fringe of reeds and water vegetation holds sedge and reed warblers.

Just round the turn of the lake, on the wood edge, lie the remains of an old temple brought from the Roman city of Leptis Magna in Libya by King George IV in 1827. The walls and pillars are draped in bramble and ivy and provide nesting places for robin, wren and spotted fly-catcher in spring. The path following the southern shores of the lake runs through the edge of superb ancient woodland, splendid examples of mature oak, beech, sweet chestnut and hornbeam growing on sandy soil, with much Scots pine and some birch scrub. The ground cover varies but is largely bracken and heather.

Past the ruins there are two large cedars of Lebanon; they grow near the start of Frost Farm Plantation which is now a declared SSSI because of its spectacular array of rare insects and fungi. In autumn a superb display of fungi may be found throughout the ancient woodlands, while summer brings some thirty-three species of butterfly out and about in the park and forest. This southern heathland area has Holly Blue around the masses of ivy in May, White Admirals and Purple Emperors in late June, and Silver-studded Blue and Grayling in July. Beetles are a special feature of these ancient wood-lands: over 2,000 species have been identified at Windsor, rivalling the New Forest as Britain's foremost insect site.

Scan the tree-tops through Frost Farm Plantation for crossbill, goldcrest and coal tit in the pines, and siskins and redpolls in

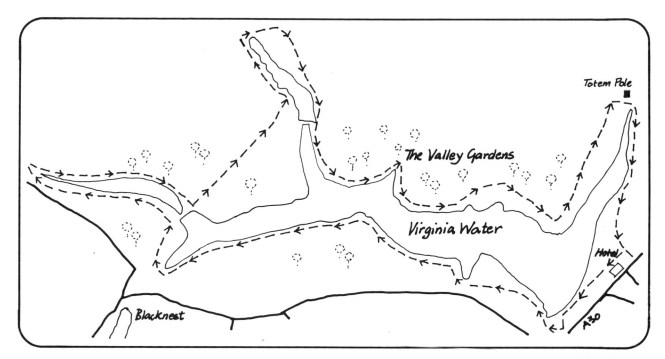

the birches. In May and June the woods are filled with bird-song – willow warbler, blackcap, chiffchaff and garden warbler, along with several pairs of fiery redstarts.

The path then bends back towards the Ascot road and the traffic noise near Blacknest Gate, running through a large stand of huge sweet chestnut trees. Grey squirrels forage for nuts in autumn, while across the quiet waters of the lake echelons of gulls fly in to roost at the reservoirs around Staines, crossing a constant stream of traffic travelling in the other direction as it leaves Heathrow Airport.

Turn from Blacknest Gate towards the long stone bridge over the lake and, at the bridge, turn left down a grassy ride. This is a quiet corner of the park with mixed conifer plantations on both banks, with spruces, firs and even Chilean pine. Goldcrests and crossbills are frequent here, while woodcock breed in the damp woodlands. Watch the wood-edge for hunting sparrowhawks, and if you move quietly, the open ride itself for a glimpse of fallow, roe or muntjac deer.

The western arm of the lake narrows, and is filled with alder and sallow thickets; siskins and redpolls often frequent these in winter, while lesser spotted woodpeckers prefer the alders in which to hollow out their nesting holes. Return along the northern side of the lake to the bridge and then aim diagonally across an open lawn of heather which lies before two red-brick houses – here swallows and martins dip and dart over the open ground for insects, while on warm summer evenings hobbies, breeding in the southern Windsor Forest pines, hunt dragonflies and the occasional swallow. Greenfinches

and even hawfinches feed in trees along the ride which leads to the north-western corner of the lake. At the signpost turn right along the lakeside, past the National Holly Collection and a really beautiful house and boathouse with sloping lawns to the lake.

The path runs down into the Valley Gardens, a magnificent collection of azaleas, rhododendrons and magnolias in a beautifully landscaped, natural stream valley. These gardens, developed since 1950, are full of colour in spring and autumn and abound in woodland birds – long-tailed tits, marsh tits, woodpeckers, nuthatches, tree-creepers and thrushes all year, with warblers and redstarts in summer.

From the wide open vistas of the lake by the Valley Gardens' edge, the path turns north through mature beech-woods, the woodland floor carpeted with beech-cushion moss (Leucobryum). Holes in these ancient trees provide homes for little and tawny owls, whilst a pair or two of redstarts may be seen in summer. Green woodpeckers are regulars here, often rooting through the leaf litter on the forest floor looking for ants. Four hundred yards (365m) bring you to the Totem Pole, given in 1958 to HM the Queen to celebrate the centenary of British Columbia. It is exactly 100 feet (30m) high. A sparrowhawk sometimes uses the top as a look-out post. The world-famous Savill Gardens are signposted one mile north; 1,000 acres (404ha) of the Great Park surround these gardens and since 1979 efforts have been made to restore the red deer – the herd now numbers 300.

Turn back over the lake at the Totem Pole to return to the car-park in half a mile.

The Boat House, Virginia Water

4

The New Forest
HAMPSHIRE

Address of Site/Warden

Mainly administered by the
Forestry Commission
New Forest Office,
Lyndhurst,
Hants

Highlights and Features

Outstanding area of ancient
woodland, heathland and
lowland bog. A wealth of
woodland birds including
Dartford warbler, hobby,
honey buzzard, firecrest and
crossbill. Many deer,
badgers and other
mammals. Top site for
woodland and heathland
insects.

Facilities

Well-known tourist area, with
many camp sites and other
accommodation of all
standards. Car-parks, forest
walks. Reptillary near
Lyndhurst.

Photo Tips

Patience and long telephoto
lenses will provide pictures
of deer, foxes, badgers etc,
but only if carried out at
dawn and dusk. Medium-
zoom lenses for insects and
New Forest ponies. Close-up
lenses for flowers and small
insects. Tripod essential.
Flower spike (spike with
tripod head attached to push
into soft ground) useful.

*Owned by the people of
the New Forest, but wild
in behaviour patterns, the
New Forest pony plays an
important part in forest
ecology*

The New Forest is one of the most extensive and important ancient lowland forests in the whole of Europe, covering some 145 square miles (375sq km). Preserved for hunting by the Norman kings, the Forest of Domesday Book times was already a complex of woodland and open heath; since the fifteenth century man has continually exploited it for timber, largely for military purposes. Forestry management cycles have continued down the centuries, but despite this the whole Forest has a natural air. Parts are still designated 'Ancient and Ornamental Woodland' and may be remnants of the original forest that covered lowland Britain in prehistoric times.

Heathland is actually the most extensive habitat. Valleys in the heaths are largely treeless bogs and shelter many rare plants and insects. The New Forest remains one of the finest sites for wildlife in Britain, a reminder of the woodlands destroyed elsewhere. Pressure from tourism is heavy but for the most part well-controlled by the Forestry Commission. Two wildlife walks are described, the first through a variety of rich woodland in the south-east of the Forest, and the second onto a wilder open heath in the north-west near Ringwood.

Wildlife Walk I: Denny Lodge,
Lady Cross and Whitley Ridge (A 5-mile (8km) round walk on level ground.)
Take the B3056 from Lyndhurst to Beaulieu. Turn right uphill from Matley Bog and pass through the Denny Wood camp-site. Park half-a-mile beyond this at a 'No unauthorised vehicles' notice.

These woods consist of ancient oak and beech with holly, and in early summer the birds are almost overwhelming: redstart, willow warbler, chiffchaff and blackcap can be seen; all three species of woodpecker; nuthatch, tree-creeper and hole-nesting titmice are numerous. Quiet exploration of these woods at dawn will reveal fallow deer.

Stay on the left-hand track between Denny Lodge and a cottage on the left. Small 'wet' meadows have been cleared behind the houses and are full of marsh marigolds in spring; the gate leads over a small stream into Denny Lodge enclosure – piles of timber line this main forestry access point. The track runs through alternate blocks of conifers, spruce and fir, of varying ages. This part of the forest is well over a mile from any road and is quiet and secluded.

Bird sounds change in character since it is the conifer woodland species which prevail: coal tit, goldcrest, crossbill and the occasional siskin – even firecrests, which always favour the larger conifers along this track.

Three hundred yards (274m) further and the pines change to oak on the left. Try exploring some of the many side-tracks here – walk half-a-mile into the heart of the silent forest and you will find that deer are more numerous than people; you should see fallow, sika and roe deer if you are quiet. Birds are most numerous at the junction of conifer and broad-leaved woodland: woodpeckers, nuthatch, redpolls, warblers, tits and goldcrests are all present in some numbers, and sparrowhawks regularly hunt the rides.

Nearly a mile beyond Denny Lodge a gravel track goes left towards Beaulieu and reveals a superb stand of unfenced, mature oaks with all the high forest birds, including redstart and wood warbler, especially in summer. Tall spruce line the track down towards the main London–Bournemouth railway line – a number of large wood ants' nests may be found by the side of the track here. A gate and a bridge lead over the railway line with a long grass 'lawn' running the full length of the cutting for two or three miles (4km). New Forest ponies, found everywhere, are always here in photogenic groups. Several acres have been cleared, and the low scrub is ideal habitat for whitethroat, lesser whitethroat and tree pipit. This is also an excellent spot for woodland butterflies with Pearl-bordered Fritillaries in May and June, and Silver-washed Fritillaries and White Admirals in July. Foxgloves and marsh thistles line the paths in midsummer.

Cross the bridge and continue for half-a-mile to Lady Cross Lodge and the Brockenhurst–Beaulieu road. Turn right towards Brockenhurst, and at the right-angled bend in the road, strike left for a hundred yards (90m) to the edge of the Lymington River – here a lovely fern-lined stream running through fine woodland. This is a well-known picnic site and the birds are positively tame – nuthatches and

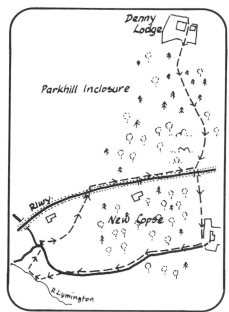

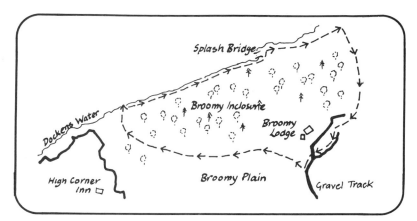

tits will take food from your hand and there are kingfishers and grey wagtails along the stream. The track along the bank is peaceful England at its best. Return by the same route or via Whitley Ridge Lodge and along the railway.

Wildlife Walk 2: Dockens Water and Holly Hatch (A 4-mile (6km) round walk, very muddy in places: wellies useful.)

Drive from Lyndhurst through the great trees of Bolderwood, under the A31; turn right, signposted Broomy Lodge and Holly Hatch, along a gravel track. Park among high gorse at the boundary of Broomy Inclosure. Wide heathlands spread to the horizon.

This is a splendid spot where Dartford warblers frequent the gorse, and tree pipits and curlew breed on the heath. Strike west downhill through gorse and open grass 'lawns' where at dawn fallow and roe deer can be seen feeding, retreating to the quieter woodland as people stir. A thousand yards (914m) takes you down to a bridge and a clear stream running into the inclosure at High Corner Wood. This is a lovely spot with groves of tall Scots pine. A huge badger sett with ten or more holes occupies the woodland bank at the corner of the inclosure. This used to be one of the quietest parts of the forest, but bad planning has allowed the High Corner Inn building development which, although screened by trees, causes constant disturbance to a wide area of great wildlife importance.

Avoid this and turn right to Dockens Water. This is one of the high peaty-brown moorland streams of the New Forest and teems with life: trout lurk in the clear olive pools, and grey wagtails nest under tiny bridges. A dense belt of alder and sallow runs along the stream, sheltering many

warblers and tree pipits in summer, while winter brings siskin and redpoll in flocks to eat the seeds. Half-a-mile brings you to Splash Bridge and a gravel track up onto the wild open heathland, and it is worth walking the mile to Latchmore Brook and back. From the open hillside scan the skies for birds of prey: buzzards, hobbies and sparrowhawks are frequent breeding birds and even the rare honey buzzard sometimes soars over these high forest woods. Nightjars, stonechats and a few curlew breed on this heath; redshank and snipe prefer the bogs along the brooks, whilst woodcock have nesting sites in all the woods and may be seen at dusk in spring 'roding' around their territory.

For the botanist these bogs are rich with marsh St John's wort, three species of sundew, bog asphodel, marsh gentian and the rare bog orchid. Wild gladiolus grows under the bracken in June.

Return across Splash Bridge and walk up through Broomy Inclosure keeping the conifers and a fence on the right, and mature, ivy-clad oaks on the left. The last three hundred yards (274m) of track are fairly steep and indistinct before the gravel path, back and to the right, is reached, to return you to your car.

Fallow deer are numerous in the Forest, best seen early and late in quiet rides

The Dorset Heaths

*The sand lizard is now
very rare and found in
only a few heathland
localities in Britain*

The sandy heathlands of Dorset have largely succumbed to pressure from farming and strip urbanisation. Planners tend to regard heaths as 'wasteground', and you only have to follow the A31 around Poole Harbour to appreciate the extent of the destruction – supermarkets, DIY stores and amusement parks all replace a rare and vanishing resource. Studland Heath National Nature Reserve and the RSPB reserve at Arne have fortunately been saved. On the Purbeck peninsula they form a dramatic contrast to the high chalk and limestone downland of the nearby southern coast, comprising gorse and heather heaths; they are the low-lying slopes which border Poole Harbour, which is itself a wonderful wildlife site at all seasons.

These heathlands are of national importance to wildlife since they are sanctuaries for some of our rarest birds, many rare insects and for all six species of British reptile, including the very rare smooth snake and sand lizard. Brownsea Island is owned by the National Trust and lies nearby in Poole Harbour itself, roughly between Studland and Arne. This island, accessible by boat from Sandbanks, is open from April to September and provides superb views of the wildfowl and waders of Poole Harbour. It has a heronry of nearly a hundred pairs, the second largest in Britain; there is also an isolated colony of some sixty red squirrels, and Brownsea Island is one of the best places in Britain to see them.

The wildlife walk described takes the explorer round the dunes and into the woods of Studland.

Wildlife Walk: Studland National Nature Reserve

Park in the Knoll Car Park, just north of the Knoll House Hotel in Studland Village. Walk out to the beach via an old pill-box, a deep erosion hollow and the beach huts. Walk north up the beach for about three hundred yards (274m) to a yellow post and a bollard which mark the beginning of the nature trail. Although Studland has almost unlimited access, it is a good idea to avoid disturbing the breeding birds which nest around the large land-locked freshwater lake – so keep to the trails. In summer common terns, various gulls and cormorants will be offshore, while oyster-catchers may be seen along the tide-line.

Walk up over the first ridge – Zero Ridge – looking for animal tracks in the sand, and descend into the first hollow which is really a long dune slack between two ridges. Here a proper dune 'sward' has appeared and the ground is moist in winter. Occasional clumps of heather and cross-leaved heath can be seen, with many insectiverous sundews, and now and again a small Scots pine has established itself along with gorse, sallow and a few birch trees.

Up onto the second ridge crest – called 'First Ridge' before the last war when it *was* the first ridge – and drier heath conditions begin to prevail. Pipits, stonechat and willow warbler are all present as are heath butterflies, particularly grayling and Silver-studded Blue in July. Smooth snakes may occasionally be seen here, although they do occur anywhere on the reserve. Adders are more numerous but your chances of seeing either are small – early morning, when they need to bask in the sun to gain warmth, is the best time.

The next dune slack is much wetter, with a number of 'bomb-crater' pools, and the track goes back along it towards the car-park. Marsh orchids are numerous in summer and the vegetation is altogether richer and more vigorous than nearer the beach; large clumps of the rare royal fern may be found here. Bog myrtle is the main shrub around the pools, together with great tussocks of purple moor grass in which harvest mice often make their nests. Over twenty species of dragonfly and damselfly have been seen here during the summer, including rarities.

Follow the fence line here – a good spot for reptiles – and continue on through woodland, past a pond where toads abound in spring. After 400 yards (365m) you will come to the southern end of the 'Little Sea', a large freshwater lake nearly a mile-and-a-half (2km) long. This is a lovely reed-fringed lake surrounded by gorse-covered ridges and with a dense, wet, alder-sallow forest called 'carr' at its southern end. In winter the 'Little Sea' acts as a refuge for up to 4,000 wildfowl of many species. All the common ducks are found and a regular sprinkling of rarer birds occur, including divers, grebes, smew and long-tailed duck. In summer, apart from mallard, coot and moorhen,

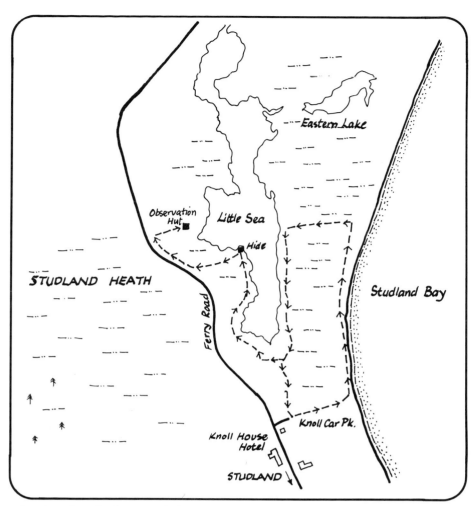

other breeding birds around the water include great crested grebe, dabchick, shelduck, water rail and many reed and sedge warblers. Roe deer are frequent, especially around the lake.

By taking a track from the southern end of the lake left across heather moorland, you come to an observation screen set upon a hill, perhaps 400 yards (365m) distant. This provides superb views of the whole of the Little Sea and across much of the heathland. Summer birds include nightjar, stonechat and breeding Dartford warbler – a real prize, though restricted to a few pairs on these southern heaths. A track west for 200 yards (182m) returns you to the road, and it is then an easy mile walk back to the car-park.

Studland Heath National Nature Reserve is a marvellous mix of beach, dune, lake, marsh, heath and acid bog on Bournemouth's borders

6

Breckland
NORFOLK

Address of Site/Warden

Several reserves belonging to the Nature Conservancy Council and the Norfolk Naturalists' Trust. Norfolk Naturalists' Trust: 72 Cathedral Close, Norwich, Norfolk NR1 4DF Norfolk Naturalists' Trust: East Wretham Warden, The Nature Reserve, Thetford, Norfolk IP24 1RU

Highlights and Features

Quite unique area of sandy heathland, with large conifer plantings. Near continental climate means many rare flowers, insects, birds. Especially good for stone curlew, red-backed shrike, woodlark, long-eared owl, crossbill, siskin, hawfinch and even golden pheasant. Very good for mammals, with red squirrel, red and roe deer and otter on rivers.

Facilities

Weeting Heath National Nature Reserve has hides for viewing stone curlew. East Wretham Nature Reserve has nature trail and hides overlooking Ringmere.

Photo Tips

Long telephoto lenses for birds and mammals. Wide-angle zoom for flowers.

Introduced for fur and meat, the rabbit has spread throughout the country in a few centuries

In the heart of East Anglia, centred largely on Thetford, lie 300 square miles (777sq km) of dry, sandy heathland, stony fields and 'new' pine forest. This is Breckland, deriving its name from the local word 'breck' which described an ancient field, cultivated and then abandoned as the soil became exhausted. The landscape is thus largely man-made with Scots pine 'shelter' belts around the 'brecks' – the new conifer forests are recent plantings run by the Forestry Commission, and a large central area is used extensively as a military training area; some of it is inaccessible.

For hundreds of years Breckland was inhabited mainly by rabbits and sheep which controlled all vegetation, but now rabbits have declined except on some less disturbed heaths and the sheep are largely grazed elsewhere. Hot summers and long, cold winters make Breckland one of the driest parts of Britain, with a unique flora and fauna which repays extensive exploration. Some of Britain's rarest birds and flowers are found here and the mammal population is superb.

The wildlife tour includes the nature reserves of Weeting and East Wretham Heaths, and a number of other good sites within the boundaries of the Brecks – East Wretham has some particularly good wildlife walks. The best time for a visit is May to July, although winter here has its own special bleak appeal.

Wildlife Tour

The tour starts at Weeting Heath which is reached from the B1106 north of Brandon. Take a minor road west out of Weeting village towards Hockwold and park on the left after about a mile, by the warden's caravan. This reserve is managed by the NCC and the Norfolk Naturalists' Trust, and the warden is resident only in the summer. Two hides are available, but access to the heath itself is not allowed. The speciality here is the very rare stone curlew which is usually present from late March until mid-August; several pairs breed on the stony, sandy heath. The heath itself has been restored by fencing in large enclosures to encourage large rabbit populations, and provides ideal habitat for the several breeding pairs of wheatear, lapwing and the ubiquitous skylark. The old shelter belts of Scots pine hold a few pairs of crossbill, although these are more easily seen nearby at East Wretham.

The rich chalk/heath vegetation elsewhere on the reserve attracts many breeding butterflies including Essex Skipper, Brown Argus and Holly Blue in some numbers. Several rare plants grow on the reserve, and these include maiden pink and spiked speedwell which are protected from the rabbits by wire cages.

Leave Weeting Heath eastwards and travel about four miles (6km) to Santon Warren just north of the railway line at Santon Downham. This is a good area for a variety of common woodland birds and the young plantations scattered over the Warren often hold woodlark. An interesting 'extra' here is the golden pheasant – a thriving colony has existed in Breckland for many years, and this is a good spot to see them. Three miles (4km) north again is West Tofts Mere, one of the loveliest of the Breckland meres, filled with reeds and bullrushes and surrounded by sallow; teal, mallard and tufted duck breed here regularly.

Take the side-roads north of Thetford (bounded on all sides by 'MOD – Keep Out' notices) and after ten miles (16km) you will come to East Wretham Heath. This is a lovely Norfolk Naturalists' Trust reserve of some 370 acres (150ha); together with the large area of Croxton Heath, Forestry Commission forest, East Wretham makes up one of the largest blocks of land available for wildlife in the Brecks. Stop at the warden's house and get a leaflet, then take a walk along the Drove Road. This crosses the reserve from east to west and the nearby lay-by gives good views of Ring Mere, an open 'breck' mere with much fringing vegetation – gadwall, pochard, shoveller, teal, mallard, tufted duck and dabchick almost certainly breed here, and you may see a kingfisher perching briefly or a migrant osprey hovering over the lake. Passing waders appear in spring and autumn, with common, green and wood sandpipers, greenshank and spotted redshank all regular visitors. Woodcock breed in many of the woods and at dusk can be seen probing the mere margins.

The Drove Road is a good track and a public right of way; there is open heath on one side with birch scrub, and after a quarter of a mile you come to the lovely water of Long Mere which is overlooked

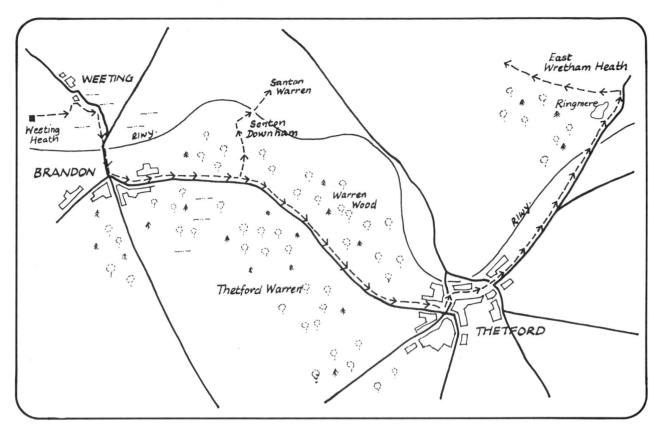

by a useful bird hide to the north. Long Mere, like Ring Mere, often holds a variety of waterfowl; behind it is a stand of mature Scots pine which stretches down and eventually meets the Drove Road – open silver birch and hawthorn heath, with a ground cover of heather, bracken and wavy hair grass, runs up to this pine plantation. Tree pipit and willow warbler are numerous on the heath and there are many breeding pairs of stonechat, whinchat and wheatear; dusk in summer brings the 'churr' of nightjar, reeling grasshopper warblers and the mournful hoot of long-eared owl. Both long-eared and tawny owls breed in the pines.

The Drove Road meets the superb old Scots pine plantation at an entrance where there is special provision for blind people; this includes an excellent trail with rails continuing for several hundred yards, so that disabled people can feel and hear the life of the Brecks all about them. This is a lovely place – the huge, gnarled old pines were planted at the time of the Battle of Waterloo – so treat it quietly: you may still see a red squirrel, although the grey is gaining ground, roe deer and rabbits are quite common and rabbit predators, the stoat and the weasel, may also be seen by those willing to sit still and remain silent. Crossbill, siskin and redstart breed either in these pines or across the Drove Road in Croxton Forest, and woodlark may be seen along the forest edge.

The main Drove Road continues beyond the reserve through great plantations of Corsican and Scots pine – red squirrels and roe deer use these forests as a retreat. Try and plan your visit so that you can walk back along the track towards your car at dusk; although the reserve closes at 5pm the Drove Road is public and this is the time to see the delicate roe deer step gingerly out onto the track before you, twitching its nose to scent the air.

Midsummer brings the haunting, moth-like shapes of nightjars displaying in the sunset, and the silent, gliding owl or the swift sparrowhawk looking for prey. Winter too has a special appeal: hundreds of thrushes, redwings, fieldfares and blackbirds feed on the hawthorn berries – so too will waxwings in an 'invasion' year when their winter food in Scandinavia has failed. There are innumerable finches in large, mixed flocks which include brambling, siskin and crossbill, and sometimes hawfinch joining the even more numerous chaffinches, bullfinches and yellowhammers. Large, open heaths with concentrations of small birds like this in winter, especially in East Anglia, attract the occasional large hawk such as a hen harrier or perhaps a small falcon like the merlin.

East Wretham is a remnant, precious in its rarity, hemmed in by great tracts of foreign conifer forests, NATO training grounds and the thunderous air bases of the flat East Anglian countryside. Go and explore it.

The stone curlew was once widespread in southern England but is now confined to a few Breckland nature reserves by modern farming practice

7

The Forest of Dean and the Wye Valley
GLOUCESTER AND HEREFORD

Address of Site/Warden

Forest of Dean
Forestry Commission Office,
Crown Offices,
Coleford,
Glos
RSPB Nagshead Reserve:
Warden:
6 Stompers Row,
Parkend,
Lydney,
Glos GL15 4JL

Highlights and Features

Ancient royal hunting forest allowing continuity from original forests. Now large area of mixed woodland, with oak and beech as standard. Superb area for woodland birds and insects, especially pied flycatchers. Good herd of fallow deer, also good for many other woodland mammals, including dormouse.

Facilities

Various information centres, country pursuit centres. Well known tourist area with full facilities.

Photo Tips

Woodland bird photography only possible with time and preparation. Excellent area for woodland flowers and insects. 28–70mm and 80–200mm lenses best here.

The Brown Hairstreak is an uncommon butterfly flying in late summer, whose larvae live on blackthorn

The Royal Forest of Dean is bounded on the south by the River Severn and on the north and west by the lovely River Wye, and rolls like a rumpled green carpet over a huge tract of hilly ground between England and the Welsh border. Set aside by Saxon and Norman kings alike for hunting, the Forest has survived today because of the deer that hide in its shadowy coverts. The rocks on which it lies are varied, leading to a rich mixture of woodland types and much of the woodland is of ancient origin. The area of some 27,000 acres (10,926ha) is now administered by the Forestry Commission, although in 1938 it was declared as Britain's first National Forest Park. Commercial forestry still flourishes but is carried out with a strong bias towards the conservation of wildlife and the provision of amenities for the general public. There are dozens of walks of varying lengths; two are described here, one taking in the western boundary River Wye with its wonderful wood and hill scenery, and the other through the RSPB Nagshead Reserve in the ancient heart of the Forest.

Wildlife Walk 1: Symonds Yat Rock and High Meadow Woods

Leave the A40 about five miles (8km) north of Monmouth on a minor road signposted to Symonds Yat Rock, which is probably the best known viewpoint in the Wye Valley. The road is single track with passing places and the car-parks at the Rock are often crowded in summer. The round walk described is four miles (6km) long and steep in parts. A visit at anytime of year is rewarding, but early summer brings the most by way of woodland breeding birds, flowers and butterflies. Walk back from the car-park past the wooden footbridge over the road to the viewpoint. A stunning view appears far below, with high cliffs running south where the river has cut its way through a layer of limestone. Peregrines have nested on this cliff for the past three years, returning to one of their traditional sites. The RSPB provides a warden and a superb lookout from the Rock, and the birds may be watched hunting the Wye Valley, feeding their chicks and generally lazing about later in the autumn. This is the best site in Britain to watch this bird without fear of disturbance.

Return over the wooden bridge to the Log Cabin refreshment hut and descend a steep, stepped path marked 'Wye Valley Walk' to a sloping gravel track – ignore the continuation of this path with its sign 'to river and boats' and instead turn left down the track. The woodlands here are thick and luxuriant with a dense scrub layer, and are a somewhat strange mixture: predominantly beech with sessile oak, ash, wych elm and lime which grow on successive layers of limestone and sandstone, often on steep bluffs; and there are whitebeam and wild service trees, as well as larch and pine plantations.

As you descend the gravel track towards the river the woods in early summer will be filled with birds: all the common species, woodpeckers, nuthatch, treecreeper, tits and goldcrest may be seen, besides several warblers, especially chiffchaff, willow and wood warblers. Several pairs of redstarts and the odd pair of pied flycatchers provide exotic colour. The river banks are lined with ferns – hartstongue fern in particular is rampant – and also giant bellflower and Himalayan balsam, while the limestone clefts hold various spleenworts; buddleia bushes line the track and ivy, traveller's joy and bryony grow in tumbling profusion down the slopes. In summer butterflies of a dozen or more species occur here with fritillaries, Red and White Admirals and even Holly Blue coming to the flowers to feed. Further down, the River Wye is much used for canoe instruction but before the crowds come out you may see grey wagtail and the secretive kingfisher.

Some 600 yards (548m) along the river turn left at the first, major, arrowed track. This is a superb spot, full of woodland birds. From the river the path rises steadily through rich mixed woodlands lined with meadowsweet and butterbur; if you are quiet you may see a shy fallow deer – check the muddy paths for their footprints, and for those of fox and badger. After three-quarters of a mile the path divides at a huge block of Old Red Sandstone, point 9 on the Symonds Yat Nature Trail. Here the soils are acid sandstones and the trees are great Douglas firs. Join the red-arrowed trail which runs through open groves before entering a dense and silent, young plantation. Conifer-loving birds are here in profusion, with breeding pairs of goldcrest, crossbill, siskin, sparrowhawk and long-eared owl, and just the chance of a rare firecrest to be seen sometimes in the forest. However, the interior of the young fir plantation is dark and almost lifeless compared with the outer clearings.

For half-a-mile the path runs first through the firs and then through a mature plantation of cypress trees before returning to the car-park along an open wooded ride of mature oaks. Sparrowhawks hunt regularly along this avenue of trees.

Wildlife Walk 2: Nagshead RSPB Reserve

The Nagshead Reserve entrance lies a quarter of a mile west of Parkend village and the Woodman Inn, opposite the Whitemeads Country Club. From the car-park the Information Centre (open only from April till August) is down a birch-lined track; the reserve itself is open all year, although early summer is still the best time to visit. From the Centre the longer nature trail, some two miles (3km) or so in length, turns right after 200 yards (183m), past an old Nissen hut half-hidden in the undergrowth – take the minor track between the holly trees and not the major woodland ride.

The woodland here is primarily mature oak on sandstone. The path runs down into an extensive dell, a valley with a little stream and a pool where dipper, grey wagtail and kingfisher can be seen along the stream. As you walk the damp oak paths, woodcock are a possibility and breed regularly in this damp woodland habitat. These woods have a very varied shrub layer of rowan, yew, and holly, and much bracken. Less visited than much of the Forest, Nagshead often shelters groups of fallow deer, slipping softly through the trees – walk quietly and your chances of seeing one or two are high. Fox, badger and dormice are all resident but are more nocturnal, although a dusk walk could reveal all three – dormice in particular like a many-layered woodland, with lots of different types of nuts and berries to provide food throughout the season. Use one of the several seats along the main ride and watch quietly. The track from the dell rises to the main ride at a stile and a 'dog-flap'; turn right here and follow the pink-arrowed trail. Sparrowhawks and buzzards hunt this angled wooded valley where the track turns at the far end of the nature trail.

Flowers on sandstone are less varied than on limy soils but bluebells carpet the woods in May, while great spikes of foxgloves line the rides later in the summer. Butterflies may be seen throughout the reserve with Silver-washed and Pearl-bordered Fritillaries and graceful White Admirals in late June. Holly Blues

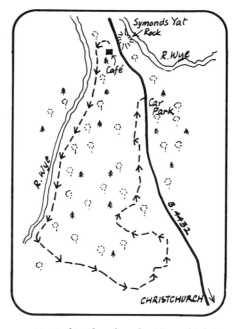

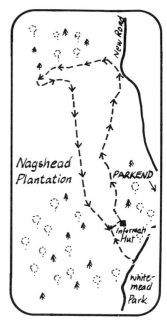

are attracted to the abundant ivy which in September grows in flower-filled fountains up many trees.

Returning towards the Centre the path runs through some open heath clearings with birch and gorse where whinchat, grasshopper warbler and tree pipit are found; the path then climbs through a conifer plantation inhabited by goldcrest, crossbill and coal tit, all typical of these trees.

Nest-boxes have been placed throughout the wood; these are used in spring by some forty pairs of pied flycatchers on their return from Africa, and sometimes by redstarts which also breed in the mature oak and beech. Find a nest-box with a flycatcher or redstart and sit and watch the comings and goings as these rather special birds raise their hungry broods.

The nocturnal badger is found throughout Britain, preferring rich woodlands such as in the Dean Forest

8

The Wyre Forest
WORCESTER

Address of Site/Warden

National Nature Reserve
Nature Conservancy Council,
West Midland Region
Attingham Park,
Shrewsbury,
Shropshire SY4 4TW

Highlights and Features

Large area of mature oak woodland on the coal measures. Consequent wide variety of plants and insects. Good for woodland butterflies with rare fritillaries. Excellent for woodland birds with breeding redstart, wood warbler, woodcock, and long-eared owl.

Facilities

Permits only away from footpaths.

Photo Tips

Close-up lenses needed for flowers, insects. Medium zoom for butterflies and a wide-angle zoom for forest habitat shots.

Common in open woodland the foxglove provides the source for the cardiac drug, digitalis

So little of Britain's ancient forest remains that any really large area is particularly precious, providing the only remaining examples of wildlife and vegetation whose development has been unbroken since the primeval forest which once clothed the whole country before the advent of man. Those large areas that have survived, the New Forest, the Forest of Dean and the Wyre were all royal hunting forests, and this is really why they have survived into the modern age. Plantagenet and Tudor kings liked the Wyre and hunted from the royal palace at Tickenhill. By the time the industrial revolution was destroying the rest of our ancient woodland to fuel its furnaces, royal forests had developed an aura of Victorian conservation which happily ensured their continuing survival.

With Birmingham and the industrial heart of the Midlands a few short miles to the north, the Wyre is one of the most important woodland wildlife sites in Britain. One round walk of some five miles (8km) is described, mostly over level ground with one or two short steep paths. It can be very muddy and wellies are essential in anything other than prolonged dry weather.

Wildlife Walk

Access is from the Forestry Commission Visitor Centre with a large car-park some three miles (5km) west of Bewdley on the A456 – the car-park straggles through the edge of the wood and is itself a good spot for woodland birds. The Centre is open for some five hours each day. Visiting is good throughout the year, but particularly in early summer when all the breeding song-birds are present. There are many walks throughout the two main blocks of forest which are separated by the B4194, running north-west from Bewdley. Much of the area is run by the Forestry Commission as commercial woodland, but fortunately the central rich heart of the forest along the Dowles Brook is a national nature reserve of 750 acres (303ha). The woodlands lie on the many varied rocks of the coal measures, including sandstones, marls, conglomerates and bands of limestone. Most of the soils are acid, but limestone is the base of the national nature reserve, and here the variety of native trees and flora is very rich.

Take the left-hand wide gravel track away from the Centre, using the well-marked forest trail. This runs through a very mixed woodland, with considerable conifer plantings of varying ages and large groves of mature Douglas firs. The red-marked forest trail, still well outside the main national nature reserve, dips to a water course, then climbs an eroded path through these firs. Crossbill, goldcrest, siskin and owls are seen here, and sparrowhawks hunt the main ride. In summer the young plantations, full of bracken and heather, are frequented by scrub birds such as grasshopper warbler, whitethroat and numerous willow warblers; long-eared owls sometimes breed in the groves of firs. In about 400 yards (365m) the path loops back right-handed to the main ride, and oak now predominates. The Wyre is a meeting-place of many woodland types and both sessile and pedunculate oak form large woods, originating from ancient coppiced stumps but growing now as high forest. Coppicing was the original method of harvesting the forest and dates back to the Middle Ages.

Although the soils are acid, the summer flora of these woods includes wood sage and lily of the valley among heather and bracken, unusual because these are usually found on lime-rich soils. The path runs down towards the Dowles Brook through wonderful woodland of oak and beech – birds are typical and numerous, with all three woodpeckers, nuthatch, tree-creeper, warblers, the bright black-and-white pied flycatcher and the fiery redstart. After a mile or so the red-arrowed trail turns off the main track, but ignore this and continue on for a few hundred yards. Splendid forest valley views to the left afford good opportunities to see passing buzzard and sparrowhawk. The NNR sign is just beyond Park House, and 400 yards (365m) further on is a footbridge over Dowles Brook.

This is by far the richest part of the forest, growing on a band of limestone on lime-rich soils. A small outcrop of rock lies by the path. Dowles Brook itself is a wide bubbling stream of crystal-clear water, sufficiently clean to hold crayfish and brook lamprey as well as trout and salmon. Kingfishers are frequent, attracted to the abundant food; the brook has cut a deep stream valley, with steep oak-clad sides.

Turn right beyond the footbridge and the vehicle ford, and use the paths which follow the brook eastwards. Pied fly-catchers are frequent, busy hunting insects all summer, with grey wagtail and dipper along the brook edge. Along the stream valley the shrubs are very varied and include hawthorn, blackthorn, hazel, guelder-rose, rowan, alder and willow thickets, dogwood, and the rare small-leaved lime and the wild service tree. The dense, layered vegetation provides a prime habitat for dormice although the chances of seeing one are very slim. All along the brook paths the variety of woodland birds is a delight in high summer; by autumn there are thrushes cropping the berries and also roving bands of tits, tree-creepers and goldcrests.

Some 400 yards (365m) east of the footbridge a major junction of several paths occurs alongside an experimental pond dug by the Nature Conservancy, a likely site for frogs and toads in spring with common lizards basking on the banks. Turn right following the brook, where the clearings are a delight, full of meadow-sweet and agrimony among the stands of pendulous sedge in high summer. The brook and the main rides support a wonderful variety of butterflies: Silver-washed and High Brown Fritillaries, White Admiral, Orange-tip and many more flit through the woodlands throughout the summer. These base-rich soils also en-courage many rare flowers: several species of orchid appear in the clearings, with green-veined and narrow-leaved helleborine as prime examples. Most of the valley woods are filled with dogs' mercury and primroses, but here and there are columbine, lily of the valley, wood and bloody cranesbill, yellow rattle, meadow saffron and adders' tongue.

When you reach the flat wooden bridge stand and watch the brook, partly hidden by the steep mossy bank. Kingfishers pass this way regularly, while more nocturnal animals leave their tracks in the muddy path — badger, fox and fallow deer. Walkers who are quiet may see fallow deer anywhere in the forest, but the Dowles Brook area is probably best when animals come to feed on the lush grasses and drink from the streams.

Continue through high forest above the brook until the muddy path returns to water level and a further NNR notice. Turn right here following the red-marked bridle trail south for 400 yards (365m) to NNR notice number 15 on the track of the old railway. Cross this and continue down the red-marked bridleway, which now becomes a wide clay track running along the bank of a tributary to Dowles Brook. The track heads southwards back towards the Forest Centre some two miles (3km)

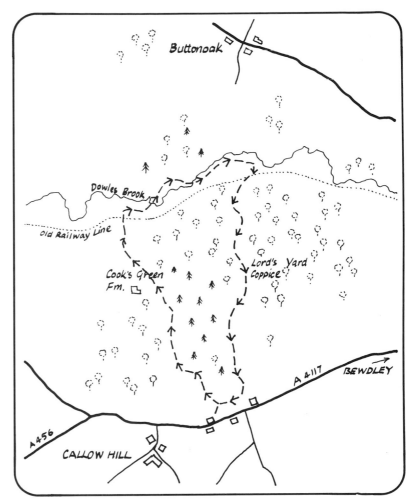

distant. Many side paths enable explora-tion of the whole woodland, which is sufficiently extensive to demand a simple compass to avoid getting lost. Otherwise stay on the main track which leads through groves of huge Douglas fir where crossbill, siskin and goldcrest can fre-quently be seen. The last half-mile is a well marked forest trail and runs through some uninspiring young conifer plantations.

The blackcap, a tiny warbler of the scrub layer, arriving from Africa in April to rear its family

9

Dinas and Gwenffrwd
DYFED

Address of Site/Warden

RSPB Reserve
Troedrhiwgelynen,
Rhandirmwyn,
Llandovery,
Dyfed SA20 0PN

Highlights and Features

West coast sessile oak-
woods, rushing streams and
high craggy moorland.

Facilities

Small car-park. Information
centre open Easter to
August. Nature trail open all
year.

Photo Tips

Wide-angle lenses here for
scenic shots. Use a tripod for
flower and fungi pictures.
Most birds will be distant.
Try ferns on rocks, with a
wide-angle lens to show the
distant hills.

*The tawny owl is the
most numerous of the
British owls, and is found
in many woods and
copses in the countryside*

Drifting along the moorland edge, suspended on an invisible thread between
earth and sky, flies a red kite, its long,
mobile, white-patched wings and twisting,
elongated forked tail proclaiming its
identity. It flicks a wing to spill air from its
primary flight feathers and side-slips down
the hillside to disappear down the deep
chasm of the valley's torrent. This sight is a
rare wildlife privilege in Britain where less
than forty pairs of red kites survive in the
coastal mountains of Wales. Like vultures
and some eagles, the red kite has declined
even throughout Europe because it lives
largely on carrion which is now less
available because farming practices are
better. However, at Dinas and Gwenffrwd
this otherwise rare sight of a graceful red
kite coasting along the hills is frequent;
indeed one of the best places to watch is
from the Dinas RSPB car-park – scan the
hillsides while you sit and eat your lunch.

Dinas Wood is the easiest of these
reserves to visit but the surrounding
wooded valleys, especially where the
woods are ancient oak woodlands and not
new conifer plantations, all have good
walks in search of birds, plants and
animals. Dinas, much smaller than Gwenffrwd, is open at all times; Gwenffrwd,
however, is open only during the period
Easter till August, when intending visitors
must first report to the Dinas Information
Centre, situated a few miles north of
Llandovery on minor mountain roads
towards the Llyn Brianne dam. There is a
small car-park.

Walking boots and waterproofs are
needed in these rain-swept rocky valleys,
and full mountain equipment for Gwenffrwd which is thoroughly mountainous.
Best time to visit is early summer when
most of the wildlife is seen more readily.

Wildlife Walk: Dinas Hill and Wood

The tiny car-park under Dinas Hill is
situated in a lovely, narrow green valley
surrounded on all sides by huge hills. As
you park your car a cascade of chaffinches
will probably descend to see if you have
brought some food. The River Tywi
crashes down in a series of cataracts a few
yards away; after heavy rain, quite frequent here, the sound of tumbling water is
a constant companion as you walk.

At the start of the footpath lean on the
post and scan the open hillside in front of

you: two valleys with a high hill saddle join
together here and red kites often appear
over this saddle, while buzzard, raven and
peregrine all hunt along the hills. Buzzards
are particularly numerous and the whining
calls of the chicks in early summer show
just how common they are – there is a pair
nearly every half-mile around these
wooded valleys.

To avoid damaging the wet valley bog
vegetation the first 500 yards (456m) is a
raised boardwalk, often wet and slippery;
the steeper sections have had chicken
wire nailed to the boards to give a
foothold. Way above, the hanging sessile
oak-woods cover the conical dome of
Dinas Hill, while alder, hazel and sallow
grow in the boggy valley – marsh marigold, yellow flag and bog asphodel grow
here in profusion. Grey squirrels sometimes forage for hazel nuts and marsh and
willow tits are frequent. An occasional
lesser spotted woodpecker may appear in
the alders while early spring brings redpoll
and siskin to feed on the seeds.

Turn right off the boardwalk following
the white arrow to start your circuit of the
hill. This is a rocky, slippery, steep walk of
a mile and a half, which will take you
nearly two hours even if you are in a
hurry, and all day if you are not. The
mature oaks which grow in the valley floor
are full of birdsong in spring and summer;
this open woodland is ideal for redstart,
and for tree pipit on the forest edge. The
high-pitched trill of wood warblers should
be just about audible above the thunder of
the Tywi torrent as it rushes down its rocky
gorge.

200 yards (183m) from the boardwalk
there is an open grassy lawn beside the
river, with a seat and the view of crag,
gorge, woods and falling water is quite
outstanding. Dippers are numerous along
the rivers here – watch the isolated rocks
in mid-stream which they frequently use
as perches. Common sandpipers nest in
the tussocks along the river bank, while a
more recent resident is the goosander
which commutes to feed on Llyn Brianne
upriver and is now nesting in the larger
tree-holes on the hill. Sparrowhawks are
common in these woods and skim through
the gorge to pluck an unsuspecting chaffinch from its perch.

The rocky path now scrambles sharply
up and down the northern, steeper side of

the reserve, with the roar of the river below your feet to the right. In May these woodlands belong to the lovely black-and-white pied flycatcher, truly the woodland sprite of the bird world. Several dozen pairs use nest-boxes and the oak tree-holes, arriving in late April from their African winter quarters. As the track turns the north-west corner, a side path scrambles up a steep and difficult climb to Twm Sion Catis Cave, linked by legend to the real-life Welsh hero born in 1530 in nearby Tregaron. A seat on a high corner overlooking Junction Pool gives splendid views of the valleys of the Rivers Tywi and Doethie – the two rivers meet here and flow past the reserve, less of a cascade than before but still powerful. Dippers and grey wagtails haunt the river while the lucky visitor, out very early, may see an otter.

The acid soils of the reserve mean that flowers are few but because of the high rainfall the trees and boulder-strewn hillsides in the woods are carpeted with ferns and mosses. From this seat go searching among the nearby rocks for the twelve species of fern which grow here, some quite rare and delicately beautiful. Common species such as male fern, hard fern and polypody are numerous, but you should also find the rarer lemon-scented mountain fern, lady fern, golden-scaled mountain fern, oak, beech, rusty-backed and Wilson's filmy ferns. Autumn, though quiet for birds, brings a superb display of woodland fungi and ferreting out the various ferns and fungi can be very rewarding after the summer birds have flown. In spring the woods are filled with bluebells, while bracken covers the more open areas. From the vantage point of this same seat high above the river a quiet visitor, watching for the elusive otter, may glimpse an equally elusive polecat, quite common in these Welsh hills but rarely seen.

The path swings away from the river for the last half mile, through more mature trees on deeper soil. Here the woodland birds are much in evidence: woodpeckers, tits, nuthatches, tree-creepers, warblers, flycatchers and redstarts vie for attention. Butterflies are often numerous in mid-summer with Small Pearl-bordered and Silver-washed Fritillaries among the commoner Ringlets, Tortoiseshells and Meadow-Browns. Purple Hairstreaks are frequent throughout the oak woodland. Bog pools near the car-park bring forth the lovely Golden-ringed Dragonfly in June while the rushing streams are good for Demoiselle Agrion damselflies, unmistakeable with their fluorescent blue-green wings.

Back in the car-park watch the hills again for the soaring red kite, whilst not

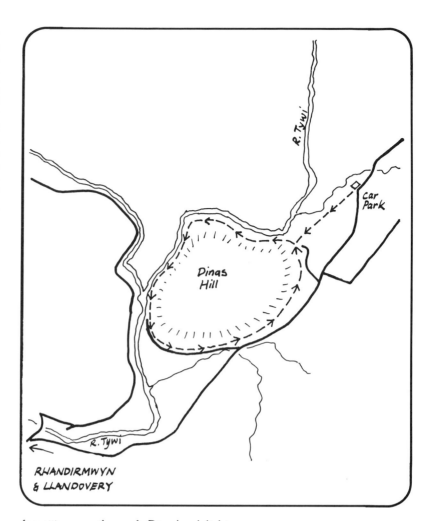

forgetting another of Dinas's delights: feeding crumbs to chaffinches, tame enough to collect them from the top of your car mirror.

Separate access to the hills of Gwenffrwd must be arranged with the warden, but most of the birds can be seen by turning right two miles (3km) south of Dinas over the iron Towy Bridge, and right again beside the Inn. This narrow road runs westward through more hanging oak-woods under the Gwenffrwd hills.

Once very rare the polecat is slowly spreading from its last stand in the mountains of Wales

10

Address of Site/Warden

Abernethy Forest:
part is National Nature
Reserve
NCC Head Warden,
Achantoul,
Aviemore PH22 1QD
Loch Garten RSPB Reserve
Warden,
Grianan,
Nethybridge,
Inverness PH25 3EF

Highlights and Features

Large remnants of the great
Forest of Caledon. Extensive
Scots pine forest with
heather, bilberry and juniper.
Probably the best area in
Britain for Scottish woodland
birds, with many crested
tits, Scottish and common
crossbills, capercaillie, black
and red grouse. Many birds
of prey including golden
eagle, goshawk and hen
harrier. Famous osprey nest
site at Loch Garten.
Mammals include red
squirrel, red and roe deer.

Facilities

Forest Office at Glenmore
Lodge for forest information.
RSPB Centre manned March
to September at Loch
Garten with observation hide
for ospreys. Well-known
tourist area with many
facilities.

Photo Tips

Long telephoto lenses for all
birds, and deer. Medium
zoom for red squirrels. Flash
possibly useful for latter.
Tripod essential.

Abernethy Forest and Loch Garten

HIGHLAND

The whole of the forested area around the Cairngorm massif is excellent for wildlife with many places to stop, walk and watch. The famous RSPB reserve of Loch Garten forms part of the much larger Abernethy Forest and is situated on a minor road between the villages of Boat of Garten and Nethybridge. Abernethy Forest also contains much of the Glenmore Forest Park, a large tract of forest situated to the north of the Aviemore–Cairngorm road and managed by the Forestry Commission. Most of the extensive forest is a remnant of the ancient Caledonian pine forest which once stretched right across the Highlands.

There are five distinct habitats within the area: Scots pine woodland, moorland, peat bog, open loch and farmland, and the main features of the area were formed 10,000 years ago during the last Ice Age – hollows filled with peat and water surrounded by moraines of sand and gravel.

Two wildlife walks are described, one through the main part of Abernethy Forest and the other taking in the RSPB reserve and the open water of the lochs. May and June produce all the breeding birds, but late October is a splendid time to visit for winter birds arriving from the north.

Wildlife Walk 1: Abernethy Forest

Access is straightforward from Nethybridge: drive down the road which leads directly south from the telephone kiosk in the village centre; after a mile you will see Dell Lodge on the left and the road becomes a track – there are several places to park cars on the edge of the forest. *Do not drive on* down the track as you will miss the specialities of this area – the track belongs to the Forestry Commission and you will disturb the wildlife.

Walk south. The fields here see much wildlife: early morning brings roe deer out to crop the sweet grass, and large flocks of redwing and fieldfare use them in autumn. Three hundred yards (274m) further on a pylon line splits the forest in two; a walk westwards along this line is very worthwhile as there is a three-mile 'forest edge' created by man, always a favourite habitat for birds and animals. This is one of the best places in Britain to see red squirrels – they really are numerous and the piles of eaten cones on pine logs will testify to their number. Try the woods just south of

the pylons in the early morning and late afternoon – they are often quite approachable and easily photographed; but take a flashgun, as the light in the woods is poor. Half-a-mile west along the pylons there is an extensive open area where capercaillie may be seen – in spring a 'lek' occurs nearby, but to see the male display and attract his hens will need a 4am start.

Back on the main track, and after half-a-mile a broken hummocky area of birch and rowan scrub can be seen on the left with rocks on the slopes. The grass and herb sward between the trees is a favourite area for roe deer which may often be seen at quite close quarters. Redwings and fieldfares in large numbers feed on the rowan berries on arrival in late October, and black grouse may often be seen here. Scots pine forest now dominates both sides of the track. In spring this forest has large populations of the common birds associated with conifers: coal tit, goldcrest, chaffinch, wren and treecreeper; blue tits are numerous along the forest edge. There are also some special birds found only in the Scottish pinewoods: crested tit are frequent, as are siskins; Scottish crossbills breed in early spring in many places and band together in midsummer to form noisy feeding flocks.

After a mile-and-a-half one emerges into an open area of moorland with views straight to the northern slopes of Cairngorm. The intervening valley is used by many birds passing from mountain to forest and back. Golden eagles are seen occasionally although they have become less frequent due to 'people pressure' on the ski-slopes of Cairngorm. Buzzards are quite common, breeding in the forest and hunting the open moors and farmland for rabbits. From April to September an osprey passing along the valley is not unusual.

Wildlife Walk 2: Loch Garten

'To the Ospreys' is a famous sign-post on Speyside, and thousands of people have come for thirty years to see this glorious fishing hawk, ever since the first pair nested there in 1954. The RSPB observation hide is easy to locate and parking round the loch side is usually possible, although crowded in summer. The ospreys arrive in April and by August, with

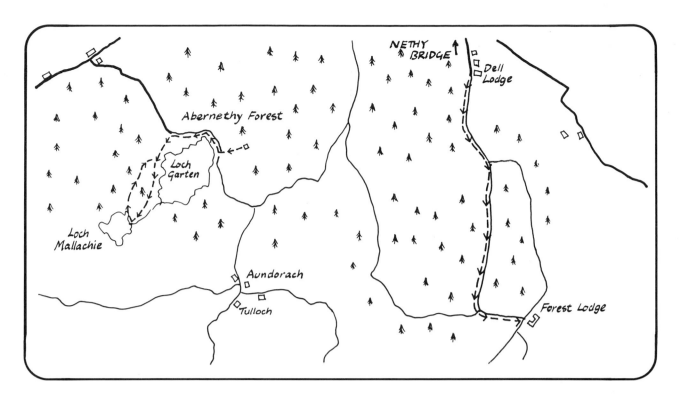

chicks flying, there are several birds in the area. At least one other pair breeds locally. By far the best place to see an osprey catch fish is at the loch belonging to the trout farm at Aviemore; Loch Insh to the south is another favoured place.

While no disturbance is allowed around the breeding ospreys there is a large area of pine woodland, birch scrub and moorland accessible towards Nethybridge and around the southern end of Loch Garten itself. Keep to the marked paths. Crested tits are the gem of this woodland, breeding in old tree-stumps in some numbers, capercaillie are also resident and black grouse breed on the moor edge. Summer migrants add variety with several pairs of redstarts in the larger open trees and willow warblers extremely common in the scrub. Try walking through the woods around the loch. Red squirrels are common and become quite tame in summer since so much food is provided by visitors. By October, with the first snows the squirrels spend most of their day in windproof holes between the rocks. Wildfowl have nesting sites all around the loch, but in particular use the reeds at the southern end — mallard, teal and tufted duck are all breeders, with the occasional wigeon and goldeneye using nest-boxes.

At the southern end of Loch Garten is the much smaller Loch Mallachie, and the path from the roadside car-park runs through the pines to its edge, about a mile. Otters are sometimes seen here — look for their tracks in the peaty mud; ospreys fish this loch too, especially in August when the chicks are learning to hunt.

Flowers in midsummer are typical of highland woods with creeping ladies' tresses and lesser twayblade, uncommon orchids in the forest by Loch Mallachie. Mountain Ringlet butterflies appear in late June while Scotch Argus butterflies are seen over the moor a month later. October means no ospreys, but also no people so you can have the glorious colours of the Highland autumn all to yourself. Birch trees seem to cascade gold over all the hillsides. Loch Garten is directly in the line of migrant wild geese heading south down the Spey Valley — great skeins of pinkfeet and grey-lag geese pass southwards every day to head out over the mountains towards their wintering grounds. About 1,000 grey-lags stay on to feed on the local farmland throughout the winter, using the loch as a night-time roost. Moving down the Spey at treetop height come redwings and fieldfares by the thousand, feeding on the rowan and escaping from the High Arctic winter.

The red squirrel is now largely restricted to the north and west, surviving best in large areas of forest

A regular winter visitor, from Scandinavia, the goldeneye has recently begun to colonise the Highland lochs and rivers

GRASSLANDS AND DOWNLANDS

As the traveller to Britain flies in above the clouds, he is greeted with a panoramic view of the countryside, a patchwork of different shades of vivid green. The green is mostly the grass of farm fields and of common and downland, dotted here and there with woods and copses. The wide open spaces of the British lowland grasslands were created by man when he felled the forests, so the glorious scenery of our 'green and pleasant land' is in fact largely man-made. The character of grassland areas has changed most dramatically in the last two or three decades due to technical advances in modern farming. Whether one looks on it as good or bad, farming methods and the political pressures of the European Common Agricultural Policy have destroyed large areas of ancient flower-filled meadows, all replaced by 'improved' grass.

Now that the forests have largely been removed, all Britain's lowland grassland requires management to prevent the re-establishment of scrub and woodland. Farm fields are constantly tended to maintain the grassland environment. Ancient open downland has been kept as such for centuries by grazing, because grasses are adapted to survive the removal of their leaves by animals, unlike most other plants. Therefore grazing eliminates the potentially invasive scrub and maintains the grass.

Grazing in Britain is provided by cattle, sheep and rabbits, all animals introduced by man as a food source several thousand years ago. This clearly demonstrates the artificial nature of grassland, provided that such grazing has been a long-term policy, although a balanced semi-natural habitat is in fact created since a wide diversity of plant species is encouraged. Long-term grazing by sheep on chalk downland has been responsible for the rich chalk-plant community found here.

In southern and eastern England, a bedrock of chalk stretches from Purbeck in Dorset to Flamborough Head in Yorkshire, with spurs lying east–west along the North Downs to Dover and the South Downs to Beachy Head. The thin layer of soil covering the surface is rich in lime and has a high pH value, meaning that it is strongly alkaline in nature. Chalk and limestone are both made from the same basic rock of calcium carbonate, and their porosity allows water to seep quickly through to layers below. The surface soils are thus usually very dry and this, together with the poor nutrient value of the soil which has only a limited supply of nitrogen and phosphates, determines the plant species that can survive. The fact that chalk and limestone grasslands are rich in species shows that the alkaline nature of the soil is very advantageous to plant growth.

Old downland is identifiable by its anthills. The location of these is quite deliberate, built by the ants in full sunshine to provide a centrally heated home for their nest and the subsequent rearing of broods. Old, untouched downland usually has many such anthills, giving a rough guide to the age of the surrounding grassland. The anthills encourage a special habitat, prohibiting the 'rosette' form of chalk plant which needs its growing point above the soil, but providing ideal conditions for plants such as thyme and rock rose which trail over the surface.

Many plants are characteristic of chalk and limestone soils and are rarely found elsewhere. It is thus possible by a quick scan of the vegetation to tell whether the rock below is filled with lime. Among the plants characteristic of lime-rich soils are rockrose, thyme, salad burnet, harebell, bird's-foot trefoil and traveller's joy. Grasses include quaking grass, sheep's fescue and red fescue; the coarser upright brome grass is found where grazing has been limited.

Many orchid species are also found only in chalk or limestone grassland, and their rarity and the beauty of their flowers make them much prized by photographers and naturalists generally. Some are so rare that they suffer from unscrupulous and illegal collection by the selfish few, and need constant protection during their midsummer flowering period. Typical chalk species include bee and man orchids, burnt orchid, early and late spider orchids, musk and frog orchids.

Most of the best localities for flowers are also good for butterflies. The blue butterfly family is typical of the downs, and in good years drifts of blue butterflies of several species occur on the sunny slopes from May through to September. The Common Blue is the most numerous overall but where colonies of Chalk-hill Blues exist they may number many thousands. The much rarer Adonis Blue is limited to a few localities in southern Britain, while the Small Blue, although widely distributed, is everywhere fairly scarce. Habitat destruction has reduced these species dramatically in the last three decades, so that colonies are often isolated by many miles and cannot be sustained by influxes from elsewhere. Even the strong-flying Dark Green Fritillary exists only in pockets along the downland hills. This isolation has become one of the main threats to species in many habitats, and chalkland butterflies are just one example.

In Britain, the largest area of chalk downland

survives in Wiltshire, largely by courtesy of the army on Salisbury Plain. Porton Down, part of this area, is very rich in wild flowers and butterflies. Other excellent sites on chalk downs include Martin Down and Butser Hill in central Hampshire; Hod Hill in Dorset which has a spectacular range of butterflies; Castle Hill near Lewes in Sussex with colonies of unusual butterflies and orchids; Box Hill in Surrey with an excellent flora and with Silver-spotted Skipper butterflies – despite hordes of picnickers; Tottenhoe Knolls in Bedfordshire; and Devils Dyke in Cambridge, an old earthwork built of chalk and now holding rare flowers.

In the north and west the chalk gives way to the much harder but still very porous Carboniferous Limestone. Chalk has very few natural exposures (the river cliff at Box Hill, Surrey, is an exception) but limestone outcrops frequently, and there are important sites at Cheddar, Ebbor and the Avon Gorges in the Mendips; Millers, Lathkill and Dovedales in Derbyshire; and many more in the northern dales, especially around Malham and Gordale in Yorkshire. Limestone pavement, much abused for rockery stone, is found at Gait Barrows near Arnside and at Hutton Roof and Southern Scales Fell on Ingleborough.

Limestone hills have a broadly similar flora to that of the southern chalk downland, with some additional species in the north. On the northern fells, however, sheep are the traditional type of mainstream farming and huge numbers graze the grasslands; plants tend to survive best where the sheep cannot reach them, in limestone outcrops or hidden two feet down in the grykes of limestone pavement. This pavement is particularly exciting to explore as there is no knowing what rarity may be growing in the next gryke. Special flowers of these areas include the dark red helleborine, tutsan, angular solomon's seal, and bloody cranesbill.

Neutral grasslands are often referred to as meadow grasslands because their chief use was for hay or a combination of grazing and hay cutting. They occur on soils neither very alkaline, nor very acid, and are mostly found on clays or loams. All are extensively managed by man, some as flood meadows along rivers, some as man-made washes in the East Anglian fens, some as water meadows maintained by a series of sluices and ditches and now rarely seen, and others as damp grasslands on clay soils. These flower-rich hay meadows are now extremely rare in Britain because herbicides and fertilisers have been used everywhere to 'improve' the sward for cattle feed, nowadays usually harvested as silage.

Conservation of the last remaining remnants of these habitats is now urgent. Each piece of downland newly ploughed or sprayed with fertiliser is a permanent loss, and so unnecessary in our over-productive countryside. It is unreasonable to add to the mountains of grain stored at vast cost to the taxpayer when with a little forethought the same taxpayer might have woollen products from sheep grazing the downland grasses.

Lathkill Dale, in the White Peak, with shining, unpolluted river, and largely unimproved chalk grasslands

11

The South Downs
HAMPSHIRE AND SUSSEX

Address of Site/Warden

Old Winchester Hill National
Nature Reserve:
Southern Regional Office,
Nature Conservancy Council,
Foxhold House,
Thornford Road,
Crookham Common,
Headley,
Newbury,
Berks RG15 8EL
Beachy Head:
Eastbourne Borough Council
Nature Trail:
Town Hall,
Eastbourne BN21 4UG.

Highlights and Features

Old Winchester Hill:
National nature reserve with
very rich chalk down flora
and insects
Beachy Head area:
southern sea-cliff ramparts
of South Downs with superb
chalk flora and butterflies.
Prominent position into
English Channel means that
it is excellent for bird
migration in spring and
autumn. A ringing station
operates during migration
periods.

Facilities

Old Winchester Hill:
interpretative centre and
wild-flower garden.
Beachy Head area:
well-known tourist area.
Nature Centre on headland,
and another nearby at
Cuckmere.

Photo Tips

Both areas are best for
downland flowers and
insects. Close-up and wide-
angle lenses useful for
flowers, while medium
telephoto zoom, say
80–200mm, is ideal for
butterflies. Table-top tripod
useful for low-growing chalk
flowers.

The South Downs are easy hills to explore: paths criss-cross them in all directions and the tops are linked by one of the most ancient ridgeway tracks in Britain. The South Downs Way runs for 80 miles (129km) from Buriton near Petersfield eastwards to Eastbourne, with the sea almost constantly in view to the south. Old Winchester Hill forms the westernmost section, while the switchback downs of the Seven Sisters and Beachy Head above Eastbourne are a formidable rampart against the sea on the east. The hills are chalk, and much more open and wind-swept than the well-wooded downs to the north. Two wildlife walks are described.

Wildlife Walk 1: Old Winchester Hill, Hants

Old Winchester Hill lies at the western end of the South Downs between Portsmouth and Winchester, and was made a national reserve in 1954 to protect its exceptionally rich variety of chalk flowers and insects. The wildlife walk follows the nature trail laid out by the Nature Conservancy Council. *Do not stray from the path*: there are still live mortar bombs on the reserve – 263 were discovered during the last search in 1980. The best times to visit for orchids and for butterflies are late May, early July and early August.

Travelling south down the A32, take the second tiny road on the left in West Meon village, and follow it for a mile and a half. There are several small lay-bys for cars at the top with reserve notices and leaflets; also a grassy picnic area so please eat your picnics only here. The view south and west reveals extensive arable farmland with dense but rather isolated woods of yew on the edge of the reserve. Behind you on the other side of the road is a stand of mature beech with green and great spotted woodpeckers, and nuthatches; white helleborine and bird's-nest orchids may be present in June.

After three hundred yards (274m) the track bends south along the spine of the hill and enters a dense stand of yew, where most of the trees are nearly 300 years old. In autumn and particularly November, the berries attract large numbers of migrant redwing and fieldfare, also thrushes and blackbirds, as they move west along the downs. The mixed scrub-lands at the edge of the yew woods and in the dell below have many breeding birds in spring and summer – most prominent are bullfinch, chaffinch, willow warbler, whitethroat and yellowhammer.

The path leaves the yew wood and rejoins the chalk track round the edge of the reserve. Wide arable fields stretch to the horizon in all directions over the rolling Hampshire Downs, leaving Old Winchester Hill as an 'island', last example of how all the surrounding countryside once looked. Rabbits are numerous now on the reserve and the track along the edge acts as a highway for stoats and weasels as they hunt out into the grass-land; they pass this way frequently.

Another hundred yards (91m) brings you to where the open spur of the hill begins. The whole hill-top is an Iron Age fort with a splendid earth rampart and ditch around it; some rough pasture here is given over to nesting skylarks, which sing constantly on the wind high above. Electric fencing has been installed around the downland slopes and along the fort's ramparts to ensure that the sheep graze only selected areas. A chalk turf rich in flowering plants needs hard grazing; with the rabbit all but eradicated by myxoma-tosis in the 1950s, extra grazing became necessary and the Nature Conservancy Council used these sheep for this purpose.

The fences also encourage people to keep to the edge of the sensitive plant-rich slopes. The rampart itself has a wonderful display of chalk flowers from April through to October and includes many rarities; fourteen species of orchid alone grow on the reserve, with large colonies of fragrant, bee, frog and greater butterfly orchid – there is also a large colony of the rare round-headed rampion. Over thirty species of butterfly can be seen here regularly: Common, Small, Adonis and Chalk-hill Blues, Dark Green Fritillary, Marbled White and Duke of Burgundy; many migrant butterflies may be seen.

Leave the hill fort and take the lower path down steps towards the Information Centre. The yew woods above hold several badger setts and roe deer are frequent, especially early in the morning. As you return to the car-park, watch the hill-top woods for hovering kestrels and for swooping sparrowhawks using the downland air-currents.

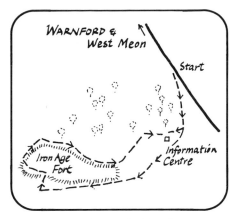

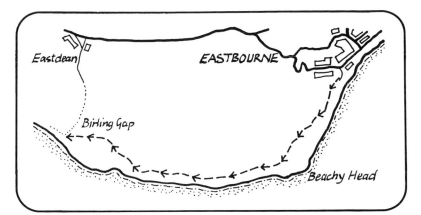

Wildlife Walk 2: Beachy Head to Birling Gap

This is a six-mile (9.5km) round walk which can start at either end, and it is easy to continue along the coastal path at Birling Gap to Cuckmere in another three miles (4.8km). The walk is renowned for its chalk flowers and butterflies and has the advantage of being a good site for bird migration, with a ringing station in Whitebread Hollow. Start from Duke's Drive at the western end of Eastbourne and take the lower cliff path which runs through privet and thorn scrub to the Hollow in half a mile. This is a sports field used for cricket in summer, set in a steep-sided, wooded dell.

Bird migration can be excellent here in spring and autumn: the Beachy Head Ringing Group then spend most weekends catching and ringing the hundreds of small passerine migrants. The common warblers are most frequent, with blackcaps often outnumbering all others; redstart, nightingale and ring ouzel are regulars and the spring passage of terns, skuas, ducks and waders east up-channel can be a marvellous sight when the wind is south-easterly.

Leave Whitebread Hollow by climbing the paths up towards the top of the hill on the western side. This is a fairly steep chalk slope, but soon you are 500 feet (152m) above the sea and walking on springy chalk turf along the cliff-tops, with the cliffs below gleaming white in the sunshine. Spring flowers appear from late April onwards with early purple orchid as one of the first. Burnt-tip orchid and green-veined orchid, dwarfed a little by the cliff-top exposure, are quite numerous in the grass towards the top in May. Thereafter a wonderful succession of summer flowers follows quickly one after the other: pink centaury, yellow-wort, common spotted orchid, carline and dwarf thistles, common and chalk milkworts, mignonette, viper's bugloss, bee orchid, round-headed rampion and autumn gentian among a whole array of chalk flowers. Coastal plants are also found with sea campion and sea lavender in clumps on the western section of the path.

Looking down at the red-and-white lighthouse, itself 142ft (43m) high but seeming a mere toy from the 520-foot (159m) high cliff, constitutes one of the most famous views in Britain. Layers of flint can be seen protruding at intervals down the cliffs allowing holes and ledges for nesting jackdaws. A few pairs of fulmars are now established and even the occasional peregrine has been seen flying along cliffs which used to be occupied by this magnificent bird.

Descend towards Belle Tout Wood; the chalk butterflies are much in evidence from May onwards: Chalk-hill, Adonis, Common and Small Blue all fly here, with Brown Argus, Marbled White and Dark Green Fritillary. Migrant moths and butterflies from the Mediterranean area, including Red Admirals, Painted Ladies, Clouded Yellows and even Humming-Bird Hawk Moths are seen every year, sometimes in huge numbers when conditions are favourable. Belle Tout Wood, beyond the old lighthouse, can be rewarding for observing migrant birds, as can the gorse and scrub which descend the hill to Birling Gap car-park – with its toilets, refreshment kiosks and crowds of tourists. Return is by the same general route, using different paths.

The South Downs are filled with chalk flowers, like mignonette, throughout the summer

Now found in scattered colonies along the chalk of southern Britain, the Chalk-hill Blue butterfly has declined due to farming pressure

The North Downs
SURREY AND KENT

Address of Site/Warden

Surrey Wildlife Trust,
Hatchlands,
East Clandon,
Guildford GU4 7RP
Kent Trust for Nature
Conservation,
The Annexe,
1a Bower Mount Road,
Maidstone,
Kent ME16 8AX

Highlights and Features

Ranmore Forest and Down:
Mixed Forestry Commission
woodland and downland
beech-woods on chalk down
ridge. Excellent for woodland
butterflies. Good for
mammals, especially roe
deer. Ranmore Down has
superb chalk flora, with
many orchids and many
butterfly species.
Queensdown Warren:
Steep chalk downland with
many rare chalk flowers,
especially orchids, and many
butterflies.

Facilities

Car-parks only.

Photo Tips

Medium zoom lenses for
butterflies. Tiny table-top
tripod for chalk flowers.
Wide-angle lens gives flower
close-up with downland
background.

*The Brimstone butterfly is
the sulphur-yellow
harbinger of spring in
woods through most of
England*

The North Downs sweep right across the counties of Surrey and Kent in a great arc from west to east, terminating in the spectacular white cliffs of Dover. These are chalk downs with short turf and all the flowers and insects characteristic of this habitat. To the north lie the clays and aggregates of the Thames basin, while south are more sands and clays which form the richly wooded Weald. The downs create a dramatic southern-facing scarp slope.

The North Downs Way traverses the ridge from Farnham as far as Dover, with many excellent short stretches of accessible downland. Two of the best nature walks are described, one in Surrey, the other in Kent.

Wildlife Walk 1: Ranmore Forest and Down, Surrey

This may be regarded as one continuous circular walk of some three miles (4.8km) through Ranmore Forest and along Ranmore Down, providing an amazing diversity of wildlife in a compact area. There are numerous side paths away from the described route; midsummer in late June or July provides the best variety. Park in the Forestry Commission car-park, complete with picnic tables. Pass through the gate at the western end and take the first path south towards the scarp, with a belt of tall larch on the right and open oak-woods with thin holly scrub on the left. After two hundred yards (183m) a wide east-west cross ride is encountered – this is an excellent place to stop and just sit on the grass and watch.

Grey squirrels are numerous, and roe deer are often seen in this ride when it is quiet – their slots show clearly in any damp ground. In May and June the woods, because of their variety, are filled with birdsong: blackcap, garden warbler, whitethroat, wood warbler, willow warbler and chiffchaff all sing within a few yards of each other; all three British woodpeckers, nuthatch, tree-creeper and all the woodland tits are common. Goldcrests nest high in the spruce branches, redpolls have a small, scattered colony and if you are lucky you may see a redstart – rare in Surrey.

Butterflies are a speciality of the whole walk and the area is rated in the Nature Conservancy's top ten sites. In May, Brim-

stones and Orange-tip flit through dappled sunlit rides, while in July White Admirals and even Purple Emperors glide among the honeysuckled boughs. Continue towards the downland slope – the path becomes steeper; soon you can see the open hillside falling away through the trees. Perched on the side of the scarp and hidden by three large yew trees is an old wartime pill-box – still in good order.

Take the wide, level path east through thin beech and oak, running along the top of the downs – badger tracks are frequent here. After half a mile the path goes through a pair of 'kissing gates' and on the left you might notice a new and single badger hole, larger than the many rabbit holes. This is a mixed beech and yew wood with many magnificent old yew trees – filled with berries in winter, attracting fieldfare, redwing, blackbird and other thrushes to the forest. Through another 'kissing gate', over a stile and out onto open Ranmore Down. The view is glorious, with Dorking nestling in the gap to the east, the whitewashed walls of Westcott village just below, and the wooded greensand ridge across the southern horizon. Rooks and jackdaws feed on the valley fields in hundreds, while the occasional sparrowhawk swoops out from the high down wood to hunt across the valley.

Follow the path straight along the top of the grass slope towards Dorking. From spring to autumn there is a succession of butterflies and chalk flowers which continually delight the eye. The whole walk offers wonderful opportunities to photograph the flowers and butterflies of downland. The secret of success with butterfly photography is to move in slowly and avoid casting a shadow directly onto the insect; and be persistent – if it flies away, follow it and try again.

Drifts of blue butterflies abound at Ranmore – Common, Chalk-hill and the rarer Adonis Blue; in late June hundreds of Marbled Whites and Dark Green Fritillaries sweep the downland slopes. Green Hairstreaks, migrant Red Admirals, Painted Ladies, Peacocks, Browns and Skippers – the list of butterflies is thirty-six strong.

Orchids – man, fly, bee and pyramidal orchids are all found on the open slope, together with a wonderful display of fragrant and spotted orchids on the western side; hard by the last stile up to Ranmore car-park you will find bird's-nest orchids hiding behind the fence beneath the shady beech.

Buy an ice-cream from the ever-present 'Mr Whippy' van and drift back through the woods the mile-and-a-half to your car.

Wildlife Walk 2: Queensdown Warren and Bredhurst, Kent

Park at the top of the Warren by a complex cross-roads of narrow lanes; a gate opens southwards immediately onto a steep slope of short chalk turf.

This is an orchid and butterfly spot 'par excellence'. Once a commercial warren in the time of Henry III, a rich array of chalk flowers is found here now throughout the spring and summer. Simply wander along the slope at will, although be careful where you put your feet – the whole slope can be covered in rare orchids. Here a changing pattern of colour shows the true beauty of chalk downland: thousands of cowslips and violets are succeeded by the typical herbs of chalk soil – thyme, basil, marjoram, milkwort, trefoil, horseshoe vetch, rock rose, yellow rattle and bell-flower, all of them alive with bees and butterflies.

A splendid succession of orchids occurs, starting with the early purple in late April. By 1 May, dozens of rare early spider orchids spread right across the slope; May itself brings fly orchids along the wood-land edges, and green-veined, man and burnt-tip orchids in the grass – all un-common or rare in Britain. As May turns to June, spotted, fragrant and bee orchids take their place on the slope with white, broad-leaved and violet helleborine in the woods; pyramidal orchids appear later in the month.

The woods all around vary from blocks of high-forest beech and oak to coppiced sweet chestnut with ash, birch and wild cherry. One mile to the west is Kemsley Street, a downland wood and a carefully protected NNR; entry is by a well-marked path from the gate. An open chalk slope below the wood holds bee, fly and man orchids, and the wood itself is mainly beech and oak. Its greatest glory is its large colony of lady orchids, with flower spikes as large as hyacinths – both rare and beautiful. By late May the wood is full of bluebells, by which time the hundred or so lady orchids are in full bloom; here and there in sunny spots a greater butterfly orchid raises its white-spurred flowers towards the warmth.

At both sites the chalk slopes abound with butterflies: Chalk-hill and Common Blues, Marbled Whites and Dark Green Fritillaries are numerous in June and July.

Adders are quite common on the lower slopes and are often found basking in the

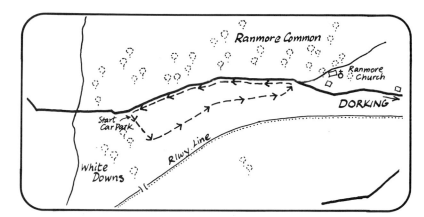

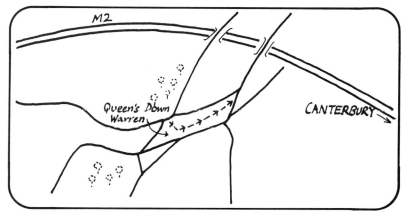

sunshine early in the mornings – their main food, the common lizard, is present in some numbers. The turf is still kept short by a large population of rabbits, which in turn attracts an unusual concen-tration of predators – stoat, weasel and fox are often seen hunting the woodland edge.

Characteristic of downland, the Marbled White butterfly too is now isolated in scattered pockets by intensive farming practices

13

The Chilterns
BUCKINGHAMSHIRE

Address of Site/Warden

Berks, Bucks and
Oxford Naturalist Trust,
3 Church Cowley Road,
Rose Hill,
Oxford OX4 3JR

Highlights and Features

Chalk downland with high-
forest beech-woods. Good
for birds in summer and
quite superb for chalk
flowers and insects. Also
good for woodland
mammals, including badger,
fallow and muntjac deer,
dormice.

Facilities

Warburg Reserve has
information centre open
intermittently in summer.

Photo Tips

Butterflies and flowers are
the speciality here. Take a
wide-angle zoom lens, such
as a 28–70mm for the
flowers and a 80–200mm
zoom for the butterflies.

*Common spotted orchids
are often numerous in
undisturbed chalk
grassland*

West of the great London basin and stretching in a 45-mile (72km) arc from Goring-on-the-Thames, the gentle, beech-clad hills of the Chilterns run north-east round Luton to the slopes of Sharpenhoe Clappers.

There are several excellent sites conserving the flowers, trees and animals of these ancient chalk downs but sadly much has been ploughed up or improved to provide high grass yields for grazing.

Wildlife Walk: Warburg

From the A423, turn north to Bix some two miles (3km) west of Henley-on-Thames and follow the single track road for two miles to a small car-park beyond Valley Farm. This is a BBONT reserve with an information hut and a leaflet dispenser. The reserve has a wide range of chalk flowers, insects and woodland birds, and is best visited from May to early August, with June probably the best month. There is a nature trail but it is indistinct in places, and it has several cut-offs to bring you back to the car-park in a shorter distance than the full round walk of some three miles (4.8km).

Behind the car-park turn right uphill through mixed woodland for a hundred yards (91m) into a long open chalk clearing below Great Hill; this is full of chalk flowers from spring to autumn with a continuous succession of colour. Common flowers predominate with milkwort, bird's-foot trefoil, vetches, ragwort, St John's wort, marjoram and musk mallow. Thyme grows on the ancient anthills while early summer orchids include common spotted, fly, bee, fragrant and greater butterfly orchid. This narrow belt of grassland is an excellent example of the stages in succession from grassy flower meadow, through invading scrub seedlings to climax woodland. Rabbits are the only grazing animals left here and the ride is mown every few years to keep the turf short. Sheep are also used, strip-grazed to assist with the autumn flush of grass.

Follow the path through a wooded strip where white helleborine and twayblade grow nearby; chalk scrub plants form dense thickets with privet, dogwood, rose, hazel, maple and wayfaring tree. Clematis, or traveller's joy, which will only grow on chalk or limestone soils, climbs over the shrubs. The path crosses the sunken track

of Hatch Lane and enters another long, flower-filled clearing. Woodland birds are excellent: all three woodpeckers, nuthatch, willow and marsh tit, wood warbler, chiffchaff, blackcap, tree pipit and redstart are all present; woodcock breed in the damp undergrowth while sparrowhawks nest high in the conifers.

This slope is also a good place to see the common lizard, and sometimes an adder or slow worm. The trail then turns left, emerges onto a gravel track, turns right and after five hundred yards (456m) turns left at a tree stump which is obviously used by squirrels as a 'table'. Follow the path through high beech-woods and across two ancient flint boundary banks – redstarts and wood warbler sing in the beech-wood edge, while deer and badger tracks cross the field layer of dog's mercury; fallow and muntjac deer are frequent, while badgers have several setts in the undisturbed woodland. On top of the ridge the beech-woods are tall and mature; bird's-nest orchids can be found here in June, while the rarer helleborines appear in July – the path is wide here and descends to Hatch Lane past clumps of violet helleborine.

Turn right at the cross-roads between high hazel hedges, and follow along a muddy bridleway; after three hundred yards (274m) turn left over a BBONT stile and then quickly right round a tall, solitary Norway spruce. A long flower-filled downland meadow returns you to the car-park in three hundred yards (274m). Butterflies are numerous, with blues, brimstones and fritillaries throughout the summer.

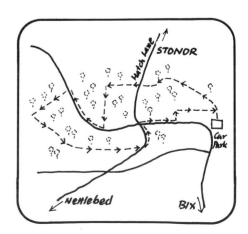

The Mendips
EBBOR GORGE
SOMERSET

Above the marshy wetlands of the Somerset Levels the Mendips rise to the north in high, rolling downland hills formed mainly from carboniferous limestone, harder and older rock than the chalk of southern England. The highest point is barely 1,000 feet (305m) above sea level, and yet through the action of water, these hills contain some of the most spectacular rock scenery in Britain, with huge gorges and limestone cliffs, the best known of which is Cheddar, a nationally famous beauty spot with cliffs rising to 450 feet (137m). Six miles (9km) to the southeast near Wookey Hole lies Ebbor Gorge, much smaller, almost unknown, and quite unspoiled.

Wildlife Walk: Ebbor Gorge
Access to the mysterious Ebbor Gorge is from the National Trust car-park on the steep hill south from Priddy village, six miles (9km) east of Cheddar. The two-mile trail through Ebbor Gorge is steep, rocky, and strenuous and requires good walking boots, as it is often muddy and slippery besides.

The path descends at once from the reserve sign down a hundred long steps through thick, luxuriant woodland, mainly ash with some oak. The shrub layer consists of hazel with many ash saplings, while bluebells, dog's mercury, enchanter's nightshade, primrose, wood anemone and celandine carpet the woodland floor. Badger paths run through the wood about half-way down the steps; foxes and badgers are common here and there are several setts nearby.

The path turns left at the bottom past an old tree-stump full of polypody fern; here, the shorter one-mile trail will return you to the car-park. However, if you follow the signs to the Gorge the walk is longer; you will first cross over a wooden footbridge with a tiny stream trickling down the valley. Surface water in the Mendips is unusual, and it is running here because the earth movements of some 270 million years ago pushed a layer of hard millstone grit beneath the valley floor.

The path now leads into the Gorge proper between high-forest woodland, mainly very tall ash with some oak, wych elm and whitebeam. In midsummer great tangles of honeysuckle, ivy and traveller's joy spread themselves riotously over a limestone shrub layer of hawthorn, dogwood, privet and many more. The path soon begins to climb into the rocky Gorge, the wayside strewn with ferns. The most prominent are great clumps of hartstongue fern but the damp shade of the Gorge encourages brittle bladder fern, maidenhair fern, maidenhair spleenwort, rusty back, wall rue and the rare Tunbridge filmy fern. Hard shield fern, lady fern, male fern and broad buckler fern complete a superb list of unusual species.

Here the limestone cliffs rise to 100 feet (30m) and the path climbs steeply over wet and slippery rock to a point where the walls close in so much that only single file is possible. Woodland birds, wrens, tits and nuthatches drink from the trickles of water. Above, the path levels out to run through woodland to the return loop waymarked by a large fallen log.

At the next T-junction the path turns right by an old dead tree much used by woodpeckers and full of holes, and then runs down to a scrap of grass overlooking a steep 100-foot (30m) cliff. The cliff is dangerous but the grassland supports rock-rose, thyme, fairy flax and several orchids. Butterflies are spectacular here in summer with White Admiral, Dark Green, Silver-washed and High Brown Fritillaries, Marbled White, Chalk-hill and Silver-studded Blue and the rare White-letter Hairstreak in the elms. Buzzard and sparrowhawk hunt the wooded valley.

The path now descends some 125 long steps to rejoin the gravel track in the valley floor before turning left and climbing out towards the car-park with more steps to slow the weary.

Address of Site/Warden

Ebbor Gorge:
Nature Conservancy Council,
Roughmoor,
Bishops Hull,
Taunton,
Somerset TA1 5AA

Highlights and Features

Limestone gorges. Exceptional limestone flowers and insects. Also good for woodland birds and mammals.

Facilities

Apart from information boards and leaflets, none. Many local tourist facilities nearby.

Photo Tips

Flowers and insects are the speciality as well as scenery. Use a 28–70mm wide-angle zoom for the flowers and the scenery and a 80–200mm zoom for the insects.

Wild, overgrown and mysterious is limestone Ebbor Gorge, a nature reserve given to the nation in memory of Sir Winston Churchill

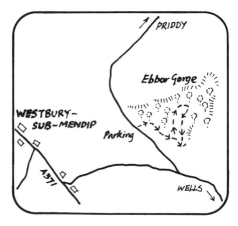

15

The Purbeck Downs
DORSET

Address of Site/Warden

Information from
Dorset Naturalist Trust,
39 Christchurch Road,
Bournemouth,
Dorset BH1 3NS

Highlights and Features

Mixture of chalk and limestone downland with superb flora and many butterflies. Many rare species including orchids. Good cliff colonies of auks, including a few puffins, kittiwakes and other seabirds. Several rare mammals especially bats.

Facilities

None on walk given.

Photo Tips

Close-up and wide-angle lenses for downland flowers and insects. Table-top tripod useful for low growing flowers.

Many bats, such as this whiskered bat use caves to hibernate during the winter. Do not disturb them!

The Isle of Purbeck is Dorset in miniature, its chalk hills reaching the sea at Studland cliffs with the shining stack of Old Harry rock offshore. Alongside the chalk runs a band of tougher limestone with beds of Purbeck marble which has been extracted and used in churches all over Europe. Purbeck is a wonderful place for wildlife despite the crowds of summer tourists that throng its beauty spots; the southern coastal path runs from the Devon border into Purbeck at Lulworth and in spring the banks are filled with celandine and primroses.

Between Lulworth and St Aldhelm's Head are the bays of Worbarrow and Kimmeridge; the gault and blue lias clays here are famous worldwide because the fossils are so easily exposed, but they are not so dramatic as the rolling chalk downs and steep two-hundred-foot (61m) cliffs which stretch eastwards to Durlston Head. Northwards lie the Dorset heaths of Studland, Arne and the Poole Harbour borders – such a range of habitats is unique in such a small area.

One wildlife walk is described starting at Worth Matravers, taking in the coastal path to Durlston Head and returning either by the same route or, for the physically exhausted, by the 144 bus from Swanage. Worth Matravers to Durlston Head is about six miles (9km) and there are some steep sections – if you return by the outward route the last climb into Worth is shattering. However, the views and wildlife are superb. Take food and cold drinks in summer, and good walking shoes are essential. The distance can be halved by walking to Dancing Ledge and then returning.

Park in the Worth Matravers village car-park if possible (30 cars maximum), turn left past the pub and after two hundred yards (183m) take the path south in front of some bungalows – don't be put off by the gate. Pass through a field alongside a drystone wall, towards a clearly visible signpost. Turn left over the wall following the track marked 'Seacombe ¾', between arable fields; this quickly arrives at the top of a coombe which leads down towards the sea – take the steep path into the coombe, easy going down but exhausting on return. This is a lovely peaceful valley where Friesian cows might be grazing the upper pastures near the farm, and with cowslips on the grass slopes. At the stile there is a National Trust sign 'Easington', and a tinkling stream with bog flowers at its edges runs down the middle of this lovely valley.

Walk towards the sea following the stream; the left-hand hillside is covered with gorse and dense thorn scrub. Migrant birds pass northwards through this valley in spring from the sea-shore and late April may see seven or eight species, warblers, chats, redstarts and flycatchers moving up through the gorse thickets. Linnets and goldfinches are numerous residents. Ten minutes along the stream and the sea will suddenly come into view. The coastal path is signposted and can be walked either way – climb the eastern slope and the view westwards opens out along the two-hundred-foot (61m) cliffs to Winspit. Fulmars glide the up-currents and, together with a few pairs of kittiwakes, nest on the ledges of these cliffs. Breeding pairs of shags and cormorants occupy the lower ledges in small numbers, but the ubiquitous herring gull is *the* bird of these cliffs, breeding on many inaccessible ledges.

Once you are over the upper stile and have turned east out of the coombe, a glorious four-mile (6km) stretch of chalk and limestone cliffs comes into view; the path travels right along the edge, protected by an unobtrusive wire fence. The cliffs are between one and two hundred feet high (30–60m), dipping in folds to the lower level – this is one of the finest cliff walks in all Britain.

The Purbeck downland rolls upwards from the cliffs – broad sheep pastures bisected by drystone walls – everywhere the song of skylarks and the cry of gulls, floating on the ever-present breeze. Several small streams filter down through the chalk creating damp places along the path (usually provided with a fixed plank to bypass the wetter bits) – butterflies, especially 'blues', drink from these in summer.

These chalk downlands offer a superb selection of wild flowers and butterflies from April right through to September. They are best known for an extensive colony of early spider orchids, usually in flower by 1 May and found very close to the path along Dancing Ledge (about a mile from the first cliff stile out of the

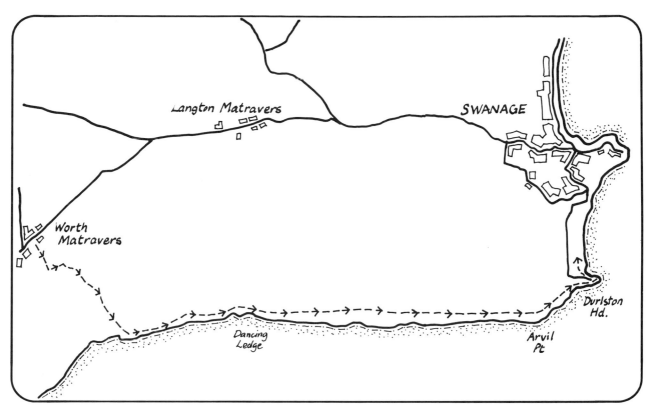

coombe). A stream runs down to it from Spyway Barn creating a wide ledge and dropping to a small, pebbly beach; a wide variety of orchids is found on these downs. Do be careful where you walk – orchid colonies are likely to be wiped out by incautious feet. Bee orchid, green-veined orchid, fragrant, pyramidal and several others throng the chalk turf in May and June, and there are other notable flowers here including autumn gentian and Italian arum.

The butterflies are a delight on a warm June day – drifts of blues, Adonis, Chalk-hill, Common and Small Blue; in July the handsome Dark Green Fritillaries glide on brilliant orange wings along the downs while innumerable Marbled Whites flit among the flowers. Migrant butterflies are often numerous along the coast and late May can see a wave of Red Admirals and Painted Lady butterflies arriving from the Continent; in good years Clouded Yellows, too, arrive in large numbers. The real rarity here is the Lulworth Skipper, found around Lulworth Cove itself but also along the cliff path right down towards Durlston Head. It is possible to see thirty species of butterfly here on a warm summer day.

From Dancing Ledge the cliffs are slightly higher and there are more sea-birds: scan any visible rock ledges and look closely at the birds on the sea because there are a few pairs of puffins among the small colonies of guillemots and razorbills. These are probably the only breeding puffins surviving on the whole south coast of England.

A mile past Dancing Ledge an area of broken ground, with much gorse and thorn and many flowers, reaches down the hillside to the cliff edge. Stonechats and wheatears breed among this landslip while adders and lizards bask in the sunshine – adders can be frequent in these quiet coombes so be careful where you put your feet. Once past the two radio masts stuck high on the cliffs, Durlston Head is just a mile (1.6km) along the clifftop.

Throughout the length of this walk, breaks in the cliffs reveal cave openings – pale-grey limestone of old mine-workings against the white gleam of the chalk. Some of these caves have small colonies of bats, and the very rare Bechsteins bat is found (usually by experts) in one or two Purbeck caves. *Do not* enter and disturb these bats which really have become rarities.

At Durlston Head the Tilly Whim caves are a tourist attraction in their own right. Spring and autumn bring migrating sea-birds in some numbers past this headland; scan the sea for streams of common, Arctic and Sandwich terns pursued by the dashing Arctic and the more ponderous great skuas, all on passage up the English Channel.

The return to Worth Matravers is either by bus from Swanage, or the six miles (9.6km) back along the Dorset coastal path – as the fulmar flies: but not so easily!

Differential erosion by the sea has scooped out the soft Weald clays of Lulworth Cove and left the limestone cliffs to tower around it

*Orange-tip butterflies are
numerous in the
limestone dales of the
White Peak in early
summer*

The Peak District National Park

DERBYSHIRE

Although the Peak District actually touches six counties, to most people it means Derbyshire. There are really two Peak Districts: the northern Dark Peak, formed from hard Millstone Grit crags; and the softer southern White Peak of gleaming limestone – at all events, rock dominates the landscapes of both. For half the population of England this area is only a day-trip's distance away, and with upwards of 20 million annual visits it is the most heavily used of Britain's national parks. Its 542 square miles (1,404sq km) has seen much change, and despite national park status it is still threatened by man's activities, notably the quarrying of limestone. Both coal and formerly, lead have been mined here.

Two wildlife walks are described to cover both the high northern peat moorlands, and the softer downland of the southern limestone.

Wildlife Walk 1: Grindslow and Hartshorn Tor, Dark Peak

This is a strenuous fell walk of some six miles (9.6km) skirting the blanket peat bogs of the Kinder plateau. Start at the information centre in Edale. Turn right down the sunken track past the old cemetery, through a blue gate and on for half-a-mile to Ollerbrook Farm. Turn sharp left out of the farmyard and up the right-hand side of the field to the boundary of the moor; continue over the stile and on for 300 yards (274m) until you reach a fork in the path. The Ollerbrook alongside may have dippers and grey wagtails; swallows hawk insects up the valley.

Turn left up the old sled road, used in the past to bring down quarried stone – the path climbs steeply up to the Nab. Scan the skies for buzzard and kestrel. The commonest bird by far, however, is the meadow pipit which nests in the tussocks and heather. The surrounding moorland may hold a mountain hare. Look back to appreciate the fine views south of Edale, with the badly eroded Pennine Way ascending Grindsbrook to the right, on the first part of its long trek northwards. Follow the path north for half-a-mile under the rocky outcrops of Ringing Roger; wheatear, stonechat and the occasional ring ouzel or whinchat may be seen here.

Turn left at the top of the Golden Clough valley and follow the path along the crag edge. This is high moorland country with superb views on a good day but needs care, especially in poor weather. Follow the path past Nether Tor and on to the top of Grindsbrook Gorge. Moorland birds here include red grouse which clatter away from the heather tussocks at your feet; the black grouse is now much rarer, but there are still a few in the Dark Peak. Although curlew and golden plover do breed on some of these moors in spring, they are declining due to disturbance.

Cross the stream and continue to the western fork of the Grindsbrook to join the Pennine Way as it emerges from the valley. These gritstone edges provide good sites among the cotton and moorgrasses for the less common northern plants: bearberry, cloudberry, oak and beech fern all occur. In boggy places along the brooks look for the spikes of yellow bog asphodel and for sticky-leaved sundews.

Follow the Pennine Way, badly eroded by constant use (to which you are contributing), down towards Edale a mile away. The Pennine Way actually starts here at the Nags Head: you have walked the base of Britain's backbone.

Wildlife Walk 2: Lathkill Dale, White Peak

The wildlife of the limestone is in total contrast, and as regards flowers and insects, far more fruitful than the surrounding gritstone moorlands – Lathkill Dale is a national nature reserve maintained largely for its wonderful array of flowers and insects. The scenery typical of the White Peak is well demonstrated here, with rolling downland cut by the steep-sided, well-wooded dale.

Access is from a car-park in the village of Over Haddon three miles (4.8km) west of Bakewell. Descend the 'No through road' past tiny St Anne's church, and in 400 yards (365m) you will come to the entrance of the Dale by the River Lathkill. There is only space for some six cars near the entrance for those who cannot manage the steep hill. A well made limestone grit path runs along the flat valley floor with the Lathkill river close on the left and continues for some two miles

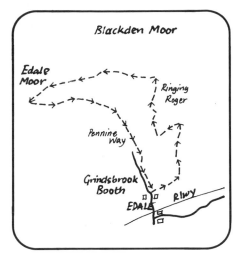

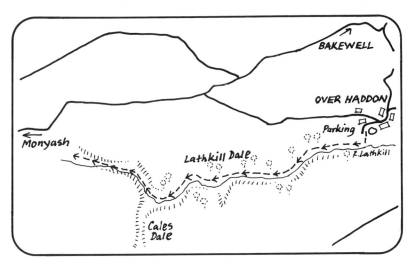

to the dale-head; return by the same path.

The river rises and flows wholly within the White Peak and is crystal-clear, regarded as one of the cleanest and most pure rivers in Britain. Trout and grayling are easily observed, with every mark on a fish visible even when it is two feet or more down in a deep pool. The beneficial effect of the lime in the water and the lack of pollution are amply demonstrated by the wonderful display of water and marginal plants in the shallows; large numbers of mayflies, stoneflies and other insects in the river support fish and birds alike.

Several small limestone outcrops to the right of the path in its first 400 yards have a rich flora in early summer, with thyme, rock-rose, meadow cranesbill and biting stonecrop. Two ancient lead-mine entrances are passed after a short distance: they are both dangerous, so *keep out*! Spring sandwort grows on rocks around the mines.

The dale now becomes well wooded with the leaf canopy meeting overhead – the river, some five yards wide here, gurgles and splashes down a series of tiny limestone shelves. Outside the normal peak tourist times this is a lovely peaceful place – kingfishers hunt the brook, while grey wagtails and dippers catch insects above and below the water which is so clear you can actually watch the dipper walking on the river bed.

The main woodland of Palmerston Wood consists of ash and wych elm, with hazel, dogwood, hawthorn and bird cherry as shrubs and dog's mercury and wild garlic covering the ground. There are several large wet clearings along the river where meadowsweet, ragged robin, meadow cranesbill and red campion grow in luxuriant clumps; marsh marigolds are a feature in spring. Examine the muddy patches for deer tracks – roe deer will usually only come out when it is quiet most probably at dusk and dawn when fox

and badger too may be seen. Just over a mile from the entrance the wood opens out on the right and steep grassy hillsides are revealed, with outcrops of broken weathered limestone – these also occur a half-a-mile beyond Low Wood at the head of the valley.

These slopes are filled with flowers throughout the spring and summer: thyme, rock-rose, milkworts, violets, harebells, primroses, orchids and mulleins produce a veritable rock garden. The outcrops have good colonies of bloody cranesbill, melancholy thistle and dark red helleborine.

Butterflies similar to those of the southern chalk downs occur with blues, Brown Argus, Orange-tip and Dark Green Fritillary.

Wheatears nest in the rocky outcrops and drystone walls, while the rich woods support a wide variety of birds including redstart, pied flycatcher and wood warbler.

Grey wagtails hawk insects for their chicks, along the Lathkill stream

The Yorkshire Dales National Park

MALHAM COVE AND GORDALE SCAR

Address of Site/Warden

Yorkshire Dales National
Park Committee
Colvend,
Hebden Road,
Grassington,
Skipton,
North Yorks BD23 5LB

Highlights and Features

Huge limestone cliffs and
outcrops. Spectacular
limestone scenery. Many
unusual limestone flowers,
especially in the grykes of
limestone pavement.

Facilities

Well-known tourist area with
many facilities in Malham.
Malham Tarn Field Studies
Centre nearby. Large
information centre in
Malham with excellent
interpretative display.

Photo Tips

Wide-angle lenses best here
for plants, scenery and
combination of both. Tripod
essential.

*A great mullein, one of
many rare and unusual
flowers restricted to chalk
and limestone soils*

The Yorkshire Dales National Park is a glorious mixture of pastoral valleys, green lanes, old grey barns, tumbling becks, gritstone fells, patterns of drystone walls and villages of limestone nestling snugly in the steep-sided valleys. Strewn across this scene as if in gay abandon lies the framework of the landscape, exposed in great limestone cliffs and gorges and in an intricate pattern of limestone pavement left by Ice Age glaciers. Water running off the uplands has dissolved the softer rocks, and now beneath the green face of the Dales lies an underground world of caves and tunnels all of great beauty but seen only by a few.

The Yorkshire Dales present the finest area of limestone scenery in Britain and are of international importance in the understanding of the geology of limestone country. The wildlife of the Dales, with its upland birds and above all with its superb and special flora, is of national importance. One wildlife walk is described around Malhamdale. The best time to visit is in midsummer when the limestone flowers, butterflies and upland birds can be best appreciated. A short-cut may be taken to reduce the walk to four miles (6km), otherwise the total distance is eight — steep sections are inevitable to cover the whole walk.

Visitor pressure can be a real problem here as the lanes are narrow and become readily jammed with cars. It is essential to leave your car securely locked in one of the visitor centre car-parks and walk.

Wildlife Walk: Malham Cove and Gordale Scar

Use the National Park information centre and its car-park at the southern end of Malham village. Cross the tiny stone bridge over Malham Beck, next to the forge a few yards away; turn right along the beck and continue over a number of ladder stiles, designed to safeguard the ancient drystone walls which they surmount — the path follows this part of the Pennine Way for 300 yards (274m) and then turns left to join Gordale Beck at Mires Barn. Continue for three-quarters of a mile through flower-filled meadows and across more ladder stiles — spotted orchids are numerous in the meadows in June. The stream soon acquires a marshy valley with marsh thistles, marsh orchids and grey wagtails along the waterside, but the valley sides steepen as you enter Wedber Wood through a kissing-gate and become more a wooded gorge, the path picking its way between moss-covered limestone boulders.

This is a lovely mixed wood with beech, wych elm and ash, and a dense ground flora. Birds include woodpeckers, tree-creeper, nuthatch and flycatchers, with dipper and kingfisher along the clear limestone stream. You must keep to the footpath as the wood is fragile and suffering from visitor pressure — half-a-mile brings you to Janet's Foss, a lovely water-fall only fifteen feet (4.5m) high, set in a greenly dappled glade and splashing into a deep circular pool.

Gordale Beck is rich in dissolved lime-stone which is precipitated as yellowish tufa rock along the stream; an 'apron' of tufa has been laid down over Janet's Foss. In early summer the woods around the falls are full of the white lily-like flowers of wild garlic.

Go through the gate onto the road and turn right to Gordale Scar path. Already the great cliffs of the Scar will be opening up before you. The footpath is good, newly laid for the half-mile or so that it leads into the gorge, finishing just below the waterfalls. Although an ancient right-of-way exists up the falls and through the top of Gordale Scar, it is little short of sacrilege to clamber on the delicate and easily eroded tufa deposits. There are less damaging routes to the hill tops.

Gordale Scar is one of the wonders of Britain, a deep twisting ravine eroded through thick limestone beds by Ice Age streams. The present Gordale Beck is a pretty but much smaller waterfall. The 300 foot (91m) cliffs are overhanging and provide a constant shower of water drop-lets on your head as you gaze at the upper reaches of the gorge; climbers' pitons and slings still hang in two thin cracks up the right-hand wall.

Return to the road and take a footpath to the right near Janet's Foss — this climbs steeply round the northern side of Cawden Hill, towards limestone outcrops on the skyline. The lumps and mounds in the pastures denote the boundaries of ancient Iron Age fields. The path runs for three-quarters of a mile under the lime-stone crags of Stridebut Edge to join Tarn

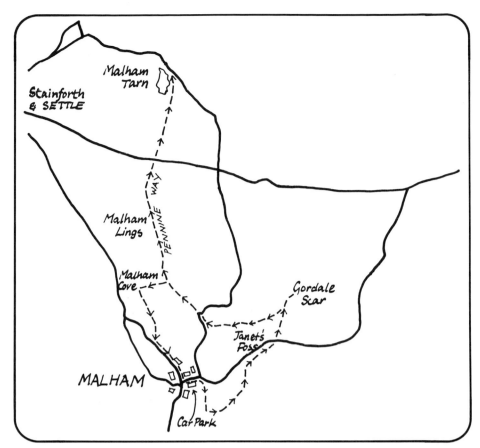

Road over ladder stiles; walk north a few yards to Shorkley Hill corner and descend the footpath towards the top of Malham Cove.

A great stretch of limestone pavement covers the area around the summit; here the deep grykes hold a multitude of limestone flowers and ferns, as do the surrounding limestone crags. Any nook or cranny inaccessible to sheep may shelter ferns such as hartstongue, rigid buckler fern or green spleenwort, and flowers like tutsan, herb robert, globeflower and dark red helleborine. Treat these precious, polished pavements with care, both because of their rarity and for the sake of your ankles.

The view from the top of the huge cliffs of Malham Cove looks back down the whole of Malhamdale to Pendle and beyond to Bowland. Here you are on the tops of the Dales, a sense of airy wide-skied beauty all about you. Below, the cliffs of Malham Cove fall vertically 300 feet (91m) to the wooded valley floor. Like Gordale Scar, this is an eroded valley cut back from the line of the Mid-Craven Fault. No waterfall exists today and the great amphitheatre is dry, the water bubbling out of the limestone hills far below. House martins nest on the cliffs here in what must be their truly natural situation, just as they must have done before the coming of man and houses.

Two alternatives face you from the top of Malham Cove! The Pennine Way goes south round the western lip and descends to the valley floor by way of hundreds of steps cut to keep walkers on one path and prevent erosion. It is then an easy walk back to Malham village, a total of four miles (6km). Otherwise, follow the Pennine Way north for two miles (3km) across the craggy roof of the Dales to Malham Tarn. Look for flowers in all the crevices. Sheep are the dominating factor in these hills; the area is too heavily grazed for flowers to flourish unless they are inaccessible because of cracks in the rock. In spring, the wild call of curlew and golden plover can be heard across these hills, while ring ouzels and wheatears nest in the rocks.

Malham Tarn is a lovely lake, one of the few natural lakes in the Dales. It lies on a bed of impervious Silurian Slate, pushed into place by movement of the North Craven Fault, surrounded on all sides by limestone. Streams feed dissolved lime into the lake waters, and the surrounding fen is exceptionally rich in plant and invertebrate life.

The internationally famous Field Centre now occupies the Victorian Tarn House, where Charles Kingsley gained inspiration for his famous book *The Water Babies*, using the tarn, the cove and the limestone terraces as the background to his story.

Gordale Scar is one of the scenic wonders of Britain, cut by water action through the hard Yorkshire limestone

Arnside Knott and Gait Barrows

CUMBRIA AND LANCASHIRE

Address of Site/Warden

Arnside:
National Trust,
42 Queen Anne's Gate,
London SW1H 9AS
Gait Barrows National
Nature Reserve,
NCC,
North-West Region,
Blackwell,
Bowness-on-Windermere,
Cumbria LA23 3JR

Highlights and Features

Limestone hills and superb limestone pavement at Gait Barrows. Excellent array of limestone flowers and butterflies including unusual woodland species.

Facilities

Only small car-parks.

Photo Tips

Wide-angle lenses useful for flowers on limestone rock and in grykes. Tripod essential. Small flash useful for flowers deep in grykes.

Angular Solomon's seal, a rare plant of northern limestone areas

The Arnside and Silverdale peninsula lies just south of the Lake District and is designated as an area of outstanding natural beauty. The richness of the area in wildlife terms is due to the underlying carboniferous limestone rock, and the mild climate. Despite its proximity to the rain-drenched hills of Lakeland, the Arnside peninsula has little more than a third of the rainfall of Borrowdale which is only thirty miles (48km) to the north, and the warming effect of the Gulf Stream ensures a relatively mild winter climate. Some of the plants and insects to be seen here are at the northerly limit of their range in Britain. Although these limestone hills are good for woodland birds, it is for their flowers, insects and the classic limestone geology that they are of national importance. They are in urgent need of protection.

Two wildlife walks are described, one round Arnside Knott in Cumbria, the other through the woods and round the limestone pavements of Gait Barrows National Nature Reserve, just over the border in Lancashire.

Wildlife Walk 1: Arnside Knott

Arnside Knott dominates the pretty villages of Arnside and Silverdale, rising 522 feet (159m) in steeply wooded slopes; most of it belongs to the National Trust. The walk described is some three miles (4.8km) with steep sections, though there are easier walks lower down. The woods of Arnside Park are adjacent.

In Arnside, drive uphill from the promenade and turn right along Redhills. Follow the signs to the Trust car-park down a bridleway called Sauls Drive – walk down Sauls Drive towards Arnside and turn right through the first stile; the path climbs steadily across high meadows through a stile in the wall, and finally to a scree-scramble onto the summit ridge at the Knotted Trees.

If you have picked a bright day dozens of butterflies will be on the wing over the limestone grassland: blues, fritillaries, skippers, Grayling and Scotch Argus will be present, the latter being nearly at its southernmost location. There is also a wide variety of limestone flowers including several orchids.

Walk east along the edge to the triangulation point on the summit: the view of the Lake District hills to the north on a clear day is quite breathtaking. Once you have recovered from the climb, turn right a little way down the hill to the north; this descends quite quickly, through a dry-stone wall and into Redhills Wood.

This is a hazel and yew wood with large groves of yew on the steeper slopes. A winter visit will find scores of blackbirds, mistle thrushes, redwings and fieldfares feasting on the berry crop – the hard seeds inside are opened by finches, great and marsh tits; hawfinches are found here regularly.

Red squirrels are frequent in this woodland – the best way to see them is to find a vantage point with a good view over the path or clearing and wait. In midsummer they are most active early and late in the day.

A wide range of birds is present in summer with many common warblers, tits and woodpeckers; woodcock breed and may be seen 'roding' around the Knott at dusk. Tawny owls are numerous and call constantly in springtime.

Continue west under the scree slopes round the bridleway. On the right, colonies of dark red helleborine, a rare orchid which will only grow in northern limestone, have been fenced off to prevent trampling – a few specimens may be found near the car-park. From the car-park, paths run west into Arnside Park, an ancient coppiced woodland of oak and ash with some birch. Wild daffodils produce a superb display in early April, while the woodland supports and shelters roe deer, badger and many small mammals.

Wildlife Walk 2: Gait Barrows National Nature Reserve

This reserve, some two miles (3km) east of Arnside, is a paradise for the enthusiastic botanist and geologist. A public footpath runs north–south through the reserve; a permit is required if you wish to leave this footpath and is provided by the Nature Conservancy Council NW office on written request – this is to avoid undue disturbance of the fragile limestone environment.

The entrance is on the Arnside–Yealand road near the junction to Silverdale; there is a small car-park a hundred yards (91m) inside the gate for permit-holders, and a warden and his assistants are always

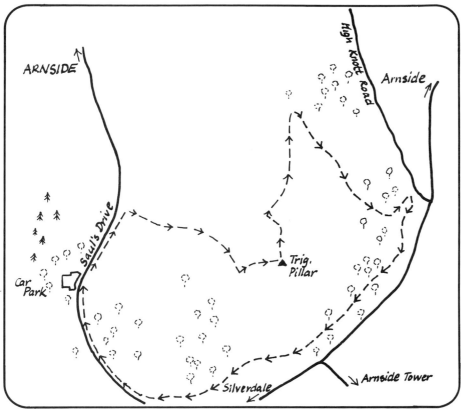

present on the reserve. A large clump of yellow loosestrife grows round the reserve sign. The public footpath goes south through a second gate with a long flower-filled meadow on the right – this is exceptionally good for butterflies on a fine midsummer's day.

A hundred yards further on another footpath turns left through the woodland, and this is for permit-holders only. It leads to a maze of paths around a large area of gently sloping limestone pavement, virtually hidden by oak, ash, hazel and yew woodland. These wonderful limestone pavements can be seen in a few other places in the Yorkshire Dales such as at Malham (see p 44) but are otherwise now gone. Large areas were broken up in the past and taken for rockery stone. The pavements were left as smooth limestone sheets by the last Ice Age. Since then the weak carbonic acid of rainwater has dissolved the softer structures, leaving deep grykes, or fissures, in the rock surface. 'Clints' are the flat blocks divided up by the grykes; 'runnels' are draining gutters into the grykes and 'solution cups' are hollows dissolved into the tops of the clints.

The sheltered, humid conditions in the grykes provide ideal growing conditions for a wonderful range of flowers, ferns and shrubs. The excitement generated by this amazing place, never knowing what rare and beautiful plant might be hiding in the next deep gryke, is immense. Some of the old, damaged areas, broken up before the declaration of the reserve, now hold good colonies of unusual plants: dark red helleborine, pale St John's wort, lily-of-the-valley, tutsan, angular Solomon's seal, biting stonecrop and a wide range of ferns, including hartstongue and rigid buckler fern, are all present.

Having used the tracks to examine this area, return to the public footpath and continue for 200 yards (183m) when you will come to several flower-filled stream-side meadows at the southern end of the reserve. These are filled with clovers, ox-eye daisy, buttercups, ragged robin and meadowsweet. Butterflies are abundant in fine weather with twenty-seven species on record. High Brown Fritillaries may be seen in dashing flight through the wood-land edge.

Cross the meadows westwards along a rather vague footpath downhill towards the woodland, and leave the reserve over a stile at Haweswater. This is a lovely reed-fringed lake just through the wood, itself a reserve of the Lancashire Trust for Nature Conservation. Bird's-eye prim-roses grow around its banks.

Continue north along the footpath, forking right through high limestone forest of oak and ash. Wooded limestone cliffs run near the path, which is wet and slippery. Go quietly at all times in these woods, roe deer and red squirrels are then easily seen. After half a mile turn right, back on the road to the reserve entrance.

Tutsan growing in a limestone pavement gryke

FRESHWATER MARSHLANDS

It rains a lot in Britain, as many of its visitors and certainly most of its inhabitants will wish to confirm. It is the rain, however, which keeps Britain green, as soon became apparent in 1976 when the rain stopped, the sun shone day after day for many weeks and the land took on a brown and desert-like appearance. On fresh-marsh fields lapwings sheltered under hedgerows out of the baking sun.

This chapter describes the normal, damp Britain – its rivers filled to bursting and its fields a squelchy quagmire. Wetlands and freshwater marshes are amongst our most precious wildlife resources and are by no means commonplace any more, as most of the marshlands have been drained for farming. The rain that falls somewhere on nearly every day of the year quickly leaves the uplands for the rivers where man makes sure that it is rushed post-haste to the sea. Lowland fields are kept similarly drained, to ditches scoured clean by the mechanical dredge so as to toss the water quickly into the sea-bound river.

Marshlands tend to form in the lower reaches of rivers where drainage is poor. Rivers pass through several stages before reaching the lowlands and a brief description is included here to provide greater understanding. The chapter does not describe any particular riverside walks although many exist throughout the country. Some appear in other chapters where their individual features are described in detail.

Rivers usually rise in the hills as small torrential streams, although some do come from lowland sources where water appears as a spring between two layers of rock. Water speed is the all-important factor, followed by mineral content and management by man. Water speed has a direct effect on the amount of oxygen dissolved in the water: where water splashes and rushes and tumbles over rocks its oxygen content is high, whilst downstream slow-running water is less well aerated and holds far less oxygen. Water speed is also responsible for the character of the river bed itself. Fast-flowing streams carry grit and pebbles and leave behind a gravel, boulder-strewn bed, while slow-flowing lowland rivers allow even fine particles to sink, forming mud and silt.

Consequently in upland, fast-flowing steams there is little life by comparison with lowland waters and it is all specially adapted to deal with the current. Thus salmon, trout and grayling are all muscular fish, streamlined to withstand its pull, plants grow clinging to the rocks and any invertebrate life lives in sheltered crevices or clings onto the rock surfaces.

Only trout live in the true headwater streams, spawning in side waters or in the lee of large boulders where the slower current leaves gravel beds. Food is limited, with only a few stonefly larvae and detritus and insects falling into the stream.

Farther downstream and nearer the lowland the water still carries much oxygen but the stream bed changes to a mix of gravel, sand and silt. This allows a few plants to take foothold. Water chemistry is now vital, as the type of plants trying to grow depend upon the minerals available. This comes from two sources, in through the roots from the bottom sediment and through the submerged leaves in the water. This may actually vary in rivers which rise for example in chalk hills but then flow across sand and gravel – the River Mole in Surrey and the Arun in Sussex are good examples.

As the river speed drops the animals needing a high oxygen level vanish. Trout still remain abundant but coarse fish such as roach and rudd may appear. The most characteristic plant is water crowfoot, forming dense masses in mid-stream and throwing hundreds of white flowers an inch or two above the surface. The main food supply is still detritus but algae may now grow on many of the rocks.

Eventually the river slows right down to run in a leisurely fashion across the lowlands. Here silt is deposited, eroded from the distant hills and stream banks, and the action of the river current on its own banks produces a meandering course, often leaving cut-off ox-bow lakes surrounded by damp marshland. Fine silts and muds allow a dense growth of aquatic plants and free-swimming algae provide food for a wide variety of animals.

The slower the water speed the more the life of the river comes to be like that of the surrounding marshland, whose water table often depends upon the adjacent river level. The wildlife of such marshland areas is outstanding, providing one of the richest sources of animals and plants possible. All of it however, may be at risk from any changes which reduce the wetness of the ground.

Wet marshlands tend to be of two main types, fen or bog. Bogs occur on acid soil, are usually more associated with uplands, and have a restricted variety of plants of which bog asphodel, sundews, butterwort and heath spotted orchid are typical. Fens occur where the soil is alkaline and are very rich in plants, dominated by tall herbs and reeds.

Apart from the freshwater marshland bordering a river's flood plain or estuary there are three other distinct types of reed-swamp. Reed readily colonises the margins of shallow artificial lakes, such as those at Chew Valley Lake, Avon and Rutland Water, Leicester. Natural lakes, too, sometimes have marginal reed fringes but these are rare, the best example being at the Fleet, alongside Chesil Beach in Dorset. In a few places reed-beds occur in silted estuaries where they are periodically flooded by high spring tides. Two good examples are at Blacktoft Sands on the Humber where a large reed-bed is now part of an RSPB reserve, and at Exminster in Devon.

Reed-swamps have only survived at all in Britain because man needed thatching material. Recently there has been something of a revival in the demand for thatch but this may only be temporary – many bird reserves are explicitly managed to provide thatching material in the best possible interests of the reed-bed inhabitants.

Thus the single most important management measure is to cut the reeds in winter, allowing the fen plants space and light to grow, and making room for the new reed stem the following year. Fen plants such as yellow flag, flowering rush, purple and yellow loosestrife, brooklime, water mint, water forget-me-not and great water dock may all grow in small fen fields. Marsh marigold, once found in the corner of nearly every badly drained field, is much more restricted now in its distribution, while the lovely marsh helleborine orchid, once fairly numerous in rich marshy soils, is now quite rare.

Wetlands and freshwater marshland provide an ideal habitat for a profusion of invertebrates, minute protozoa, worms, sponges, molluscs, spiders, crustaceans and insects. Many prey on one another, but then become food themselves for fish and birds in the rising food chain.

Worthy of mention among the insects are two specialists: the Swallow-tail butterfly whose larva lives only on milk parsley, and the Large Copper butterfly which will lay its eggs only on great water dock. There are also several dozen British species of dragon- and damselfly dependent on wetlands for their life-cycle.

These are among the easiest small animals to see on any marshland walk, but a marshland's greatest glory is its birds. Fens especially are rich in bird life, and many species have adapted to survive in extensive marshland habitats.

The threats to marshland have never been greater. Developers see it as wasteland and yet it is of utmost importance for wildlife and for the aesthetic appeal of its quiet watery places. There is so little of it left that every last square foot must be defended against development.

The 'scrape' at Strumpshaw is clean, fresh-marsh, with its banks sealed by the RSPB against pollution from the Broads

Stodmarsh
KENT

Address of Site/Warden

National Nature Reserve:
Warden:
4 Sandpit Cottages,
Wickhambreaux,
Canterbury,
Kent

Highlights and Features

Large area of reed-marsh due to mining subsidence. Fresh grazing marsh. Large populations of reed-bed birds. Close views of bearded tit from Lampen Wall. Good for birds of prey in winter.

Facilities

Car-park with small information hut not always open.

Photo Tips

Birds will usually be too distant for good pictures. Try the marsh flowers and insects in the fen, accessible from a boardwalk. Use a tripod. Try some wide-angle shots to show the plant in its marsh setting.

Dragon- and damselflies are frequent along the wet marsh ditches of sites like Stodmarsh

Stodmarsh, a few miles east of Canterbury, seems just like everyone's idea of a marsh. Great reed-beds sway in the wind, lagoons ring with bird calls, and wide marsh fields ripple with swifts and swallows throughout the summer. But all this is largely man-made, caused by the subsidence of old coal workings which has allowed the marshes of the Stour to return. In the winter months the area of marshland to the east of the reserve towards Grove Ferry is liable to flood and this whole area of extensive wetlands attracts many wildfowl.

Just one wildlife walk is described, going out through the marshes on the single track, and can be extended as far as one likes towards Grove Ferry along the bank of the river. A good idea is to amble slowly for perhaps two miles (3km) along the track and then return, making a round trip of four to five miles. By taking your time you are much more likely to see the stars of the area.

Wildlife Walk

Arriving in Stodmarsh village, from Canterbury, turn left immediately past the Red Lion Inn; there is a rough track which, after a short distance brings you to the reserve car-park. Hawthorn and oak hedges line this track and are usually busy with bullfinch, yellowhammer and tits. The walk begins at a rectangle of reed-swamp across which the NCC has built a wooden boardwalk, allowing access to the heart of the swamp itself. The boardwalk takes you onto the Lampen Wall, which is the main track out through the reserve and consists of a raised flood barrier providing excellent views. However, the swamp must not be neglected; take your time here, be quiet and be alert – water rail, and even the rare spotted crake, may sometimes be seen. A bearded tit slipping through the reed stalks, a grass snake hunting frogs, an alder-fly laying eggs on a reed stem – this is just the place to see the 'inside' of a reed marsh, normally quite inaccessible. The flowers and insects along the boardwalk alone make a visit worthwhile.

After all too short a distance the boardwalk emerges at the beginning of the Lampen Wall; the first 200 yards (123m) consist of marshy alder-woods on the right and reed-swamp on the left. The alders are splendid bird woods with drier marshland around them. Grasshopper warblers are regulars here with several breeding pairs – listen for the 'reeling' song, a continuous rattle like a running fish reel; willow warbler, chiffchaff, garden warbler and whitethroat are all numerous. Nightingales sing here too, and in winter large chattering flocks of redpolls and siskins are nearly always found in the alders.

Walk out along the raised track and soon the wide expanse of marshland stretches far on either side. On the left, large open shallow lagoons are dotted with wildfowl, while on the right a wide wet ditch separates you from a reed-bed which seems to continue as far as the horizon. There are a number of small hawthorns dotted along the wall – sit down on the bank by one of these which will effectively break up your outline, and then watch carefully. You will see a great deal – water voles are common and inquisitive. In summer the open lagoons have many breeding great crested grebes and dabchicks. Nesting duck include mallard, shoveler, pochard, gadwall, garganey, tufted duck and shelduck. Coot and moorhen are numerous.

The reed-swamp on the other side of the wall holds hordes of reed and sedge warblers throughout the summer, and grasshopper warblers are still present if the marsh is dry. The gems of the reeds are bearded tits – numerous in most years – bitterns, which are rare, shy and secretive; and the Savis warbler, a recent colonist from Europe. The bitterns may be heard 'booming' in spring and are best seen at dusk when they fly above the reeds more often than they do in broad daylight. Savis warblers may not have survived the very cold spells of the 1986/87 winter, however – and Stodmarsh is one of only two or three breeding sites in Britain.

The bird above all else at Stodmarsh is the swift; thousands hunt the reed-beds every day from May till August, flying low in screeching flocks to scoop up marshland insects. With the swifts are swallows, house and sand martins, and evenings in late summer bring thousands of swallows to roost in the reed-beds. A sizeable roost of yellow wagtails occupies the reed-beds in early autumn, with two or three hundred birds quite usual.

After about a mile the raised track bends

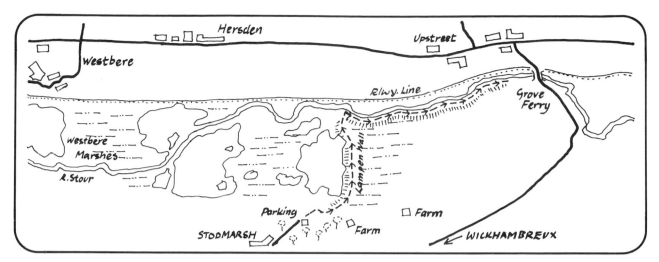

round through some scrub to run along the banks of the Stour; on the right before this is a 'wader scrape', used by a variety of species in spring and autumn. This acre or so of scrub is an excellent place for Cetti's warbler, as well as rails and thrushes in autumn. Terns fish the Stour and all the lagoons throughout the summer; a 'floating island' has been established in the largest lagoon to attract common terns to breed. Common sandpipers are frequent in spring and autumn along the Stour, while kingfishers appear regularly in winter.

After a further half-mile the reeds give way to open wet 'grazing marsh' with reed-filled ditches and grass tussocks. Lapwing, redshank, snipe and yellow wagtail all breed here, and ruff, black-tailed godwit and golden plover are often on these fields in good numbers. A glossy ibis is a regular visitor.

From April through to October marsh harriers are frequent visitors and must one day breed; ospreys pass through in spring on their way north. Winter brings rafts of pochard and tufted duck and the occasional goldeneye to the lagoons. Bewick's swans are usually to be found on the wet meadows, along with small parties of whitefronted or grey-lag geese. Several hen harriers hunt these marshes in winter with a fairly regular roost in rough ground to the south – with luck, ten or more may be seen at dusk.

Dusk is a good time to be at Stodmarsh. Two barn owls hunt the marsh in spring and summer and are joined by several short-eared owls in winter.

Sandpipers are some of the many species of birds which stop off at marshland sites, in transit between Africa and the Arctic

Wicken Fen
CAMBRIDGESHIRE

*One of the rarest
butterflies of the fens, the
Large Copper is found in
one small wet remnant,
hidden in miles of wheat
prairies*

Wicken Fen owned by the National Trust is one of the few tiny remnants of real fen left in Britain. Access is straightforward on payment of a small fee.

Wildlife Walk: Wicken Fen

The reserve covers 730 acres (295ha), a tiny island in the midst of a vast sea of arable fields. Access is by a side road from Wicken village, clearly marked, and there is a large car-park. Make your way on foot to the William Thorpe building, the main interpretative centre. Wicken Fen is marvellous for wetland birds and insects in summer, and good for wildfowl and raptors in winter.

The wildlife walk starts immediately over the little footbridge onto the fen paths. Turn right towards the restored windmill which is being used to raise water from the drainage ditches and put it back into the fen. Just past the windmill is a series of water-filled pits – the 'brick pits' – abandoned in the 1920s and now filled with a multitude of water plants. Many species of dragonfly and damselfly breed in these pits together with coot, moorhen and the occasional dabchick.

The Sedge Fen on the other side of the path is a drier, 'mixed fen' with a wide variety of plants including reed, great fen sedge, marsh thistle, yellow loosestrife, meadowsweet and many others. In summer many butterflies are found here including peacocks, tortoiseshells and Red Admirals. Sedge Fen Drove, the wide path off to the left, is one of the original villagers' paths which led to their own strips of peat. Throughout the fen these open, damp droves are filled with southern marsh orchids, yellow rattle and marsh marigold in spring and summer.

Large ash, with smaller oak and poplars, pierce the scrub. The path turns left round dense thickets of blackthorn, buckthorn and alder buckthorn, and runs out along Spinney Bank, a wide and higher, open bank heading west towards a diesel pump which is used to bring water onto the fen. Mole hills are very obvious along the drier bank. The path turns left at the diesel pump and follows Drainers' Dyke. After 400 yards you reach the other end of Sedge Fen Drove which in summer is filled with orchids and many other flowers. The whole of the thicket vegetation you have passed is excellent for birds:

in summer many different warblers breed, including willow warbler, blackcap, whitethroat, sedge, reed, and grasshopper warbler; reed buntings are numerous.

If you can be out at dusk in spring, Sedge Fen Drove is a good place to see 'roding' woodcock and listen for the mournful hoot of long-eared owls. Large roosts of starlings, buntings and bramblings use the bushes from autumn onwards.

The path continues to the Tower Hide which is a superb view-point, especially looking southwards over Adventurers' Fen (to which there is no access). The open water and waving reed-beds of Adventurers' Fen shelter a whole range of wetland birds: in summer snipe, redshank and lapwing are easily seen; marsh harrier, bearded tit, Cetti's and Savis warblers all occur and occasionally breed; water rail and garganey are present, but difficult to see.

In winter the numbers of duck steadily increase, mainly wigeon and mallard, and occasionally they are joined by parties of whitefronted and grey-lag geese – Canada geese are present all year. An occasional bittern or short-eared owl may appear. A great grey shrike is a regular winter visitor along the main paths. However, Wicken's main attraction in winter is its roost of hen harriers, up to a dozen appearing at dusk to roost on Adventurers' Fen.

From the Tower follow the bank of Wicken Lode east for three-quarters of a mile, when you return to your starting point at the footbridge.

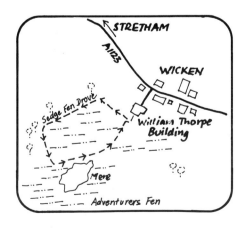

Minsmere
SUFFOLK

The RSPB reserve at Minsmere and the adjacent national nature reserve of Walberswick on the Suffolk coast total some 3,100 acres (1,254ha) and make up one of the finest wildlife areas in Britain, throughout the year.

Wildlife Walk: Minsmere

There are two approaches to the reserve. The obvious route is to enter by side roads from Westleton, down a bumpy track to the large and very well hidden car-park. The other is to park in the National Trust car-park by the coastguards' cottages at Minsmere cliffs, walk down the beach and enter the reserve across the first marsh path. Either route takes you to the centre for a permit and vital, up-to-the minute information. It is of course so easy to see birds at Minsmere that the 'served up on a plate' feeling is sometimes inevitable. Birdwatchers in hides are often amazingly noisy, but Minsmere birds appear to take no notice of the racket whatsoever, remaining quite undisturbed. Avocets stroll about a few feet from a hide re-verberating like the Centre Court at Wimbledon.

In summer a large and very prominent colony of sand martins occupies the sandy cliff which has been cut out manually next to the car park. Superb views are possible whilst eating your lunch. There are several nature trails here but probably the best is to look at the western sector of the reserve first; this includes walking back down the entrance track so as to make your way through the extensive area of woodland and across some of the heath. Access is restricted to the marked paths only, other-wise the birds you have come to see will not stay. Nearly a mile back down the track from the car-park to Scotts Hill Farm a footpath from the farm returns you towards the coast through a good mature woodland called South Belt, which holds most of the common woodland birds: all three woodpeckers, woodcock, sparrow-hawk, nightingale, redstart, tawny and long-eared owls. The heathy areas have tree pipit, stonechat, and nightjar.

Island Mere Hide lies part-way back along the wooded path towards the coast and gives excellent views over a wide expanse of reed-bed and open water. Half a mile nearer the coast the next hide is Tree Hide, on stilts and up steep steps; this also looks out over reeds and open water, and the alders of South Belt behind it have many redpolls and siskins in winter.

The reed marsh and meres hold a vast array of interesting birds: several pairs of bitterns, marsh harriers, hundreds of bearded tits, water rails, herons breeding in the reed-beds, scores of reed and sedge warblers, Cetti's and grasshopper warblers. Savis warbler is regular in small numbers, and a glimpse of kingfisher can also be had about the meres. Rarer birds such as purple heron, spoonbill and osprey are still surprisingly frequent.

A path now takes you from the car-park round four hides which overlook the famous man-made 'Minsmere Scrape' – a series of shallow, muddy, brackish pools with many islets; follow the path south checking pools and hides as you go. Avocets, common, little and occasional sandwich terns, plovers, oystercatchers and shelduck all breed here, along with many black-headed gulls. Migration periods, especially in autumn, bring in hordes of waders of at least twenty-five species to these pools. Winter always attracts many wildfowl as the water levels are raised – all the common dabbling ducks, with goldeneye and goosander on the meres and small parties of geese and Bewick's swans which appear on the grazing marshes.

Address of Site/Warden

Warden:
Minsmere RSPB Reserve,
Westleton,
Saxmundham,
Suffolk IP17 2BY

Highlights and Features

Wide variety of marshland habitats, backed by heath woodland. One of the richest areas for birds in Britain.

Facilities

Minsmere: Open every day except Tuesday 0900–2100 or sunset. Information centre. Large car-park. Many hides, including two public hides on beach. Non-members £2.

Photo Tips

Long telephoto lenses essential. Minsmere hides very good for close views many marsh birds especially avocet. Birds used to people. Sand martin colony by centre. Good for fen flowers. Try to be present when rare birds are not, to avoid large crowds.

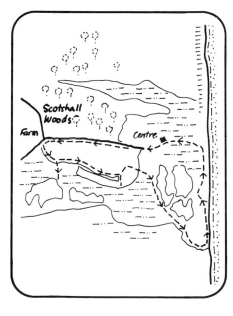

The graceful avocet has built up several small colonies on East Anglian marshland reserves

22

Ouse Washes

CAMBRIDGESHIRE AND NORFOLK

Address of Site/Warden

Ouse Washes RSPB Reserve:
Warden,
'Limosa', Welches Dam,
Manea,
March,
Cambs PE15 0ND
Welney Wildfowl
Trust Refuge:
The Wildfowl Trust,
Pintail House,
Hundred Foot Bank,
Welney,
Wisbech,
Cambs PE14 9TN

Highlights and Features

Extensive wet meadows between two parallel rivers. Many dykes and ditches. Flooded in winter. Large population breeding wetland birds in spring. Huge numbers of wildfowl in winter including 5,000 Bewick's swan.

Facilities

RSPB Reserve. Access at all times to series of hides along banks. Information centre open weekends. Toilets.
Welney Refuge. Open daily 1000–1900. Information centre shop, café. Lots of hides.

Photo Tips

Pictures in summer unlikely. Winter produces huge flocks of ducks and swans. Long telephoto lenses will give superb pictures. The Wildfowl Refuge is best in the morning as the hides face west. The RSPB reserve hides face east and are better in the afternoon.

Until the seventeenth century 1,500 square miles (3,885sq km) of north-western East Anglia was an untamed wilderness of marshland, meres and reed-beds, with small isolated communities of people on the higher ground. From 1637 onwards a Dutch engineer, Vermuyden, was engaged by the then Earl of Bedford to build a 32km straight-cut – the 'Old Bedford River' – and later a parallel 'New Bedford River' half-a-mile away, to drain the marshlands in summer. High barrier banks were raised along the rivers and the land between became grazing marshland, divided into fields or 'washes' by open ditches. Sluices are now used to allow surplus water in winter to flood onto the washes from the River Delph, the inner channel of the Old Bedford River.

Thus was created one of Europe's finest wildfowl sites which has fortunately survived, little changed, to the present day. All the surrounding marshes have long since been turned into arable farmland. Only in the early 1960s was the importance of the site recognised, since when the RSPB, the Wildfowl Trust and the local County Naturalist Trusts (Cambient) have acquired some 3,000 acres (1,214ha) of the 4,700 acres (1,902ha) available.

Spring and early summer are exciting times on the washes as the water levels recede and the eighty species of breeding birds reappear. However, the time to see the Ouse Washes at their best is after the floods have come towards the end of the year – winter brings hordes of wildfowl from the far north and east to feed and shelter here, and only if the whole area completely freezes over do the wildfowl depart for softer climes. From mid-December through to March this is a wonderful wildlife spectacle for all the family. The whole area is well served by wooden hides, which are truly welcome when the arctic winds strike straight across the fenlands like a blaze of lances. So be warned, go bobble-hatted, scarved, mittened and well wrapped against the cold.

One wildlife tour is described taking in the RSPB and Cambient Reserves at Purls Bridge, and the Wildfowl Trust Reserve further north at Welney.

Wildlife Tour: Winter
This tour starts at the RSPB reserve car-

park reached from Manea via RSPB signs to Purls Bridge and Welches Dam. The reserve notice board gives up-to-date information; there are also modern toilets – useful in freezing winter weather, and the small visitor centre is open at weekends. There are ten hides spread out along three miles (4.8km) of bank overlooking the washes, all situated on the western bank of the Old Bedford River. You can cut out some of the walking by concentrating on two hides south of the car-park and then driving to Purls Bridge and using the two or three hides accessible from there. However, Purls Bridge is a little community in its own right and you may be using someone else's official car-park space. The Ship Inn provides lunches.

After leaving the car-park go up onto the bank by the Welches Dam pump station. The large willows here are some of the few trees you will see – this is a land of wide marshland skies filled with birds. Pass through the Angling Society gate and please abide by the notice: *do not walk on top of the bank after this point* – you will see nothing if you do and may ruin a day's outing for many other people.

By this time you will have seen great flocks of duck and distant skeins of wild swans against the light. Walk along the bank of the Old Bedford River for the half-mile to the first hide which is called Rickwood Hide. There are two more hides, 'Common Wash' and 'Eastwood' at half-mile intervals farther on – if you have time and can stand the cold, all are worth a visit. You may even find that the walk between the hides warms you up and restores the circulation! North of Welches Dam there are no less than seven hides spread out along two miles (3km) of bank. All ten of these hides provide superb views over the washes, often best in the afternoon, especially on sunny days as the light will then be behind you.

Vast packs of duck crowd onto the wet and flooded meadows: wigeon far outnumber all the others with up to 35–40,000 birds at peak times; there will be 3–4,000 each of pintail, teal, mallard, pochard and shoveler. Besides these, smaller numbers of less common duck can also be seen, while the deeper ditches and the rivers attract goldeneye, goosander and cormorants which all come for fish.

Swans are present in large numbers,

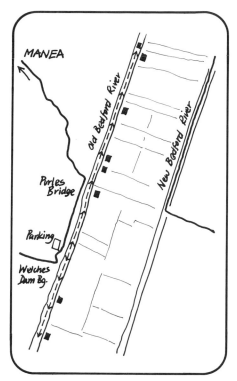

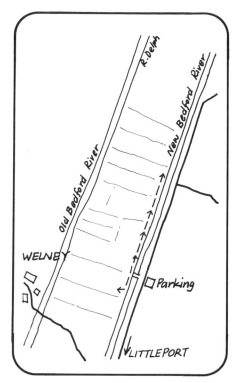

although the best place to see them is farther north at Welney – nevertheless large flocks will pass up and down the washes all day. Small parties of geese – whitefronts, grey-lags, pinkfeet and the occasional bean goose – are often to be found if the floods are not too severe and where there is damp grass for feeding.

A sudden panic among the wildfowl may mean a drifting hen harrier or short-eared owl; terrified ducks all over the sky indicate a hunting peregrine. Thousands of lapwing, snipe and golden plover use the washes in winter, with small numbers of redshank and ruff. Roosting gulls, mostly black-headed, may number 20,000 late in the afternoon.

Three or four miles (5km) further north at Welney on the right bank of the New Bedford River is the Wildfowl Trust Reserve, easily found by following the signs. This is rather more commercially organised than that of the RSPB, and includes a tiny café. Non-members may use all the hides if they pay a small entrance fee, but not the large, plush, centrally heated main observation room which is for members only. All are approached from the car-park over a covered footbridge to prevent disturbance to the birds. There are over forty small hides buried in the banks of the reserve, made from fibre-glass workhuts, together with two wings to the main observation centre.

The main lagoon is the star attraction – all the birds are wild, but really do act as if tame. Thousands of duck flock in all day, but they are completely outshone by the swans: 2–3,000 Bewick's with 200 larger whoopers and 300 mute swans. The noise and sight of the thousands of these great birds jostling and bobbing, or flighting in at such close range, will keep you enthralled for hours. These birds now know that there is supplementary food to be had here – twice a day corn and old potatoes, mostly donated by local farms, is scattered along the bank, usually by one of the wardens slowly pushing a wheelbarrow. Provided he moves slowly the birds are not afraid. As dusk falls, floodlights on a timed 'dimmer' switch slowly swell to full strength so as to light up the area for an extra hour or two into the darkness. This is one of Europe's wildlife spectacles – don't miss it.

Spring: by late March the floods have receded and the wildfowl migrate north to the Arctic. The lush wet meadows are then filled with breeding marshland birds, amongst which the prime attraction is the beautiful black-tailed godwit, usually 50–60 pairs, whose spectacular overhead display flight is worth a long drive to witness. Here, too, are twenty pairs of breeding ruff among the 800 pairs of displaying snipe, and the hundreds of redshank, lapwing, yellow wagtails, reed and sedge warblers. Barn and short-eared owls may both breed and marsh harriers are often present. Migrants stream through the wet pools, with flocks of greenshank, spotted redshank and whimbrel heading north. Black terns are regulars, as are flocks of little gulls. For what at first sight looks to be nothing more than flat, wet, fields, the bird list is quite extraordinary.

The Ouse Washes attract huge numbers of wild ducks and swans during the winter

23

The Broads
HICKLING NORFOLK

Address of Site/Warden

Warden:
Warden's Office,
Stubbs Road,
Hickling,
Norwich,
Norfolk NR12 0BW

Highlights and Features

Largest of the Broads. Huge area of reed marsh with some wader scrapes.

Facilities

Many hides, observation towers, wardened boat trip.

Photo Tips

A long telephoto lens is essential for birds. A wide-angle zoom lens will enable creative pictures of the scenery. A good place at sunset for artistic marshland photos.

A barn owl in the reeds: East Anglia is one of the few places left where hunting barn owls are still a regular sight

Created by peat-digging in medieval times, the Norfolk Broads are one of the most outstanding areas for wildlife in Britain. There are over forty Broads, formed as sea-levels rose and flooded the peat-workings, and most of them are relatively shallow, from 2 to 4 metres deep. A number of the larger areas of water are linked by navigable rivers, and in all some 125 miles (200km) of waterways discharge into a single 4-mile (6km) long estuary known as Breydon Water, near Great Yarmouth.

Changes in land use, together with increased tourist pressure, mean that the Broads no longer support much floating water vegetation except where boats and people are excluded. Hickling is the largest of the Broads, and lies just north of the village of Potter Heigham, only a few miles from the coast. 1,360 acres (550ha) of the area is a national nature reserve, consisting of the Broad itself together with large areas of sedge, reed- and grazing marsh, as well as woodland.

Two wildlife walks are described, a three-mile (4.8km) level walk along the south side of the Broad, and a shorter ramble based on the wardened Norfolk Naturalists' Trust reserve on the northern bank.

Wildlife Walk 1: The Weavers Way

Take the A149 north from Potter Heigham and after 1½ miles (2km) turn right over a level crossing to Decoy Lane. After a further mile park by a stile and gate with the national nature reserve information sign. Parking is very restricted. This walk is particularly good both early and late in the day, and should really be combined with Walk 2, around the wader scrapes on the northern side of the Broad. In summer the copse by the entrance has common woodland birds and turtle doves. Climb the stile and walk east along the bank which runs along the southern edge of the Broad and its vast reed-beds – this is part of the Weavers Way, the main East Anglian long-distance footpath.

After a hundred yards or so stand and watch the whole reed-filled horizon waving gently in the breeze. Summer will produce a drifting marsh harrier just above the reed tops, lots of cuckoos flying over the reeds looking for reed warblers' nests in which to lay their eggs, bearded tits,

grasshopper and Savis warblers, and herons stalking in the shallows. Common and little terns fish the open waters and in spring and autumn, parties of graceful black terns skim the water for surface insects. Feral Canada and grey-lag geese breed in some numbers in the surrounding marshland, whilst great crested grebes and an occasional dabchick are resident on the Broad itself.

After half a mile an oak and alder wood on the south of the path has numerous woodland birds: nightjar and Cetti's warbler sing from the thickets, redpolls are frequent and are joined by siskins to feed on the alders in winter. Several pairs of bitterns breed in the reed-beds; they are very secretive and you are unlikely to see them except at dawn and dusk, but their 'booming' calls echo across the marshlands in the half-light.

A mile further on the path bends north round Heighton Corner and reveals a large area of open water; there is an open wooden hide to aid observation. Looking south there are several wide marsh fields before the inevitable arable farmland – barn owls hunt this area and can often be seen in summer over the fields; short-eared owls occasionally join them in winter.

Fifty-five acres (22ha) of reed are harvested every year for thatching. This is normally carried out on dry reed in late winter but saw sedge is harvested for ridge thatch in summer. The fen-like vegetation created in the reed-beds encourages a lot of milk parsley, the ideal food plant for the Swallow-tail butterfly – these lovely, large and rare insects are often quite numerous at Hickling in midsummer.

Marsh vegetation is superb, with meadowsweet, purple and yellow loose-strife, hemp agrimony, yellow flag and ragged robin present in quantity. Large stands of marsh orchid occur around Deep Dyke, with smaller colonies in wet marsh fields elsewhere. The fact that two seaside plants grow here – sea milkwort and marsh mallow – indicates that sea-water is seeping in from the coast some three miles (4.8km) away.

In autumn, parties of migrant waders come in to feed and roost throughout the reserve: spotted redshank, greenshank, wood and green sandpiper. Juvenile spoonbill and purple heron often wander

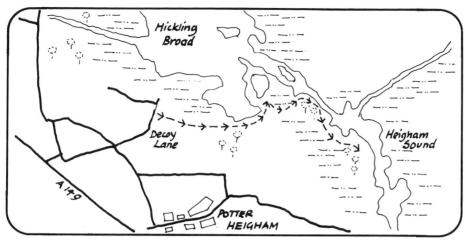

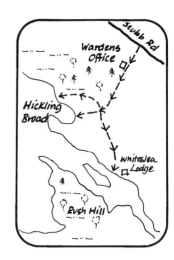

across the North Sea from the Dutch colonies at this time. Winter brings hordes of duck, 60 whooper and 150 Bewick's swans. In hard weather the open water may sometimes have the three rare grebes, Slavonian, red and black-necked, present at the same time.

The presence of unusual mammals is a feature of this reserve. Wild coypu, an introduced species, are still seen, although coypu rate as a pest and the population has been much reduced. Chinese water deer may be seen occasionally along the reed-bed margins, whilst harvest mice are frequently noted in the reed-beds and overgrown ditches.

The path continues around the edge of Whiteslea Wood, a mature oak woodland with many woodland birds, and on along the south bank of Heigham Sound, increasing the round walk to nearly six miles (9.6km).

Wildlife Walk 2: The Wader Scrapes

From Hickling Green take Stubb Road for half a mile, and then turn right down a track towards Whiteslea Lodge. There is a Norfolk Naturalists' Trust signpost. During the summer months, a 2½-hour 'water trail' by boat will take you to parts of the reserve that other visitors cannot reach, and provides close views of reed-bed and open water birds.

From the warden's hut, walking trails along damp fen paths take you to a variety of hides overlooking the reedy edge of the Broad, or the various wader scrapes constructed in recent years. A permit and a key to the hides are both necessary for these walks. Since this part of the reserve is open from 9.30am till 6pm it is best to combine a walk around the wader hides with an early or late walk along the Weavers Way (Walk 1).

Ringed plover, oystercatcher, lapwing, redshank, avocet, common and little terns all breed on these wader scrapes. Snipe, yellow wagtails, gadwall, shoveler, pochard and the occasional garganey all have their nests in the fen vegetation nearby, though shelduck have taken to breeding in the banks.

Winter can be bleak here but brings hunting hen harriers and short-eared owls to quarter the fen lands. Large roosts of gulls occur from autumn onwards with 10,000 birds at peak times.

The large, rare Swallow-tail butterfly is restricted to fenland areas of East Anglia

24

Strumpshaw Fen
NORFOLK

Address of Site/Warden

RSPB Reserve:
Warden:
Staithe Cottage,
Low Road,
Strumpshaw,
Norwich,
Norfolk NR13 4HS

Highlights and Features

A large fen with reed-beds. Alder and willow swamp and damp woodland. Large area of fresh grazing marsh. Rich marshland for birds, animals and flowers.

Facilities

Open daily 0900 to 2100 or sunset. Information centre. Three hides including observation tower.
Another winter hide at Buckenham for bean geese.

Photo Tips

Large flocks of wildfowl in winter need long telephoto lenses. Remember to compensate for the light sky when taking pictures of birds in flight. Lovely mute swans on nest in fen environment need 200mm zoom lens. Good for fen flowers with wide-angle zoom.

Primroses, once very common spring flowers, but now much rarer, flourish well in open marshy woodlands

Strumpshaw Fen is part of the lower tidal section of the polluted River Yare. In 1975 the RSPB leased 320 acres (129ha) of the fen, and now, having purchased several other sections of neighbouring marshland, controls a reserve of some 600 acres. Banks have been strengthened against pollution from the river and management has been designed to enlarge the water areas, dig out the derelict dykes, create water scrapes, limit reed-cutting to selected areas and prevent an expansion of sallow carr.

As a result of twelve years of intensive work the RSPB has produced a superb marshland reserve with all the broadland habitats intact: open water, fen, sallow and alder carr and oak woodland. Every habitat requires continual rotational management to maintain this pleasing state of affairs. The variety of animals, birds and plants has increased dramatically so that now over eighty bird species breed regularly. This is a beautiful, peaceful marsh, a delight to visit. The main wildlife walk encompasses the whole reserve, and is a 3½-mile (5km) round walk on level ground. Visiting is good all year. A short winter walk to the nearby Buckenham Marshes to look for bean geese is also described.

Wildlife Walk 1: Strumpshaw

At the eastern end of Brundall village find Low Road which leads through woodland to the reserve car-park; cross the railway line to the information centre – an adjacent hide looks out over an open reed marsh pool. From the centre, a wide track goes south through mature, damp woodland. This is a mixed wood of oak, with hazel and birch, and a rich shrub layer. Old, ivy-clad trees, full of holes, provide nesting sites for many common woodland species: all the tits and woodpeckers, nuthatch, tree-creeper, warblers, spotted flycatcher and goldcrest; turtle doves are also numerous.

The ditches alongside the path here often hold frogs, newts and hunting grass snakes, and even have European terrapin which have become naturalised in the area and may appear on a log. A wooden seat is provided to sit and quietly watch the woodland. Roe deer are frequent and Chinese water deer are also present. After some 500 yards (456m) the woodland

thins out to birch and alder carr: masses of rosebay willowherb grow along the path with primroses, bluebells and red campion earlier in spring.

The scrub here holds many breeding warblers and finches. In winter large roosts of thrushes, especially redwing and fieldfare, appear to eat the berries, while siskin and redpoll flocks may run to hundreds in the alder trees bordering the marsh. Just beyond the scrub is open grazing marsh, with the woodland on your right. Watch the marsh from the gate – herons, ducks, and breeding pairs of redshank, snipe and lapwing are all found here, and yellow wagtails nest among the grass tussocks. The rich black marsh soil is ideal for moles, and shows mole-hills and the larger 'fortresses', the mole breeding den, to great advantage.

Follow the path along the line of telegraph poles to an old chimney, and out onto the broad bank of the River Yare – the view from here across the southern area of fresh grazing marsh is excellent. This is excellent habitat for raptors: in winter short-eared owls and hen harriers quarter the meadows, and barn, tawny, little and long-eared owls all breed in the area. The fence posts are favourite vantage points, especially at dusk and early in the day, for barn and little owls – short-eared owls and the occasional merlin also use them.

Walk north along the bank of the river and take note of the wash created by pleasure craft – this, together with sewage and agricultural pollutants, has destroyed much of the plant and animal life in the river. Litter from these craft drifts into sheltered bays; cola cans and plastic bottles bob in the water. On the other side of the bank is Strumpshaw Fen with wide reed-beds and clean water, clearly showing how the area would be if it were not for the squalid habits of the human race.

The Yare is lined with massive willows, and also sallow scrub which is inhabited noisily by Cetti's warblers. Half a mile along the Yare bank there is a path which takes a short-cut back through extensive reed-beds to the centre. Explore this path just to look over the reed-beds and the grazing marsh towards the woodland – woodcock breed in the damp woods and 'rode' along the marsh edge in spring, mute swans have several conspicuous

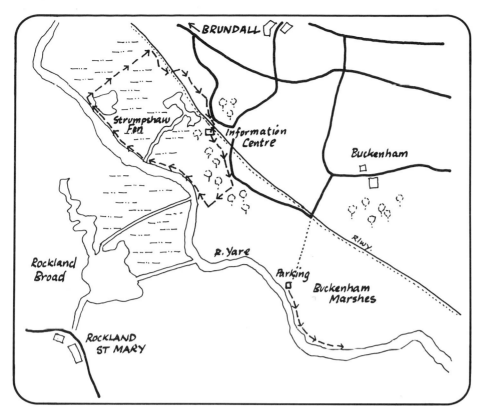

nesting sites around the marsh ditches and Chinese water deer may appear on the marsh here, early and late in the day.

Return to the Yare bank and continue north for a further 1,000 yards (912m) – old willow trees along the bank provide good nest sites. Watch the reed-beds on your right, where marsh harriers breed regularly and bearded tits are numerous. Cetti's and grasshopper warblers build their nests where the reed blends with sallow carr, and look out for Savis warbler which has bred and may occur regularly. Cuckoos fly the reed-bed in search of reed warbler nests in summer.

At the north-western corner of the reserve a tower-hide built on stilts overlooks the marsh with twenty-two steps to gain access. A new and extensive wader scrape has been excavated directly in front of the tower which is well screened by tall willows – there are wide views over the reed-bed and fen. Great crested grebes breed on the 'cut' on the Yare bank near the tower, and Canada geese have already colonised the scrape and its islands.

Because the purity and condition of the water has been so much improved by sealing the banks against the Yare, wildfowl and waterbirds breed in increasing numbers: kingfishers and water rails, dabchick, mallard, shoveler, pochard, gadwall and tufted duck are all present. Winter sees large flocks of wildfowl, snipe and lapwing using the marshlands. The new wader scrape already attracts 'fresh' marsh species, such as green and wood

sandpipers, and greenshank on migration, and many more will turn up in increasing numbers as they get used to its availability. On quiet days a lucky visitor may even see an otter, and almost certainly mink or coypu, all of which are resident. All the common mammal species of wood and marsh are present.

From the tower-hide the path crosses the open fen towards the railway. In summer, Swallowtail butterflies are frequent, while many dragonfly species occur. Finally the path recrosses the railway and returns in half a mile, down a wooded track to the car-park.

Wildlife Walk 2: Buckenham

This is primarily a winter walk when peak numbers of wildfowl are present. The Buckenham Marshes, protected by the RSPB, now have the only regular wintering flock of the rare bean goose in Britain. The flock has increased since it has been protected from winter shooting, and now some 300 bean geese are found here from late November until March. A few whitefronted geese are also present; 6–8,000 wigeon use the Buckenham Marshes for winter feeding, while hen harriers and short-eared owls are regulars.

From Brundall take the Hassingham road and turn left after a mile to Buckenham Station. Drive on for half a mile and park where the track reaches the river. Walk along the riverbank footpath to the RSPB hide beyond the old mill which gives good views over the marshland.

Great crested grebes breed on many freshwater sites in the south and east of England

Radipole Lake
DORSET

*Large numbers of
wildfowl gather at
Radipole Lake in winter*

Radipole and Lodmoor are two RSPB reserves right in the heart of Weymouth and as such are quite unique in Britain.

Wildlife Walk: Radipole

Radipole consists of 200 acres (81ha) of reed-bed and open, shallow freshwater, at the northern end are some water meadows of the River Wey. What is so surprising about this beautiful place is its surroundings – busy, brash Weymouth.

Park in the large municipal Swannery car-park opposite the bus station. An excellent RSPB interpretative centre is at the top corner by the lake.

Mute swans, mallard, coot and moorhen are here all year, joined by large rafts of tufted duck and pochard in the winter months. The whole of the large shallow lake is attractive to grebes, with two or three pairs of great crested and dabchick breeding, while larger groups come in to shelter in winter.

Take the path north into the reed-beds from the centre. The whole path system has been well laid out for the handicapped. Fifty yards (46m) will bring you to some gravel paths on the right – these run for 400 yards (365m) through extensive reed-beds and alongside the deep eastern channel.

In spring and summer hundreds of reed and sedge warbler breed in these reeds, together with the much rarer Cetti's warbler, and some twenty pairs of bearded tit. If you penetrate 100 yards into these reed-beds you can enjoy a mixed chorus of dozens of warblers overlaid with pop-music from the funfair. Two hundred yards and the music has merged with the low murmur of the town – the warblers have won.

In places the tracks are lined with dense thickets of blackthorn, bramble and buddleia. Butterflies flock to the buddleia in summer – twenty-six species already seen on a wetland reserve! Red Admirals, peacocks, tortoiseshells, Painted Ladies and Clouded Yellows occur – all the most colourful of British butterflies to please the eye; there are even Marbled Whites on the chalk grasses.

It is half a mile to the first hide, Buddleia Hide, with its fine views over reeds and open water. Two small artificial islands have been built to attract terns. Old tyres have been anchored at the reed-bed edge to provide nesting sites for coots.

The track continues for another 600 yards (548m) over a small bridge at the western gate to Island Pool Hide which looks out over a lovely pool surrounded completely by reeds, with sallow thickets to right and left. Look in the reeds for bearded tit – especially feeding from the reed-tops in winter. A further 500 yards (456m) along the western edge of the reserve is North Hide. Return to the car-park is straightforward.

All these hides and trails provide superb views. Sometimes great flocks of birds may be seen – huge numbers of swallows, martins and swifts feed over the reserve from May until late August. Late summer is undoubtedly a special time here, when thousands of swallows gather to roost in the reeds prior to their southward migration. They are joined by many thousands of starlings and up to 3,000 yellow wagtail – and the whole roost will almost certainly attract a sparrowhawk or migrant hobby. Dusk at Radipole in late August or early September can be a bird experience to remember.

Kingfishers and water rails breed in less disturbed parts of the reserve, and grasshopper warblers, whitethroats and lesser whitethroats prefer the thickets along the paths.

Winter brings large roosts of gulls and rarer wildfowl to the lakes. Thousands of starlings and nearly 1,000 pied wagtails roost in the shelter of the winter reed-beds.

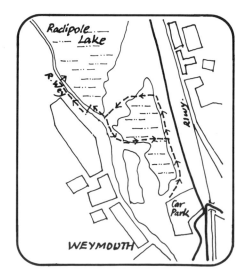

Slapton Leys
DEVON

The South Devon peninsula from Kingsbridge to Dartmouth provides one of the widest ranges of birds to be seen in Britain, especially in migration seasons.

Slapton Leys, only seven miles (11km) to the east of Kingsbridge, are a superb series of freshwater lakes with extensive reed-beds, run as a carefully managed reserve by the Field Studies Council.

Wildlife Walk: Slapton Leys

Park in the car-park facing the Lower Ley in Torcross village. There is a public bird hide just before Torcross on a sharp bend, but it is possible to view the Lower Ley from the car-park. There are in fact three main leys, freshwater lakes, here behind a shingle ridge which is inaptly named Slapton Sands. However Beesands Ley, half a mile south of Torcross village, is not part of the local reserve and suffers disturbance from a local caravan park.

Having examined the Lower Ley, drive a mile north along the road on the shingle bank and park among the tourists in a pay car-park. Although the ley is visible from here, there are far better views to be had – walk over the bridge which separates the main lake from the Higher (and drier) Ley. Simply standing on the bridge provides excellent views of extensive reed-beds on one side and the superb freshwater lake on the other.

There is a ringing hut by the bridge. This is an important nature reserve, and the people who work on it will happily advise on what to see. Take the path directly in front of the ringing hut. This runs along the bank of the Higher Ley for three-quarters of a mile, usually above it along the sides of farm fields, and offers splendid views over reed-beds and a central channel of water. It has a fine marsh 'edge', and lots of sallow thickets mixed with blackthorn; the fen is full of marsh marigold and yellow flag in spring. The whole of the Higher Ley, despite its closeness to the road, is a quiet, secret marshland world. Otters are seen here occasionally, and mink are now firmly resident.

Breeding marsh birds include a number of Cetti's warblers with their loud, explosive call, one or two pairs of Savis warblers, and grasshopper warblers with their somewhat similar 'reeling' call, and bearded tits 'ping-pinging' away as they slide down the reeds. Dozens of pairs of reed and sedge warblers breed here, while one or two pairs of water rails live secretively in the Higher Ley. Great crested grebes nest on the main lake.

Return to the bridge and walk along the path hugging the back of Slapton Ley. One or two stretches are short, steep climbs, but most of the path is along the lake shore, below steep banks and full of bluebells, stitchwort, red campion and gorse in early summer. After 400 yards (365m) the remains of an old gun emplacement make a good look-out spot, even providing views into Ireland Bay and over the reed-bed. Buzzard, sparrowhawk and raven are resident all year round in France Wood above the Bay, with all the usual woodland species including lesser spotted woodpecker. Continue a further quarter of a mile to the Field Centre gate by the reed-bed.

Spring and autumn bring a wide variety of migrants both in the Leys and passing offshore, including huge numbers of swallows which roost in the reeds in autumn.

The Leys are thus a superb complex of habitats providing a rich wildlife cross-section. The main Ley itself gives valuable shelter for sea-birds and wildfowl in winter.

Address of Site/Warden

Slapton –
Slapton Ley Field Centre,
Slapton,
Kingsbridge,
Devon TQ7 2QP

Highlights and Features

Slapton Leys:
A series of freshwater pools behind shingle ridge of Slapton Sands. Excellent reed marsh birds and migrants.

Facilities

Slapton Leys – Field Studies Council Field Centre plus bird-ringing hut.

Photo Tips

Zoom lenses plus tripod to take pictures of sea-cliff and marsh flowers. Birds need telephoto lenses. A small flashgun may be useful for pictures of birds in the hand caught by the Slapton Ringing station.

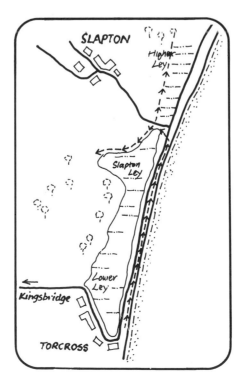

The elf-like little owl breeds in hedgerow trees and marshland willows throughout southern Britain

Somerset Levels

Address of Site/Warden

West Sedgemoor
RSPB Reserve
Warden:
Hadleigh,
White Street,
North Curry,
nr Taunton,
Somerset TA3 6HL

Highlights and Features

Low-lying wet meadows, partially flooded in winter. Rich plant-filled ditches. Used as hay meadows and grazing marsh. Woodland on southern hill border. Large populations of wetland birds, insects, flowers and mammals. Many breeding waders. Huge flocks waders and many wildfowl in winter. Large heronry visible from hide.

Facilities

Two hides, one on marsh and one in woodland overlooking small pool and up to heronry. Open at all times.

Photo Tips

Birds can be quite close at woodland pool, but not the herons which are high in the trees. Long telephoto lenses may give pictures of birds at pool. Wide-angle zoom for superb marshland flowers in ditches.

Many pairs of redshank breed in the wet meadows of the Somerset Levels

Between the Mendip hills and the Quantocks lies a little known area of rich grazing marshes and meadows – the Somerset Levels. Used for centuries for traditional hay-making and grazing, it is a wonderful reservoir of wetland plants, birds and animals. Unfortunately modern farming methods have drained much of the wetland and only small segments of the original grazing meadows remain. It is vitally important to maintain these quite unique marshlands – apart from large populations of breeding marshland birds, they hold nationally important stocks of wetland flowers and many scarce insects. In winter parts of the area flood, and the whole then becomes a haven for thousands of birds driven westwards by severe weather. If these last western wetlands are drained, birds needing winter shelter and marshland feeding will have nowhere else to go.

One wildlife walk is described at the RSPB reserve of West Sedgemoor. This is probably the easiest point of access, although King's Sedgemoor and North Moor near Bridgewater are important. The entrance lies one mile east of Fivehead on the A378 out of Taunton; park in the tiny car-park (ten places!) cut from the edge of the wood. If visiting in winter the wood holds many wintering birds and may be viewed at once. If visiting in spring, leave the wood until you have walked the marsh. May is an excellent time to visit, and January to March for winter birds.

Walk down the steep, narrow road out of the wood – do *not* take your car down here as it is a dead-end in a private farmyard. The road has steep banks filled with flowers in spring: bluebells, primroses, stitchwort and yellow archangel. The open flat levels quickly appear, while behind you a high wood caps the limestone ridge. A large rookery occupies the northern edge of the wood overlooking the moor, and there is always a constant stream of rooks to and from the marsh.

Under half a mile brings you to Eastwood Dairy Farm on the right; from here, walk to the barn on the edge of the marsh, in the shelter of which the RSPB has built a wooden hide, giving an excellent view over the area. Have a quick look inside the barn itself, as collared doves nest on the eaves while dozens of jackdaws pick up tit-bits; pied wagtails often breed in the

rafters, and there are swallow trays in the roof.

A large pool has been excavated a hundred yards in front of the hide, and the wet meadows extend some two miles (3km) to the hills around Stoke St Gregory. The levels consist of a network of raised tracks called 'droves', lined by ditches, called 'rhynes', all of which border wet grazing meadows. Pollarded willows border the rhynes which are filled with reed, bullrush and yellow flag. They are cleared only every five years or so, therefore allowing their vegetation to become dominant.

Next to the hide is Swell Drove. Walk down it across the marsh watching carefully all around – be aware of movement. Mute swans nest out on the levels and are usually visible from some distance away. In spring and early summer the meadows and ditches are a riot of colour, filled with marsh marigolds and ladies' smock, followed by ragged robin, meadowsweet, pepper saxifrage, angelica, yellow flag and yellow rattle. Thousands of marsh orchids flower in June.

In spring the marshland breeding birds will be all around you. Lapwing, redshank, snipe and curlew all breed in these fields, the first three species in some numbers which makes this one of the most important sites in Britain for 'freshmarsh' waders. Swallows and house martins swoop across the marsh feeding on the multitude of insects; skylarks, too, are very numerous, spiralling upwards in full song.

Walk Swell Drove for nearly half a mile until you are stopped by an RSPB notice and a ditch: some parts of the marsh are kept completely undisturbed. Return to the hide and take the very rutted and usually muddy track left, eastwards, along the back of the marsh. Herons will be a considerable part of the constant traffic to and from the wood, since this contains Somerset's largest heronry in its tree-tops (80 pairs in 1986).

A thick thorn hedge over a ditch runs alongside the track with small copses and old trees at intervals. Summer brings sedge and grasshopper warblers, bullfinch, chaffinch, linnet and long-tailed tit in the hedge; willow warblers and chiffchaffs in the copses; and redstarts, tree sparrows and little owls in the tree-holes. The ditch banks shelter wild arum and hartstongue fern, and clumps of mistletoe hang in the willows.

After 400 yards (365m) you will come to Broadway Drove which extends for half a mile into the marsh; however, continue along the back of the marsh and leave Broadway for your return journey. On the main track several large clumps of cowslip appear in May, together with a cowslip/ primrose hybrid. A large old oak on the marsh edge is often used as a perch by hunting owls at dusk, as similarly an old elm stump nearby provides a vantage point for birds of prey. An old barn, next to a crowfoot-filled pool by the track, is also used by the occasional owl.

Just past the barn take the unnamed drove and walk for half a mile to a gate with RSPB 'Private' notice – use the gate-posts as cover: two or three pairs of black-tailed godwit nest here, making this a prime site for this rare breeding bird in Britain. Yellow wagtails and whinchats breed in some numbers.

Large flocks of whimbrel migrate through these meadows in spring from mid-April to mid-May – as many as 2,000 have been seen heading for their roost in Bridgewater Bay. Small numbers of green and wood sandpipers and greenshank also pass in spring and autumn.

From late April onwards hobbies may be seen hawking insects, especially dragonflies, over these fields and one or two pairs now breed locally in the hill-top woods. They are most likely to be seen at dusk, and join one or two barn owls hunting the marsh. Buzzards are frequent, circling the marsh on wide-spread wings, and breed in many woodlands nearby; kestrels and sparrowhawks are local residents.

Winter floods bring thousands of birds to these marshes: lapwings are most numerous, with upwards of 25,000; cold weather further north and east can bring as many as 10,000 snipe, 1,000 jacksnipe and 1,000 dunlin; and 2,000 golden plover are usual among the hordes of lapwing.

Birds of prey attracted by these winter congregations include several short-eared owls, one or two peregrines, merlins and hen harrier. Bewick's swans may reach a hundred strong in cold weather.

Leave the marsh either by the same route or by Broadway Drove and return to the woodland car-park. This is a mature and ancient wood of ash and oak – only a hundred yards from your car a hide looks up at the heronry, which is clearly visible before the leaves break in May; twenty nests are easily observed from the hide. A small pool attracts nuthatches to collect mud for their nests and woodland birds to drink – all three woodpeckers, marsh and long-tailed tit and tree-creeper are

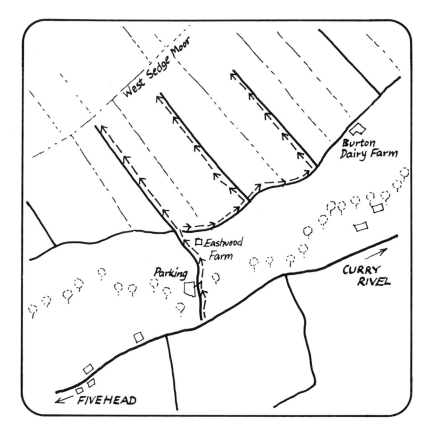

resident. Blackcap, chiffchaff, willow warbler, redstart and nightingale are numerous in summer.

The woodland is filled with primroses and false oxlips in early spring, and by June has produced a variety of orchids, in particular greater butterfly and bird's-nest orchids which can be seen clearly from the half-mile circular track through the woods.

If you can stay till 10pm on a warm May evening you may see badger and roe deer. Walk the track at dusk, take a torch to light you back, sit on a tree-stump in the dark and wait. Nightingales will sing all around you.

Pied wagtails may nest in the outbuildings of Sedgemoor farms

28

The Midlands Marshes
FAIRBURN INGS YORKSHIRE

Address of Site/Warden

Fairburn RSPB Reserve:
2 Springholme,
Caudle Hill,
Fairburn,
Knottingley,
Yorks WF11 9JQ

Highlights and Features

Marshland and open water created by mining subsidence. Extensive land reclamation. Winter brings large flock wildfowl. Good for breeding ducks and waders. Lots of marsh flowers.

Facilities

Good information centre open weekends 1000–1700. Several hides open all times.

Photo Tips

Wildfowl come to feeding point. A 200mm lens will suffice here. Otherwise good for marsh flowers. Use a light tripod.

An occasional spoonbill, drifted across from the nearest colonies in Holland, may take up residence on marshland to its liking

These man-made marshlands of the Midlands demonstrate the possibilities for wildlife conservation in industrial areas; this is especially true of Fairburn Ings which lies in the heart of a heavily populated industrial area. Fairburn Ings belongs to the National Coal Board and is leased by the RSPB.

Wildlife Tour: Fairburn Ings
Fairburn lies just off the A1 north of Pontefract and Castleford. Leave the A1 four miles north of the M62 junction. The Ings are a series of shallow lakes and 'flashes' caused by mining subsidence. They are visible to the west of the A1 and are approached through Fairburn village, which straggles along the eastern and northern banks for half a mile or more. Subsidence of the old coal workings continues and more than one third of the reserve is now open water – some of the reed-beds have vanished altogether due to this increased flooding. Several artificial floating islands have been installed to try and compensate for the loss of 'edge' habitat.

A footpath runs from Cut Lane in Fairburn village for a mile along the SE corner of the reserve; a small car-park is situated off Cut Lane. The path is screened by thickets of hawthorn and sallow and runs between two waters, Cut Bay on the left and Village Bay on the right. Three hides give wide views across stretches of open water.

Birch, alder and oak woodland, planted since the establishment of the reserve in 1957, now disguises many of the old coal spoil heaps opposite the village; most of this work was carried out by local school parties and naturalists' organisations.

An amazing total of over 300 species of plant has been recorded. Along Cut Path good clumps of yellow toadflax and meadow cranesbill, and large stands of bullrush, yellow flag and the rare sweet flag are found. Beyond the Cut, where the path runs through the wooded area, foxglove and greater willowherb have colonised, with elephant hawk moths frequenting the willowherb. The woodland, largely silver birch, is kept open and many willow warbler, blackcap, garden warbler and lesser whitethroat come here to breed. Winter brings large flocks of redpoll and siskin to feed on the birch

seed, while fieldfare and redwing flocks prefer the hawthorn berries.

Wooded Priestholme Island opposite Village Bay Hide supports a large colony of black-headed gulls as well as being the main nesting site for many of the reserve's ducks: mallard, teal, shoveler, gadwall, tufted duck and pochard all breed on the reserve with an occasional pair of garganey.

In winter, the areas of open water attract enormous flocks of wildfowl and a large gull roost. A herd of over a hundred whooper swans is now regular. Golden-eye and goosander are often quite numerous, while the more common ducks such as teal, mallard and tufted duck may number many hundreds.

After leaving the hides, drive westwards through Fairburn on the Allerton road, screened from the Ings by tall hawthorn hedges; after a mile a lay-by gives excellent views over the whole of Main Bay. The RSPB has installed an identification board for local people, and this is where they come to feed the ducks.

Hordes of Canada geese and mute swans together with many common duck gather here in summer, and in winter the numbers are even larger. 'Wild' Canada geese will happily feed from your hand. A few exotic birds have been released here, and the several black swans are comparatively striking.

The view south from the lay-by is not inspiring, backed by huge cooling towers, pylon lines and power cables. Rounded piles of bare slag emphasise the need for land management and conservation. Yet here, even on the bare slag itself, several pairs of little ringed plover actually breed – they are often seen on the wet marshy edges, presumably washing their feet!

Flocks of swallows, swifts and martins use the area for feeding, with large autumn roosts in the bullrush beds. Migration periods bring large groups of common, arctic and black terns, with some little gulls, especially after easterly winds have driven them up the Humber Estuary.

Half a mile further west, beyond the lay-by, is the reserve information centre, much used by schools mid-week and otherwise open at weekends. An excellent boardwalk runs around a superb small marsh, full of wetland plants. Reed, bullrush, yellow flag, great willowherb and

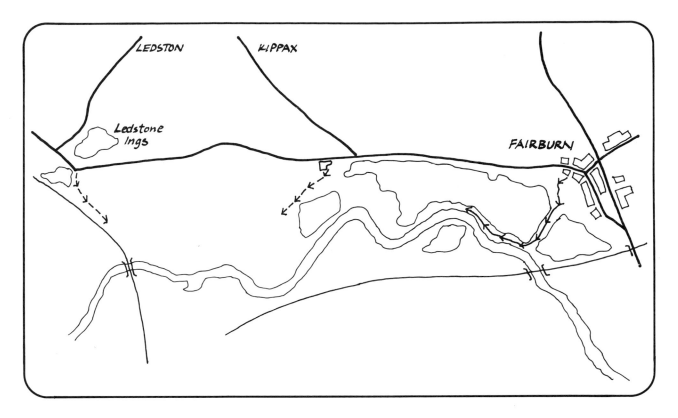

masses of nettles attract a wide range of birds and insects. Water voles are numerous here, and harvest mouse nests have been found in the dense vegetation. Reed warblers breed around Pickup Pool at the end of the boardwalk and can be viewed from a wooden hide.

Beyond the centre several extensive 'flashes', shallow pools surrounded by marshy fields, run alongside the road for nearly two miles. These 'flashes' are very attractive to waders, with breeding redshank, snipe and lapwing, and many migrants such as greenshank, wood and green sandpipers in spring and autumn.

A car-park at the western end of the reserve under the pylon line gives access by a well screened path to Spoonbill Flash Hide with good views over the marsh.

Just westwards is the main road to Castleford.

The ubiquitous field vole found in grasslands throughout the country, forms the staple diet of many predatory birds and animals

29

Martin Mere
LANCASHIRE

Address of Site/Warden

The Wildfowl Trust,
Martin Mere,
Burscough,
Ormskirk,
Lancs L40 0TA

Highlights and Features

Large mere re-created by the Trust, with wide area of fresh grazing marsh around. Wader scrapes and wet ditches. Large captive wildfowl collection in nice grounds. Superb for wintering ducks and pinkfooted geese. Up to 10,000 regularly in winter months.

Facilities

Information centre, shop, café, large car-park. Many hides. Beautifully laid out grounds. Open 0930–1730 or dusk.

Photo Tips

This is *the* place for close-up views of large flocks of wild geese in winter. Thousands come in to feed around the lake especially when extra food is put out. 200mm zoom lenses will give good pictures of all the captive birds and the flocks of wild ones.

Lapwings breed on undisturbed fields throughout Britain, but everywhere are in retreat and numbers have declined alarmingly

As the climate warmed and the last Ice Age withdrew, the whole of south Lancashire became a complex of lakes and tundra marshes. Peat was formed in great quantity and as the temperature rose further the tundra turned to woodland. Until the end of the seventeenth century the Mere was upwards of twenty miles (32km) in circumference, but inevitably it was drained and in Victorian times a steam-pump at Crossens dried out the last of the land except for winter floods.

Large numbers of pinkfooted geese have visited southern Lancashire for centuries, and in 1972 the Wildfowl Trust acquired 363 acres (147ha) solely to save their marshland habitat, the last of which was almost gone. Although the original interest of Sir Peter Scott, the trust's founder, was in the geese, Martin Mere has since become one of the best sites in the country to see large numbers of wildfowl and scarce waders at close quarters.

One wildlife walk is described using the track and hides of the Wildfowl Trust. Winter is by far the best time to visit, although summer always provides something of interest.

Wildlife Walk

The reserve is well sign-posted from all directions and is situated two miles (3km) along Red Cat Lane on the north side of Burscough. There is a large car-park and an excellent visitor centre, with a café and bookshop. Outside there is a fine collection of the world's wildfowl in beautifully landscaped grounds. Once you have walked round the waterfowl collection and fed the ducks, go through the gate marked 'Nature Trail' near the main building – beyond the high fence surrounding the waterfowl collection lies the main area of the reserve, and the trail runs round this on a level asphalt track. There are large observation hides at intervals and all except one, which by its very nature needs steps, have excellent access for disabled people. Just beyond the gate is a butterfly garden, packed with plants to attract butterflies in season, buddleia, ice plant and Michaelmas daisies; an identification board shows the species.

Walk the half mile to the farthest hide – Miller's Bridge Hide – a large, two-tiered structure which looks out over wild marshland. In summer the ditch on the left of the approach path is full of marsh plants, including water soldier, yellow flag and marsh marigold. A kingfisher pool which was excavated just to the left of the main hide has now matured; it is screened by willows and has a secluded sandbank, and kingfishers may be seen regularly on nearby posts.

Immediately in front of the hide is Vinsons Marsh, with Horseshoe Scrape, a ten-acre muddy water pool. This is a superb area in winter and produces hordes of waterbirds, one of the reasons being that the régime of hay production, the cutting and intermittent flooding of the area, provides maximum food production for wintering birds; this is further supplemented by waste potatoes which are dumped in the fields. Thousands of wildfowl come flocking to these marshes, the pinkfooted geese arriving in late September and the ducks, especially wigeon, teal and pintail, building up in numbers before Christmas.

The wader pool, Horseshoe Scrape, often attracts a lot of birds – at least 150 black-tailed godwit come regularly from June onwards, with many ruff throughout the year – these breed regularly, and over 200 spend the winter here. Little ringed plover nest on the artificial islands, but often spend some of their day running about on the asphalt path.

Although the marsh may appear comparatively quiet in summer, mallard, teal, shoveler, shelduck, gadwall, tufted duck, snipe, redshank, lapwing and oystercatcher all breed in some numbers, while sedge warbler and reed bunting are very numerous.

A wide variety of migrant birds are seen: green and wood sandpiper and greenshank come frequently; little gulls and black terns are regular summer and autumn visitors, sometimes in sizeable flocks; and the occasional marsh harrier has begun to spend the summer months in the area.

Return along the path, taking in the other nine available hides spread round the ¾-mile semi-circle of asphalt track – you are screened from the Mere itself by a hedged bank into which the hides are built, and even the hedges consist of many 'birdy' shrubs all specifically chosen to provide food and nesting sites.

Opposite Hale Hide is the 'Duckery', where chicks from the waterfowl gardens are reared in summer. Rose thickets along the path here are especially good for redwing, fieldfare and other thrushes in winter, feeding on the hips. Perhaps the best view over the Mere is provided by the Catty Bank Hide just through the nature trail gate, and also the Gladstone Hides, some 300 yards (274m) further south: both have the Mere edge only twenty feet away. The North Gladstone Hide is used daily as a feeding spot for wild swans in winter.

The nest-boxes attached to the Gladstone Hides are in fact bat boxes, with the entrance slit in the base. Bats are becoming rare due to man's interference in the environment and conservation measures are urgently needed.

Walk two hundred yards further: all the way you are screened from the waterfowl gardens by the ancient Catty Bank willow trees in which there are bird nest-boxes, and then you come to two hides, one on each side of the path – Carum Field Hide looks out over a willow-fringed area of the Mere, and Crawford Hide over arable farmland.

The Great Manchester Hide is the last, on the tip of the semi-circular track, a two-tiered tower with ten steps at the entrance and providing superb views over the marsh and Mere. On arrival in winter all the pinkfooted geese of the north-west coast converge on Martin Mere. Some then disperse to nearby wintering grounds such as the Ribble Estuary, but nevertheless, 16,000 winter regularly on the Mere and the peak total can be 34,000, usually in autumn.

Since the establishment of the reserve, wild swans which were once rare now return for the winter in increasing numbers, current New Year maxima being 300 Bewick's and 250 whooper swans.

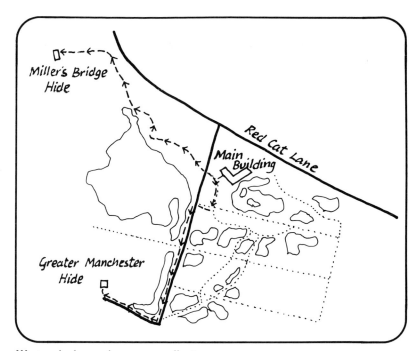

Winter duck numbers are really impressive, flocks of them attracted by the superlative feeding provided by the rich, flooded hay meadows – teal, pintail and wigeon number 10,000 each by the New Year.

Huge numbers of freshmarsh waders occur in winter: snipe come in clouds – a thousand in the air together is not unusual; several thousand lapwings and golden plover; and in spring, golden plover in full breeding plumage, often of the dark northern form, pass through in large flocks. This concentration of birds inevitably brings winter predators. Peregrines are frequent, besides hen harrier, short-eared owl and merlin which all hunt the marshes – and sometimes the hapless victim is not a bird, but one of the Mere's large population of water voles, often seen in the ditches along the paths.

Pinkfooted geese arrive en masse from their Arctic breeding grounds, in late September, to spend the winter in the north

30

Leighton Moss
LANCASHIRE

Address of Site/Warden

RSPB Reserve:
Warden:
Myers Farm,
Silverdale,
Carnforth,
Lancs LA5 0SW

Highlights and Features

A large area of reed swamp with lovely open meres below a backdrop of limestone hills. Dense alder and willow thickets. Superb for breeding marsh birds with Britain's largest number of bitterns. Well screened from people so still has otters. Wide variety of birds throughout the year. Large colony of black-headed gulls.

Facilities

Information centre. Shop. Open all days except Tuesday, 0900–2100 or sunset. Five hides plus one on the public causeway open at all times.

Photo Tips

Good spot for close views of marsh birds from the hides. Especially good for gulls and ducks in summer. Long telephoto lenses essential.

Driven out of quiet waterways by boats, people and pollution, the otter is now rare in all but the far northern islands. Leighton Moss still quiet and clean, houses a few

Leighton Moss is situated just back from the sea near the beautiful village of Silverdale; part of its western boundary nearly abuts the other RSPB reserve of More-cambe Bay at Carnforth. The two are in total contrast. At 6,000 acres (2,428ha), Morecambe is one of the largest RSPB reserves, while Leighton Moss, only 321 acres (129ha), is one of the smallest. Whereas Morecambe Bay is a great tidal estuary, Leighton Moss is a lush green gem of reeds and willows, full of fresh clear water bubbling from the wooded limestone hills around.

Finally purchased in 1974, the reserve was intensively managed to produce the present equilibrium from open mere, through fen vegetation to mature wood-land, and this management policy is con-tinual. The freshmarsh now has a wide range of breeding birds and the largest population of bitterns in Britain. It is a haven for wetland mammals. Many of the birds, especially waders, gulls and terns, alternate between the Moss and More-cambe Bay for feeding – one flap of a harrier's wing takes it from one reserve into the other.

A visit is productive here at any time, but spring and summer are best to see the breeding marsh birds. As well as More-cambe Bay, the glorious, flower-rich lime-stone hills nearby are themselves sites of national importance (see p 127). One wildlife walk is described – a round walk of three miles (4.8km) on level ground.

Wildlife Walk

The reserve centre is just east of Silverdale village, near the station; a small car-park and toilet facilities are available. The reserve splits neatly into two, the western entrance being behind the centre.

The path runs at once through a narrow woodland strip with mature, ivy-clad ash, oak and willow, excellent for woodland birds and scrub warblers. It then divides, left will take you to the YOC hide in a few yards, and right in 500 yards (456m) to Grizedale and West Hides. By the path junction is a permanently sited mercury vapour lamp for moth identification. At the last count 308 species had been recorded, including several hawk moths.

The YOC hide overlooks a large mere with wide reed-beds. Dense fen vegeta-tion includes bullrush, marsh horsetail in

the shallow bays, and great clumps of yellow flag; several verdant islands have been taken over by a large black-headed gull colony. Because of its proximity to the centre this is the most popular viewing place.

Towards West Mere and its two hides the path runs alongside a flowering ditch backed by mature hedges and trees. The shrub layer is full of marshland flowers, and woodpeckers, tits and reed warblers live in close proximity. The path then turns away from the hedge and crosses 300 yards of reed fen – some of the reeds reach ten feet (3m) in height, and fen flowers include yellow flag, bulrush, great water dock and meadowsweet. If you are patient, there is a reed screen across an open marsh ditch to allow possible views of bittern, rails or kingfisher.

Grizedale and West Hides both look out over smaller meres, which together are known as West Mere. These are very shallow, and waders of several species call in regularly on migration – ruff, green-shank, spotted redshank, green and wood sandpipers are frequent. There must be a dozen breeding pairs of bittern; bearded tits now number forty pairs, while reed and sedge warblers are abundant. Lap-wing, snipe, redshank and yellow wagtail all have nesting sites in the fen. Wildfowl breeding around the meres include scores of mallard, with teal, shoveler, pochard, tufted duck, gadwall and garganey. Water rails breed regularly but are difficult to see, as are the bitterns. Best bittern time is approaching dusk when they occasionally fly over the reeds.

Late summer dusk brings back great clouds of birds to roost in the reeds – starlings, swallows, sand martins, pied and yellow wagtails; starlings alone may reach 50,000. Birds of prey drop in frequently at this time, drawn by the roosting birds, and include sparrowhawks, owls and pere-grines, all of which breed in this vicinity. Buzzards hunt over the reserve daily and marsh harriers now spend much of their summer over the reed-beds.

Return to the centre, go out into the road and turn right; walk for half a mile to the public causeway which crosses the reserve – a high willow and thorn hedge shields the mere from disturbance. Throughout the reserve emphasis has

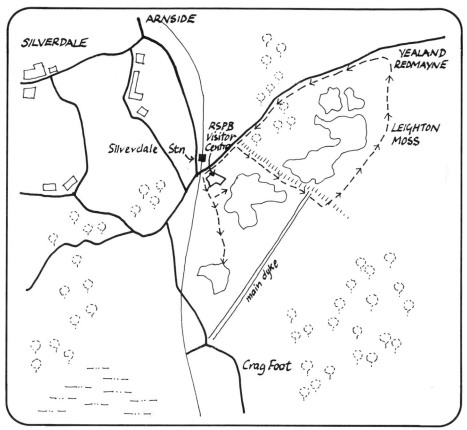

been placed on this, with the result that many shy birds and mammals may be seen. Do not yatter in noisy groups in these hides – you will disturb both wildlife and other visitors, and not see very much at all. Half-way down the causeway a public hide looks north over the main mere, a large expanse of open water with several islands and hidden bays.

Beyond the public hide the causeway crosses the main dyke and ends at the foot of the limestone hills and a farm gate. Turn left along the eastern edge of the reserve – this path runs through lush fen vegetation and may be very wet. A side path towards the mere after half a mile goes to Lower Hide, through wide reed-beds. This offers the most isolated view of the mere and is one of the best places in Britain to see wild otters. A notebook hanging in the hide is for otter observations. You need dedication to be an otter watcher – you may visit dozens of times and see nothing, and then see a whole family playing in the water for several days in succession. Dawn (4am in summer!) and dusk offer the best chances. Buzzards are often visible over the limestone hills opposite Lower Hide.

Autumn brings black terns and little gulls over the mere, while the numbers of wildfowl steadily increase with the onset of winter: 5,000 assorted duck may congregate on the main mere in the New Year, though teal dominate with 3,000. Being shallow, the Mere itself freezes

quickly, but the springs still run even in the worst weather, so the area still attracts hordes of waterfowl.

The path continues along the edge of the reserve beyond Lower Hide across three small plank bridges. Water runs across the path in many places and 'wellies' are advisable. Frogs and toads are abundant in the ditches but snakes are rare, even the marsh-loving grass snake.

The fen vegetation is superb, both along this path and as you walk round to the drier, slightly higher northern section of the reserve: willow and sallow scrub, with alders and hawthorn, grow among reeds and sedges; tussocks of panicled sedge and meadowsweet are nearly overrun by abundant yellow flags; large clumps of northern marsh and spotted orchids, with many hybrids, are found along the path in summer.

Grasshopper warblers, redpolls, flycatchers and tits breed here abundantly, and autumn and winter bring large flocks of siskin and redpoll to feed in the alder trees. Red, roe and fallow deer all find shelter in the dense scrub. In late summer this area supports good numbers of butterflies, especially on the drier limestone rock, including the rare High Brown Fritillary.

The path runs out of the fen through woodland, with visiting red squirrels, onto the road through a green gate. The reserve centre is to the left in just over a mile.

The rare and elusive bittern is rarely seen, but Leighton Moss supports a large proportion of the British stock

31

Loch Ken and the Dee Valley

DUMFRIES AND GALLOWAY

Highlights and Features

In summer, wide variety of habitats – loch, freshmarsh, moorland and forest provides wide variety of breeding birds. Winter brings many wildfowl along with hunting raptors in some numbers. Excellent site for barn owls. Particularly good goose country in winter.

Facilities

Several hides.

Photo Tips

Long telephoto lenses essential.

Barn owls have declined to danger level in all but a few places like the Ken-Dee marshes

The marshlands of the Dee Valley above Castle Douglas have long been known as a wonderful wildlife site, with many breeding waders in spring, and more importantly, hordes of wildfowl in winter. The marshland increased many years ago when the Electricity Board dam was built at Townhead of Greenlaw. This 'backed-up' the waters of the Dee to form Loch Ken, a ten-mile (16km) long meandering stretch of water with marshy bays and wet meadows.

The surrounding district contains a wide variety of habitats, including hill pastures, arable farmland, conifer forests, broad-leaved woodland and high moorland. The scenery of hill, wood and water is quite splendid, and the wildlife of the area is correspondingly rich. For sheer variety of bird species this must rank as one of the best areas in Britain.

One wildlife tour is described which takes in two nature reserves, the RSPB reserve of Ken/Dee in the north and the Threave Wildfowl Reserve of the National Trust for Scotland in the south. Much of the area is private farmland; please respect it, as the area can be well covered by roads and public paths.

Wildlife Tour: Loch Ken and Dee Valley
Carlingwark Loch, just west of Castle Douglas on the A75, begins the tour. The loch itself is 105 acres (42ha) with several wooded islands; great crested grebes breed here and there are always lots of mute swans. Wildfowl increase in winter, with 300 each of tufted duck and pochard and up to a hundred goldeneye and goosander – a hundred whooper swans regularly spend the winter here, and in freezing conditions will come for bread at the lochside. Photo possibilities are good because the locals feed the ducks.

Just north of the main road here is a rounded, grassy hill called Hightae Drum, which until recently was the wintering ground for *all* of the British grey geese and the main site for the flock of bean geese which used to come in for the winter. These have declined dramatically over the last few years, although up to fifty can usually be counted after the turn of the year. View the 'Drum' from the track to Threave Castle.

The nearby marshland and grazing fields of Threave Wildfowl Reserve (open from 1 November to 31 March) hold large numbers of wintering geese and wildfowl. Two car-parks allow access to five hides, four of which are primarily screened observation points. Wildfowling takes place regularly in the area and wild geese are likely to be 'jumpy'.

Use the car-park at Kelton Mains Farm, signposted to Threave Castle one mile west of Castle Douglas. A track runs north from the A75. Walk north from Kelton Mains Farm for half a mile to the river and turn north. The hide, overlooking the meadows of the Blackpark Marshes as well as the river, is situated half a mile away along the bank. In winter the dominant species are grey-lag geese (1,000) and wigeon (4,000); Greenland white-fronts flight in to roost at dusk. The river has goldeneye, goosander and red-breasted merganser, and the last two breed in the woodlands. Kingfishers are regular on this stretch of the river.

Returning towards the car-park, an observation screen just south of the Castle path overlooks pools on the river and a small island which is used regularly by grey-lag geese. Three more screens have been placed along the disused railway to the south, and are accessible from a car-park spot (two cars only!) by a little humpback bridge at Lodge of Kelton Farm. The best view is to be had from the furthest screen to the west, reached by crossing the old railway bridge. Loch Ken is easily viewed from the road. At Townhead of Greenlaw, take a minor road north which follows the west side of the loch for four miles (6.4km) to the Mains of Duchrae, where the road, now very narrow, turns sharply left.

Wide views of the rushy bays of the loch can be enjoyed across small fields of barley or hay meadows where breeding pairs of lapwing, snipe, curlew, redshank and oystercatcher are common. A large colony of black-headed gulls now occupies islets near Bridgestone. The road is single track with passing places, so find another space for your car and then walk. This is the best area to see overwintering whooper swans and geese: 500 Greenland whitefront, and 200 whoopers have been recorded. Otters are present and they are occasionally seen in the quieter bays; mink are widespread. Teal, mallard, shoveler, tufted duck and goosander all breed here, while common sandpipers nest along the shoreline.

On the eastern bank, the A713 runs along the shore for ten miles (16km) from Crossmichael to New Galloway, with many car-park spots. This is lovely rolling countryside, lush and green in spring with birch and oak hedges and copses between high meadows. Curlew breed in some numbers and woodland birds have excellent nest sites in the large old oaks.

The RSPB has a reserve on the western side of the loch, reached by rounding the top of Loch Ken through New Galloway and driving south down the A762. Visiting is by arrangement with the warden (Midtown, Laurieston, Castle Douglas, Dumfries and Galloway); a charge of £2 is made. Much of the area can be seen from the road, although the damp alder and birch woods hold a wide variety of small birds – flocks of siskin, redpoll, willow tit and thrushes in winter, and these plus many breeding warblers in summer. Grasshopper and sedge warbler join the common woodland species; redstarts, tree pipits and a few pied flycatchers also breed here.

One mile south of New Galloway a woodland walk follows the side of New Galloway Golf Course and the massive Cairn Edward Forest. In the forest the cleared areas and rides are the most productive of wildlife, while the golf course edge has many woodland species along the walkway. Siskin, crossbill and redpoll all breed in the conifers, with wood warbler and redstart in the open areas.

Two miles further south a minor road turns right towards Stroan Loch at Bennan. This is a Forestry Commission Forest Drive, emerging after several miles at Clatteringshaws Loch to the west, and is a toll road (£1) open only from May to October. All the forest birds may be seen along this route but in fact the best area can be reached easily on foot all year round. The more open Stroan Loch offers suitable habitat for black grouse and hen harriers to roost in winter with ten or twelve birds appearing at dusk. The whole area is good for raptors, with buzzard, hen harrier, peregrine and merlin all regularly seen. Barn owls still survive here in reasonable numbers, and at dusk one may appear anywhere hunting the marshlands.

Roe deer are numerous and may be seen in many of the fields bordering the loch early and late in the day.

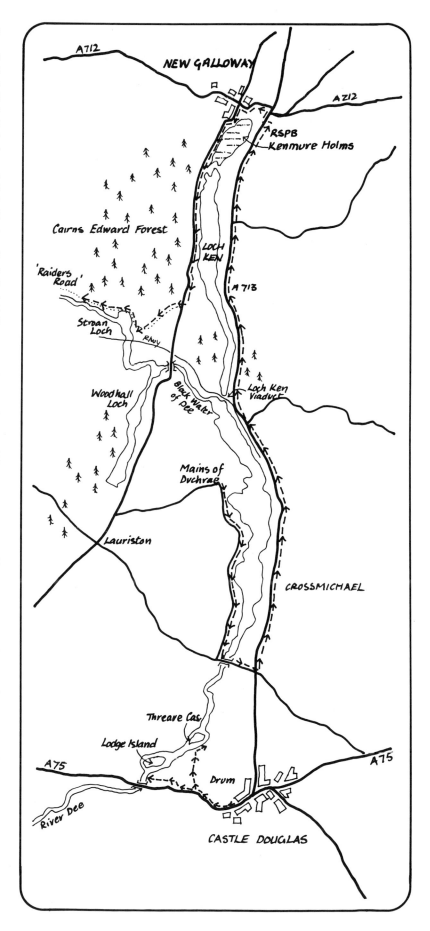

ESTUARIES AND COASTAL MARSHLANDS

This chapter describes a number of estuaries which are among the best wildlife sites in Britain. It also discusses several localities which are really coastal marsh, since like estuaries, they too are determined by the sea and its immediate proximity. Many of these marshlands have lagoons of brackish muddy water near the shore, and their visible wildlife is often similar to that of a true tidal estuary. Only a mile or so inland the same marsh may be dominated by fresh-water and hold dense reed-beds. The dividing line is rarely straightforward and a gradation from salt- to freshmarsh is often the result.

Estuaries are river mouths through which fresh-water is passed into the sea, where salt- and fresh-water mix to produce a zone of variable salinity known as brackish water. In Britain there are over 300, of which a hundred are large enough to carry a tidal flow at least four miles (6km). Some, like the Severn, carry a huge volume of fresh-water combined with a large tidal range so that there is a long section where sea- and fresh-water mix; others may have such a negligible amount of river water that the estuary is largely saline.

Estuaries are relatively sheltered, which leads to deposition of sand and mud, exposed in large inter-tidal flats at low water. These inhospitable and empty-looking flats in reality teem with life. Enormous, incalculable numbers of worms, molluscs and crustaceans colonise the mud and sand. These together with eel-grass and green algal weeds form a food source for millions of waders and wildfowl, especially during the winter months.

In the most sheltered places where the currents are weak, the mudbanks become stabilised and salt-marsh develops; this usually takes place above the level of neap tides. A careful examination of the plants which have become established shows that the different species grow in zones depending upon their exposure to the sea: algaes and eel-grass grow only on the mud covered daily by the tide; glassworts are next, colonising mud that drains quickly near the high-tide line. In the formation of marsh, mud particles are trapped by these establishing species and the mudbank slowly rises, making inundation less frequent. Rice-grass then becomes dominant and eventually the marsh is only covered by the highest tides. Sea aster, seablite, sea lavender and sea manna grasses create a salt-marsh sward which raises the level of the marsh still further, so that the sea-water flows in creeks and runnels. Grey sea purslane will then grow along these runnels, marking their course. A coloniser of drastic proportions is cord grass or spartina, a hybrid deliberately introduced in the last century to aid reclamation. It has overwhelmed some smaller estuaries and now needs constant management.

By the very mechanics of deposition the inner parts of estuaries tend to be muddy as the finer sediments settle out. Nearer the sea the tidal currents ensure that coarser material is deposited last, so sand or shingle spits develop at the river mouth.

The density of invertebrate life in the mud and sands is phenomenal, and scientists regard estuaries and salt-marshes as the most highly productive natural habitat, far more so than a heavily fertilised field or a woodland. Measurements in Morecambe Bay showed densities of 50,000 per square metre for a small bivalve mollusc, macoma; 40,000 per square metre in colonies of a small snail, hydrobia; and 5,000 per square metre of ragworms. Average densities for a whole estuary may reach 10,000 items per square metre.

Many other commercially important species are found in vast populations: oysters, mussels, cockles, shrimps, flounders and herring are all characteristically estuarine species. This vast food resource is used by countless birds, with estimates of two million waders and a million wildfowl in British waters in winter. Adjacent habitats are important, with fields nearby taking huge roosts of waders when tides are highest.

Coastal marshlands are formed wherever sea-water still permeates the sub-strata, even though prevented from actually flooding low-lying ground by shingle spits or sea defences. Good examples of this exist at Cley in Norfolk where salt-water filters through the shingle spit to form a series of brackish pools, and at Minsmere in Suffolk where the man-made scrape is now a brackish lagoon.

The very nature of land reclamation around Britain's estuaries means that coastal marshland may form inside the sea-wall boundary. Similarly, where streams run into the sea in low-lying areas, marsh-land may build up within the confines of the surrounding stream valley. The River Fleet near Golspie in Scotland has extensive alder-marsh which has backed up behind a man-made barrier. In such cases the estuary may be just over the sea-wall from a coastal marsh of largely fresh-water.

The coastal marshland year begins in February when many of the birds, although still in winter flocks, are obviously paired. Display starts in earnest when days become milder, with lapwings 'tumbling' across the marsh fields and wintering swans and goldeneye yodelling in tide-filled creeks. Salt-marsh itself is used for breeding by only a limited number of species, mainly redshank, oystercatcher, mallard, eider and shelduck; but just over the sea-wall in grazed marsh fields and dykes a wide variety of birds will breed with lapwing, redshank, yellow wagtail and snipe in the grass tussocks, and ducks such as pochard and shoveler in the reed-filled ditches.

Seabirds come to nest on sand and shingle banks, and in the salt-marshes too – black-headed gulls are the most numerous and the most noticeable. Large colonies of 10,000 pairs or more are found in the Keyhaven salt-marshes near Lymington in Hampshire; also at Needs Oar Point, at the mouth of the Beaulieu river, and on the Ribble estuary. Terns tend to prefer sand and shingle. Many of the best sites are described in the text, but the 3,000 pairs of sandwich terns which usually nest on Scolt Head Island in Norfolk are worthy of mention here. Common tern colonies which although more frequent, are usually much smaller, are found in sites such as Coquet Island in Northumberland and the Loch of Strathbeg, Grampian.

The rarer little tern uses beaches, and good colonies are found at RSPB reserves at Tetney marsh in Lincoln and along the North Wales coasts, but because these are likely to be disturbed by people they need summer protection.

By mid-July the seabird chicks will be fully grown and wader juveniles born early in spring will be gathering together in post-breeding flocks. Early migrants appear from farther north; these are usually 'failed' breeding birds, with ones and twos of greenshank, godwits and sandpipers still in summer plumage. By early August waves of birds are drifting south from marsh to marsh, estuary to estuary, feeding on the wide mudflats. Curlew, redshank, grey plover, oystercatcher and many more gather in large groups at high tide, spreading out to feed in leisurely fashion as the flats are exposed. Terns, ducks and gulls often join these roosts on the highest shingle ridges, out of reach of the waves.

In late summer and autumn seals appear inshore, with common seals using estuarine sandbanks on which to produce their single pups; and grey seals can be seen feeding on inshore fish prior to the late autumn breeding season.

Throughout October seabirds and waders from the high Arctic continue to pass southwards in huge numbers towards warmer climes. The estuaries of the British Isles are on the Western European migration flyway, and although perhaps three million wildfowl remain to winter here, many millions more move south into Africa. Thus estuarine development in Britain may threaten birds of many countries.

As autumn changes to winter so great flocks of wildfowl join the waders in escaping from the bitter continental weather. Although on a cold January day it might not be obvious that Britain has a mild winter climate, compared with the freezing temperatures always found in Russia, the Baltic states and the Low Countries, Britain is positively warm. Huge wintering flocks of waders descend upon the mudflats: knot, dunlin, bar-tailed godwit, curlew, oystercatcher, grey and ringed plover – all depend on the restless tides. Offshore, rafts of sea-duck, scaup, goldeneye, long-tailed duck and scoter dive for mussels.

Huge numbers of dabbling ducks, mallard, shelduck, pintail, teal and wigeon feed at the tide's edge or ride the waves – periodically large parties move inland to feed on fields adjacent to the river, over the sea-wall. This winter grazing also attracts geese of several species and they may also descend on fields of winter wheat making them extremely unpopular with farmers. Brent geese tend to live on the south and south-east coasts, pinkfeet in the north and barnacles in the north-west; grey-lags occur in large winter flocks in the north. Those grey-lags elsewhere are often feral birds present all year; whitefronted geese show a patchy distribution but tend to be a southern Britain species.

It is now urgent to protect all the remaining unspoiled estuaries and coastal marshes left in Britain, and to try and improve the pollution situation existing in many others. They are quite vital both as wildlife habitats and as the source of vast stocks of commercial fish. We must ensure they are maintained for the wise use and benefit of future generations.

Estuarine mudflats, such as these at Pagham harbour in Sussex, seemingly empty, teem with unseen life, feeding large numbers of wading birds and wildfowl

32

The Thames Estuary
KENT

Address of Site/Warden

Main estuary – none.
Northward Hill RSPB
Reserve
Warden:
Swigshole Cottage,
High Halstow,
Rochester,
Kent ME3 8SR

Highlights and Features

Splendid for birds and
mammals at all seasons.
Grazing and arable farmland
behind sea-wall of Thames
estuary. Large flocks of
waders and wildfowl from
September to April, including
up to 2,000 whitefronted
geese.
Good for woodland birds in
Northward Hill RSPB
reserve. Largest heronry in
Britain.

Facilities

None. Parking difficult at
Northward Hill, although
easy at Cliffe.

Photo Tips

All birds and mammals likely
to be at a distance. There
are many derelict buildings,
ex-wartime huts etc which
make good hides. Patient
photographers may find
these useful.

*Wigeon in thousands
descend on British
estuaries to escape the
arctic winter*

The Kent shore of the Thames estuary has long been famous for its birdlife. The change in farming policy from grazing marsh to draining for arable fields has dramatically reduced its wildlife value, but nevertheless birds flock to these shores in thousands at all times of the year. Spring brings a flood of summer visitors, autumn a tide of returning waders and sea-birds, while winter draws huge flocks of wildfowl, waders and their attendant birds of prey. The Thames marshes have a wild spirit of their own despite the oil-tanks on the northern shore and the great ships which pass just a stone's throw away. The area divides conveniently into three, with Cliffe Pools as the western segment, the Halstow marshes and Northward Hill in the middle and Allhallows in the east.

Allhallows is the least attractive, with its new caravans, waterskiers and the nearby Grain oil refinery. Two wildlife walks are therefore described, although both can be joined up by walking along the sea-wall. Alternatively a private but usable track out across the marsh at Cooling Castle divides the marsh in two.

Wildlife Walk 1: Cliffe Pools and Lower Hope Point

Take the B2000 into Cliffe village, then drive out north onto a very rough track westward along the marsh edge. On the left an overgrown chalk quarry filled with hawthorn and ivy often shelters long-eared owls in autumn. Park on the wide track overlooking the first series of flooded pits, formed by the past extraction of clay for cement. The pools occupy nearly a square mile, and have a bush-lined path between them running down to the shore – the rough track continues along the northern side of the pits which means they are all still easily workable. Some infill has taken place on two of the pits, providing muddy conditions ideal for waders, and one or two are used for water-sports in summer.

The best time to visit is from August through to May, and on an incoming high tide; birds are then driven from the extensive mudflats of the estuary to roost on the pools and fields behind the sea-wall. Walk south round the pit along the track by the disused quarry; after 300 yards take the track out through the middle of the pits. The bushes here are hawthorn, blackthorn

and bramble, and are often filled with birds in autumn and winter: redwing and fieldfare, together with a wide variety of woodland species – bullfinch, goldfinch, brambling, redpoll, tits and buntings – make this an excellent spot.

Scan the first pit with its small, bare islands – in summer common terns and black-headed gulls nest on these, and dabchicks and great crested grebes breed in the thin reed-beds; and spring and autumn bring common and green sandpipers to its edge. There are always scores of cormorants. Winter brings thousands of duck throughout these pits, but they are usually all found using just one pit at a time, which may change daily with the weather. Cold January days mean great rafts of tufted duck, pochard, scaup, pintail, teal and shoveler. With a rising tide there is constant movement between pits and river mouth.

Along with these winter regulars comes a sprinkling of rarities, divers, grebes, long-tailed duck, smew, goosander; and the predators, a drifting hen harrier, a short-eared owl or a peregrine scything the sky. And just to brighten up the scene, a gathering of 'escaped' Chilean flamingoes has haunted the pits for some years.

After a mile through the pits you will come to the sea-wall. Before you, the Thames itself is about a mile wide, but the mudflats are quite small; a jetty runs out at this point. Walk eastwards along the sea-wall for three-quarters of a mile to Lower Hope Point. The coast bends south here, the mudflats widen, and it is a wonderful place for 'migration watching', especially with a rising tide. In August and September, terns stream to and fro, sometimes in thousands, and with black terns frequently amongst their numbers. October brings large groups of arctic, great and even pomarine skuas, kittiwakes and little gulls, and winter Bewick's swans, storm-driven auks and wild geese. This is a truly exciting spot. Return along the sea-wall, back along the track and past the coastguards' cottages on the northern side of the pits.

Wildlife Walk 2: Egypt and St Mary's Bay and Northward Hill

Take the tiny road (one car wide) down to Swigshole Farm from High Halstow. A short steep hill at the Northward Hill

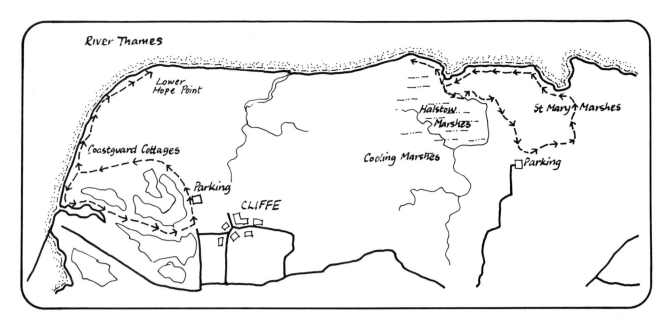

entrance may be ice-covered if the weather is very cold: if you think this might be so, stop before you get to it and walk. Parking is almost non-existent and visitors few. Climb the stile at Swigshole Farm and take the track slightly left out across the marsh which is criss-crossed with reed-filled ditches. Shade House, recently rebuilt, stands on the left in the middle of the marshland.

The gravel track runs for three-quarters of a mile and then stops just before the sea-wall of Egypt Bay; go through the two farm gates to get onto the wall. Stretching back to Northward Hill is a long, superb reed-bed with open water, to the north is rough salt-marsh and Egypt Bay, and then the wide mudflats and open river. It is possible just to sit here for a full day and see a constant stream of birds. Marsh harriers often appear over the reeds, and the number of birds that breed here is enormous: bearded tits, also dabchick, coot, moorhen, mute swan, garganey, pochard, water rail, reed and sedge warblers; snipe, redshank, lapwing and yellow wagtail prefer the fields; on the seaward side, ringed plover and oyster-catcher choose the tiny shell beaches of the bays. Common and little terns can be seen fishing the dykes along the sea-wall.

In spring and autumn there is always a stream of migrants: whimbrel, green-shank, stints and sandpipers are all regular; waders of twenty-five species can occur on this walk in any one year; and the occasional rarity is thrown in for luck – a storm-tossed phalarope in Egypt Bay or a pectoral sandpiper driven far from its American shores. As autumn changes to winter so the mudflats teem with dunlin, grey plover, curlew, knot and godwit; all may roost on the fields between the bays at very high tides.

Winter can be bleak here. Two thousand whitefronted and brent geese come regularly to feed on the wheat fields, and great flocks of surface-feeding duck appear in the bays – 10,000 mixed shelduck, mallard, wigeon, teal and pintail are usual.

The route is circular and returns east along the sea-wall, the mile to St Mary's Bay and then south across the marsh towards Swigshole – keep your eyes open on the marsh for harriers, short-eared owls and merlins. A brisk mile back from Swigshole is the RSPB bird reserve of Northward Hill. Here, a large heronry occupies the tree-tops in summer, there are breeding pairs of long-eared owls, and a roost gathers in the hawthorns in winter – the warden will usually point them out. Nightingales and warblers of ten species are the gems of the reserve; walk the paths as quietly as you can and listen.

Halstow is genuinely one of the few 'hundred species in a day' spots in Britain.

The graceful common tern has isolated colonies around the south and east coasts, but return to the warmth of Africa in the autumn

Elmley Marsh
SHEPPEY KENT

Highlights and Features

Fresh grazing marshes, large flooded scrapes, sea-walls and Swale estuary. Superb for birds at all seasons. Many breeding marsh birds. One of Britain's top sites for large flocks of wildfowl in winter. Very good for winter birds of prey. Marsh frogs in ditches.

Facilities

Car-park and toilets at Kingshill Farm. Hides are two miles (3km) from farm. Five hides. Open daily, except Tuesday, 0900–2100 or sunset if earlier.

Photo Tips

Birds at some distance, but often in large numbers. Use long lenses from the hides.

A few rough-legged buzzards from the arctic north haunt the east coast marshlands during winter

Elmley Marsh is an RSPB reserve on the south-west corner of the Isle of Sheppey, with the estuary of the Swale along its southern flank. It is a superb bird-marsh at all seasons of the year, and also has an interesting array of insects, flowers and mammals. It is the nearest 'large' RSPB reserve to London and, being in the overcrowded south-east, is very popular.

Access is by a very rough, two-mile track across open grazing marshland – the track needs careful negotiation in view of the size of the pot-holes. Parking space is at Kingshill Farm. This is a working farm and a selection of inquisitive farm animals will greet you, including two very large turkeys and several extremely friendly cats and their offspring. One original feature: there are toilets in a small new block where swallows nest a foot above the doorway; these can be watched at very close quarters feeding their chicks whilst you occupy the loos as a hide. After all, there is little privacy on the open marsh except for distance and curves in the sea-wall . . .

Wildlife Walk

Elmley is a land of wide skyscapes brimming with birds. Just before you get to the car-park, stop by a large green water tank and scan the open grassland to the east for low-flying raptors and owls. Hen, marsh and Montagu's harriers may all be seen, though the hen harrier is most frequent. Short-eared and barn owls are winter visitors – watch the ditches and banks as the best spots. There are two solitary oak trees near the farmhouse where little owls can often be seen, and there are always tree sparrows, finches and buntings busy in the foliage. The bushes around the farm also provide close views of redwing and fieldfare on the berries in winter.

Past the farm, the field on the right is usually a wheat-field which positively shimmers with swallows in summer, and thousands more in early September. In winter the field is ploughed which attracts lots of lapwing and up to 200 golden plover. After 400 yards (365m) the track bends round by the Swale sea-wall. Lapland buntings may be found here in winter, with up to fifty feeding on or near the track, and twite are regular along the seawalls at this time.

Do not walk on the sea-wall, just peep over it, as there will be lots of waders at all times of the year. Low tide leaves vast expanses of mud and birds in the distance.

A tumble-down barn and a 'counter wall' mark the entrance to the 'floods'. Just before this, on the right, are ditches and dykes which hold dabchick, redshank and snipe in summer, green and wood sandpipers in autumn and lots of snipe in winter. When the floods freeze in winter these grasslands will hold all the duck and geese, including 15,000 wigeon and 2,000 whitefronts; if the cold spell is prolonged, many of the birds move away from the frozen marsh completely.

The little 'knoll' with its convenient seat provides the best all-round view of the reserve. Waders pour across here at high tide to roost on the open pools before you, and from late September through to March there is always the chance of seeing a peregrine giving chase – there are usually two on the reserve, and they sometimes hunt the high-tide roost together.

Three well-placed hides round the floods are often crowded at weekends. For good photographs try the Counter Wall Hide with large flocks of wildfowl side-lit in flight. Two thousand mixed ringed plover, grey plover and dunlin, together with stints and sandpipers at the right season, roost every day in front of the Well-wall Hide, and may be photographed at close range. Larger waders are often further out but include 300 black-tailed godwit, 200 spotted redshank and 50 greenshank; numerous rarer waders turn up, besides 3,000 curlew and 1,000 redshank which roost in the grasslands around the floods.

There is a resident flock of 500 feral grey-lag and Canada geese; in winter these are joined by 2,000 whitefronts on the grazing marsh and 2,000 brent geese on the Swale. All of these provide superb opportunities for flight photographs.

A pair of marsh harriers breed on the reserve and hen harriers are frequent in winter – several may be seen each day. One or two rough-legged buzzards drop in during most winters, and there are often two or three merlin to be found, which brings the total complement of birds of prey for this area to one of the best in the country. Two more hides overlook the estuary, the furthest being at Spitend

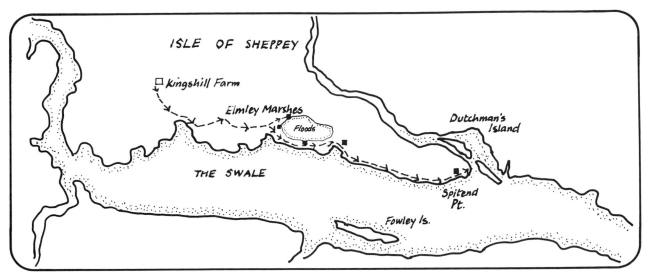

ISLE OF SHEPPEY

Kingshill Farm

Elmley Marshes

Floods

Dutchman's Island

THE SWALE

Spitend Pt.

Fowley Is.

Point, and these are both good places to see the chance merlin as it hunts the shimmering mudflats for dunlin.

Merlins, peregrines and short-eared owls like to perch on fence-posts in the grasslands, so scan all posts carefully. As you walk from one Swale hide to the next, peep over the sea-wall occasionally – this stretch is good for snow and Lapland buntings and stonechats in winter, and for wheatear and whinchats in the autumn. Look out over the grazing meadows to the left for geese, harriers and peregrine, and for large flocks of curlew at high tide. The far hide at Spitend overlooks a salt-marsh island with a large black-headed gull colony and some common terns in early summer.

From April through to July the marsh has a high population of breeding wetland birds, with many lapwing, redshank, mallard, shoveler and pochard, with some gadwall, tufted duck and garganey. Ringed plover and oystercatcher breed on the floods and at Brickyard pools, while snipe and dozens of yellow wagtails breed in the meadows. Rare breeding birds include marsh harrier, occasional ruff, avocet and black-tailed godwit. Spring at Elmley is a season of drumming snipe, tumbling lapwings and drifts of sulphur-yellow wagtails.

In autumn, terns, skuas and other sea-birds are seen in the Swale, usually coming up-river at high tide – Spitend and Swale Hides offer good views. Winter brings mergansers, eider, goldeneye, grebes and divers.

For the best opportunity to see all this varied birdlife the time to visit is with a high tide in the early afternoon.

Mammals are rewarding here. Hares are common in the extensive, open meadows and can sometimes be seen and photographed from the tumble-down barn. Rabbits are very numerous and often feed among the ducks, and because these populations are healthy stoats and weasels are also fairly common and can sometimes be seen exploring the sea-wall warrens. Water voles are elusive but are found in most of the dykes, which in spring attract marsh frogs; spring is also the time to see grass snakes hunting in the ditches.

The very noticeable buzz on the reserve in summer is produced by Roesel's bush cricket. There are the usual grassland butterflies but Small Tortoiseshell and Peacock are often numerous on the clumps of nettle along the dyke edges. Migrant Red Admirals, Painted Ladies and Clouded Yellows are frequent, not surprising in view of the reserve's proximity to the Continent.

In winter Elmley is largely for the birds! Be warned – this is wild marsh and uncompromisingly cold in winter. Wellies and thick anoraks are essential; don't leave your lunch in the car – it is a long walk back. Spitend is a seven-mile (11km) round walk from the car-park.

Preying on rabbits, the stoat is particularly common in the eastern counties

Rye Harbour
SUSSEX

Address of Site/Warden

Rye Harbour Local
Nature Reserve:
Warden:
1 Coastguard Cottages,
Rye Harbour,
East Sussex

Highlights and Features

Shingle ridges, river mouth.
Gravel pits now flooded.
Superb shingle flora in
summer. Large colonies of
black-headed gulls and little
terns.
Good for wildfowl and
grebes on pits in winter.

Facilities

Small information centre.
Large car-park. Access to
area at all times. Centre
Open April to September
daily 1030–1730.
October to March –
weekends and Wednesdays
1200–1600.
Two hides overlooking pools.

Photo Tips

Good site for shingle flora.
Use low tripod and wide-
angle zoom lens. Good site
for breeding terns and gulls
which need long telephoto
lenses used from the two
hides.

*Herons fish the marshy
shallows of the lagoons*

At first sight Rye Harbour Nature Reserve looks a bleak and bare expanse of shingle, but a day spent walking its footpaths and using its bird hides will soon show that this is a place for the wildlife connoisseur. It consists of shingle ridges built up by major storms over four centuries. Successive ridges can be dated and this enables a time scale to be put upon the vegetation succession from bare storm crest to stable grassland a mile inland. Rye has one of the finest examples of shingle vegetation in Britain, with many rare flowers.

Much of the area around the reserve consists of disused gravel pits which provide homes for a variety of water-birds. The reserve lies a few miles to the west of Dungeness, that enormous shingle fore-land jutting south into the English Chan-nel. The whole area, being so close to the Continent, receives hordes of migrant birds at all times of the year. In spring particularly Rye and Dungeness are first landfall for tired bird migrants heading north.

For the bird-watcher, almost any time of year is rewarding at Rye, but to see the greatest variety of animals, birds and plants, midsummer is the best time to visit. The wildlife walk described takes in the whole reserve and covers some five miles (8km) of level ground.

Wildlife Walk

Start at the large car-park by the remains of a Martello Tower and at the entrance to 'Frenchman's Beach Caravan Park'. Try and ignore this and take the narrow roadway south along the banks of the River Rother. Areas of tidal salt-marsh and fresh-water creeks are found within two hundred yards. Sea-purslane is the most abundant plant here, with stands of grass-like spartina, blue sea aster and the succulent shoots of five species of marsh samphire. Redshank, dunlin and ringed plover use the salt-marsh runnels, and in the reclaimed fields on the right lapwing and redshank both breed; common and little terns fish the river.

After half a mile the road leads onto the shingle. Look for plants which character-ise the different stages of this beach – some rare, others common, but all adapted for life on the sea-shore. Sea-pea, quite rare, covers the main storm ridge with carpets of deep pink flowers in June;

from May onwards yellow-horned poppy, sea-kale, sea-rocket, brilliant yellow patches of wall-pepper, large blue spikes of viper's bugloss and many more occupy niches in the shingle ridge.

After three-quarters of a mile you will be at the river mouth which is a great place for sea-birds. In summer the usual five common species of gull – black-headed, common, herring, lesser and great black-backed – are all present. Mediterranean and little gulls are regular visitors and kittiwakes pass on migration; Sandwich terns join the common and little terns to fish the sea off the river mouth.

A wide variety of visiting wildfowl occurs, with common scoter migrating eastwards in spring, eider and merganser offshore in winter and small parties of wild geese 'coasting' during migration.

A look back inland and you will see how the landscape has changed over the centuries. Three miles away the old cliff line is clear, when Rye was a sea-port, with Camber Castle (1539), the Martello Tower (1803), and two 1939–45 block-houses clearly visible.

Walk west along the shore and after half a mile turn inland, using the clearly marked footpath towards Ternery Pool and the bird-hide which is sunk into a bank at its eastern end. Around you are rows of electric fences, and the whole shingle over many acres seems littered with them. These are to protect the nests and chicks of birds on the shingle from clumsy feet and from night-time foxes – terns, ringed plover and oystercatcher breed here. Protected by these extensive measures the Rye Harbour little tern colony has now increased to become one of the largest in Britain with over 70 pairs – nonetheless, there are still under 2,000 pairs in the country as a whole. Also breeding here, especially on islands in Ternery Pool, are 65 pairs of common terns and 40 pairs of Sandwich terns (1986 figures). The strongest breeding colony is the black-headed gull with over 1,000 pairs – and as you peer out from the hide across the pool, it is obviously the dominant bird. Herring gulls nest too, but in small numbers.

The pool has a fringe of reeds and rushes which provides dabchick, tufted duck, shelduck and reed warblers with enough nesting cover; there is another

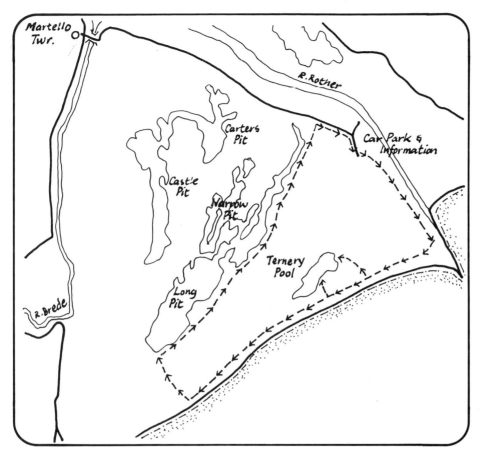

hide on the pool's southern bank.

Return to the Southern Water Authority's new asphalt track along the beach and continue westwards past the 'Atmospheric Corrosion Testing Station'. Watch for migrants at all times, and for nesting wheatears in rabbit holes in the summer.

The most noticeable daytime mammals are rabbits, especially in the more stable inland areas, and brown hares, which are often seen rushing across the shingle ridges. Towards dusk, bats of several species hunt the pools for insects; the larger ones are noctule and serotine bats and the smaller, pipistrelle and Daubenton's bats – the latter glide close to the water's surface in flight. You will almost certainly see foxes on the reserve at dusk.

After a mile there is a footpath which takes you back north, away from the shore, across a stile between grass fields; it joins a track at the start of a series of gravel pits which are now all disused and flooded. On the left is a small wood with a heronry – herons are around the marsh all year. This wood is excellent for migrant birds, and long-eared owls are regular here in autumn. Take the track back towards Rye Harbour village keeping to the southern side of the gravel pits. Marsh frogs are numerous in summer.

The 'Narrow Pits' nearest the village are large, filled with reeds and edged with sallow. Breeding grebes, duck, reed and sedge warblers are all present in some numbers, and kingfishers can be seen here throughout the winter. Cold weather often brings rare ducks to these pits. All the bramble, elder and sallow bushes along the track should be scanned for migrant birds – these may be their first bushes since France. Warblers, chats, thrushes, goldcrest and firecrest are frequent.

Follow the track back into the village and turn right into the car-park.

Ternery Pool at Rye Harbour, created by gravel extraction, now houses a large colony of black-headed gulls

35

Pagham Harbour
SUSSEX

Address of Site/Warden

Pagham Harbour
Local Nature Reserve:
Warden:
Selsey Road,
Sidlesham,
Chichester,
West Sussex PO20 7NE

Highlights and Features

Good for birds all year but best in autumn and winter. Large flocks brent geese often in front of hide at Sidlesham Pool. Splendid shingle flora best in June. Good for insects, especially butterflies migrating inland or along the coast.

Facilities

Information centre open at weekends. Large car-park with one hide overlooking Sidlesham Pool. Reserve area open at all times, except tern colony in summer.

Photo Tips

Hide provides good views of waders and geese at Sidlesham. Use long lenses here. Insects excellent in late summer with many migrants. Use medium-zoom lens 80–200mm and perhaps small flash gun.

Red Admiral butterflies migrate in waves north from Africa, moving inshore over the south coast from May onwards

Long stretches of the Sussex coast have been heavily developed, and in particular the wild estuarine coast of west Sussex has recently become one of the most densely populated suburban districts in Britain, with sprawling towns running one into the other from Chichester west to Southampton. However, carefully nurtured between this industrial area around the Solent and Langstone Harbour in the west, and the holiday towns of Bognor and Worthing in the east, lies Pagham Harbour Local Nature Reserve, 1,100 acres (445ha) managed since 1965 by West Sussex County Council.

Pagham has become an essential wildlife reserve for breeding, wintering and migrating wetland birds, and is a positive delight to its visitors since it represents one of the very few areas of marshland left anywhere in southern England.

In fact it has been reclaimed for farmland once already, in 1873, but in 1910 the shingle ridge was breached by the sea in massive storms and it has remained a salt-marsh ever since. Two or three small streams run into the marsh, maintaining low water channels.

An excellent information centre, with a substantial car-park and picnic spot, is sited at Sidlesham Ferry. There are a number of access points for people who wish to avoid long walks but Sidlesham Ferry is undoubtedly the best starting point. A public footpath runs right round the embankment for those who wish for a long walk. One wildlife walk is described.

Wildlife Walk: Pagham Harbour
Take the B2145 south for six miles from the A27 Chichester by-pass to get to Pagham. Use the car-park at the information centre.

Two or three acres around the picnic site are full of seed-bearing flowers favoured by birds for food – ragwort, nettles, thistles and willow-herbs grow in great abundance. Hundreds of butterflies and other insects are attracted to this area, especially in late summer, and close views of at least a dozen butterfly species are likely. Late autumn and winter bring large flocks of linnets, goldfinches, and greenfinches to eat the seeds.

A wooden hide overlooks Ferry Pool which lies at the end of this area 200 yards (183m) south from the car-park. It is next to the road and a reasonable view can be had from the paved footpath, but less disturbance is caused by using the hide. Ferry Pool attracts a large variety of waders in autumn and winter, and over forty species have been recorded. July onwards produces parties of black-tailed godwits, curlew sandpipers, little stints, greenshank and many more, all of which can be studied at close quarters. Winter brings large flocks of commoner waders at high tide, 1,000 brent geese in the fields and several avocets.

From the hide bear left onto the harbour's southern sea-wall – the black sluice-gate marks the access. The highest tides fill the whole harbour right up to this point. Walk along the sea-wall which follows the harbour edge for some half a mile; alongside on the left there is a deep mud channel, backed by large undisturbed areas of salt-marsh and a long narrow fresh-water fleet and reed-bed on the right.

In summer, the fleet has breeding mute swans, dabchick, reed and sedge warbler; oystercatcher, redshank and lapwing breed on the salt-marsh. The mud-banks attract many waders, with whimbrel, curlew, redshank and oystercatcher frequenting the runnels; wintering avocets also use this low tide creek.

The salt-marsh of the harbour is easily viewed from this southern sea-wall. The dominant plant is cord grass (spartina), though the slightly raised areas are drier and support sea purslane, seablite (suaeda) and glasswort (salicornia). The inter-tidal mud contains huge quantities of worms and crustaceans, a wonderful food source for wintering waders and wildfowl. A winter walk round this sea-wall will reveal 2,000 brent geese, several hundred wigeon, shelduck and pintail, and thousands of waders.

Low hedges of gorse and blackthorn develop along the sea-wall, while arable fields extend south to Church Norton. Extensive scrub of briar, bramble and thorn bushes borders the sea-wall for two hundred yards; in between, deep ditches filled with reeds provide good cover for water rail and sedge warbler. Green sandpipers may be flushed from these ditches in autumn, and wild mink are found along the banks.

The bushes and trees are very important

in an otherwise treeless landscape, providing shelter and food for a variety of migrant birds and insects. After half a mile the path runs down onto the shingle deposited round the harbour edge – the highest tides will make this wet and muddy.

The mudflats are nearer now, separated by only fifty yards of salt-marsh and the main central channel too can be seen more clearly. In winter geese, ducks and waders will be well spread out at low tide, though the high tides tend to push the ducks into shelter away from the wind. Slavonian grebe, goldeneye and red-breasted merganser are regular visitors to the main channel in winter.

The path dives beneath the low branches of some spreading oaks and runs the last 400 yards (365m) to the shingle ridge alongside a high hedgerow of blackthorn, bramble, and sallow. Passerine migrants are often numerous in this hedge: in spring warblers, chats, fly-catchers and the occasional redstart may be seen moving north, while from late July the direction is reversed as the autumn emigrants flood southwards out of Britain.

A footpath runs 100 yards west to Church Norton through the trees. There is space for a few cars by the church for those wishing to avoid a two-mile (3km) round walk. Continue on towards the shingle ridge: this is closed to the public from late April until 31 July to allow the 70 pairs of rare little terns to breed undisturbed. Common terns also breed and both may be watched fishing the nearby harbour ditches.

This south-easterly facing shore, filled with flowers and prominently exposed in the English Channel, draws migrant insects by the thousand. Red Admirals, Painted Ladies, Peacocks and Clouded Yellow butterflies join resident gatekeepers, blues and whites. Hundreds may occupy a single large bramble bush in flower in early August. In good years large numbers of dragonflies may also move alongshore in autumn, flitting over the ditches and reed-beds.

The path runs on top of the shingle ridge with extensive reed-beds and freshwater pools stretching alongside. Teal, shoveler, water rail, bearded tit and kingfisher are often seen here in winter, and birds offshore usually include eider, merganser, common scoter and red-throated diver.

The ridge supports interesting plants, with scattered clumps of sea-kale, sea-campion and yellow-horned poppy, best seen after the beach opens on 1 August.

It is possible to return via footpaths across the intervening farm fields to Sidlesham, but far easier to return along the

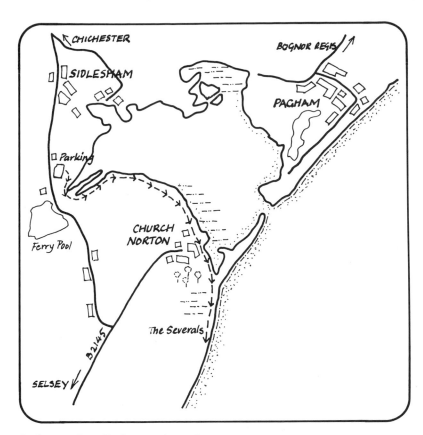

harbour edge. Dusk may bring hunting barn owls over the marsh, and one or two pairs still breed locally. More surprising is a small roost of ring-necked parakeets in the trees at Church Norton.

Kingfishers often move to coastal marshlands in the winter months

81

36

Langstone Harbour
FARLINGTON MARSH HAMPSHIRE

Address of Site/Warden

Farlington Marsh
Local Nature Reserve:
Hampshire & Isle of Wight
Naturalists' Trust,
8 Market Place,
Romsey,
Hants SO5 8NB

Hightlights and Features

Fresh grazing marsh and
large fleet bordering large
area mudflats, creeks and
salt-marsh islands.
Summer: large colony
breeding little terns on
islands.
Autumn and spring:
many migrants.
Winter: huge numbers
waders, especially knot and
dunlin. Prime site on south
coast for wintering waders
and wildfowl, especially
brent geese with up to
8,500.

Facilities

Small car-park. Information
centre open intermittently.
Access round sea-walls at all
times. Islands are RSPB
reserve and landing is
forbidden.

Photo Tips

Brent geese are very
approachable here. Use
200–300mm lenses from
sea-wall, or from old pill-box.
Use a shoulder pod for flocks
in flight.

*Dragonflies, harmless to
man, are predatory
creatures, catching and
eating smaller insects*

Langstone Harbour is the most important estuarine site on the whole of Britain's southern coast. It is continuous with Chichester Harbour to the east and together they form an enormous area of inter-tidal mudflats and saltings. The harbour is best viewed from Farlington Marsh Local Nature Reserve which is an integral part of the whole locality. Most of Langstone Harbour itself is an RSPB reserve. The walk described takes in Farlington Marsh, with wide views across the harbour; access points on Hayling Island also provide good views. The distance is about 2½ miles (4km).

Wildlife Walk

Access is off the M27 motorway which forms a noisy northern boundary. Leave the M27 on the roundabout marked Farlington, and on the left-hand side of the *roundabout itself* turn sharp left into a signposted gate – it is easy to miss, and find yourself heading for Portsmouth. Park anywhere along a very bumpy track. You can sit and bird-watch from your car here – a good spot for lunch; in winter, with no other shelter available, this is worthwhile!

Before you lies the Broom Channel of the harbour, at low tide filled with birds. In winter when the tide is high a hundred or so brent geese are always to be found paddling about below the car-park, and they are often very tame. Take the track past the reserve notice-board out along the sea-wall which is usually muddy except in high summer. On the left is a large area of dense thorn bush, mainly hawthorn, bramble and gorse, growing on rough pasture. The ground here has not been ploughed since 1600 and supports a large number of unusual plants including nearly 50 grass species (out of 150 in the whole of the UK). There are several ponds, some made by bomb-craters; the ones nearest the road are fresh-water and have colonies of frogs and toads.

It is normally possible to walk anywhere within the bush area but in most autumns a number of long-eared owls arrive from the Continent and like to roost in the bushes; the warden will usually try to point them out so as to avoid disturbance. Scrub warblers, greenfinches, yellowhammers and other common species breed here, and in autumn and winter, especially with harder weather further east, hordes of redwings and fieldfares feed on the berries.

After 500 yards the marsh opens out with a fine reed-fringed lake on the left. Beyond this is another stream of fresh-water with a considerable reed-bed, and beyond this again is a large and obvious area of grazed rough pasture. The mud-flats of Langstone Harbour on the right complete the scene.

This spot is perhaps at its most exciting in midwinter, and at a nearly full tide because enormous flocks of waders use the rough pasture as a high-tide roost. You will have a much closer view of them by the time you reach the far point, which is marked by a lone hawthorn bush and a post. This post is often used as look-out point by kestrels and short-eared owls; very occasionally it might be occupied by a wintering merlin: scan all fence-posts here in winter.

In winter the lake attracts hundreds of duck, with pintail, shoveler and teal at 300–500 apiece. Bearded tits arrive in the reed-beds in autumn and stay the winter, escapees from cold East Anglia. Large numbers of gulls come to bathe in the fresh-water at all times, and as the water level reduces in autumn, many migrant waders are encouraged to alight, including green, wood and curlew sandpipers, stints and greenshank. Spotted redshanks may be seen all year except in the midsummer months, with up to a hundred in autumn. Reed warbler, sedge warbler and reed bunting nest in the extensive reeds behind the lake and along the stream; and coot, moorhen, mallard and pochard all favour the reed-bed edges in which to build their nests. Midsummer brings drifts of dragon-flies of several species along the ditches.

If you simply turn around from looking at the lake, the mudflats behind you will almost certainly have many dunlin, red-shank and godwits in winter; there are usually several wintering avocets in this channel too.

The sea-wall bends east after a further 200 yards, the reeds are left behind and the marsh behind the sea-wall becomes pasture, dotted here and there with cattle. From October to March hordes of wild-fowl and waders use this at high tide, and it is a good idea to sit down behind the wall as the birds fly in – gates and stiles are useful camouflage. In spite of all the

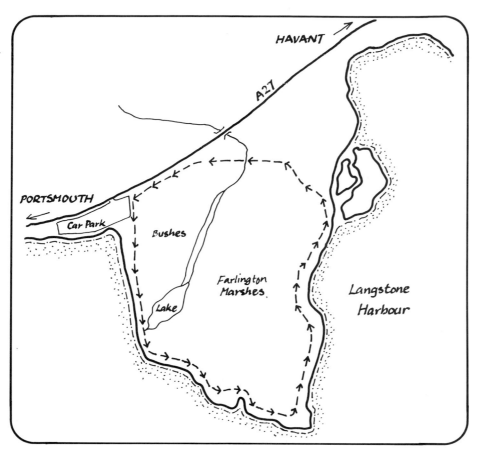

waders the bird of the marsh here throughout the winter is the brent goose: recent counts have been as high as 9,000. As the tide recedes, enormous flocks will move out to feed on the mud of Langstone Harbour; other flocks descend on local farm fields and yet more crop grass on the sports' fields around Portsmouth and Havant. They are not popular with local farmers.

Many hundreds of wigeon crop the grass alongside the brents, the number rising dramatically with harsh weather on the east coast. Short-eared owls are frequent winter visitors, and if there are long-eared owls in the thorns, dusk may produce the unusual sight of both species hunting the reserve together.

About a mile from the car-park you reach the south-eastern tip of the reserve. From here there is a wonderful view of most of Langstone Harbour and on a rising tide, birds will be streaming over the wall to roost on the marsh. Secondary high-tide roosts occur on the two islands facing you, Bakers and South Binness Islands. The number of birds in winter here is very high; a count on 13 December 1986 produced 15,000 dunlin, 2,000 knot, 1,500 oystercatcher, 1,000 lapwing, 800 grey plover, 500 each of ringed plover, bar-tailed godwit and also black-tailed godwit — this flock of 500 black-tailed godwit represents nearly 20% of the UK total. Also redshank and curlew — and all this along with 7,750 brent geese.

Great masses of waders wheel and shimmer in the sky, like smoke clouds shaking out over the saltings. You are unlikely ever to forget the sight of so many birds, but you will only see it as the tide nears its high point. At low tide all the waders are spread out over miles of mud.

In summer these rough pasture fields have many pairs of snipe, redshank, lapwing and yellow wagtail. This must also be one of the best places in Britain to watch rabbits — there are hundreds of them — and because there is no disturbance they are out and about throughout the day. Many can be watched closely from the sea-wall.

From October until March the channels of Langstone Harbour are excellent for rarer duck and grebes: Slavonian and black-necked grebes are regular in small numbers, while mergansers may exceed 200 — these are often to be seen fishing at high tide from the south-eastern tip of the reserve.

Follow the sea-wall back round towards the distant motorway. After half a mile or so there is a footpath on the left which takes you down onto the open marsh; this path passes back through the edge of the thick bramble and thorn scrub, and provides more opportunities to see warblers such as whitethroats in summer and feeding thrushes and finches in winter.

The coot is found in wetlands all over the country

37

The Exe Estuary
DEVON

Address of Site/Warden

Dawlish Warren, Warden:
c/o Teignbridge District
Council,
32 Courtenay Street,
Newton Abbot,
Devon TQ12 2QR

Highlights and Features

Extensive southern coastal
estuary with six miles of tidal
mudflats and sand-bars from
Exeter to the sea. Fresh
grazing marsh at Exminster
and large sand-dune area at
Dawlish Warren. Excellent
for winter wildfowl and
waders, and good for
migrant waders and terns in
spring and autumn.

Facilities

Well-known tourist area.
Good interpretative centre
at Dawlish Warren Local
Nature Reserve. Bird-hide
overlooking estuary mouth.

Photo Tips

Use the hide at high tide.
Large numbers of brent
geese and waders
congregate here then. Be in
hide early and use long
telephoto lens. Sand-dune
flowers need tripod and
wide-angle zoom lens.

*The marshlands of the Exe
Estuary in Devon, form
the most important
estuarine site in the whole
south-west peninsula*

The River Exe, tidal as far as Countess
Wear on the edge of Exeter, contains
some six miles (9.6km) of wide mudflats;
the tidal mud is well mixed with sand in
the mouth of the estuary to create extensive sand-bars at low tide. This is the most
important wetland in the whole of the
south-west peninsula, and furthermore on
the western tip, the longshore drift current
has pushed sand-dunes eastwards for
nearly a mile, creating excellent dune
conditions in Dawlish Warren.

The mudflats are thickly covered with a
green seaweed, *enteromorpha*, and much
eel-grass which is the favoured food of the
brent goose. Winter is the best season
here when thousands of birds pack this
estuary, though spring and autumn can be
exciting with migration in full swing.
Summer is often the quietest time and
anyway the area is full of tourists, causing
disturbance.

Two wildlife walks are described, one at
the local nature reserve of Dawlish
Warren, and the other extending along the
west bank of the river. Timing is important
here: a rising tide, already half-full, is ideal
with perhaps three hours to high water –
low tide means that all the birds will be a
mile or more away.

**Wildlife Walk 1: Exminster Marshes and
Powderham**

This is a round walk of some seven miles
(11km) but may be split into two, motoring
between Exminster and Powderham
Church. Just south of Exminster take the
left-hand turning at a roundabout past the
Swan's Nest Inn, go over the railway
bridge and park after half a mile.

Several reed-filled ditches shelter
breeding sedge and reed warbler, mute
swan and Canada goose in summer. In
winter these marshy grazing meadows
have to accommodate several thousand
birds at high tide – hundreds of wigeon,
teal, pintail and shoveler, together with
5,000 lapwing, 300 golden plover and
200 snipe. The wintering flock of over 600
black-tailed godwit roosts in the Exminster
grazing meadows, and constitutes Britain's
second largest wintering flock. Redwings
and fieldfares feed on these marshes in
hundreds.

Follow the track alongside the old
Exeter Canal for just over a mile to Turf
Lock. Wintering kingfishers often sit on

posts and lock gates, as do short-eared
owls – five or six of these can be seen
hunting the freshmarsh on winter after-
noons, and the occasional barn owl too.
Try to time your arrival at Turf Lock to
coincide with the rising tide. Cross over
the lock, and the regular wintering flock of
50 avocets may well be immediately in
front of you – if not, they are probably
further north nearer Topsham where the
mud is softer. Afternoon with the sun over
your shoulder provides the best light.

In early spring a few garganey may be
seen moving north together with the first
wheatears. Scores of whimbrel appear
from mid-April onwards and are found
both on the grazing marsh and along the
sandbanks at Dawlish.

Continue from Turf Lock on the
embankment which runs south alongside
the estuary towards Powderham Church.
In winter the wide mudflats from Turf Lock
support an enormous number of waders –
the mud off Powderham is still softer than
the sandy mixture at Dawlish. Large flocks
of long-billed waders are predominant
here with 700 curlew, 600 black-tailed
and 300 bar-tailed godwit; there are also
500 redshank and a scattering of wintering
greenshank and spotted redshank. These
last three species all roost on the meadows
along the River Kenn in Powderham Park,
south of Powderham Church.

The embankment follows the estuary
bank, leaving the railway to skirt a large
area of grazing marsh with scattered trees
which provide look-out posts for the
occasional peregrine, two of which always
spend the six winter months hunting the
mudflats. As the river fills at high tide, so
the duck confined to the main channel
spread out to feed. In summer these may
be no more than a handful of off-duty
shelduck, but winter brings 50 goldeneye,
50–100 pintail and hundreds of mallard
and teal.

Two hundred yards before Powderham
Church the track crosses the railway line
through gates, so beware of migrant trains.
Pass the lovely old church and continue
along the road for half a mile – the estuary
is no longer visible because of the railway
track. A footpath runs along the north side
of the River Kenn, past the castle, home of
the Earl and Countess of Devon, and
thence back to the church road. This
detour enables you to examine the local

wader roost more closely: hundreds of redshank with smaller groups of greenshank and spotted redshank; some greenshank and the occasional green sandpiper prefer the pools along the river. Kingfishers are frequent here, and so are herons – there is a heronry of 40 pairs in the large trees in the park.

Return is either back along the sea wall or round the shorter route by road to Exminster.

Wildlife Walk 2: Dawlish Warren

Although this is still part of the Exe Estuary proper, its character is sufficiently different to warrant a separate walk in its own right. Take the side road left, south of Starcross, to Dawlish Warren Station. Drive under the bridge and park in the extensive car-park behind the hundreds of massed beach-huts. Ignore the holiday parks and the amusement arcades and head east from the far end of the car-park. From April to September the area is well used by holidaymakers – winter, bleak and cold, will produce only the occasional bird-watcher or dog-walker.

After 100 yards pass the new Nature Reserve Visitor Centre, and follow the track alongside the pool and reed-bed with sand-dunes on the right. The dunes have great clumps of bramble and thickets of sallow, especially round the reed-bed. Gorse runs along the drier, and higher, edge of the golf course.

Spring brings many migrants to these isolated bushes, and whitethroats, willow, reed and sedge warblers can be heard singing in the thickets. Sandwich, common, Arctic and little terns pass along the shore, eastwards up-channel. A speciality of the area, and a really prize bird, is the cirl bunting which breeds in these bushes and flocks in winter in the bramble and tree lupins.

The wet dune slacks support large numbers of marsh orchids in June and the very rare sand crocus in early May.

Winter, however, is still the most bountiful season. By following the golf-course fence one soon comes to a sign to the bird hide which overlooks a semi-circular bay in one direction and the whole of the northern estuary in the other. High tide is the best time; thousands of birds are obliged to come very close in under the hide because of the incoming water: 2–3,000 brent geese, 4,000 dunlin, 1,000 oystercatchers and several hundred grey and ringed plover; also knot, sanderling and turnstone. Fifty each of goldeneye and merganser, a dozen Slavonian grebes and 8–10 red-throated divers are regular winter visitors; great northern and black-throated divers are often seen in ones or twos off the river mouth.

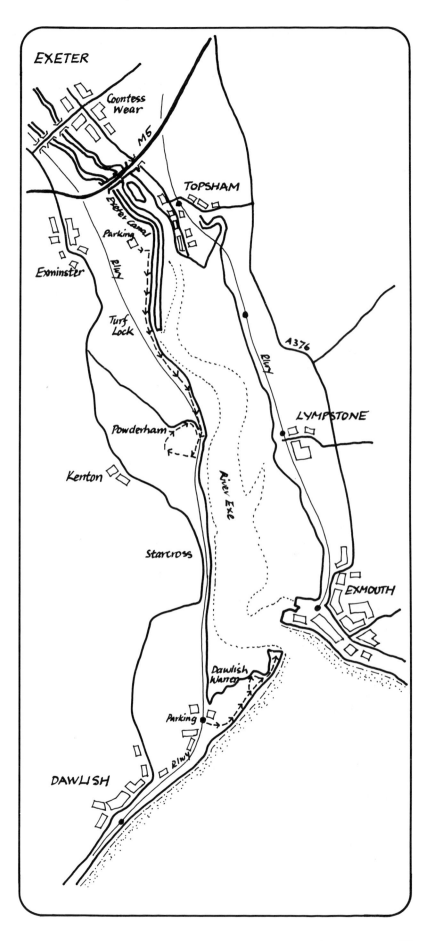

38

The Taw-Torridge Estuary
BRAUNTON DEVON

Address of Site/Warden

Braunton Burrows National
Nature Reserve
Warden:
Broadeford Farm,
Heddon Mill,
nr Braunton,
North Devon EX33 2NQ

Highlights and Features

Estuary good for waders,
especially oystercatchers,
whimbrel and sanderling.
Possibility of otter.
The Burrows superb for
flowers and insects
throughout summer but best
in June when thousands of
marsh orchids are in flower.

Facilities

Car-parks only.

Photo Tips

This is a place to take flower
photographs. Use a wide-
angle zoom ie 28–70mm
and a tripod. Try some low
angle shots.

*Widespread throughout
the country, Palmate
newts return to their
breeding ponds in early
spring*

Braunton Burrows is a huge area of sand-dunes which extends northwards from the estuary of the Rivers Taw and Torridge. The Burrows are a national nature reserve covering the southern two-thirds of this enormous dune system; parts are leased from the estate owners by the Ministry of Defence for military training – this is where American troops practised their Normandy landings. Fortunately such training – and the subsequent destruction of the superb dune flora – is infrequent; red flags are then flown at all entrances and access is restricted.

Do not touch any metal objects in the dunes: unexploded missiles are still found from time to time.

Braunton is the northern coastline of the wide, shining estuary of the two rivers, the Taw and the Torridge. The combination of estuary habitat, excellent for birds, and the dune system which is superb for flowers and insects, provides a rich area of wildlife exploration. Despite the proximity of holiday resorts both north and south, Braunton and the estuary have a truly 'wild' feel about them.

One wildlife walk is described which explores the three main habitats – the extensive dunes, the main estuary and the fresh grazing marshes behind the estuary sea-wall. The walk is based on the car-park at Broadsands Beach, and may thus be split into two; the round distance is 5 to 6 miles (9km).

Wildlife Walk

In Braunton take the road left at the traffic lights, marked 'Braunton Burrows and Crow Point'. After one mile take a lane right over a tiny stone bridge with two white notice boards; this goes through a toll-gate on a driveable road to a large car-space at Broadsands, and avoids the 'American Road', a very rough track two miles long and full of large holes.

From the extreme western end of the car-park the NCC has built a 400-yard long wooden boardwalk out through the dunes at Crow Point to prevent a recurrence of serious erosion problems. Use this for the half-mile round dune walk – do not stray off the boardwalk.

The dune sward here is made up of many low-growing plants such as thyme, dune storksbill, restharrow and eyebright; there are large stands of evening primrose

which flower in the latter part of the summer. Many clumps of viper's bugloss also flower in late June or July. The larger dune slacks are usually water-logged in winter, and the plant community is typical of these damp conditions – creeping willow is the dominant plant, with many marsh orchids and marsh helleborines in June and July, and also marsh pennywort, water-mint, round-leaved wintergreen and sharp sea-rush.

Once at the end of the boardwalk the view of the estuary is extensive, from Crow Point across to Appledore and Westward Ho! A high-tide wader roost occurs here in winter, with the birds moving to inland marsh fields on the highest tides. From late August onwards waders gather in the estuary, oyster-catchers being the most numerous species with 3–4,000 birds at peak times. Dunlin, ringed plover, curlew and sanderling are present all winter from October onwards, and this is a good area for sanderling who particularly favour the sandy tide line. Migration periods, especially autumn, bring whimbrel, grey and golden plover, and godwit to the estuary.

Take the 'American Road' – a wide, rutted track reinforced with rusty steel mesh – north from the start of the board-walk. This runs the full eastern length of the Burrows but acquires an asphalt surface only at Sandy Lane, two miles north, where there is another car-park. After a mile another broad track strikes north-west into the dunes through a red-painted military steel barrier. This is called 'J Lane' and runs right to the beach, and you may walk along this except when the flags are flying. It is unnecessary to leave the track to see all that the dunes can offer, and in this way you can help to safeguard such a fragile environment. One or two natural pools – probably filling very old bomb craters – have been supplemented by NCC digging to provide a string of boggy pools along this track.

The butterflies, flowers and dragonflies here are superb, with great clumps of marsh marigold in May, followed by thousands of marsh orchids and marsh helle-borine in midsummer. Many of the drier areas are covered with yellow biting stonecrop, while the blue spikes of viper's bugloss and great stands of yellow even-ing primrose cover many slopes. The

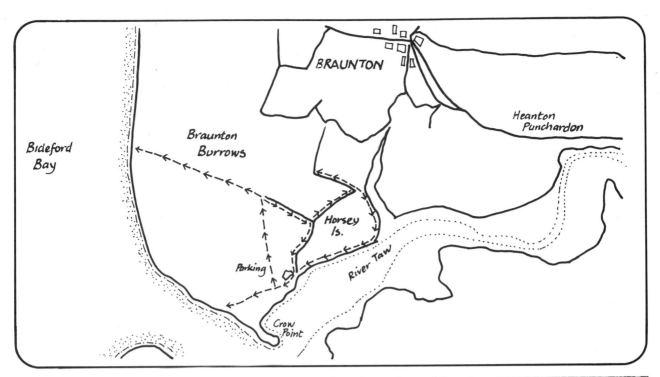

higher dunes have carpets of bird's-foot trefoil and wild thyme, and rare plants include sand pansy, sand toadflax and round-leaved wintergreen.

The most noticeable animal here is the rabbit, although the numbers even so are not high, and you may meet a visiting fox or a hedgehog at dusk or dawn. Braunton is part of the story of *Tarka The Otter*, and otters do occur here from time to time, usually in winter.

As you walk 'J Lane' the commonest birds will be skylarks and meadow pipits. Also breeding in the dunes are a few shelduck and wheatear, both using old rabbit holes, stonechats prefer the bramble thickets along with whitethroat and willow warbler, and the occasional sedge warbler in the thickets of sallow and privet near the pools. The pools themselves are very attractive to amphibians with common frog and palmate newt especially numerous. Grass snakes and adders hunt the marshy slacks.

Butterflies in midsummer are one of the glories of Braunton and thousands are attracted to the flower-rich dunes, including Common and Holly Blue, Marbled White, Green Hairstreak, Grayling, Dark Green Fritillary, Tortoiseshell, Red Admiral, Painted Lady and Clouded Yellow. Thirty-five species have been seen so far.

Dragonflies are numerous too in summer and over a dozen species are seen regularly, the most striking being the large and handsome Emperor dragonfly and the Golden-ringed dragonfly.

If you get lost in the Burrows the solution is to nip up a dune and locate the large central flagpole in the middle of the system, and then the twin chimneys of Barnstaple power station. This will enable you to return eastwards to the 'American Road' and thence to the car-park.

From the car-park head eastwards along the sea-wall past the White House. The salt-marsh between this and Crow Point attracts waders at all seasons, and there is a large freshmarsh with open water which lies immediately behind the White House on Horsey Island. Reed warblers breed in the small reed-bed.

Continue on round Horsey Island which has excellent views of the whole estuary. After a mile the sea-wall rejoins the main track from the toll-gate, and here it is possible to take a track straight out across the fresh grazing marsh, returning to Marsh Road in about a mile. This provides good views over the dykes, ditches and open meadows. Mute swans, coot, moorhen, mallard and dabchick all breed in these marsh dykes, along with reed bunting, reed and sedge warbler where reed-beds occur.

If you are lucky you may see a barn owl quartering these marsh ditches, while in winter short-eared owls are regular visitors. Passage seasons bring greenshank, whimbrel and green sandpiper to the ditches, while redshank and lapwing are year-round residents, joined for the winter months by a vast influx of new arrivals.

The Burrows and the estuary provide a wonderful combination of wildlife at all seasons, the peace only occasionally shattered by the Hawks and Harriers of RAF Chivenor as they circle the area to land on the airfield nearby.

The grass snake, thoroughly at home in water, lives mainly in marshy places

39

Slimbridge
GLOUCESTER

Address of Site/Warden

The Wildfowl Trust,
Slimbridge,
Gloucester GL2 7BT

Highlights and Features

World's largest captive waterfowl collection. Large area grazing marsh on Severn estuary. Large flocks of duck in winter, but most famous for 7,000 whitefronted geese and 700 Bewick's swan in winter. Good for birds of prey.

Facilities

Research centre. Information centre. Shop, café. Lecture hall. Many hides. Very large car-park. Open 0930–1700 or dusk, daily.

Photo Tips

One 200mm zoom lens will provide many wildfowl pictures, both wild and tame. Longer lenses will give good pictures of large flocks of wild birds from the hides in winter.

A flock of several thousand whitefronted geese spend every winter on the Slimbridge marshes

In 1946 the young Peter Scott, home from the war, discovered a couple of rare lesser whitefronted geese among the regular winter flocks of common whitefronts on the fresh grazing marsh at Slimbridge. He had been searching for a while for a site to house his growing collection of waterfowl and establish a wildfowl centre, so he decided to make his home here, in the old farmhouse that looked out across the marshes, and here was founded the Wildfowl Trust, some ten miles or so south of Gloucester off the A38.

Now, the pools and pens of Slimbridge house the greatest collection of wildfowl in the world with some 2,500 tame birds of nearly 200 species. Large feral flocks of grey-lag and barnacle geese are also based here from birds bred on the reserve.

Beyond the wildfowl collection lie the grazing marshes of some 1,250 acres (505ha) where wild birds come in thousands, especially in winter. Many of these also flight in to join the tame birds, especially if there is food to be found, and then it is often difficult to tell wild Arctic birds from the local residents.

The best time to visit is in winter, and the grounds are open from 0930 to 1700 (or dusk). It will take you all morning to walk round the captive collection, past the world's six species of flamingo – four of which actually breed here – and even through a tropical bird house. Dozens of collared doves, chaffinches and other common birds steal the grain put out for the ducks, and are catered for as extras by the Trust's staff. Facilities include a research centre, lecture hall, art gallery, shop, restaurant and many money-raising ventures for the Trust's conservation activities. Try 'doodling a duck' and add your masterpiece to the famous duck doodles pasted to the wall, from the royal family, Sir David Attenborough, Gerald Durrell, Rolf Harris and many more.

As you walk between the wildfowl pools watch the water margins and the grain trays – Slimbridge is quite the best place in Britain to watch the endearing little water vole; some are so tame they may take a piece of apple from a slow-moving finger tip – they like apples (and hopefully not fingers).

At the furthest point from the centre, right at the end of the collection, is the Acrow Tower which at 50 feet (15m) provides a high viewpoint out over the wild marshland (there is also a lower level at 28 feet (8m)); 60 steps will take you to the top. The view from the tower takes in a great sweep of the Severn marsh and estuary. Below are two hides, the Lathbury and the Barclay, and the latter, reached by a short boardwalk, is surrounded by a muddy scrape which is particularly good for seeing migrant waders in autumn, with greenshank, ruff, black-tailed godwit and spotted redshank coming in as regular visitors.

In the depths of winter the view from this spot will be one of constant movement, with thousands of wildfowl from all corners of the Arctic winter migrating here: 7,000 whitefronted geese, usually present in their greatest numbers from Christmas onwards, 5,000 wigeon, and thousands of other ducks, mallard, teal, pintail, gadwall and shoveler which will graze on the marsh fields of the Dumbles. Shelduck, curlew, bar-tailed godwit and dunlin all flight into the marshy scrapes and are joined by thousands of gulls, right in front of the hides.

Walk left through a wooded dell from the Acrow Tower over a little footbridge to the gate to the South Finger Hides. An electric fox-proof fence surrounds the waterfowl collection, but is turned off during the day. Just beyond the gate a little green fibre-glass hide peers out over a cropped grass field surrounded by long hedges. These fibre-glass hides, taking just three or four people, are built into the banks of many of the Trust's far-flung reserves. Watch the hedges here in autumn for a drifting short-eared owl, or a white barn owl ghosting past at dusk.

Continue down the track using the three large hides provided, the Van de Bovenkamp, Loke and Jack Death Hides which are hidden in the raised earth banks, with high hawthorn hedges screening both track and hides.

Winter brings in countless birds to the marsh fields, including thousands of lapwing and golden plover, with fieldfare and redwing cropping the berries above your head.

Directly in front of the Van de Bovenkamp Hide is the sea-wall, lined by a straggling hedge and topped out by two wartime pill-boxes. An old dead tree provides a good vantage point for hawks and falcons, and if you are lucky you might see a peregrine since one or two always winter on the marshes from late September round till March, preying on the huge flocks of ducks and gulls. Keep scanning all the posts, tops of pill-boxes, bits of driftwood on the far shore as many hawks, peregrine, sparrowhawk, kestrel, merlin and short-eared owl, regularly hunt the marshes from these vantage points. Watch the lines of hedgerows, used by these birds of prey for a swift yet stealthy approach – sudden panic with a whirlwind of wings means a peregrine is on the hunt.

Rare geese appear regularly in the flocks of whitefronts; pinkfooted and bean geese in occasional small parties, and lesser whitefront and red-breasted geese, one or two of which appear most years.

The Jack Death Hide at the end of the South Finger provides good views across marshland and down an avenue which is bounded by tall willows on the right and hawthorns on the left. Thrushes, buntings and finches haunt the trees while rabbits colonise the earth banks. The hide is a favoured spot for watching hunting owls, including little owls which breed in the willows, and sparrowhawks zipping along the hedges after small birds.

Return through the waterfowl collection to the Centre and take the northern path signposted to the Rushy Pen and Swan Lake. Along with the huge flocks of wild geese and ducks come Bewick's swans from their breeding grounds in far Siberia. Active conservation has increased their numbers in Britain with the largest group, several thousand strong, on the Wildfowl Trust's reserve at the Ouse Washes in Cambridge. Here at Slimbridge the occasional wintering group recorded in 1946 has grown to a flock of 700, studied intensively by the Scotts and their staff for over twenty years.

Before you reach the Rushy Pen and Swan Lake, there are some excellent 'Tadpole and Tiddler' pools to show pond life at really close quarters.

The original wooden tower, the Gazebo, overlooks the Berkeley New Duck Decoy which was used from 1834 to 1929 by the owners of Berkeley Castle – the benevolent owners of the Wildfowl Trust grounds, to catch ducks for the table, and is now used for ringing and migration studies. Close views of water rail, spotted flycatcher and sedge and reed warblers may be obtained by peering through the observation slits by the Decoy in summer. Three more hides run out to the Holden Tower in some 400 yards to provide further superb views of skeins of geese and swans.

This then is Slimbridge and the Wildfowl Trust, now expanded into six other centres nationwide, some mentioned else-

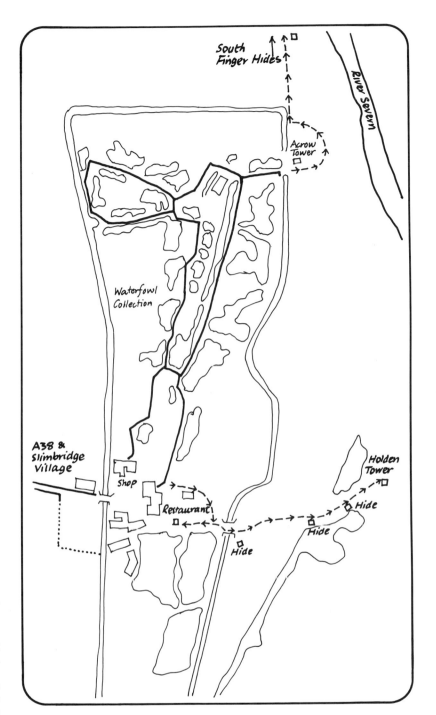

where in this book: Martin Mere (p 66), Caerlaverock (p 108) and Welney (p 54).

This is the crowning, personal achievement of Sir Peter Scott, knighted for his services to conservation in his capacity as co-founder of the World Wildlife Fund, for his abilities as Olympic yachtsman, international glider pilot and MTB flotilla commander in World War II with two DSCs and an MBE; for being a renowned wildlife artist, author and broadcaster, and father of Britain's conservation movement; it is perhaps fitting to use his description of his Slimbridge as 'the biggest bird-table in the world'.

Cley and Salthouse
NORTH NORFOLK – EAST

Address of Site/Warden

Cley: Norfolk
Naturalists' Trust,
Warden:
Watchers Cottage,
Cley,
Holt,
Norfolk

Highlights and Features

Probably best known bird
site in Britain. Marsh,
brackish pools and shingle
ridge. Large reed-beds. Huge
variety of migrant birds at all
seasons. Many breeding
avocets, some black-tailed
godwits. Breeding bittern
and bearded tit.

Facilities

Information centre open
daily except Monday
1000–1700 April to
October.
Winter visits need arranging
with warden. Ten hides
overlook many wader pools
and reed-beds. Whole area
can be well seen at all times.

Photo Tips

Very close views of many
waders, ducks, geese, swans
and reed-bed birds from
hides. Long telephoto lenses
will provide many pictures.

*Cley Mill, a familiar
landmark on the north
Norfolk coast, looks out
over wide marshlands*

Of all the superb wildlife areas along the north coast of Norfolk, Cley is probably the best known, at least to the bird-watching community. It was here in 1926 that Dr Sydney Long and friends acquired 400 acres (162ha) of marshland and the Norfolk Naturalists' Trust, the first in the country, was formed. The conservation movement was on its way.

Apart from the nature reserve itself the whole of the Cley marshland, shore and nearby countryside is a wonderful wildlife site. Its fame is international, especially for its non-stop supply of rare birds. Unfortunately, owing to the increased number of visitors, one of the marshland's mammal stars is now a rare visitor – the otter used to live in these marshes, but droves of bird-watchers out all year and often before dawn have largely driven it away.

Two wildlife sites are described, one a circular tour of Cley Marsh and sea-shore, the second taking in the marsh at Salt-house and Salthouse Heath to the south.

Wildlife Walk 1: Cley Marsh

Stop at the visitor centre on the A149 at the eastern end of Cley Village and buy a permit to enable you to use the various hides. Most people start here, but half a mile further east is a little car-park on the left from where a ¾-mile raised bank runs out towards the shore. This is East Bank, and is perhaps the most famous bird walk in Britain. If there is a really rare bird here, East Bank can look like a miniature Wembley Stadium.

Before you set off along East Bank, walk a hundred yards east past the lovely reed-fringed pool, Snipes Marsh, on the right and climb the short path through gorse and thorn to the Walsey Hills Migration Watchpoint. This is open daily (except Mondays) in summer and week-ends in winter, and it has all the local news. These low scrub-covered hills attract migrants throughout the year. They also have a good population of adders, often easily visible.

Walk out along East Bank with wide reed-beds on the left, and a ditch and open wet fields on the right. Watch the reed-tops for bearded tits. Bitterns breed in the reeds and may sometimes fly near the Bank, especially around dawn and dusk. Reed and sedge warblers are numerous in summer, and yellow wag-

tails, redshank, lapwing and snipe breed in the meadows. This is also a breeding site for black-tailed godwit, and their spring display can be seen at quite close quarters. Two hides in the reeds, Bittern and Pool, often give good views of small birds like rails and snipe, but are not the best sites.

Continue on towards the beach. After half a mile the wet fields on the right give way to a large brackish pool with several islands fronting the shingle ridge. This is Arnolds Marsh. On the left a deep ditch separates the reed-bed from further brackish pools. Kingfishers, dabchick, mute swans and herons are seen frequently along the ditch – watch the tops of posts for the kingfishers. The brackish pools and especially Arnolds Marsh are superb for waders throughout the year. The islands hold breeding black-headed gulls, common and little terns, and many terns use the islands for resting and preening.

Avocets are to be seen here from March to October, and quite a breeding colony has built up on the 'scrapes' of the main reserve. All sorts of waders appear on Arnolds Marsh, especially in autumn – anything from a USA sandpiper to a USSR plover. In winter there are flocks of duck in good numbers, with many goldeneye and red-breasted merganser. The shingle ridge, especially on the landward side where seeds gather, is good for snow and Lapland buntings in winter.

The beach overlooking the North Sea is a good watchpoint, although the gannets, skuas, kittiwakes and so on which pass just offshore at Blakeney Point are here further out to sea.

Turn west along the shingle towards the coastguard's look-out at Cley Beach; this allows access to North and Maynard's hides. These have excellent views south over a large scrape with breeding avocets, lots of migrant waders and winter duck. An extensive rabbit warren exists all around these hides, and very close views may be obtained; hunting stoats are therefore frequent. Wheatears breed in the rabbit holes along the beach.

Cley Eye, together with the Eye Pool and the Eye Field, are just west of Maynard's Hide. The field is a good opportunity to see geese and golden plover in winter, and dotterel, singles or even parties, occur here every year. Snow

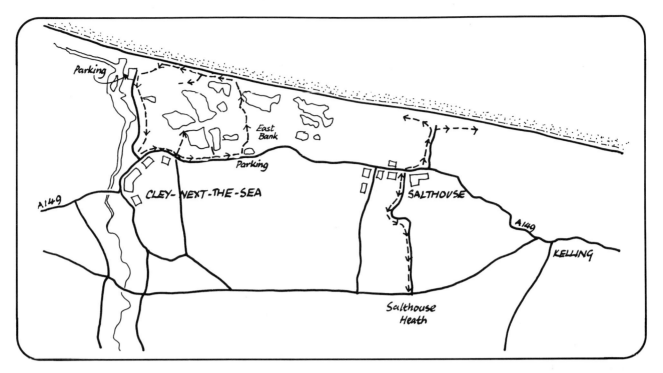

and Lapland buntings are found on the field and sometimes even in the car-park in winter.

The coastguard's look-out is an excellent spot for sea-watching. The worse the weather is here, the more you are likely to see. For a small fee you can use the look-out, but most birders shelter behind the collection of boats pulled up on the shingle ridge. Northerly gales in late autumn will produce streams of sea-birds along the shore, with little auks, Leach's petrels, little gulls, sooty shearwaters and many more.

Return towards Cley village along the salt-marsh bank on the west of the road. In Cley, turn east to complete the square, crossing the fields through a gate to a fine group of three hides overlooking three of the main scrapes. These are Avocet, Dauke and Teal hides, and are excellent for waders and wildfowl throughout the year. The reeds nearby are not quite so dense as the main beds, and are extremely good for views of bearded tits.

Walk the last half a mile along the road to East Bank, using Richardson and Irene hides to see the last of the man-made 'scrapes'. In winter hen harriers, short-eared owls, merlins and the occasional peregrine regularly hunt the area, while marsh harriers are a daily occurrence from spring right through to autumn. Barn owls appear at dusk on many days throughout the year.

This is a four-mile (6.4km) round walk on level ground.

Wildlife Walk 2: Salthouse Marsh and Heath

The birds of Salthouse Marshes are similar to those seen only a mile along the road at Cley. It is actually quite simple just to turn east instead of west at East Bank beach and walk to Salthouse, returning via the main road. However, by car from East Bank take the Beach Road just east of Salthouse village – a number of ornamental ducks are kept 'on the village pond'.

Open grazing marshes with wet pools and ditches lie on both sides of Beach Road – these are excellent for brent geese in winter with up to 2,000, and these are often nearly within touching distance.

For many years a glaucous gull, known as George, spent the autumn and winter on these fields. 'He' vanished in 1981 but another individual, nicknamed 'Boy George', has taken his place.

Park by the shingle ridge. The nearby pools are excellent for small waders such as stints and sandpipers. Shore larks and snow buntings are nearly always to be found in winter between the car-park and the string of grassy knolls on either side.

Back through Salthouse village and up the little hill by the public house, brings you in half a mile onto Salthouse Heath, an extensive area of gorse, heather and birch scrub perched a hundred feet above the marshland.

This adds a new dimension to the bird habitats here, with many common woodland species present, plus breeding nightjar, nightingale and long-eared owl. Hen harriers roost here, while a great grey shrike is often present in winter.

Usually seen as a blue streak zipping down a stream, the kingfisher is truly the most dazzling of British birds

41

Address of Site/Warden

Holkham National
Nature Reserve:
Warden:
7 Kelling Road,
Holt,
Norfolk
Blakeney National
Trust Reserve:
Warden:
35 The Cornfields,
Langham,
Holt,
Norfolk NR25 7DQ

Highlights and Features

Dunes, pinewoods and
extensive freshmarsh. Wide
variety of birds and animals
at all seasons. Particularly
good for variety of geese in
winter when six species may
be present.

Facilities

None other than convenient
car-parks.

Photo Tips

Birds rather distant. Medium
lens, say 80–200 zoom for
opportunist pictures.

*Canada geese, once
introduced, now breed in
many parts of Britain. A
large flock is based on
Holkham Lake*

Holkham and Blakeney
NORTH NORFOLK – CENTRAL

The central section of the lovely north Norfolk coastline presents the widest possible diversity of habitats together with the largest land area given over to wildlife on the Norfolk coast. Holkham is the largest coastal nature reserve in England, whilst Blakeney with its mile-wide salt-marsh, great tidal harbour and sand-dune point adds these habitats to the freshmarsh and woods of Holkham.

Two wildlife walks are described, although the Blakeney 'tour' is easier by boat at high tide.

Wildlife Walk 1: Holkham

Holkham is an exceptionally rich wildlife area split neatly in two by the little town of Wells-next-the-Sea and its harbour channel. The western section has two walks, starting either by the lifeboat station car-park one mile north of Wells town centre, or from the car-park at the end of Lady Anne's Road, one mile west of Wells and opposite the main entrance to Holkham Hall.

Each walk, on level ground, travels westwards to Gun Hill and back: a 5-mile (8km) round trip from Lady Anne's Road, 8 miles (13km) from the life-boat car-park. It is probably worthwhile firstly to have a look at the wet area known as the 'Dell', two or three hundred yards west of the 'boating lake' by the caravan park, as many migrant birds reach this first after coming in from the east off the North Sea. A long water-filled pit farther along this path on the right is also good. Crossbills are often found in this area.

Take the path which follows the southern edge of extensive pinewoods, skirting areas of scrub and brambles for a further mile to Holkham Gap at the end of Lady Anne's Road. This is the alternative start for the shorter walk. The track here is bordered by a grove of poplars on its south side, and by the pines on the dunes to the north – these are Corsican pines and were planted a century ago to stabilise the dunes and protect the fresh grazing marsh already reclaimed. The pine belt here is perhaps a hundred yards wide and worth exploring – there are a few red squirrels, and crossbills are regular.

The path continues along the landward side of the pines, past a small reedy pond and provides excellent views of the fresh-marsh fields. Dense bramble and briar scrub along the path edge provides cover for tired bird migrants. The little pool has a pair of dabchick breeding, with reed and sedge warblers in the vegetation. In hard winter weather this pool will often shelter goldeneye, smew and pochard.

Watch the marsh fields along here. In summer redshank, lapwing, snipe and yellow wagtails all breed, whilst in winter large flocks of geese use these fields to feed – brent may reach 5,000, with a thousand each of pinkfeet and grey-lag; the grey-lags are actually from the feral flock based on Holkham Park. Many Canada and Egyptian geese breed on these marshes and are present in winter, also from Holkham Park. Flocks of white-fronts are regular from November to March and the rare bean, red-breasted and lesser whitefronted geese have all been seen – a great goose-gathering place. Up to a thousand golden plover and two thousand lapwing may use these fields in winter – watch the winter flocks to pick out the smaller golden plover.

The pines have a variety of woodland birds, with tawny and long-eared owls, woodpeckers, tits, nuthatch, goldcrest and redpoll all breeding. However, it is for rare migrants that these woods are famous. In spring and autumn and as long as the winds are easterly, hundreds of chats, flycatchers, warblers, firecrests, shrikes, wrynecks and dozens more may suddenly appear. Early morning is best to observe these birds, before they move on or are disturbed by holiday 'strollers'. If the winds are south-westerly however, you may spend a whole week here and see hardly anything at all.

Meals House is passed on the left and the track runs out onto extensive dunes, along the inland edge to Gun Hill which you will reach in a further mile. Just after leaving the protection of the pines several small pools on the left shelter a small colony of natterjack toads. Gun Hill is a large dune with a broken and eroded top which overlooks the extensive creeks and salt-marshes of Overy Staithe; these creeks usually hold small numbers of the common waders, including curlew, bar-tailed godwit and grey plover in winter. The hollows or 'slacks' of the stable dunes have a good flora, with bee and pyramidal orchids and various marsh orchids in

June. Creeping ladies' tresses orchid may be found in the pinewoods.

From Gun Hill you can return along the north side of the pines, along the foreshore. The tide recedes a long way into Holkham Bay at low tide, leaving a vast expanse of dazzling sand. Walk near the tide line and throughout the year, apart from the short midsummer period, there will be migrant waders here – it is a favourite place for scores of sanderling, tiny waders with twinkling feet, skipping through the very edge of the tide.

Wildlife Walk 2: Blakeney Harbour and Point

This is one of the most famous 'bird walks' in Britain. In summer it is possible to cross by boat from Morston Quay at high tide after a very muddy walk from the car-park. These boats will also take you out to 'see the seals' at a suitable price, and small numbers of common seals may often be seen watching the birders at Blakeney Point on the rising tide.

May and June at Blakeney Point belong to the terns. Four species breed, although there are only one or two pairs of Arctic terns; little terns may reach fifty pairs and roseate terns may sometimes make the fifth species. The majority are Sandwich and common terns, with two or three thousand pairs of each in a good season. Sandwich terns are notoriously fickle and in some years the whole colony may move ten miles (16km) to join the ternery at Scolt Head. A hide is specially placed to give good views of the terns. Oystercatcher, ringed plover and redshank all breed on the marshes, while quite reasonable numbers of shelduck rear their pie-bald families in rabbit burrows in the dunes.

This unique shingle ridge and sand-dune point projecting into the North Sea inevitably collects a large share of passerine migrants brought in from the rest of Europe by northerly and easterly winds. It is also ideally placed to observe large-scale sea-bird, wader and waterfowl movements along the coast. To get a close enough view of the migrants it is usually necessary to walk the full length of the shingle ridge from Cley Beach. This is a seven mile (11km), rather tiring, round walk; one way can be traversed along the hard sand at low tide, but if a 'fall' of migrants has occurred you will find it essential to walk along the inner rim of the shingle ridge. This has extensive areas of suaeda scrub, especially where shingle and mud have consolidated and migrants will be found flitting about these bushes, especially in autumn. Views across the harbour for waders, duck, geese and birds of prey are excellent.

Halfway House, literally two miles

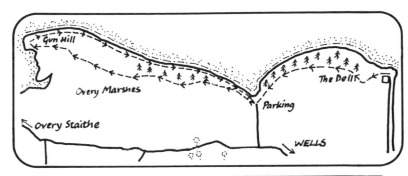

(3km) along the shore, has an area of dune grassland which is good for seeing Lapland and snow buntings in winter. Keep walking at the point where tree lupin thickets grow in the dunes, and you will see a tiny plantation of pines near the summer tea-rooms – these bushes are like magnets to tired birds, and can hold hundreds of redstarts, flycatchers, warblers and chats on a good day, along with a scattering of rarities such as bluethroats, wryneck, barred and Icterine warblers and Ortolan bunting.

Northerly winds in autumn will bring large coastal movements of terns, skuas, gannets, kittiwakes and shearwaters, and rarer species are frequent. The best place to sea-watch, comfortably out of the wind, is from the dunes at Blakeney Point itself. Here, skuas and gannets may be nearly overhead.

Pochard breed in small groups in fresh marshes, augmented by a large winter influx from the Continent.

Holme and Titchwell
NORTH NORFOLK – WEST

From the RSPB reserve at Snettisham on the east coast of the Wash, the main A149 turns the corner at Hunstanton and heads east for over 30 miles (48km) to Cromer. Most of this fascinating coast consists of nature reserves owned by various conservation organisations, and is a wild landscape of marsh and mud, sea and sky, sand and shingle. Facing north, it takes the full brunt of the worst weather the cold North Sea can throw. Thus, despite the little flint and pantiled villages nestling under the coastal hills, the land still belongs to its wildlife and above all to its birds.

A dozen or more reserves are strung out along the coast, most consisting of stretches of freshmarsh backed by a sand or shingle beach and often enclosing extensive saltings. Holme and Titchwell are the first of these coastal reserves eastwards from Hunstanton.

Wildlife Walk 1: Holme Reserve
(Norfolk Naturalists' Trust)

Holme is a lovely marsh and sea reserve quite different in character from its near neighbour at Titchwell – the prime habitat here is an extensive dune system backed by grazing marshes. From the A149 at Holme-next-the-Sea, take the beach road and at the 'Police – No Parking' sign, turn sharply right along a gravel track and continue down this for ½ mile. There is a car-park at the reserve entrance, on the edge of Lavender Marsh and substantial sand-dunes, although the track continues for nearly a mile more to another car-park by 'The Firs', the large, white warden's house and Holme Bird Observatory.

The salt-marsh creek and the dunes of Lavender Marsh are always worth examination. The dunes continue beyond the mouth of the creek and stretch right round the shore of the reserve. Extensive areas of that invasive shrub sea-buckthorn occupy the inner zone of the dune edge, finally giving way to a hundred-year-old grove of Corsican pines surrounding the observatory. The combination of an isolated pinewood and dense shrub vegetation makes this spot particularly attractive to incoming bird migrants.

The several dune ridges show a succession from bare sand, through marram-stabilised dune to shrubby grassland. The high shell content of these dunes means that many chalk-loving plants can be found here. Dry areas may have reasonable colonies of pyramidal and bee orchids in June, along with carline thistle, storksbill and bird's-foot trefoil. Wet dune slacks in the hollows have splendid displays of southern and early marsh orchids and in June and July there is marsh helleborine to be found in places.

By autumn the bright orange berries of the sea buckthorn provide food for flocks of immigrant thrushes, especially fieldfares, though the other thrushes tend to prefer the hawthorn scrub which is also present.

From the car-park in front of 'The Firs' a nature trail runs through the edge of the sanctuary area around the Heligoland trap and netting sites of the Bird Ringing station. It is often possible to watch the warden catching and ringing the thousands of migrant birds which pass through the area when you can obtain really close-up views of birds in the hand, detained for a minute before flying off with their tiny identification rings.

Between the car-park and the open grazing marsh is a series of pools and scrapes, mostly man-made, around which are seven well planned wooden hides. These pools are excellent for observation, with migrant waders in spring and autumn; several pairs of avocets now nesting in summer, along with ringed plover and oystercatcher; little tern which breed on the shore and feed over the pools and bearded tit which breed in small numbers in the Broadwater reed-bed.

Spring and autumn bring hordes of birds, especially on favourable east or north winds – warblers, ring ouzels, redstarts, black redstarts, wheatears, flycatchers and even firecrests are all regular, and waders and birds of prey pass through in reasonable numbers. Easterly weather in autumn may bring large 'falls' of migrants overnight to shelter in the bushes, and rare birds are surprisingly frequent at Holme.

If you sit in the dunes overlooking the sea at high tide, autumn can provide a wide variety: terns, immigrant wild geese, ducks and waders moving down the coast. Winter brings divers, grebes and diving duck offshore, with hen harriers and short-eared owls hunting the grazing marsh; from November till March about a thousand brent geese use the fields for feeding. Twite, snow bunting and shore lark are all fairly regular winter visitors to the dune slacks and the shore.

Rabbits occur in scores in the dunes, so that their main predator, the stoat, is quite frequent. The rare natterjack toad has recently been introduced into the pools, and happily the tiny colony is beginning to expand.

Wildlife Walk 2: Titchwell Marsh

This is a delightful RSPB reserve of wide skies, reeds and open water; a signpost just west of Titchwell village takes you into the reserve car-park. The interpretation centre here describes how the reserve of some 510 acres (206ha) has been transformed from salt-marsh into its present highly productive state.

A dense thicket of willow, hawthorn, briar and bramble between the car-park and the marsh provides good birds while you eat your picnic. Sedge, willow and grasshopper warbler, blackcap, chiffchaff and lesser whitethroat are all present in summer, with many common finches. Marsh harriers often appear over the car-park, while in winter a barn owl may sometimes be seen here at dusk.

One path leads from the centre and in about half a mile takes you to the beach, along a raised bank which offers wonderful all-round views. Several hides overlook the main freshmarsh and lakes on the east, and there is a summer hide overlooking the tern colonies in the dunes.

In contrast to nearby Holme, much of this marshland is flooded, some by the tide and some by holding back the fresh-water through a series of sluices. Marsh and water birds abound here: in summer thousands of black-headed gulls nest on the islands; little gulls are frequent with flocks on passage; common and little terns breed along with oystercatcher, ringed plover and avocet. The extensive reed-beds have two pairs of breeding marsh harriers, several pairs of bittern, dozens of bearded tits and scores of reed and sedge warblers and reed buntings. Water rails breed but are difficult to see. Spoonbills and black terns come regularly onto the main area of open water.

In autumn thousands of swallows and martins fly in to roost in the reed-beds while the water level of the whole area is lowered to attract migrant waders. Twenty to twenty-five species may be present at peak times in August and September and close views can be obtained from the bank and the hides. Offshore, once you have reached the beach, terns of several species fish in summer. With the onset of autumn, passage can be continuous with gulls, terns, kittiwake, gannets and skuas passing eastwards.

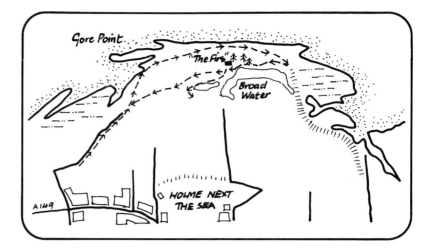

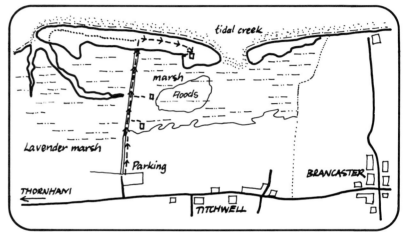

Winter brings eider, scoter, divers and grebes offshore, with twite and snow bunting in good numbers in the dunes; large flocks of common duck appear on the waters of the marsh and a roost of hen harriers, with up to ten birds, settles in at dusk. High tides in winter can move waders in large numbers from Thornham Island eastwards onto the reserve beach.

Titchwell is one of the best all-year-round bird spots in Britain.

Migrant ruff pass through the marshlands in some numbers every year en route to and from Africa

The Wash
SNETTISHAM NORFOLK

Address of Site/Warden

Snettisham RSPB Reserve
Warden:
18 Cockle Road,
Snettisham,
King's Lynn,
Norfolk PE31 6HD

Highlights and Features

Vast expanse of mud and
sand of Wash at low tide.
Reserve includes long
shingle beach with flooded
gravel pits, used by up to
80,000 waders at high tide
in autumn and winter.
Breeding black-headed gulls
and common terns in
summer.

Facilities

Large car-park on beach
with 1½-mile walk to four
hides round pits. Open at all
times.

Photo Tips

Wonderful place for pictures
of huge flocks of swirling
waders at high-tide roosts.
Use hides and long lenses.
Hides face both east and
west so light not a problem.
Remember to allow for the
bright sky when setting light
readings.

*Snettisham supports a
colony of black-headed
gulls around its gravel pits*

The Wash, that great tidal estuary between East Anglia and the Lincolnshire coast, is recognised as a site of international importance for its huge numbers of wintering waders and wildfowl. It supports more birds than any other estuary in Britain except Morecambe Bay. Vast flocks use its wide, flat sands from August right through to mid-May, and only June and July are relatively quiet times here – even during these months considerable colonies of gulls and terns breed on the RSPB reserve at Snettisham.

Out on the far sandbanks of the Wash a large colony of common seals produces pups in midsummer. Normally the seals cannot be seen at all from the shore, but local boatmen provide 'See the Seal' trips. One or two salt-marsh inlets on the Norfolk coast are noted for high-tide parties of seals, but these are usually all on private land, which is perhaps fortunate.

The Wash, because of its vast size and the difficulty of access to much of its coastline, is not easy to work for its birds. Snettisham makes up for all these problems and is a wonderful place to see huge numbers of waders and wildfowl, from autumn arrival to spring departure. One main wildlife walk is described.

Wildlife Walk: Snettisham RSPB Reserve

The reserve lies on the eastern side of the Wash and comprises some 3,250 acres (1,315ha), much of which is intertidal sand and mudflats. Some 300 acres (121ha) are salt-marsh. Only a small strip of real *land* is included, but this contains five large, brackish lagoons totalling over a hundred acres (40ha), produced by past shingle extraction. Leave the A149 at the southern end of Snettisham village and drive for three miles along the beach road. This ends in a large car-park amid holiday chalets, caravans and the various other accoutrements of beach holidays. You must *not* park along the roads through the chalets – they are private and the RSPB has established good local co-operation which is vital for the success of such a reserve.

A three-mile (4.8km) round walk is now necessary to reach the best viewing places – four hides overlooking the southernmost pits. An alternative route is a footpath from Dersingham village, but this is a five-mile (8km) round trip. Best times for a visit

are September to November for peak wader numbers, and throughout the winter months for a combination of large wader totals and lots of wildfowl. It can be extremely cold. Timing is also very important – a rising tide with perhaps a couple of hours to high tide is ideal, as low tide will find all the birds spread out over fifty square miles (130sq km) of sand.

Walk up onto the top of the shingle ridge out of the car-park. North is an area of low dunes with bramble and gorse, and there is also a small pool and some reeds. This spot can produce unusual migrant birds attracted by the bush cover. Having examined this little corner, turn south and follow the track along the shingle ridge; after half a mile the first two pits are easily viewed, either from the path which runs between them or by peeking round the chalets.

Continue on past the yacht club either along the service road or, better still, along the beach if possible. In winter there are birds all the way here with a variety of wildfowl on the pits and as the tide rises, waders streaming along the coast. Snow buntings, with the occasional Lapland bunting or shore lark, are found along the beach – even the car-park is worth a look for these on a bitter January day.

Walk past the last blue-painted bungalow and through the reserve gate. The grass along the path is kept 'mown' by scores of rabbits and Snettisham is one of the best places to watch them – a favourite pastime while waiting for the tide to bring in the roosting birds. The path, which now avoids the skyline, passes through some sea buckthorn and dense gorse with the two best pits a few yards to the left.

In summer these pits are a marvellous site to see breeding birds: nearly 150 pairs of common tern, scores of black-headed gull, and many oystercatcher, redshank and ringed plover. Most nest on the artificial shingle islands situated in the middle of the pits. Wheatears can occasionally be found among the chunks of concrete left from the defunct shingle company's roads; pairs of great crested grebe also display on the pits while linnets, reed buntings and stonechats prefer the bushes.

The path runs up to the first hide which overlooks the sands of the Wash in one direction and the lagoons in the other;

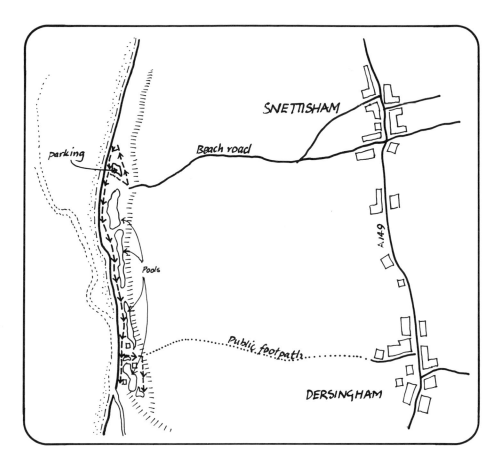

there are three more hides on both sides of the pits. Migrants increase in autumn with a fresh influx of waders from late July onwards, and numbers build to a peak by September; terns and marauding Arctic skuas are then frequent too. As the tide covers the Wash sands, huge flocks of waders congregate here – depending upon the height of the tide all may roost on the reserve lagoons, or the roost may be split with large groups along the beach and even as far back as the car-park.

Autumn and winter high tides at Snettisham are not to be missed and provide a wildlife spectacle which must be unsurpassed in western Europe. You may see 100,000 waders at peak times, although the totals are usually smaller. Survey counts have shown the following peak totals and peak months: knot 74,000 November; dunlin 52,000 October to March; oystercatcher 19,000 September; bar-tailed godwit 8,300 September; curlew 6,600 August; turnstone 1,000 September; and ringed plover 550, also in September.

Some of these totals represent 20–25% of the total British count for the species.

There are also large numbers of other passage waders including several hundred sanderling, black-tailed godwit, spotted redshank and greenshank.

Snettisham is a truly magical place as the huge flocks swirl and twist across the sands in a display of massed formations.

As autumn turns to winter so the wild-fowl numbers build up too, although some of the wader totals decline a little. Wild-fowl counts here have shown internationally important flocks of shelduck, brent and pinkfooted geese on the Wash sands: shelduck, returning from their moult in November, reach a winter peak of 14,000 in January, brent geese may number 10,000 and pinkfooted geese 8,000. The pinkfeet often use the fields near the pits for feeding, along with perhaps a thousand brents, where they eat remnant potatoes and sugar-beet left after the harvest. From November onwards small flocks of whooper and Bewick's swans appear in the pits or the neighbouring fields.

Rarer ducks, grebes and divers may appear in cold weather – smew, long-tailed duck, Slavonian grebe and many more may all come in for shelter. Large flocks of mallard, wigeon, teal and pintail can be seen offshore. Common scoters with small groups of eider can be seen feeding on the mussel beds off the main car-park.

The common seals tend to drift inshore more in winter and may sometimes be seen swimming alongside the beach usually in ones or two – the Wash, however, support 5–7,000 seals, which is the largest population in Britain.

Several thousand common seals live on the sandbanks of the Wash

44

Ynys Hir and The Dyfi Estuary
DYFED

Address of Site/Warden

Ynys Hir RSPB Reserve:
Warden:
Cae'r Berllan,
Eglwysfach,
Machynlleth,
Dyfed SY20 8TA
Ynyslas Dunes National
Nature Reserve:
Warden:
Information Centre,
Ynyslas,
Dyfed

Highlights and Features

Ynys Hir has wide range of habitats with many breeding birds, especially pied flycatcher. Very varied bird-watching over estuary. Good for butterflies, mammals, with chance of otter, polecat.
Ynyslas Dunes has superb flora during summer, best in June.

Facilities

Ynys Hir: Information Centre and toilets. Reserve open daily 0900–2100 or sunset if earlier. Several hides.
Ynyslas has Information Centre and nature trail open daily 0930–1700 April to September.

Photo Tips

Ynys Hir. Long telephoto lenses needed from hides. DON'T disturb birds in nest-boxes. Butterflies and dragonflies worthwhile with medium lens, say 200mm and small flashgun.
Ynyslas – good for flowers. Use wide-angle zoom and tripod.

As you explore the many beautiful places described in this book some will stand out as very special. Ynys Hir, to my mind, is a gem, its wonderful mosaic of wood, hill and marsh quite delighting the eye.

The Dyfi estuary, the traditional boundary between North and South Wales, has a complete range of habitats from extensive dunes at Ynyslas to a surrounding ring of mountain tops. Ynys Hir is an RSPB reserve of well over 1,000 acres (405ha), which despite being primarily a bird reserve, also has high appeal for those interested in butterflies, dragonflies, flowers and mammals. The variety of birds around the estuary is enormous, and the whole locality must rank as one of Britain's few 'one hundred bird species in a day' places.

One wildlife walk round the reserve is described. The nearby Ynyslas National Nature Reserve, a large expanse of sand-dunes at the mouth of the Dyfi, has a superb range of dune plants including thousands of marsh orchids and marsh helleborines in June, but this area is under severe pressure from the 300,000 annual visitors who use its sands on holiday.

Wildlife Walk: Ynys Hir RSPB Reserve

The entrance is on the north side of the A487 in Furnace village, some seven miles (11km) south of Machynlleth, right next to the mill and its beautiful waterfall. Where the cascades of the little River Einion tumble through the village, there are always dipper and grey wagtail to be seen, with common sandpiper and kingfisher nearer the mouth.

Follow the bumpy track for a mile through farm- and woodland to the small car-park, where there is an Information Centre and toilets. The reserve is open from 0900 to 2100 daily, and visiting is highly rewarding all year round. Turn right out of the little wicket gate by the Centre, down a muddy path through open oak copses and parkland. Wellies are a good idea as the whole walk, some four miles (6½km), is wet in places and steep down through the woodland.

A farm gate takes you about 300 yards (274m) past rocky outcrops and some sheep pasture, with nest-boxes set up in many of the trees. The results for 1987 are posted in the Centre and speak for themselves: 288 small boxes in place, used by 80 pairs of pied flycatchers, 23 pairs of blue tits, 18 great tits, 2 coal tits, 7 redstarts and 2 pairs of nuthatches; while 10 large boxes were used by kestrel, tawny and barn owls, jays and grey squirrels.

The path crosses the railway bridge (the line crosses the reserve along the marsh banks) and continues through some splendid ancient oaks with fine views from the hilltop out across the estuary. More nest-boxes here include some especially for tree-creepers, and for bats. Amusingly the bats – noctule, pipistrelle and long-eared – prefer the bird-boxes, while tree-creepers use the bat-boxes.

The first hide, reached some half a mile from the Centre, is the Marian Mawr Hide, perched on an outcrop and looking out over a series of reed-fringed scrapes, the wide sweep of the estuary down to Ynyslas dunes, and round the wooded hills above Aberdyfi. The Saltings Hide, which used to be right out on the marsh, has been taken down.

This is a glorious place, filled all the year round with birds, and in summer with butterflies, other insects and the rustle of mammals in the wood edge. A wide variety of waders uses the scrapes, especially at high spring tides when birds are pushed up from the estuary mouth.

Buzzard, kestrel and sparrowhawk hunt the reserve all year and all breed in its woods. As you cross the boggy valley to the next hide, the avenue of trees around you is particularly good for hunting sparrowhawks zooming down from the hills. Heronry Hide, overlooking the main river, is so-called because of the seven or eight pairs of herons which nest in the trees, and is therefore closed from February till July. Check the fence-posts along the river for watchful kingfishers, barn and short-eared owls, and also buzzards. From Heronry Hide scan the tawny uplands, as you might well glimpse a drifting buzzard, and even the occasional red kite.

Return to the Centre wicket-gate to see the rest of the reserve. The Penrhyn Mawr Hide is close by, a tower-hide up twenty-four steep steps which allows close views of woodland birds, especially pied fly-catcher, redstart and woodpeckers as they raise their families high in the trees. Two hundred yards along the top track the path

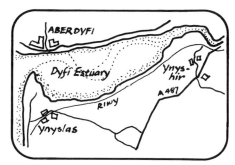

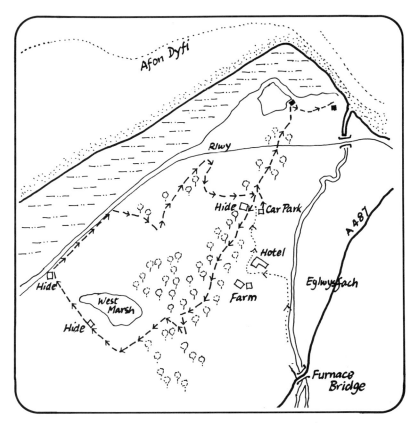

enters the woodland through an iron gate. Here the high rocky outcrop is clothed with oak, mixed with some fine specimen trees, and a dense shrub layer of hazel, rowan and bracken. A wooden seat on top of the hill is dedicated to the previous owner, Hubert Mappin, who maintained it as a wildlife sanctuary, and the view down through the steep, hanging oak woodlands out across the estuary is quite stunning.

Wood warblers, flycatchers, redstarts and other woodland birds abound here; and if you sit quietly at dusk there is always the chance of watching a badger making his way past you, or a polecat, or a hedgehog ferreting for its supper. Dormice love these many-layered woodlands, while summer brings innumerable butterflies: Silver-washed and Small Pearl-bordered Fritillaries, Orange-tip, Green and Purple Hairstreaks, Speckled Wood and Holly Blue in the woods, and meadow species along the marshland paths, totalling thirty-one species in all.

Quite suddenly the track falls very steeply through the honeysuckled woods to a wide path and a conifer plantation at the base of the hill. A sign points to West Marsh; follow this, turning right on a gravel track, and after 200 yards, left on a new (1987) track to Ynys Eidiol and Breakwater Hides. The track passes through Covert Du, the reed-swamp and willow thickets. Many wetland birds breed here with reed, sedge and grasshopper warblers and the occasional water rail in the reeds, lots of willow warblers and redpolls in the scrub, and willow tits in the old tree-stumps.

The path crosses West Marsh ditch by a wooden footbridge, where water voles are frequent, and turns right towards the estuary. After 300 yards (274m) the Ynys Eidiol Hide looks out over a freshmarsh pool which has the edge of the reed-bed, the oakwoods and the tawny moorland as a backdrop. This is a likely spot to see the now rare and nocturnal otter, a few of which do live on the Dyfi although only one or two are ever seen each year. The variety of birdlife from this one hide is amazing, with marsh, woodland and upland birds as well.

Five hundred yards beyond (456m) lies

Breakwater Hide which can be reached by a wooden footbridge over the marsh ditch, next to the railway line. The hide is a 'double-decker' with views across the salt-marsh and the river, and back across the wide freshmarsh fields. Winter is the best season at this hide when wildfowl and bird of prey numbers are high. About 100 Greenland whitefronted geese spend winter on the Dyfi, often appearing in the Ynys Hir fields. Duck numbers are quite respectable, with 3,500 wigeon, 1,600 mallard, 1,000 teal, 300 shelduck, 80 red-breasted mergansers and 50 goldeneye. Two or three hen harriers hunt the marsh along with the resident buzzards, while peregrines are attracted because of the steady supply of gulls and waders which provides them with prey.

From Breakwater Hide follow the path along the bottom of the railway bank for some 600 yards (548m) and then turn right through a strip of pine trees. Buzzards sometimes breed here while grey squirrels collect the cones. The path returns round a slate outcrop in half a mile to the Centre.

The hill of Foel Fawr immediately above Furnace village is also part of the reserve and may be reached by walking up a side road just north of the reserve entrance for 200 yards (183m) and then turning left along the rocky hillside footpath. Summer brings breeding whinchat, stonechat and wheatear to the hilltop and there are usually nightjars at dusk.

The long-eared bat is the prettiest of an unusual group of useful mammals, now strictly protected due to their drastic decline

45 Newborough Warren
ANGLESEY GWYNEDD

Address of Site/Warden

National Nature Reserve:
Warden:
'Serai',
Malltreath,
Bodorgan,
Anglesey,
Gwynedd LL62 5AS

Highlights and Features

Dunes, forestry plantations and salt-marsh. Good for birds at all seasons. Roseate terns frequent visitors. Superb dune flowers all summer and into autumn.

Facilities

Two public hides including an observation tower. Access to NNR by permit only from warden.

Photo Tips

Best for dune flowers and insects in summer. Use range of lenses or wide-angle zoom 28–70mm to provide variety. Butterflies best with 200mm zoom to avoid disturbing insect.

An introduced species from North America, the ruddy duck has spread rapidly in Britain

From the southern end of the Menai Straits westwards to the wide salt-marsh of the Cefni estuary the national nature reserve of Newborough Warren, together with the Forestry Commission's forest stretches for over three miles (4.8km). This is a land dominated by the prevailing north-west winds and by the sand carried by the winds across the roads and farms. The longshore drift has carried the dunes out into the Strait at Abermenai Point enclosing a huge salt-marsh bay. Newborough Forest was begun in 1948, and now some 2,000 acres (809ha) of mainly dark Corsican pines have helped to stop the sandblows.

Sand-dunes are a very fragile environment easily destroyed by visitor erosion. It is possible to walk all round the area in a day but the described tour includes four walks, each of about two or three miles, joined by short car trips. Please keep strictly to the footpaths, clearly posted on the ground. Autumn and winter are probably best for birds but summer produces a magnificent display of dune flowers. A permit is required to walk the dune paths, obtainable from the Nature Conservancy Council.

Tour: Newborough Warren

Park at Malltraeth Cob, in a lay-by on the bridge over the River Cefni. The Cob is a raised bank built by the great Victorian engineer, Thomas Telford, who also built the Menai Bridge.

At high tide waders roost on the land-spit by the bridge and on the banks of the river back towards the viaduct. Curlew, lapwing and golden plover also use the surrounding fields, with several hundred present for much of the year. Cormorants are frequent on the river, and in winter divers, grebes and sea-duck occur, sometimes in good numbers.

Go through the kissing-gate and walk along the Cob, watching the salt-marsh on the right and the extensive Malltraeth Pool, fringed with vegetation, on the left. Many duck come here, especially in winter, while in summer shelduck and mallard breed. Migrant waders use the pool, with both species of godwit, greenshank, ruff and spotted redshank sometimes numerous.

The salt-marsh and the bay have large flocks of oystercatcher throughout the year, while all five species of breeding tern occur offshore – the rare roseate tern is particularly worthy of mention, because the colony just north up the coast on offshore islands is the largest in Britain. Sandwich and little terns have colonies nearby and often fish inshore.

It is possible to walk on round the forest path, but on reaching the large sallow clumps near the end of the Cob, return and collect your car, watching the marsh-lands for ravens which are numerous here, and in winter hen harriers, short-eared owls and barn owls and other birds of prey. This is an especially good spot for barn owls at dusk, when two or three may hunt the marsh.

Drive the car back a mile towards the forest and park on the right by the footpath sign. Follow the muddy path through the pines and along the back of the salt-marsh. This is actually dune soil and you will see that already plants such as creeping willow occur along the path; there are excellent views from here across the salt-marsh of the Cefni Estuary. Several thousand waders, oystercatchers, curlew, godwit, dunlin and redshank feed on the mudflats, except in midsummer. Above the dark canopy of pines the deep calls of raven are a constant sound, while lower down, goldcrests and coal tits forage for insects. A mile round the track an observation tower gives splendid views right across the wide estuarine flats.

Where the salt-marsh reaches the lime-rich dune sand, a rich fen vegetation exists, in a thin strip just out from the dunes, with quantities of yellow flag, meadowsweet and water-mint. Sedge and grasshopper warblers occur here in summer, while autumn brings a rich flush of fungi along the wood edge.

Return to Newborough village and turn right at the second crossroads just past the garage, signposted to Trearth and Llanddwyn Beach. As you enter the forest a ticket-machine eats your £1 coin to entitle you to car-parking space at the road's end. A mile of good Forestry Commission access road, lined with yellow evening primroses and crossed by hump-backed 'sleeping policemen', takes you slowly to the large car-park, complete with toilets and forest walks information, carefully hidden behind the dune ridge. Go through the cutting directly onto the beach and turn right, round a lovely dune- and forest-fringed bay towards the rocky headland of Ynys Llanddwyn.

Waders hunt the strand line on the sandy beach; little flocks of sanderling with twinkling feet rush after each receding wave; turnstones and oystercatchers flick the seaweed, while ringed plover and dunlin probe the firm sands. From a distance the headland looks like an island, but two rocky bluffs at the gap together with the high storm beach mean that the walk is still easy, and that an island only occurs on the highest tides.

The headland, largely covered in bracken and rising to some 50 feet (15m), is composed of Pre-Cambrian rock over 600 million years old, some of the oldest rock in Britain. Rocky islets at the far end by the squat white lighthouse have breeding groups of shag and cormorant, while the grassy top is covered with blue spring squill in April. It is a good place for birds in winter, with turnstone and purple sandpiper on the rocks, while divers and rare grebes are frequently seen offshore.

Return to Newborough and drive east to the little roundabout, turning sharp right towards the 'dead end'; this is actually the national nature reserve entrance, and there is a tiny car-park. An adjacent grove of willows screens a hide and the large fresh-water lake of Llyn Rhos-ddu – this has dense fen vegetation and a variety of waterfowl, including, surprisingly, ruddy duck, great crested grebe, dabchick, mallard, coot and moorhen all breed in the dense stands of yellow flag.

From the car-park, a footpath runs towards the distant shore along the fence, past several experimental grazing enclosures and stolid penned sheep. Since the crash of the rabbit population it is essential to graze the dunes correctly to prevent scrub invasion.

The flowers which grow along this damp dune path are very varied, with creeping willow, ox-eye daisy, yellow rattle, silverweed and many more. Turn left after some 600 yards (548m), through a new kissing-gate, and take the clearly marked path through a second gate into the line of dunes. The path cuts into the dunes by the red-painted fire-beaters, a good signpost.

And now, the variety of flowers is simply staggering. June and July must be the best months for colour, with thousands of marsh helleborines and marsh orchids in the damp slacks, and the extraordinarily rare dune helleborine on the drier sandy slopes. All summer long brings carpets of thyme, eyebright, trefoils, vetches, rest harrow, ladies' bedstraw, dune pansy and dozens more. Late summer and early autumn fill the dune slacks with the waxy white flowers of grass of Parnassus, along

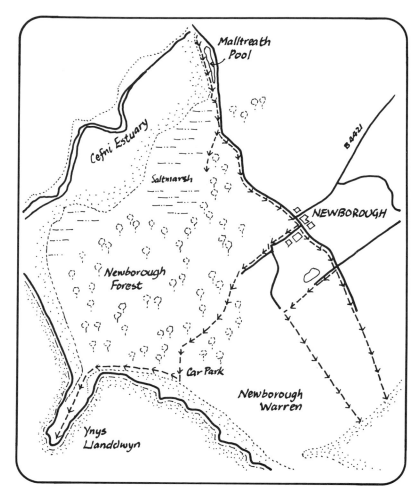

with millions of the formerly rare round-leaved wintergreen in spiky white carpets between the covering of creeping willow. A wide and colourful variety of fungi appears from mid-September onwards.

Birds breeding in the dunes in summer include shelduck, which nest down rabbit holes; lapwing, curlew, oystercatcher and ringed plover in the dune slacks; and skylarks and meadow pipits in the marram tufts. Small numbers of herring gulls also breed in the outer dunes. Watch the fence-posts here for hunting barn or short-eared owls and kestrels.

Back at the roundabout turn right again to another little car-park, and take the path which is clearly marked by white-topped posts out through dune slacks and ridges towards the Menai Strait. The salt-marsh of the Braint estuary is spread out before you from the top of the dune ridges, and across the Strait lies Caernarfon Castle, a magnificent backdrop. The dune flora is quite superb, there will be dozens to see: bee orchids, fairy flax, carline thistle, felwort, autumn gentian and viper's bugloss. Butterflies abound in summer with Common Blue and Dark Green Fritillary particularly abundant.

This is a fragile earth – please keep to the footpaths.

The rare and beautiful grass of Parnassus is found in profusion in the dunes of Newborough Warren

The Ribble Estuary

LANCASHIRE

46

Address of Site/Warden

National Nature Reserve:
Warden:
Old Hollow Farm,
Banks,
Southport,
Merseyside PR9 8DU .

Highlights and Features

Summer. Large numbers breeding redshank. Good displays salt-marsh flowers and also marsh orchids. Prime winter site with huge flocks waders and pinkfooted geese.

Facilities

None, although nearby Southport has full holiday facilities. Access at all times to sea-walls.

Photo Tips

Flowers may be good in summer. Use wide-angled zoom 28–70mm and tripod. Winter: birds all at distances but flocks very large, so may get pictures with long lenses.

Oystercatchers use their dagger-like bill to open shellfish, such as cockles and mussels, on which they feed

The Ribble river runs into the Irish Sea between Blackpool and Liverpool, creating a wide, sandy estuary backed by a flat flood plain managed largely as farmland. However, the southern shore of the estuary has been set aside as a national nature reserve of some 5,700 acres (2,306ha) and fresh grazing marsh nearby provides winter wildfowl feeding areas. The Ribble is an estuary of international importance for wildfowl and waders, supporting one of the largest wintering and migrant populations in Britain.

A tour and wildlife walk along the southern shore is described, which includes the national nature reserve, and a short car tour along the northern shore gives you the chance to see additional bird species. It should be noted that shooting is traditional along the marsh from 1 September to 20 February, controlled by the Nature Conservancy Council by licence to the local wildfowling club. Access along public footpaths, sea-walls and paths in the nature reserve is unrestricted, except for the salt-marsh study zone opposite Old Hollow Farm, and Hesketh Out Marsh.

The southern shore is only six miles from the Wildfowl Trust reserve at Martin Mere, and bird populations may use both areas for feeding and roosting. Autumn and winter are the best seasons to visit.

Southern Shore Tour

On the A565 in Southport turn into Marine Drive at the Plough Inn roundabout. Drive two miles west towards Southport Pier as far as the Marine Lake, watching the marshes and estuary for concentrations of birds. Pinpoint these and then return along Marine Drive, parking wherever you can – otherwise use the Sand Depot, half-way along the drive, and return on foot to view the wildfowl already noted. This road is a 'freeway' – it is also a real switchback, although it appears flat, with tarmac laid on sand, so *take care*.

A rising tide is best here as the low tide line may be two miles away. The vast expanse of sand in the estuary provides a feeding ground for thousands of waders from early August through till late spring. At low tide in winter, large flocks of pinkfooted geese may roost on Horse Bank Sands, but go to feed on the extensive grazing fields between Marine Drive and the town.

At high tide the movement of waders here is remarkable, with upwards of 100,000 birds airborne in the estuary looking for roosting sites. Throughout the winter 70,000 knot, 20,000 dunlin, 10,000 oystercatchers, and 5,000 mixed curlew and bar-tailed godwit are found here, with smaller numbers of grey and ringed plover, and redshank.

Pinkfooted geese may peak at 20,000 although 10,000 are more usual; up to 200 Bewick's swans use the freshmarshes for feeding but sometimes move to Crossens Marsh across Marine Drive.

At high tide, winter duck are the most obvious with an internationally important flock of 4,000 pintail, usually in company with 15,000 wigeon and teal. Sea-duck offshore include 500 common scoter with small numbers of velvet scoter; goldeneye and red-breasted merganser are often numerous and divers, in particular red-throated, can usually be seen in small numbers in the estuary.

Autumn brings migrant stints and sandpipers, often along the ditches of the freshmarsh, with golden plover on the wetter fields. In late autumn there are enormous numbers of seabirds moving south down the Irish Sea, and westerly gales can bring large flocks into the estuary, especially at high tide. Thousands of kittiwakes, with a scattering of little gulls, skuas and even petrels are then usual.

An extensive walk is possible on the national nature reserve, and again, it is preferable to choose a rising tide in winter. Tide-time is less important in summer for seeing the breeding birds and marsh flowers.

Marine Drive ends at the Plough Inn roundabout. Turn left towards Banks and after 400 yards (365m) park opposite the Crossens Pumping Station (but do *not* block the gates!). A stile and a public footpath lead out onto the sea-wall where there are extensive freshmarsh fields contained within, and the 'greenmarsh' (summer-grazed salt-marsh) on the seaward side. There are high-tide wader roosts here and keep an eye out for hunting harriers and peregrines which are frequently about.

The sea-wall extends for fully five miles (8km) from Crossens Pumping Station round Banks Marsh and back to the road at Hundred End, two miles north of Banks village. It is equally possible to drive to Hundred End through Banks village and walk in the reverse direction – the time of day and the quality of light and shadow determines the best route, so as to avoid silhouettes of bird flocks against the sky.

In early summer the spring migrants hurry through, swelling the slowly departing winter flocks to a peak of over 100,000 birds again. The marsh of the national nature reserve now becomes an important breeding site – from April till July 7–8,000 pairs of black-headed gulls and 100 pairs of common tern nest in the marshes. Although the gulls are obviously the dominant feature, there are also 200 pairs of breeding redshank.

Most of the reserve is grazed deliberately to produce the best conditions for wintering birds. However, part of Crossens Marsh is fenced to conserve the saltmarsh plants that are destroyed elsewhere by the grazing cattle. A full range of such plants can therefore be studied, including sea-aster, thrift, sea-purslane, seablite, orache and sea arrowgrass. From the Crossens Marsh sea-wall it is possible to walk out into this carpet of colour, provided care is taken to avoid the nesting birds. Many insects are attracted to these plants, especially Tortoiseshell and various 'brown' butterflies.

Old Hollow Farm, two miles round the sea-wall from the pumping station, is the reserve office. Nearby, and usually accessible, are several carefully grazed meadows, which in late May and June are ablaze with thousands of early and southern marsh orchids.

Northern Shore

The northern shoreline is much more urbanised than its opposite bank. Blackpool Tower dominates the skyline to the northwest. From Blackpool and its hordes of tourists the main road swings south past holiday camps and all the trappings of a 'sea-side holiday', towards the beach town of Lytham St Annes.

On a cold winter's day when the holiday-makers are long gone, the sands which stretch from Squire's Gate three miles south to Lytham hold thousands of waders: amongst these the 3,000 sanderling and 2,000 black-tailed godwit are of particular note, though in autumn additional migrants may double these totals – 4,000 black-tailed godwits would represent the largest flock in Britain. The marine drive along the shore from Squire's Gate to Church Scar rocks gives unrivalled views of the estuary. Sea-watching on a high tide is best from the westernmost tip, the beach-shelter by Pontins Holiday Camp!

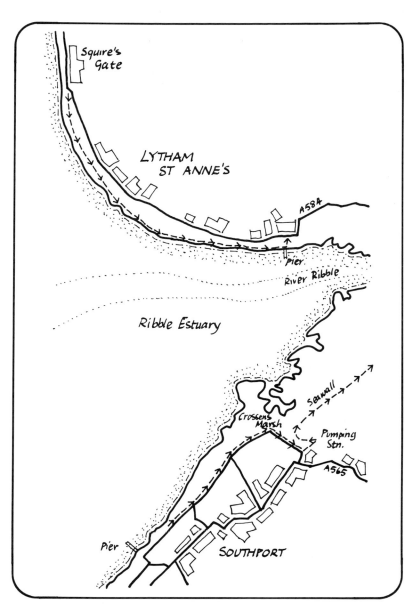

Pinkfooted geese fly daily to and from the estuary to roost

47

Morecambe Bay
LANCASHIRE AND CUMBRIA

Address of Site/Warden

Part is RSPB Reserve:
c/o The Warden:
Leighton Moss Reserve,
Myers Farm,
Silverdale,
Carnforth,
Lancs LA5 0SW

Highlights and Features

Vast area of sand-banks and mud-flats at low tide. Most important area for wintering waders in Britain with up to 300,000. Many high-tide roosts which are best places to see them, otherwise scattered over 120 square miles (310sq km) of mud. Large flocks wildfowl which attract birds of prey in winter.

Facilities

Two hides near Carnforth belong to the RSPB. Open at all times.

Photo Tips

High-tide roosts provide splendid pictures of massed flights of waders. Use long telephoto lenses. High-tide times essential.

A solitary lapwing on a salt-marsh pool, the very spirit of the wild marshlands

This huge estuary between the Cumbrian hills and the populous Lancashire coast is the largest and finest site in Britain, especially for wintering waders. Nearly a quarter of a million use its wide expanses of sand from September through to March. On a clear day the extent of Morecambe Bay is best seen from one of its northern hills – Arnside Knott, towering some 520 feet (158m) above the shore, gives commanding views. Far to the west lie the cranes of the Barrow shipyards, south the low shores to Morecambe's promenade, east the shining Kent river with its long viaduct, and north the Lakeland hills appear in serried ranks.

The bay is made up of the estuaries of the Wyre, Lune, Keer, Kent and Leven rivers. At high tide, especially in bad weather, the bay becomes part of the Irish Sea with waves thundering up the pebble beaches; at low tide 120 square miles (310sq km) of sand and silt lie exposed, while the channels of these five main rivers meander through the glistening sand-banks. Apart from the obvious mussel beds, the birds feed on a tremendous density of invertebrate life in the seemingly empty sands. Around the bay are the limestone hills of Silverdale and Grange, themselves wildlife sites of great importance with a wealth of flowers and insects (see pp 46 and 47).

June and July are the quietest times, with breeding birds on the surrounding marshes and the winter flocks absent; August sees a growing influx of migrants and by October a quarter of Britain's wading birds may be present on this one bay.

One wildlife tour is described taking in the most important access and vantage points. Timing is absolutely vital here: fortnightly spring high tides are best – at low tide all the birds will be seven miles (11km) away at the sea edge. A round tour of all the best sites involves nearly a hundred miles of driving!

Morecambe Bay Tour

From Knott End-on-Sea at the north of the River Wyre a footpath runs east along the sea-wall for three miles to Fluke Hall, where another car-park makes the walk reversible. A large high-tide wader roost usually occurs on the salt-marshes, near Fluke Hall.

Further north beyond Cockerham a narrow lane from Thurnham heads westward for two miles; a footpath then follows the shore south to Cockersand Point and the rocks of Plover Scar where there is a high-tide wader roost and concentrations of scoter, eider and merganser on the mussel beds at high tide. This is the mouth of the River Lune and large numbers of terns gather here in August and September – several hundred little terns are often present. As the waders are forced off the sands by the rising tide, birds also gather on the Middleton salt-marshes on the opposite bank of the River Lune.

Drive north on the A5105 coast road through Heysham and Morecambe; Heysham harbour, though not very picturesque itself, frequently has purple sandpiper and turnstone on the rocks, especially north to Half-Moon Bay. Autumnal gales drive sea-birds onto this north-facing coastline, when kittiwakes, little gulls and skuas may appear; Leach's petrel can be numerous in really bad weather.

At Hest Bank there is a huge high-tide roost on the salt-marsh from August through to April. Cross the railway line at the level-crossing and park on the foreshore, which is the southernmost tip of the RSPB Carnforth reserve. Footpaths lead along the back of the marsh north to Wild Duck Hall, but by far the best view, sometimes encompassing as many as 100,000 birds, is to be had by the car-park: packs of oystercatcher, dunlin, curlew, redshank, bar-tailed godwit, turnstone and ringed plover gather here in whirling 'clouds'. Grey-lag geese, pintail, wigeon, mallard and shelduck also occur in some numbers in winter, and these roosts inevitably attract peregrines, merlins and harriers – a peregrine 'beating up' the shore will put all 100,000 birds into the sky together.

Take the minor road from Carnforth north towards Silverdale, and at Crag Foot take the track under the railway bridge to a small RSPB car-park. Here two hides have been placed alongside newly constructed pools, the Allen Pool and the Eric Morecambe Pool where a wide variety of waders may be seen, often at close range. Shingle islands have breeding black-headed gulls, oystercatchers and ringed plover, and a few terns in summer.

The lower Kent estuary is best viewed from the promenade at Arnside, a pretty village backed by the high limestone woods of Arnside Knott and there is a footpath which leads west along the shore to Blackstone Point. A huge gull roost occupies the estuary off Arnside, while the main Kent channel runs near the road. Good views of feeding waders, herons and wildfowl may be obtained, even at low tide.

The northern shore of the Kent estuary can be seen best from Kents Bank. Just north of the station on the coast road there is a footpath signposted 'To Promenade and Grange', which runs for two miles right along the coast; for part of the way it is sheltered by high garden walls and affords superb views.

A mile or two further on, the narrow road to Humphrey Head runs out onto the foreshore, west of Kents Bank. A footpath runs along the back of the shore to Out Marsh where there is a medium-sized wader roost. Humphrey Head itself has a North Yorkshire County Council Field Centre – you can take a footpath which leads onto the 150-foot (45m) high limestone headland, superb for limestone flowers in summer. The view from the Head, which juts a mile into the bay, is quite marvellous.

The last of the five minor estuaries to be examined is that of the River Leven, best viewed from Park Head, west of Holker Park and one mile north of Flookborough. There is an RAC caravan site in Old Park Wood, but this is unobtrusive and does not spoil the view. The Holker Estate has provided a little car-park by the shore. A track goes south towards the sea-wall and the Severn Viaduct for half a mile, providing excellent views. Purple sandpipers may be found in the rocky areas in winter.

Beyond Ulverston the A5087 runs along the shore, or near it, for several miles. Good access points are Bardsea Country Park, by the Old Mill Inn, and a footpath north for half a mile along the shore to Wadhead Scar. The mussel beds here attract numbers of common scoter, eider, scaup and velvet scoter in winter. A wader roost also occurs here.

Four miles farther south at Newbiggin the road again runs along the shore, and a high-tide wader roost is visible from the roadside. Winter brings small numbers of red-throated divers into the Leven estuary.

The western tip of Morecambe Bay culminates in Walney Island, west and south of the industrial town and dockyards of Barrow-in-Furness (see pp 185). In summer the Cumbria Naturalists' Trust reserve has huge colonies of herring and lesser black-backed gulls, easily studied

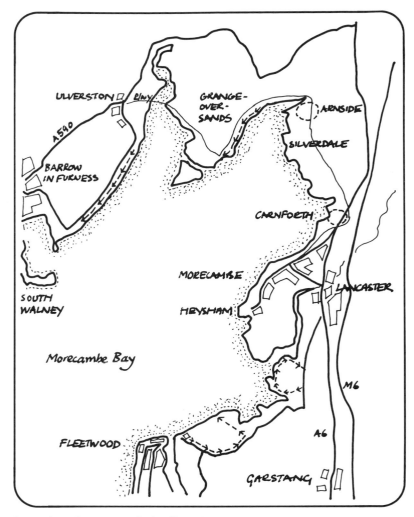

from the observation hide. Passage is exciting in spring and autumn with a variety of rare birds.

For steam-train buffs the Cumbria and Furness Railway runs regular services with LNER stock across the viaducts of the bay, to Barrow, affording superlative views of wader flocks at high tide.

The noisy, piebald oystercatchers gather in large flocks as high tide fills the estuaries

Lindisfarne

NORTHUMBERLAND

48

Address of Site/Warden

National Nature Reserve
Warden:
Tel: Belford 386

Highlights and Features

Dunes, salt-marshes and mudflats with large flocks waders and wildfowl in winter. Good populations of breeding waders and terns in summer.
Dune flowers and salt-marsh flowers very good, best mid-June.

Facilities

Small information office open intermittently. Nearby Holy Isle has usual tourist facilities. Good car-park places provide good views.

Photo Tips

Long lenses should give good pictures of winter flocks of geese and wildfowl. Since there are no hides use car as hide. Flowers in summer need wide-angle zoom lens.

Migrant sanderling patter across the Lindisfarne sands with twinkling feet

Along the wild Northumberland coast the dunes, salt-marshes and mudflats are some of the finest in Britain, together making up a national nature reserve which stretches from Goswick Sands in the north to Budle Bay in the south. This is one of the world's special places; this is Lindisfarne, the Holy Isle, where the historical and religious associations are strong. In 634 AD St Aidan founded the first monastery in a setting of peace and isolation; this was destroyed by Viking invasions in the eighth and ninth centuries, and was only restored to a full religious community by the conquest of England by the Norman kings.

The island's most famous resident was St Cuthbert who, finding Holy Island too busy, left to live on the Farne Islands. One wonders what he might think about it now!

The area is full of wildlife interest throughout the year, but as a late autumn and winter site for waders, wildfowl and migrants it must rate as one of Britain's best.

One wildlife tour is described, part by car and part on foot. The walking is easy but winter is best for wildlife, when it can be uncompromisingly cold.

Wildlife Tour: Lindisfarne

Turn east from the A1 at the Plough Hotel onto a minor road signposted to Beal and Holy Island – the Scottish border is only a few miles north, at Berwick. The road goes for two miles through farm fields and the little village of Beal before running out onto the flats of Lindisfarne, with the causeway to the Holy Isle, crossing a huge area of inter-tidal mud and sand, straight ahead. The notice by the roadside is unique: 'This bridge is totally submerged at high tide'. You have been warned! Despite this one or two unwary motorists get an involuntary bath each year, and how St Cuthbert would laugh to see the motor-car turned back by nature's power. Tide-tables are posted, and it is quite safe to cross three hours either side of low water. Tourists flock to Holy Isle in summer and it becomes very crowded, with queues of cars crossing the causeway.

The first site across the causeway is the Snook, an area of marram-covered dunes. The road runs along the inner foreshore and it is a simple matter to park and walk, a good spot being on the 'bulge' near the nature reserve sign. In summer the area is a mass of flowers, with many acres of salt-marsh along the roadside covered in pink thrift and white scurvy grass, providing good cover for breeding redshank, lapwing and oystercatcher.

From the reserve sign walk into the dunes, being careful to stick to paths, even if these are only rabbit tracks. The lime-rich flora is particularly good in mid-summer, with dense clumps of brilliant bird's-foot trefoil, viper's bugloss and houndstongue. Damp dune slacks grow masses of prostrate creeping willow, grass of Parnassus, and a superb show of orchids such as marsh helleborine, spotted orchid, early and northern marsh orchids.

Hundreds of rabbits occupy these dunes and are thriving since they are relatively isolated from the mainland, although foxes have been seen crossing the causeway and even hedgehogs appear with surprising frequency.

Common, Arctic, roseate and little terns breed around the undisturbed beach areas and on the island of Black Law, fishing the shallows at high tide.

Half a mile's walk across the Snook to the sea and you will probably be able to see grey seals that have hauled themselves out of the water onto Goswick Sands.

From this same car-park spot on the Snook in winter the only tourists will probably be bird-watchers who have come to enjoy the dramatic sight of huge flocks of wildfowl and whirling clouds of waders thronging the mudflats. Although a tour round the area is obviously well worthwhile, just pause and count the species visible from here.

Internationally important flocks of dunlin (50,000), knot (20,000) and bar-tailed godwit (5,000) use the flats, with rather smaller flocks of grey and ringed plover and lapwing, while golden plover are numerous in the farm fields. Wigeon peak at 40,000, making this their most important coastal site in Britain, while other dabbling ducks – shelduck, teal, mallard – total several thousand. You may see up to 500 whooper swans which would be England's largest group, with Bewick's swans joining them but in smaller numbers. Britain's largest flock of pale-bellied brent geese winter on the flats, up to 2,000 dependent upon the severity of the weather.

This huge assembly of birds of course attracts predators with peregrine, merlin, short-eared owl and hen harrier making frequent appearances. And in the depths of winter, all this variety and movement may be visible from this one observation spot.

Continue to Holy Isle village, jammed with people in summer but almost deserted on a cold December day. In summer a few fulmars nest on the walls of the Priory and also four miles south at Bamburgh Castle, but winter wildfowl appear in great rafts offshore. Footpaths lead from the village car-park at Sandham Lane and take you the mile to Emmanuel Head, where you can sit by the obelisk and watch the restless waves.

Red-throated divers and Slavonian grebes are often numerous offshore although black-throated divers and red-necked grebes are less usual. Cormorant, shag and large flocks of red-breasted merganser, eider, long-tailed duck and common scoter are often present in winter.

Walk down to Sandham Bay where you can watch groups of snow-white sanderlings as they rush to and fro at the tide's edge. Return across the causeway, ensuring you have allowed time for the tide. A footpath along the inner shore allows good views for late afternoon light, and you might appreciate the anti-tank barricade from the last war which provides at least a modicum of shelter in cold easterly winds.

Continue south down the A1; minor roads will take you to the shore either at Fenham (after a mile) or at Fenham-le-Moor (after two miles). The next easiest access is at Ross: from the A1 turn east on a minor road to Elwick and Grange, and then fork left to Ross, a tiny hamlet around Ross Farm. Park on the left-hand side of the lane where there is a public footpath allowing access to the shore; this runs directly from the end of the lane and then across Ross Links – the latter are strictly private farmland.

Two long shelter belts of conifers have been planted to run north-south across the links for over a mile – these are strictly private, but can be seen from the path. Harriers, owls, falcons and sparrowhawks use the edges for hunting, while migrants seek food and shelter in the trees.

The path reaches the shore within a mile and then runs in both directions overlooking Ross Back Sands. Four thousand grey-lag geese use the fields in winter and a few pinkfeet are usually found with them. The beach always attracts snow buntings in winter with a

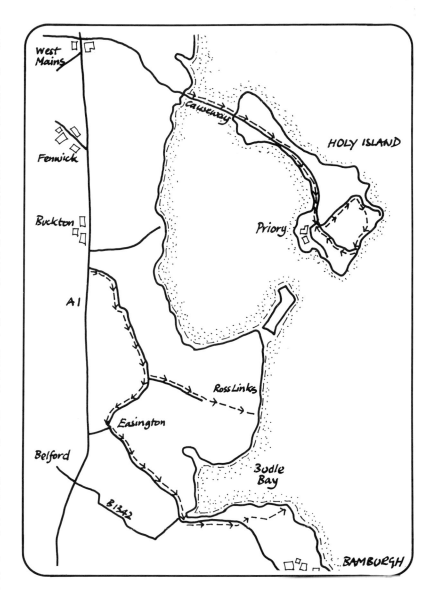

regular 2–300, although their travelling companions Lapland buntings and shore larks are quite rare. Divers, grebes and many sea-duck can be seen offshore.

Drive south for about three miles through Easington and you will come to the large tidal inlet of Budle Bay, with the B1342 running from Waren Mill along its southern shore. Footpaths run to the shore from the Mill, Heather Cottages and across Budle Golf Course to Budle Point. This is a fine sea-watching spot and also provides good views of the bay. If there is any shooting on the Lindisfarne flats in winter, Budle Bay can act as sanctuary for thousands of wildfowl. Passage sea-birds in late autumn include large numbers of the common species including gannets, auks, terns and kittiwakes, along with numerous arctic skuas and small parties of great and pomarine skuas. Autumnal east winds can quite often drive large falls of migrant land-birds – chats, warblers and flycatchers – into all the bushes for shelter.

Marsh orchids grow in profusion in the protected Lindisfarne dunes

49

The Solway
DUMFRIES AND GALLOWAY

Address of Site/Warden

The Wildfowl Trust,
Eastpark Farm,
Caerlaverock,
Dumfriesshire DG1 4RS
National Nature Reserve
Warden:
Tadorna,
Hollands Farm Road,
Caerlaverock,
Dumfriesshire

Highlights and Features

Superb winter site for
wildfowl. Large flocks of
barnacle geese are main
speciality.
Colony of natterjack toads in
summer along with marsh
orchids but site normally
closed.

Facilities

Excellent information centre
and many hides at Eastpark
Farm. Nature Conservancy
Council has tower hide here
too.
Eastpark open daily
mid-September to late April
from 0930 to 1700

Photo Tips

Superb site for close views
of large flocks geese, ducks
and wild swans in winter.
Lenses from 200mm and
larger will provide pictures.
Use the many hides.
Remember to compensate
for the bright sky when
taking pictures of flocks of
geese in the air.

The Solway Estuary is internationally famous as the wintering grounds for huge numbers of northern wildfowl. Each winter the entire population of barnacle geese from Spitzbergen arrives in late September and stays till late March or even April. Two major nature reserves now provide protection for these geese, and also for a wide variety of other marshland birds, animals and flowers. The whole of the northern shore of the Solway is a 'green marsh', or grazed salt-marsh – locally it is known as a 'merse'.

There are several major habitats here, including the estuary at high tide, the 'merse', the mudflats and farmland. The national nature reserve covers 13,593 acres (5,490ha) of 'merse' and mudflats between the River Nith and Lochar Water. In the middle of this (but not part of it) the Wildfowl Trust has a reserve of 1,495 acres (604ha) which provides superb facilities for birdwatching.

One wildlife tour of the area is described, by car and on foot. The whole area is an excellent wildlife site at all seasons but winter visits will provide you with a wildlife spectacular.

Wildlife Tour: Solway North Shore
The best place to begin is undoubtedly the Wildfowl Trust reserve at Eastpark. At Bankend, where the stream has dipper and grey wagtail by the little humpback bridge, take the tiny road – well signposted – one mile south of the village. Hedges and trees here are severely windpruned, bearing away from the south-west gales.

At Eastpark Farm, excellent facilities are available for visitors, and it is comparable to Martin Mere and the Ouse Washes, as well as Slimbridge, all Wildfowl Trust reserves. Some of the ground is leased from the Caerlaverock Estate and some is wholly owned by the Trust.

An observation tower is built into the farm itself. Folly Pool, between the tower and the marsh, is being extended in area and is therefore not yet established, but Whooper Pool, behind the tower and directly overlooked by the observatory, is a mature lake with much pondside vegetation. This one pool may hold up to eighteen species of wildfowl in winter. A 'swan pipe' just to the left of the observatory is used to catch and ring the

wildfowl, especially the growing numbers of whooper and Bewick's swans that winter here. Peak counts on this pool have been 220 whooper swans, 60 Bewick's swans and 50 mute swans; ducks include large numbers of wigeon, teal and pintail with as many as 1,000 of each directly in front of the hide.

The Trust's reserve is normally closed from 1 May to 16 September but midsummer fills the fields round Whooper Pool with hundreds of northern marsh orchids. Redshank, lapwing, snipe, oystercatcher and yellow wagtail all breed in the marshlands.

A little further along the meadow from the observatory is Teal Pool, reached by a well screened path and served by a small hide; goosander fish this pool in winter, and ducks and geese crop the meadow behind.

Two well screened paths lead from the farm – the main track runs for half a mile between banks lined with a dense sycamore and hawthorn hedge to a two-storey enclosed scaffolding tower. Sparrowhawks from the nearby conifer plantations hunt this ride regularly for chaffinches and buntings. The scaffold tower is supplemented by many small hides built into the 'merse' banks, and the tower itself provides an all-round view across wet 'flood' fields out to the slightly higher ground of the sea-wall. These fields are especially good for golden plover and lapwing in winter, when a thousand or more of each may be present.

Scan the drier tussock grass 300 yards (274m) beyond the tower: it is a good spot to see hunting short-eared owls and to appreciate the gorse of the sea-wall, and excellent for observing hunting hen harriers – there is a roost of harriers, with up to fourteen birds, near the reserve; most of these are 'grey' males.

These marsh fields hold geese from mid-September onwards. Peak numbers in 1986 were 10,400 barnacle geese and nearly 10,000 pinkfooted geese, the latter coming mainly from Iceland. Even if the winter weather over the rest of Scotland is severe, the Solway often escapes a heavy snow cover. Goose numbers may then rise dramatically – there was a peak of 35,000 pinkfeet counted in 1984. 500 grey-lag geese also use the area and small numbers of most other British geese appear. Snow goose is the most frequent rarity but confusion reigns when albino barnacle geese appear, several of which come with the winter flocks. A barnacle/emperor goose hybrid has caused great excitement when mistaken as a 'blue snow goose'.

Return towards the farm and turn left between high banks to the NCC observation tower on the edge of the tidal salt-marsh. Pools dug round here house a colony of the nationally rare natterjack toad – these have in fact spread to many of the Wildfowl Trust pools, and are easy to hear croaking in spring but much more difficult to see.

Mammal stars are roe deer which feed in the meadows, having emerged from the conifer woods nearby; and otters which live along the wild Solway coast in small numbers – you need luck to see an otter.

The NCC tower provides superb views over both freshmarsh fields and the tidal salt-marshes. Very high tides push huge flocks of waders right up to roost below the tower: 10,000 oystercatchers, 2,000 dunlin and several hundred curlew and bar-tailed godwit are quite usual. These huge flocks of birds attract other raptors. Peregrines, which breed in the Galloway hills, are frequent so watch the tops of posts and gates. Some old bits of rusted war-time iron lie just offshore in the mud and peregrines often sit on these. Merlins are regular, and one uses the top of the NCC tower as a 'bird-watching' look-out point.

Eastpark will no doubt have provided you with a surfeit of winter birds, but good views may also be obtained from a number of other sites. The B725 continues round the coast past Caerlaverock Castle; a car-park with a picnic table is

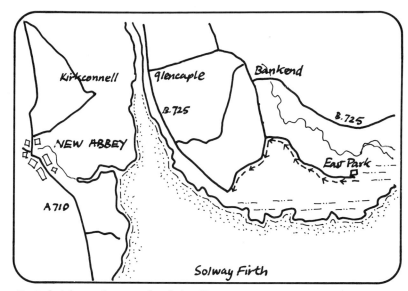

situated right at the mouth of the River Nith overlooking the 'merse' and the mudflats of Blackshaw Bank, and good views of large flocks of geese passing up and down the estuary may be obtained from here.

On the opposite bank of the Nith, at Carsethorn, sea-duck occur in winter with upwards of 500 scaup and 100 red-breasted mergansers. Drive down to the coast and scan the inshore waters at high tide – there might be a few common scoter, with a scattering of red- and black-throated divers. The shoreline is rocky and often holds turnstone and purple sand-piper.

Further north the road runs next to the river towards Glencaple where the river is still 150 yards wide (136m) and tidal. Whooper swans and pinkfeet feed on the marsh fields of Kirkonnell Merse opposite the village.

The Solway holds over 10,000 barnacle geese throughout the winter months

50

The Ythan Estuary and the Sands of Forvie
GRAMPIAN

Address of Site/Warden

National Nature Reserve Warden:
Little Collieston Croft,
Collieston,
Ellon,
Aberdeenshire

Highlights and Features

Summer – thousands of pairs of eider ducks, Sandwich and common terns. Many dune flowers. Winter – good estuary for wildfowl and waders.

Facilities

Reserve area open at all times. Information centre at Collieston open during summer unless warden elsewhere on reserve. A hide is open during the summer to watch the terns, which can be fickle and move elsewhere.

Photo Tips

Medium telephoto lens, 200mm or more will provide good shots of eider and ducklings in summer. Terns are further away and easier elsewhere.

The Ythan Estuary on the Aberdeenshire coast is famous for its terns, its salmon and its eider ducks

'The eider duck capital of Britain' is how the Sands of Forvie National Nature Reserve is known to many. In spring 6,000 eider congregate here to breed, making this by far the largest breeding colony in the country.

Forvie, however, is much more than an eider nursery. It is the fifth largest sand-dune system in Britain, and the one least disturbed by man. Because of its huge populations of breeding birds, superb wintering grounds for wildfowl and exceptional botanical interest it was one of the first national nature reserves, declared in 1959; the Ythan Estuary was added in 1979.

Forvie is a wild place where natural forces reign supreme, in total contrast to the miles of surrounding reclaimed farmland. It is easily accessible, most of the walks are on level ground and it is well worth a visit at any time of the year. It is absolutely essential to keep to the footpaths, especially in summer to avoid disturbance. One wildlife walk is described with notes on the roadside views of the estuary. Forvie Visitor Centre is on the B9003 at Collieston and should be visited for information.

Wildlife Walk

Newburgh, on the A975 ten miles north of Aberdeen, lies on the southern shore of the River Ythan. Cross the river at Waterside Bridge (a new bridge is under construction, as at late 1987) and park immediately on the north side. There are excellent views of a long stretch of the estuary which for most of its five-mile (8km) length is only 300 yards (274m) wide, and filled with mud- and sand-flats at low tide. Just to the north is the Sleek of Tarty, where the river has a 600 yard (548m) wide bulge with a tiny island, Inch Geck, in the middle. This can be viewed easily from the road or by re-crossing the bridge on foot and walking along the west bank for half a mile. A high-tide roost of waders uses the island.

There are always eider in the river, together with shelduck and in winter, groups of goldeneye and red-breasted merganser. The common waders breed, especially oystercatchers and small numbers of greenshank, and spotted redshank, ruff, black-tailed godwit and sandpipers pass through regularly whilst migrating in spring and autumn.

From the car-park walk south along the track on the east side of the river. A brake of mixed 'new' woodland, some trees fifteen feet (4.5m) high, has been planted to provide cover and wind shelter, and to the north along the main road several small plantations are already established. Look for migrants in the bushes in spring and autumn after south-east winds.

At the end of this 'new' plantation a wide track leads to the left, to 'Forvie Church and the beach'; this is known as the Rockend Track and cuts across the centre of the reserve. Continue along the river bank through the kissing-gate. It is possible to drive to the main reserve sign some 500 yards from the car-park but there is only space on the grassy bank for six cars and the estuary is much used by fishermen.

Vast areas of heather and gorse stretch away east. Hundreds of eider breed here, and in midsummer will be found escorting their broods of little chocolate-coloured ducklings for their first swim. Large 'crêches' gather on the river. The population falls in winter to about 1,000 birds, but studies here have shown that eider are quite long-lived and many may reach twenty years of age. Stonechats breed in the gorse while wheatear and shelduck use old rabbit burrows.

Almost straightaway the path runs into the huge sand-dune system. Several large dunes overlook the estuary, and fulmars will often sit in ledges in the marram grass and fly past a few feet from you down the bank. Over the heather dozens of great black-backed and herring gulls, and crows too, hang about waiting to pounce on unguarded eider eggs. Don't stray from the footpath and add to their kill.

In June, the path through the dunes is bordered by thousands of tiny blue and yellow wild pansies. The dunes may reach 60 feet (18m) high in places, with notable 'slacks' of damp vegetation between – there is always a fine show of trefoils, violets and flax.

A stepped boardwalk penetrates the dunes for 300 yards (274m) and then divides along a boundary fence – this is to protect the huge tern breeding colony. The right-hand track leads to an observation hide which usually overlooks the terns, but the winds move the mobile

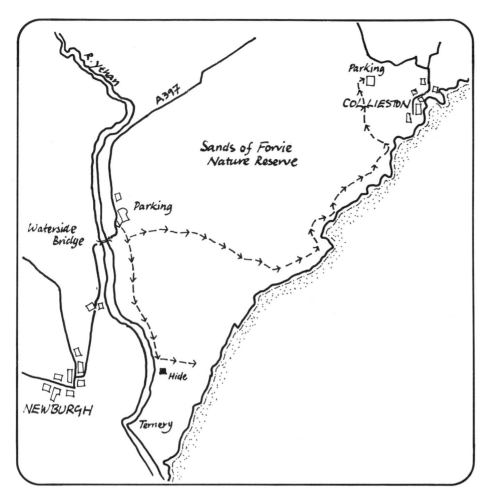

dunes around over the winter months, and sometimes the birds nest elsewhere in the system. Up to 2,000 pairs of Sandwich terns breed here, with rather fewer common and Arctic terns, but some 50 pairs of the rare little tern are also present. All these terns fish the waters of the river from time to time.

Return from the hide to the Rockend Track. In winter large numbers of wildfowl occur from October onwards: 10,000 pinkfeet and grey-lag geese appear in autumn and many stay for the winter, feeding on the estuary and the local farmland. 250 whooper swans join the mute swans while flocks of common and velvet scoter and long-tailed duck live with the eider off the estuary mouth on the mussel beds in winter. King eider sometimes turn up in the eider flocks.

Follow the Rockend Track to the beach, and turn north, along the shore-line of rising cliffs, from low dunes at Rockend to 130 feet high (40m) craggy cliffs two miles north at Collieston. This is the most colourful part of the reserve with lots of flowers on the steeper slopes in summer: thrift, kidney vetch, bird's-foot trefoil, campions, primrose, grass of Parnassus and cowslip are abundant.

The northern part of Forvie shows a variation from stable dune through to a peat moorland. Initially calcifuge plants such as crowberry gain a foothold, followed by masses of creeping willow. In still more stable conditions, a peaty soil with heathers develops, eventually gaining a few stunted birch and pine. Bog plants such as marsh pennywort, lousewort, marsh marigold and bogbean occur in the wet slacks.

Small Pearl-bordered and Dark Green Fritillary butterflies are common, feeding on violets on the cliff slopes. Emperor moths and their huge larvae are common on the heather moorland.

Curlew breed all over the moorland area in the northern part of the reserve and may be seen from the cliff path. During the summer terns from the colonies pass along the coast in a constant stream, and winter brings large flocks of snow bunting. From Broad Haven northwards sea-birds breed on the cliffs in small numbers, with fulmars, kittiwakes and a few razorbills.

In winter the main goose roost is at Meikle Loch one mile north of the reserve boundary along the A975. A short track leads to the loch, but try to avoid disturbing the geese by not appearing on the loch skyline.

Several thousand eider ducks breed in the surrounding heather of the Ythan Estuary

The Beauly Firth
HIGHLAND

A few pairs of common scoter breed in northern Scotland, but large numbers occur in winter at many places round the coast

The Beauly Firth forms the innermost basin of the complex Moray Firth system; it is sheltered by a narrow entrance directly north of the town of Inverness, and forms a site of international importance in its own right. The new Inverness to North Kessock road bridge across the bay is an effective eastern boundary. The firth proper consists of tidal mud-banks and saltings formed by the mouth of the River Beauly. Several other streams run into it, especially from the 1,000 foot hills of the Aird on its southern border, and the Caledonian Canal runs into the mouth of the firth through Inverness.

It is primarily known as an autumn–winter locality for wildfowl in tremendous numbers, though the southern shore is somewhat disturbed by wildfowlers. The whole area along both northern and southern shores is easily accessible by car and with only a little walking necessary. On foot it is a long day's fifteen-mile (24km) round walk from Inverness via Kirkhill, Beauly, Redcastle and back across the bridge from North Kessock. A tour round the whole coastline is described.

Wildlife Tour

Leave Inverness on the A862 (the old A9) after crossing Muirtown Basin at the western end of the town. The industrial area here at the waterfront is surprisingly good for gulls and often boasts glaucous and Iceland gull in autumn and winter. An old and rusting freighter moored offshore, *The Robert Baird*, is used by shags and cormorants as a roost. The road runs alongside the firth for a mile with several parking places. The firth is over a mile wide here, and wildfowl in the middle are difficult to see even with a birdwatcher's telescope.

Lots of seaweed covered rocks on the shore have regular purple sandpiper and many turnstones for most of the year. After two miles, park at Bunchrew Caravan Site. Here, Bunchrew Burn runs down from the hills to the south through woodland oak and pine. Dippers and grey wagtails are found along the burn, and the bays on both sides of Bunchrew are filled with waders, especially as the tide rises – redshank, bar-tailed godwit, oystercatcher and grey plover may all exceed 1,000, while dunlin may number as many as 5,000. From October to April

large flocks of duck also crowd into these bays to avoid bad weather: wigeon may reach 3,000, with mallard and teal slightly lower. The whole firth is noted for sea-duck, with long-tailed duck sometimes exceeding 2,000; the flocks of common scoter (2,000) and velvet scoter (500) also represent some of the largest in Europe. All are often best seen from Bunchrew since they may be well out in the bay.

After a further three miles take the B9164 signposted to Kirkhill, and then a minor road right at Wester Kirkhill. Follow this for half a mile and turn sharp right over a tiny railway bridge. The road, full of pot-holes, goes to the farms of Wester and Easter Lovat. Follow the track round. Two hundred yards past Wester Lovat there is a space to park one car – this overlooks the River Beauly just before it widens into the estuary.

The water here is brackish with some freshmarsh. Bulrush and common reed occur. Here in winter are goldeneye, merganser and goosander which come to fish in the river and which can usually be viewed closely. This is an excellent place to see whooper swans in winter, with several flocks of around 50–100 in the area, and sometimes 300 all told. These 'fresh' marshes attract migrant waders from spring to autumn with greenshank, spotted redshank, stints and sandpipers as regular visitors. Ospreys sometimes appear along the river bank, while buzzard and sparrowhawk hunt the marshlands from the woods to the south. The occasional hen harrier or merlin hunts the open marshes in winter.

Kingfishers, which are rare in northern Scotland, are sometimes noted along these banks. In the late afternoon here, enormous numbers of rooks and jackdaws flock together, and with hooded crows, fly to roost in the neighbouring woods; several thousand birds make up this roost in late autumn.

Pride of place on the whole estuary must go to the grey geese, especially the grey-lags in late October when 10–12,000 are not uncommon. Great flocks feed on the estuary mudflats or on the stubble fields of the southern shore, and large skeins may be seen quite closely, especially in stubble and potato fields near Easter Lovat. Pinkfooted geese are

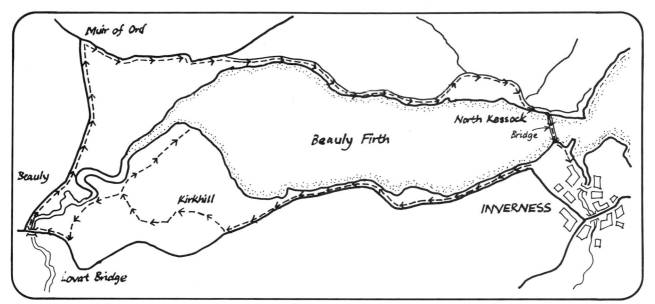

not so numerous but may number over 1,000; they often roost at Munlochy Bay, three miles north on the B9161.

The track to Easter Lovat farm is lined with large old oak trees, and at the end there is a place to park so that you can walk out along a footpath to the saltings and the beginnings of the estuary – the foreshore is perhaps a thousand yards (912m) away. This is a splendid place to view the great skeins of grey-lag geese moving up and down the estuary.

Before you cross the River Beauly at Lovat Bridge stop and walk through the excellent woods along the B9164 and skirting the railway line from Wester Lovat to Ferry Brae. These woods are primarily of birch, larch, rowan and elder and are full of berries and seeds in autumn. Good days will produce thousands of redwing, fieldfare, blackbird and songthrush feeding on the birch seed. Large flocks of migrant chaffinches with a variety of other finches also feed in these trees.

On the northern shore, two miles north of Beauly, take the A382 to Fortrose and after another two miles a minor road on the right to Redcastle and North Kessock. After a mile this road runs alongside the shore and the whole firth can be viewed closely. Out of season, large flocks of Canada geese spend July and August in this area going through their autumn moult. By autumn, with skeins of grey geese moving up and down the estuary, Redcastle foreshore is alive with sawbill ducks. From here all along the firth to North Kessock a great number of mergansers and goosanders gather in autumn, coinciding with the herring shoals which enter the bay. 5–6,000 of each species may be seen, the largest concentration of these birds in Britain.

Many other ducks and seabirds enter the estuary outside the breeding season: 500 pintail and 1,000 shelduck are sizeable populations in winter, together with smaller numbers of scaup – tufted duck prefer the river itself to the exposed waters of the bay. Slavonian grebes occur in some numbers in September and have many of their main breeding sites nearby. With the arrival of the herring come many hundreds of kittiwakes and flights of gannets, and numbers of great and Arctic skuas, dependent in turn on the smaller gulls for food.

At North Kessock the road now joins the major new route north over the Beauly Firth road bridge. Fulmars prospect the hillsides of Ord Hill and breed on the low cliffs north of Munlochy Bay.

Across the great new bridge to the south is the town of Inverness, while away to the north-west, brooding over the whole estuary, lies the snow-covered peak of Ben Wyvis. With its wide variety of sea, marsh, farm and woodland birds the Beauly Firth in winter must rank as one of the most outstanding bird sites in the whole of Britain.

Hundreds of whooper swans arrive in Britain each October to escape the rigours of the arctic winter

52

The Dornoch Firth

GOLSPIE AND LOCH FLEET

HIGHLAND

Address of Site/Warden

Part of area –
Scottish Wildlife Trust
25 Johnston Terrace,
Edinburgh EH1 2NH

Highlights and Features

Very varied bird habitats
provide many different
species throughout year.
Very large numbers of
wintering sea-duck including
eider, long-tailed duck and
scoter.
Scottish Wildlife Trust
reserve includes several
good flowers.

Facilities

Car-parks give good views.
Open at all times.

Photo Tips

Birds will be distant. Red
squirrels possible in the
pine-woods. A medium
telephoto zoom lens
80–200mm can be used for
opportunist shots.

*Eider duck are now
numerous round the
coast, especially in the
north and east*

Eastern Scotland is blessed with several large estuary systems whose rivers drain the headwaters of the Highlands nearly to the west coast. West coast rivers tend to be short torrents running through hard basalts to tumble into a craggy 'fjord'-like coastline. The wide eastern firths provide winter shelter for huge flocks of wildfowl and to a lesser extent, waders, from the far north.

Nearly all the estuaries are good for birds, even the industrialised Firth of Forth having large flocks of duck offshore in winter. Dornoch Firth and the nearby area around Golspie and Loch Fleet are no exception and are the most northerly of these sheltered bays.

A tour around both Loch Fleet and south around the Dornoch Firth is described. The bird populations of the two sites are linked and may move from one locality to the other.

Wildlife Tour: Loch Fleet – Dornoch Firth
In Golspie, turn south by the children's adventure playground on Ferry Road to Littleferry. This travels alongside Golspie Golf Links with the course on the left and farmland on the right; rocky, rounded hills clad in heather and gorse provide an inland backdrop. After the grass-clad dunes of the links, open pine plantations line the road on both sides for a mile – this open woodland is part of a Scottish Wildlife Trust reserve. A good pine-wood flora includes twinflower, lesser twayblade and creeping ladies' tresses orchids.

A sudden opening occurs in the trees and the wide flats of Loch Fleet appear on the right with a convenient car-park. Loch Fleet is a virtually land-locked basin, three miles long by a mile wide and is almost empty of water at low tide. Good views are obtained from the car-park of the eastern area of the loch, together with a pine-wood and much gorse. Shelduck, eider and Arctic tern breed in summer, with Scottish crossbill, siskin, capercaillie, woodcock, sparrowhawk, and buzzard in the forests. Eider often breed in the 'rough' on the golf course. In winter a wide variety of commoner waders occurs with many curlew and godwit.

The road continues through a further mile of plantations, lined with huge gorse bushes, and you will see the reserve car-park on the left, backed by a considerable dune system. The road ends some 200 yards (183m) further on by the row of houses at Littleferry, but the car space at the road end is needed by the householders so park in the Trust's car-park and walk.

A jetty juts out into the narrow entrance of Loch Fleet, the clear water of the river running through the middle. Many birds pass up and down this narrow channel commuting between the loch and the coast. It is a good spot for eider and red-breasted merganser all year, and king eider are surprisingly frequent here – one has been resident for several years. Others sometimes appear in winter.

From the car-park one path runs through the dunes to the shore and then north towards the golf links, while another strikes south-east down to the mouth of the main channel. Summer will have eider and Arctic tern in some numbers along the coast with a variety of passerines including redstarts in the forest edge, and autumn and winter bring hordes of wildfowl and migrant seabirds. North or north-easterly winds, especially in misty conditions, will push large numbers of kittiwakes, gannets, skuas and some sooty shearwaters inshore. Glaucous and Iceland gulls are regular. Sea-duck are a speciality of the area with 2,000 eider, 1,000 long-tailed duck and 500 mergansers. Common scoter peak at 2,000 with a hundred or more velvet scoter and goldeneye, and this is one of the best places to see surf scoter, one or two often appearing in the winter. Summer records may indicate resident birds.

Common and grey seals occur offshore and common seals may sometimes be seen on the sand-banks.

From Littleferry return to Golspie and head south on the A9 to cross the River Fleet at the Mound, which was the embankment built in 1815 to try and reclaim the estuary. There are car-parks at both ends of this causeway, giving good views of the western flats of Loch Fleet, the fresh-water and alder swamp beyond the Mound and the surrounding hills.

Fulmars breed on the craggy hills, and a wide range of woodland species also breed here, with willow and wood warblers in the light birch woods. Of birds of prey, buzzard and sparrowhawk make frequent appearances, and short-eared owl, hen harrier and peregrine all occasionally hunt the area.

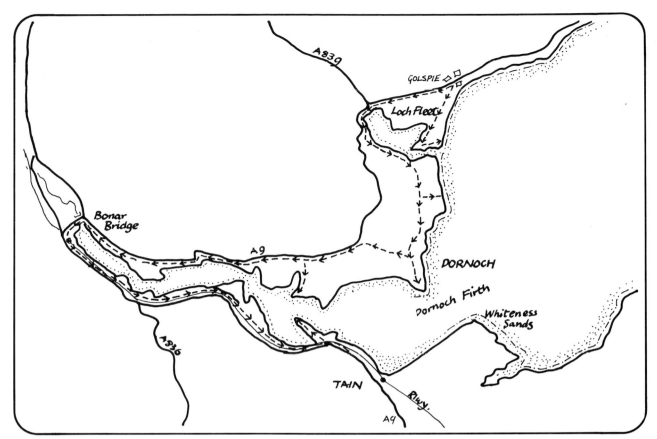

Otters are possible on the river above the Mound and on the coast in winter. The population of red squirrels is small but they can be seen in the pine-woods, while foxes are found on the links probably after rabbits.

A minor road east of the A9 just south of the Mound gives access along the loch's southern shore to a car-park at Skelbo Castle – excellent views cover the whole southern sector. This road continues for two miles to Embo, a collection of seaside huts and caravans with Coul Golf Links to the north.

Several hundred grey-lag geese and 100 whooper swans use farm fields in winter, when mixed flocks of twite and snow buntings search for seeds in the dunes.

Embo is probably best after the holiday-makers desert it in October. Many of the area's sea-duck congregate here, joined by all three species of diver in small numbers – red-throated diver is the most numerous, with often about twenty to be seen. Rarer grebes include Slavonian and red-necked grebes, sometimes in small parties.

The coastline south of Embo is quite rocky and purple sandpiper are usually present with numbers of turnstone. Fulmars haunt the low cliff coastline in summer.

There is a wide range of habitats: sea coastline, dunes, stable grasslands, conifer plantations with native Scots pine and birch, the sand and mudflats of Loch Fleet and the fresh-water and alder swamps of the river, backed by crags and heather moorland. Consequently this is one of the best sites in Scotland for species variety, not only of birds, but flowers and animals too.

Two miles south of Embo is the town of Dornoch on the north shore of the firth. Paths lead south past the small airfield to Dornoch Point with excellent views over the estuary mouth, and you can also go south by road from the A9 to Skibo Castle, Meikle Ferry and Newton Point. Ard na Cailc, a promontory cutting well into the firth, can be reached by a path across Cuthill Golf Links; the A9 runs along the inner firth to Bonar Bridge, and south along the shore for several miles.

Beyond Edderton on the southern shore a minor road at the Meikle Ferry Inn runs to Ferry Point – all these places provide good access and views of the firth. There are large conifer woods around the firth, and the huge Morangie Forest stretches for several miles south of Edderton.

All the birds around Loch Fleet may be seen at Dornoch with especially large numbers of sea-duck – long-tailed duck may reach 2,000 off Tarbert Ness in spring. Large flocks of waders use the firth with hordes of geese and other wildfowl. In summer, ospreys often fish inshore.

The narrow entrance to Loch Fleet near Dornoch hides a large, shallow estuarine basin which empties swiftly at low tide

MOUNTAINS AND MOORLAND

The most spectacular of the environments within our islands, both scenically and climatically, are the mountains. Many of the plants, birds and animals which live on them are specially adapted to do so and are found nowhere else.

The uplands of Britain are made of older, harder rocks, which withstand erosion but in consequence provide poor nutrient value to the soils, which are often waterlogged because of the high rainfall, giving rise to large areas of bog. Even the drier ridges are only able to support a range of plants specifically adapted to exposure to the elements. Many plants and animals cannot withstand these harsh conditions, and those species which do have developed so as to live on the very edge of survival.

At first sight the moors and mountains look wet, bleak and windy but because of the zonation of habitats due to the harsh conditions a variety of communities exist.

The highest zone of all, the arctic-alpine zone, is found in Britain only on the highest hills where an open community of plants grows among the broken rocks and ledges of the summits. These are either mosses, lichens or flowers with a 'cushion' habit to protect them from exposure. Snow effectively insulates them throughout the winter months.

Best plant sites are away from the exposed summits and down among screes and rock ledges, especially those protected from grazing deer and sheep. The richest alpine plant communities develop on lime-rich rocks – Ben Lawers is a classic example. Other good sites include Caenlochan National Nature Reserve near Braemar (with restricted access), Inchanadamph in Wester Ross and, actually near sea-level, the wonderful alpine flower locality of Strathnaver on the Scottish north coast.

Below the alpine zone is upland grassland, found on soils which are not too waterlogged. The grass species are very dependent upon underlying soil content and the effects of grazing. Limestone grassland, such as at Ben Lawers, develops a sward of blue moor grass with many flowers such as thyme and harebell, but dry basic soils produce a mix of fescues and bents which are the main diet of all Britain's grazing animals. Wet soils or those which have been overgrazed develop great tussocks of mat grass providing very poor grazing, and usually rejected even by sheep.

Where the hills are poorly drained, especially where a layer of boulder clay sometimes several feet thick has been left by the glaciers, the soils are permanently wet, grass fails to survive and blanket peat bogs are formed from the dead remains of 'sphagnum' or bog moss. Very little oxygen is available in waterlogged soils and so the moss becomes a spongy blanket, does not decompose and turns into compressed peat. It is usually covered with a living layer of sphagnum.

Moorland covers vast areas of the north and west and forms where peat bogs dry out and also on the better drained, acid soils of the uplands, often on former woodland areas. It is dominated by heathers of which common heather, or ling, is the main species. Other members of the heather family commonly found are bilberry, bell heather, cross-leaved heath and Arctic bearberry. Wavy hair grass, heath bedstraw and tormentil make up the commonest constituents of the grassy sward.

The mountain year begins with almost startling suddenness, as spring sends a clarion call through the valleys, corries and high peaks. The weather warms, the snow begins to melt and plants, animals and birds appear as if by magic.

Birds are the first creatures to re-inhabit the hills. Far across the moors the evocative calls of curlew, golden plover and other waders mingle with the croak of jousting black and red grouse. Dominating the moorland skies, hen harriers, merlins and short-eared owls perform their springtime aerobatic displays against an exhilarating background of mountain wilderness, while over the highest hills the majestic golden eagle stoops and soars.

The upland summer is short and everything must rush on with the process of reproduction. Ground-nesting birds such as dotterel and golden plover seek breeding sites as soon as the snow line retreats towards the summit. Returning willow warblers sing from stunted birch woods which are only just breaking into leaf.

The deer return to their moorland pastures safe, for the time being, from the telescopic sight and the bullet. The calves, nurtured all winter safe in the womb, are born in late spring, hidden in a bed of heather and within sniffing distance of the retreating snow fields.

High above, the eagle has already hatched its chicks on a remote rocky ledge, and now it scans the hills for grouse and mountain hare to feed its ravenous offspring – those on the west coast near the sea will often bring a kittiwake or puffin to the eyrie, caught along the sea-cliff colonies. Eagles begin refurbishing their eyries in early March while snow still mantles the hills.

As the snow melts from the highest ground, the

richest of the alpine screes and ledges become a mass of brilliant flowers. Purple saxifrage is one of the first to appear in April, followed by spring gentian, moss campion, starry saxifrage, alpine ladies' mantle and many more. In some localities the alpine community can be so rich that it dominates large areas – alpine ladies' mantle covers acres of the lower western slopes of Ben Lawers, while mountain avens grows in profusion on the ledges of Strathnaver.

By midsummer snow lies only in a few north-facing corries, but it will persist all year in these places, tiny permanent snow fields, only melting in the hottest summers. Apparently insignificant and yet a reminder of how near the arctic world the high tops of Scotland really are.

Upland birds range far and wide over the summer hills and curlew, wheatear, black grouse, hen harrier, eagle and raven will all be tending families. However, the prime bird is the red grouse and much of the heather moorland from Yorkshire northwards is specifically managed to provide the maximum numbers for shooting. Grouse eat heather tips and the abundance of heather over other food strictly limits populations of most other species. One bird in particular, however, is found throughout the uplands, and may be the only bird visible on long mountain walks. The humble meadow pipit lives on the sudden flush of summer insects, and may reach populations of 25 pairs per square kilometre.

Mountain mammal species are few in number. Red deer are relatively numerous in Scotland but in England are only found on Exmoor and in Martindale Common in the Lake District. A few may still survive in the New Forest in Hampshire. Mountain hares are often numerous, especially on the lower slopes of high ranges from Derbyshire northwards, while wild cats are restricted to the Highlands although they are spreading south. Fox, stoat, polecat and pine-marten are all found on the hills but often include the forests in their range. Field voles are the most characteristic small mammal, forming the main food item for many predators.

As summer turns to autumn, the hills become a fairyland of golden birch and purple heather. Autumn starts in August in the Highlands and by then most of the birds will be on the move. Waders will have left for the estuaries, warblers and wheatears will be drifting south towards their winter goal in Africa and even the pipits will be dropping down to winter in the lowlands.

By October and the first touch of snow on the tops only the eagle, the grouse and the ptarmigan will haunt the highest hills. Roaring red deer stags at rut, and calls from skeins of geese high out of the northern skies proclaim the imminent return of winter.

The sites described in the main text represent a cross section of the best upland wildlife areas in Britain, but there are many others besides: Caenlochan National Nature Reserve has a splendid range of mountain birds and animals, while Lochnagar and the surrounding mountains also hold all the traditional upland species; Ben More Coigach near Ullapool has a complete range from lochan and moor to high top; also in the north, Strathy Bog National Nature Reserve, far out in the Flow Country and surrounded by 'new' forests, has a fine assembly of bog plants and birds. Rannoch Moor on Tayside is a complex of bog, heath and remnant forest with an exciting variety of birds and animals, although it is difficult of access.

Farther south the Craven Uplands of Yorkshire are limestone hills capped with millstone grit, producing step-sided hills such as Ingleborough and Great Whernside – peat bogs on the summits and limestone flowers on the slopes.

Wales has huge areas of peat and heather moorland in the central Cambrian mountains, home of the glorious red kite which is now so rare. The Welsh hills – as elsewhere – are home to thousands of sheep, and the level of sheep grazing is critical to the appearance and wildlife constitution of the hills. Many areas have been heavily over-grazed, leading to an increase in matt grass which is thoroughly unproductive; upland grazing has deteriorated in large areas as a result, and sheep farming now depends heavily on government subsidy.

The mountain and the moorland environment is under severe threat, and not only from over-grazing by sheep. It must not be assumed that a conservationist refutes all development willy-nilly, but it is unfortunate that the best wildlife areas are usually those wanted by the developer, while less sensitive but equally usable sites are ignored.

Afforestation is the other major threat, and a cause for concern if the extensive areas needed to ensure a characteristic moorland flora and fauna are to survive.

Mass forestry planting in its early growth allows a substantial improvement in the populations of some species. Short-eared owls and hen harriers find the low-growing first stages ideal nesting territory coupled with an increase in vole numbers for food. Once the trees have reached six feet (2m) in height, however, there is a rapid decline as all the birds are forced out. All the typical upland species, divers, waders, harriers, merlins and owls are substantially reduced in numbers, even eagles and ravens since they require large areas of open moorland for hunting.

53

Dartmoor
DEVON

Address of Site/Warden

Dartmoor National Park
Authority,
Parke,
Haytor Road,
Bovey Tracey,
Newton Abbot,
Devon TQ13 9JQ
Yarner Wood and Wistman's
Wood National Nature
Reserves both from Nature
Conservancy Council,
SW Regional Office,
Roughmoor,
Bishops Hull,
Taunton,
Somerset TA1 5AA

Highlights and Features

Wistman's Wood is relict
oak-wood with vast numbers
of ferns and lichens from wet
climate. Yarner Wood is
valley oakwood full of birds
in spring – speciality is large
population pied flycatchers
using nest-boxes.

Facilities

Many local tourist facilities.
Nature trail in Yarner Wood.

Photo Tips

Wide-angle zoom lens for
close-ups of ferns and
lichens in Wistman's Wood.
300mm lens may give
pictures pied flycatcher in
Yarner Wood. Many insects
and flowers with close-up
lenses.

*The tiny, jewel-like
common lizard is found
on many dry and sunny
banks throughout the
country*

Bare grey granite, heather, bog, wind and rain – in a word, Dartmoor. This is the generally accepted description of the 365 square miles (942sq km) of Dartmoor National Park, accentuated by Conan Doyle's description in the *Hound of the Baskervilles* and aided by accounts of escaped prisoners running over bleak moorland.

Much of this land was once covered in oak woodland; it is man who has created Dartmoor as we know it today, and it is true that the highest parts of the moor do fit the common conception. Even the hard granite tors bow before the weather – centuries of frost have shattered large tors creating 'clitters', the screes of huge boulders which are so characteristic of the area.

The open moor is heavily grazed by cattle, sheep and ponies, but the 'clitters' prevent such a use and support luxuriant growth instead. Tiny relict woodlands, as in Wistman's Wood, cling close to the slopes of the moor. Lower down, the rivers have cut steep-sided valleys where the granite meets the softer rock, and these valley woods are the wildlife gems of Dartmoor.

Two wildlife walks are described – the first across the open moor for a short distance to examine Wistman's Wood, and the second looks at the glorious valley woods at Bovey Tracey.

Widlife Walk 1: Wistman's Wood

Park in the little car-park opposite the hotel at Two Bridges, itself 8 miles (13km) east of Tavistock. North, away from the main road, is a gravel track signposted 'Wistman's Wood 1¼m'; after 600 yards the track bears to the right of the little white cottage of Crockern Farm. Once past here you come out onto Dartmoor 'proper', the path largely following the 1,300ft contour line along the edge of a wide valley. The best time to visit is perhaps late May as the moor comes to life with spring green.

Wildlife is fairly sparse but it is a good idea to see this stunted relict woodland before descending to the more sheltered valleys. As you walk the springy peat turf through bracken, heather and grey rock your only companions will probably be the shaggy cattle, shaggy sheep, bouncing lambs, skylarks, pipits and the wind.

Approaching the wood the lichen-covered boulders increase, and wheatears are numerous, nesting in the crevices – so are stonechat and whinchat.

The wood is quite small and unless you are a student of lichens, will take you only an hour to explore: examine the stunted oaks, just twice the height of a man; marvel at the luxuriance of the lichens, ferns and mosses which clothe the trees and rocks, real rain-forest vegetation in a wood which may sit in clouds for weeks in winter. Written about for several centuries by geographers, historians and folklorists, this weird little wood still holds one real mystery: the oak which grows here is the typical lowland pedunculate variety, bearing acorns with stalks, and not the usual upland sessile oak.

Birds are few – chaffinches, a blue tit or a wren; overhead a raven, a drifting buzzard or a swallow slipping down the valley. Foxes are frequent visitors indicating a large vole population; adders often sun themselves in the rock piles. A quarter of a mile further on is Langford Tor with ring ouzels in the rocks.

Next stop is the valley at Bovey Tracey, ten miles (16km) further east.

Wildlife Walk 2: Yarner Wood, Bovey Tracey

This is a 3-mile (4.8km) round walk. Yarner Wood is a national nature reserve run by the Nature Conservancy Council. Access is open on marked paths but a permit is required if you wish to leave them.

Yarner is most beautiful woodland – if you are feeling jaded with city life try an early morning in Yarner Wood. Visit in early May when the trees are just breaking into green, but still bare enough to allow air and light to flood the wood. All the birds will be easily seen and, especially in the early morning, will fill the wood with birdsong.

The entrance is on the left of the B3344 travelling 2 miles (3km) west of Bovey Tracey, and there is a small car-park 200 yards (183m) off the road. Collect a 'Woodland Walk' leaflet, but before following the marked path, climb the wooden steps of the nature trail and walk out onto the open moorland, filled with heather, bracken and gorse. Stonechats and tree pipits breed here in May with an

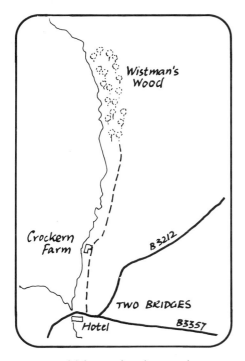

occasional 'churring' nightjar in the evening. Common lizards are numerous, sunning themselves along the track. Watch for buzzards over the conifer plantation on the left where a breeding pair holds sway most years. Follow the track round and re-enter the woodland at the gate and then take the path to the right.

A thin protective belt of young beech shimmers in bright spring leaf in front of an extensive birch woodland with much bracken and bramble – winter brings flocks of siskins to feed on the birch seed here. The path dips steeply to a lovely rushing stream, the Woodcock Stream, where the old oak woodland is open and airy, the higher branches full of wood warblers whose high-pitched, falling cadence song is audible above all else. There are nest-boxes nailed to trees throughout the wood, 10–12 feet (3m) off the ground, and the half dozen along this stretch of streamside path will almost certainly each have its pair of pied flycatchers in residence. The male is especially bright in natty black-and-white plumage, twitching his wings nervously in characteristic fashion. The colony has built up steadily since the first pair used a blue-tit box in 1955 – by 1968 there were 28 pairs, and by 1985 the total was 37 pairs. Ringing has shown that after migrating to Africa for the winter the same bird often returns to the same box next spring – and all done without the help of a huge computer! Watch for pied flycatchers throughout the wood.

Among the old oaks a few pairs of redstarts breed, so watch out for the fiery flash of a bright red tail. The cock redstart is the most handsome of British birds.

The track moves upwards through open woodland glades which have been created in the last ten years to let in more light, thereby encouraging shrubs such as honeysuckle and improving the variety of insects, especially butterflies. White Admirals and Holly Blue are frequent in this part of the wood.

Common woodland birds are all easily seen: all three British woodpeckers, nuthatch, tree-creeper and goldcrest are frequent, as are most of the tits except willow tit. Willow warbler, blackcap and chiffchaff are heard throughout the wood. Migrant summer visitors tend to arrive late in these upland valleys, the last being the spotted flycatcher which rarely comes in till early May.

The track climbs out above Yarner Stream with a lot of bramble on the drier ground. A rich growth of nettles near the stream provides food for caterpillars of Peacock, Tortoiseshell, Comma and Red Admiral butterflies. Near the ruined mine a short-cut returns you to the car-park, reducing the round walk by ¾ mile. A steep climb brings you out onto the moorland edge where you are most likely to see stonechats, whinchats, tree pipits and willow warblers, but sparrowhawks occasionally hunt the wood edge, while buzzards drift by on rounded wings.

Follow the track back towards the car-park.

If you have the time, try returning to walk the wood at dusk. You will probably have the place to yourself, in company with badgers, deer and dormice, all creatures of the night! There are several setts, so badger sightings are a real possibility here if you sit still and stay quiet.

Buzzards are widespread in upland and forested districts of Britain, and are nowhere more frequent than in the wooded coombes and hills of Devon

54

Exmoor
DEVON AND SOMERSET

Address of Site/Warden

Exmoor National Park
Committee,
Exmoor House,
Dulverton,
Somerset TA22 9HL

Highlights and Features

Lovely mixture of moorland, steep wooded valleys, rivers and farmland, with very scenic north coast with woods and cliffs. Exmoor ponies, red deer. Many woodland birds, flowers and insects. Open moorland has curlew, red grouse, buzzard, migrant raptors.

Facilities

Many and varied. Well-known tourist area. Information centre at Market House, Minehead, Somerset.

Photo Tips

Holiday area. Wide range of wildlife means variety of equipment. Flowers and insects best in summer with 200mm lens.

Wild Exmoor ponies are descendants of the most ancient British native horses, present long before the Roman invasion

Any exploration of wildlife in Britain would be incomplete without a visit to Exmoor National Park. Straddling the borders of Somerset and North Devon, Exmoor looks down over the Bristol Channel, its magnificent coastline of hogs-backed cliffs unique in their own way in Britain. Inland lies wild heather moorland, etched by deep wooded valleys and a thousand cascading streams.

Exmoor has a softer face than the high granite moorland of Dartmoor. Dunkery Beacon is its highest point, a mere 1,707 feet (519m). Man has changed this landscape dramatically over the centuries, removing the woodlands and replacing them with his farms; these spread right up onto the moor in many places so that Exmoor has become a patchwork of heather moorland, peat bog and grassy downland fields full of sheep.

The national park covers some 265 square miles (676sq km) from Combe Martin in the west to Minehead in the east. Exmoor is a land of wild red deer, soaring buzzards and the legend of Lorna Doone, a superb place for walkers and seekers after peace – especially out of season!

Three fairly short walks are described, taking in the three prime wildlife habitats: wild open moorland, high river valley woodland and the majestic northern coast – all three can be combined in an excellent day's wildlife exploration.

Wildlife Walk 1: Molland Common

Molland Common is the first main ridge of real heather moorland on the southern edge of Exmoor, rising to about 1,250 feet (370m) and stretching northwards, broken only by unfenced minor roads, for ten miles to the B3224 Simonsbath to Exford road.

From the A361 take the road to Molland through three miles of narrow lanes filled with primroses in spring. Turn left past tiny Molland church. The road climbs steeply, primroses left behind in sheltered valleys, and crosses a cattlegrid onto wild moorland – turn first right to run across Molland Common and park in a suitable spot off the road. To the east lies the little village of Hawkridge, and this name is no coincidence – recent ornithological study has shown that this first southerly Exmoor ridge attracts passing birds of prey because of its prominent position.

Late winter and spring are the best times to visit. Winter-browned heather and dry fawn moor grass give the moor a tawny look which remains unchanged until new growth sprouts green in May.

This is a splendid spot to see truly wild red deer, and Exmoor is their last stronghold in England. Exmoor ponies are to be seen here too; foals are usually produced in early spring and these little wild horses are then nearly as wary as the red deer. Use binoculars for both and scan Moorhouse Ridge as the most likely site, quiet and undisturbed.

Walk out across the moor for perhaps half a mile and scan the skies for birds of prey. Winter brings several hen harriers gliding low, merlins dashing sharply after pipits, the occasional peregrine after pigeons, and the resident buzzards hunting voles and rabbits. Spring might bring a migrant goshawk, Montagu's harrier or hobby over the ridge.

Other birds are scarce, but there are a few red grouse, and large flocks of finches, with bramblings and cirl buntings, use nearby farmland in winter. Ravens are frequent over the high moor.

In spring from early April onwards the summer visitors arrive to vary this rather sparse list of skylark and meadow pipit. Curlew and snipe breed in small numbers with whinchat, stonechat and wheatear mainly round the moorland edges, using the boundary hedges and drystone walls as breeding sites.

Wildlife Walk 2: Tarr Steps and the River Barle

This walk combines the habitats of swift stream with surrounding valley woodland, and includes a walk across Tarr Steps, the ancient clapper bridge over the River Barle. The best time to visit is in early May, before the hordes of tourists jam the road and before the tree-canopy leaves break, so you would still have good views of the newly arrived migrants.

Easiest access to Tarr Steps is westwards from the B3223 between Exford and Dulverton, but if you continue from Molland Common you can drive down through Hawkridge. Turn sharply left after the tiny church; the six-foot wide road down, with a few passing places, is a *really steep hill*. Park at the bottom, on a sharp bend by the river, where there is space for

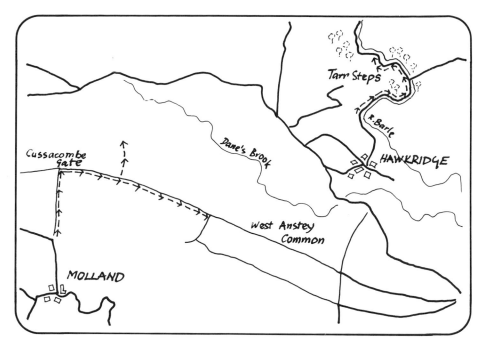

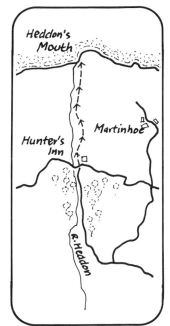

just two cars. Turning is not allowed at Tarr Steps which is still half-a-mile farther on and the official car-park is on the other side of the river. There *is* a ford running across the river beside the steps but it is deep, fifty yards of loose river gravel with a foot of water rushing over it, so don't risk your nice modern car because it is igno-minious having to have it towed out of the river by a Land-Rover.

Walk along the road towards Tarr Steps through lovely valley oak-woods filled with lichens and ferns. Dippers and grey wagtails frequent the river and in May the woods around hold many singing wood warblers; overhead watch for buzzards and sparrowhawks which both breed in the woods.

The roadside banks here are superb for flowers and ferns in May with pennywort, primrose, ivy-leaved toadflax, spleen-worts, hard fern, buckler fern and many others clinging to the walls and rocks. You will come to the river and Tarr Steps 200 yards past the unobtrusive little hotel; after crossing and returning over the clapper bridge, take the path on the left of the river and follow it along the river bank.

The rapid stream, perhaps twenty yards wide, is clear and cold and filled with trout which are easy to watch in the deeper, slower pools. Dippers buzz along its surface. The woods round about hold wood warbler, together with a few pied flycatchers and redstarts, though these rarely arrive here on the high moor till May. Walk the path for half a mile until it rises steeply to a long bracken-covered meadow below the open hillside. Tree pipits sing from the tree-tops while buzzards drift along the hills. Try and stay into the twilight – badger and deer live in

these woods and this long meadow may allow a glimpse.

Wildlife Walk 3: Heddon's Mouth from Hunter's Inn

This picturesque spot with the lovely old Hunter's Inn is also best visited in early May. The approach from the A39 is down a steep (1 in 4), narrow hill through a lovely wooded coombe, past dreamy cottages with gardens full of tulips. Peacocks call a resounding greeting as you park by the Inn.

The path to take runs for about a mile through the National Trust Estate to Heddon's Mouth, where the River Heddon rushes full tilt into the sea. The coastal path to Woody Bay, 2¾ miles away, branches to the right. The birds and animals to be seen along the way are typical of much of this glorious north coast, with pied flycatcher, wood warbler, chiffchaff and redstart frequenting the woodland path, which after half a mile runs out past a wooden footbridge over the river. This bridge allows winter access to the beach on a higher path when the river is in spate, and affords a magnificent view of the rocky downland towering high over the river, where the valley wood-lands give way to open gorse-covered hillside. Willow warblers and tree pipits sing, while high above buzzards, ravens and kestrels hang on the ever-present breeze.

Some large stepping stones across the shallow but nonetheless rapid stream give access to the granite boulder beach. Cliffs rise 300 feet (91m) all around – fulmars and herring gulls go drifting past and over the highest point you will probably see a buzzard soaring on the up-currents.

Exmoor still supports a small population of wild red deer, not above raiding local gardens to eat the fallen fruit in autumn

The Brecon Beacons National Park
POWYS

*The Brecon Beacons ride
high above the industrial
valleys of South Wales in
waves of Old Red
Sandstone*

The Brecon Beacons ride high above the valleys of South Wales in vast waves of rock. The distinctive landscape of dramatic mountain crests was created by the Ice Age glaciers which scoured out the huge corries or cwms, leaving the high ridges which face northwards towards the wild and mountainous heart of Wales.

Wildlife Walk: The Beacons Circuit

This is an all-day walk over very rough mountain country, breathtakingly beautiful in winter snows but best for wildlife in early summer.

From the Usk Valley take the road past Talybont Reservoir, through wide forested valleys, and in 2 miles turn right at Taf Fechan Forest to Neuadd Reservoir. There is a small car-park at the road end near the reservoir buildings.

The mountain views here are very impressive: facing you on the west is the apparently sheer wall of the Beacon crest – up which you have to climb; the ridge then swings round to the high tops of Corn Du, Pen y Fan and Cribin, and north beyond the reservoir the saddle up to Fan y Big.

The line of pine trees by the reservoir often holds small parties of goldcrests and siskins.

Follow the track down into the valley towards a stile, and descend still further to cross the stream – which is haunted by dipper, grey wagtail and common sandpiper. The track then continues up the line of telegraph poles towards the edge of the huge plantation running along the hills.

Here, the plantation edge offers a good chance to see hunting sparrowhawk looking for goldcrests, coal tits or crossbills; the bracken moorland around you usually holds whinchat, skylark and meadow pipit, while the damper, marshy hollows of the stream may shelter the occasional pair of snipe or curlew.

The track clambers up the wall of the Beacons alongside the plantation, a fairly short but *very* steep half mile. The reward is worth it however, and soon you will stand on the high crest of the Beacons in the airy world of the buzzard. Turn slightly left and make for the trig point of Twyn Mwyalchod; here the track leads northwards following the ridge and gives you the feeling of being on the world's edge, as the mountain crest falls vertically below

you for 500 feet (152m).

Kestrels, ravens and an occasional buzzard will drift along the edge with you, and after a mile the long valley of Cwm Crew, cut by waterfalls, falls away to the left. Ring ouzels and wheatears inhabit the glacial debris near its summit.

The ridge narrows, with slopes falling away on both sides to reach Duwynt. A short descent drops you to the saddle, and the track down would take you to the Storey Arms on the A470; however, continue on rising ground to Corn Du summit and then there is an easy 400 yards (365m) to the top of Pen y Fan with the whole of Wales laid out beyond.

Return towards the southern end of Pen y Fan summit and the view of the Neuadd Reservoirs far below. The path now has a tricky descent down a badly eroded track. The huge north-east face of the mountain falls below for 600 feet (183m) sheer to the lower slopes. At the saddle, a steep climb of some 300 feet (91m) brings you to the top of Cribin. Scan the soaring crags of Pen y Fan for passing peregrines.

From Cribin's summit, walk east down the slope to join the Roman road track at the gap in the hills which provides an easy downhill mile back to the Neuadd Reservoirs. The round walk is only 5 miles (8km) but it will take you several hours, and should be avoided in bad weather.

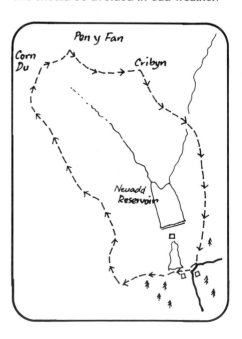

Snowdonia National Park

GWYNEDD

The stern beauty of the mountains is breathtakingly portrayed throughout Snowdonia. Spring and early summer are best when the valleys and the cwms are filled with birdsong and flowers pack the rock ledges.

Widlife Walk: Cwm Y Llan and Snowdon Summit

This is a tough walk of some 8 miles (12km) up and back by the same route. It needs care on the upper steep sections.

Start from the large car-park at the Pont Bethania south of Capel Curig on the A498. The rushing river here has dipper, grey wagtail and common sandpiper along the banks. Go through the kissing-gate by the cattle-grid on the north side of the road. Lots of sheep live in the hills, and any dogs *must* be kept on a lead. Swallows and house martins hunt the water-meadows along the valley as you walk the ¼ mile of road; this runs under a hanging sessile oak-wood, full of birds in spring but often empty in autumn – redstart, wood warbler and pied flycatcher are the classic upland oak-wood birds, with many willow warblers. Both goosander and red-breasted merganser nest in these upland woods and sometimes pass along the valley to feed on the lakes.

The drystone wall alongside the path harbours a rich flora, with wall pennywort, foxgloves, numerous ferns and a superb display of mosses and lichens. The road swings right to the farm while the footpath, clearly marked, turns left and climbs to an old iron gate. The views from here open out, with great crags all around and oak-woods wrapped around the lowest slopes. The tumbling cascade of the Afon Cwm Llan crashes down the steep, rocky valley while above, the dark crags of Craig-ddu guard the approach to the mountain.

This is a spectacular mountain valley with many mountain birds in spring. Choughs are sometimes present, tumbling along the crags in aerobatic display, but ravens and buzzards are more likely and sometimes a peregrine may pass swiftly down the valley from some high look-out crag. On a level with the waterfall, stone walls by the track are full of spleenwort ferns, while butterwort grows in the damp hollows.

An old iron kissing-gate marks the true entrance to the reserve, and smooth slabs beyond it show the marks of the glaciers. The first set of old ruins hidden in the valley above the falls are those of an old copper mill, whilst just beyond, the valley levels out past ruined slate-quarry buildings – *all* these ruins are dangerous, and should not be entered. Here for ½ mile the river runs in a wide glaciated valley, past the great polished rock used by Gladstone to deliver a speech at the age of 83 when he was still Prime Minister. Now the only voices are likely to be the chatter of wheatears and ring ouzels in the scree slopes, and the loud song of a wren nesting in a rocky cranny.

Once you have passed the ruins, with ferns growing in the lime-rich mortar, and the slate tips, with their abundance of parsley fern, the path climbs very steeply and is only for the fit and experienced. An hour's climbing up the Watkin Path will bring you to the col between Lliwedd and the Snowdon summit. This is cold mountain grassland with tufts of fir clubmoss and parsley fern among the rocks.

The last stretch of loose rock along the Watkin Path is dangerous in wet or icy conditions and needs to be treated with great care. Starry and purple saxifrages grow among the rocks, with many other arctic-alpine flowers. The path climbs onto the summit ridge and there, 200 yards (183m) away, is the obtrusive Snowdon Railway and the hideous 'hotel'. Return hastily over the ridge by the same route.

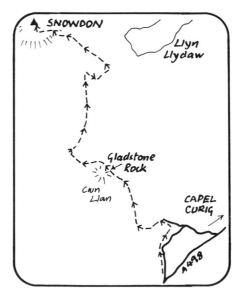

Address of Site/Warden

Snowdonia National Park Committee, Penrhyndeudraeth, Gwynedd LL48 6LS

Highlights and Features

Rugged mountain area in North Wales. Often crowded with tourists. Good for raven, chough, buzzard and other hill birds. Valley oak-woods rich in woodland birds including pied flycatcher, redstart, wood warbler.

Facilities

Many and varied.

Photo Tips

Scenic pictures are best bet, with many plants, ferns and mosses.

Spleenwort ferns grow in rocky clefts throughout the hilly regions of the country

57 Cors Caron
TREGARON, DYFED

Address of Site/Warden

Cors Caron National
Nature Reserve
Warden:
Minawel,
Ffair Rhos,
Pontrhydfendigaid,
Ystrad Meurig,
Dyfed SY25 6BN

Highlights and Features

Classic lowland raised bog. Large populations breeding waders, all common species, in summer. Excellent for birds of prey all year, but best in winter. Regular hunting area for red kites. Very good bog flora, and wide variety of insects.

Facilities

Observation tower. Access at all times along 'Old Railway Walk'. Permit needed for rest of reserve.

Photo Tips

Birds will be distant. Bog flowers and dragonflies numerous. Use medium telephoto zoom, say 80–200mm for these in view of very boggy ground.

Thousands of gulls move inland in the winter to forage on farm fields turned over by the plough

Cors Caron is a subtle place. Some of the wildlife areas described in this book are backed by great sweeps of dramatic scenery, while others at first glance may seem to be nothing but empty landscape. The Sutherland Flow country, for example, seems bleak and desolate, the spectacular mountains to the south far finer an aspect. And yet from a wildlife viewpoint, the reverse is true. The mighty hills are largely empty and the boggy Flowes teem with life.

Such is the case at Cors Caron, which is a classic example of a lowland raised bog, now very rare in Britain due to drainage. The high tops of the rain-swept Cambrian mountains nearby hold little but a few wet pipits; the bulk of the wildlife is down in the wooded valleys, along the rivers and around the bog.

One walk is described; the first section along the old railway track to the observation tower is open to all but the second section through the bog requires a permit from the Nature Conservancy Council, to limit disturbance to the wildlife. Most of the birds and animals can be seen from the Old Railway Walk; wellies are essential in the boggy areas.

Park in the roadside lay-by about 2½ miles (4km) north of Tregaron on the B4343. The wide expanse of open brown heather bog is clearly visible on the left of the road out of the town; this area comprises nearly 2,000 acres (809ha), and is roughly three miles long (4.8km) and a mile (1.6km) wide. There are actually three bogs split in two by the River Teifi, which is clearly visible from the moorland hills above the valley to the east.

Go through the wicket gate onto the track of the old railway, damaged by severe floods in 1963 and closed two years later. Turn right following the raised section of the old line.

The vegetation along the track is strikingly different to the rest of the reserve. The ballast used to build the railway was rich in lime and the flowers and hedgerows have benefitted accordingly – hazel, blackthorn, hawthorn and briar form a thick hedge, while sturdy saplings of ash and oak are noticeable. The oaks have their origins in acorns dropped by jays and grey squirrels as they transported them from the oak-woods on the edge of the eastern hillsides. Meadowsweet, yarrow,

bird's-foot trefoil and scabious along the track provide an attractive food source for butterflies. However, you will see that the vegetation out on the acid soils of the bog is quite different.

400 yards (365m) from the gate the path runs through an old and sheltered railway cutting, full of insects on a warm summer's day – Common Blue, Small Copper and common meadow butterflies occur. Adders are quite numerous on the reserve and you may often see one basking on the banks here, while common lizards may appear too.

Small birds are legion with reed buntings, finches and warblers in the scrub; autumn brings flocks to feed on seed along the railway bank with fieldfares and redwings attracted to the berries.

After half a mile the track turns past the Allt-ddu Farm, where swallows and pied wagtails breed in the buildings. The oak wood on the hillside by the road has one or two pairs of pied flycatchers and redstarts in summer, which will sometimes feed from perches along the track.

The view across the bog suddenly opens out, and it is worth scanning the whole area as visiting and breeding birds are good. In early summer there are several hundred pairs of black-headed gulls, thirty pairs of curlew, lapwing, redshank and snipe, with water rails in the ditches. In winter quite reasonable flocks of wildfowl occur, with several hundred each of teal, mallard and wigeon. Whooper swans usually reach fifty, while Bewick's swans may reach double figures. In winter, several hundred lapwing, with smaller numbers of golden plover, snipe and woodcock, plus many hundreds of gulls inevitably attract their following raptors: a dozen pairs of buzzard breed in the surrounding district and many hunt over the bog all year; red kites, the bird stars of the area, are frequent and two or three may be seen, especially in winter; peregrines breed in the hills and also hunt across the reserve throughout the year, and these are all joined by up to eight hen harriers and two or three merlins. It is hardly surprising that the area is a prime site for wintering birds of prey.

This wide valley was scooped out by the last Ice Age when a glacial moraine of debris was formed, damming the inflowing stream and creating a wide shallow lake. The lake silted up as plants and mud were carried in by the stream, ultimately producing a fen of reeds and alder scrub. This rose slowly above the level of the stream, was leached by rain and became acid, filled with sphagnum, and eventually became the raised bog.

Half-an-hour's walk brings you to a tall log tower with a wooden hide on the left of the path. This is certainly the best observation spot on the reserve and repays a patient wait – the twenty very steep steps to the hide have two good handrails to aid progress. A fast-flowing stream, the Afon Fflur, rushes into the bog by the gate, which is itself an excellent place to position yourself quietly and just watch. The long line of bushes down the track are regularly hunted by sparrow-hawk and merlin, looking for small birds. All around, the dense thickets of alder and sallow are filled with warbler song in early summer, willow, sedge and grasshopper warbler being very numerous. In autumn flocks of tits, including willow tits, gold-crests, siskins and redpolls feed in the bushes.

As long as you remain quiet, the area round the gate can be a good spot for observing mammals and the fortunate few may see a polecat, quite common on the reserve. However, stoat, weasel or water vole are much more likely. The wet pools here have lots of frogs and toads in spring, while salmon and trout spawn in the main river and its tributaries. Sometimes shoals of tiny elvers can be seen in the Afon Fflur by the gate.

Keep an eye on all fence-posts and prominent objects here, especially in winter, as buzzard, merlin, peregrine and various owls use them as watch-points – even the tower roof is worth checking as you walk towards it. Several short-eared owls are winter visitors, while two or three barn owls breed nearby and hunt over the bog.

From the tower there are good views over an excavated fresh-water scrape sur-rounded by sallow thickets. This is a favourite place for ducks and migrant greenshank and green sandpiper, and merlins often hunt the bushes in winter. A hundred yards back from the tower a kissing-gate on the right leads onto a very slippery boardwalk out across the bog for some 600 yards (548m). A permit is required for this section, but a shorter boardwalk exists along the bog edge a further 100 yards (91m) back along the fence, so that people without a permit can look at the bog flowers too. These board-walks run through very deep bog and on no account should you step off the side – moreover they can be under several inches of water after rain, so take care.

The main boardwalk is the start of a

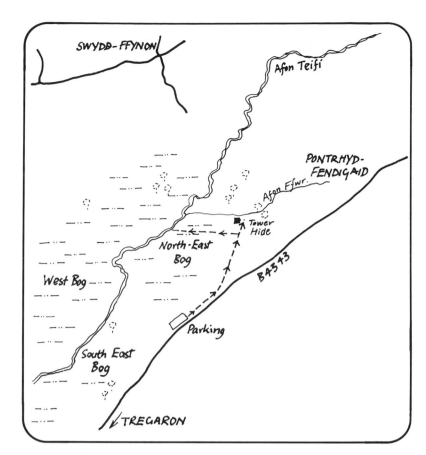

long, three-mile trail out to the River Teifi and then through the length of the reserve along its banks. The boardwalk ends after 600 yards (548m) in what appears to be the main bog, but the river bank can in fact be reached by aiming at the red marker posts, the last of these – on top of a dry knoll – is actually just by the river, hidden at this point. It is unnecessary to go further than this to see the flowers and structure of the bog – the path is indistinct and disturbance should be minimised in this fragile environment.

The other mammal star of Cors Caron, which may be glimpsed briefly by the lucky visitor who gets up early, is an otter, hunting the river.

Bog flowers along both the boardwalks are spectacular in summer: marsh mari-gold, marsh cinquefoil, bogbean, and the rare bog-rosemary; bog asphodel, royal fern, all three species of sundew, and cross-leaved heath. Bilberry, cowberry and cranberry are all common on the drier hummocks. In July, large heath butterflies may be numerous and the list of dragon-flies is a long one.

This is an active bog in that it is still forming peat, a process which is evident from the numerous brilliant green patches of growing sphagnum mosses in wet hollows. Don't step off the boardwalk or you may never be heard of again.

Cors Caron is the finest example of a lowland raised bog in Britain with a wide range of plants and animals

The Lake District
CUMBRIA

Address of Site/Warden

Lake District National
Park Centre,
Brockhole,
Windermere,
Cumbria

Highlights and Features

England's largest national
park – crags, forests, lakes.
Often crowded with tourists,
and generally regarded as
one of Britain's most
beautiful areas. Despite
tourist pressure still has
good breeding hill birds, now
including one or two pairs
golden eagles. Good for
alpine plants.

Facilities

Many and varied. Many local
information centres.

Photo Tips

Photographs of scenery
most likely. Most wildlife at
some distance.

*Canada geese bring
downy goslings to feed
and shelter on the waters
of the Lake District*

At 880 square miles (2,279sq km) the Lake District is Britain's largest national park. In its mix of mountain, moor and lakes, this small corner of Britain offers some of Europe's most dramatic scenery. Its mood may change in moments from balmy, peaceful summer greens and blues to fierce and challenging black and grey of hills lashed by a sudden squall – sent of course to scrub the fells clean for next day's batch of visitors.

Wildlife Walk: Harter Fell and Haweswater

Take the minor road from Shap to Bampton (4 miles (6km)), and at Bampton follow the signs to Mardale and Haweswater. The view soon opens out, and the large reservoir which drowned the village of Mardale Green which fills the valley before you. Despite this, Haweswater blends very well with the rugged landscape.

Along the western shore a wall of crags, Lad, Leythwate and Whetter, rear high above the lake. To the south, the great face of Harter Fell blocks the whole of the head of the valley, while the long buttresses and high wide top of High Street fill the south-west.

A small island, wooded and green and called, appropriately, Wood Howe, lies near the head of the lake and has a colony of lesser black-backed and herring gulls. Canada geese shepherd their goslings round the lake edge, while cormorants dry their wings on the island shore; red-breasted mergansers bring ducklings to the lake in June.

Park in the little car-park at Mardale Head. The fells around are huge, wild and rugged. Scan the skies, watch the hill tops: this is English golden eagle country. One pair breeds, but to date not very successfully, in the northern lakes. The crags and moorland all around are good for hill birds: ravens are frequent, buzzard, merlin and short-eared owl all occur on the high fells.

From the car-park take the path directly south up the right-hand side of Gatescarth Beck, past tumbling white waterfalls and steeply upwards for 300 yards (274m) through the upper drystone wall. The great bulk of Harter Fell and its soaring cliffs tower above you and the long Riggindale Ridge soars away to your right to join the long flat top of High Street on

the western skyline. Watch for the occasional passing peregrine which may play around the crags on the up-draughts, soaring out over the dale head.

Examine the edge of the tumbling beck for mountain plants. The Lake District fells have a fine selection where the sheep cannot get to them, and waterfall rocks are likely spots. Gatescarth Beck has brittle bladder fern, alpine ladies' mantle, purple, yellow, mossy and starry saxifrages and many plants of butterwort on peaty banks. Mountain Ringlet butterflies appear on sunny days, a rare English species; ring ouzels and wheatears frequent the jumble of rocks.

After a mile's hard going you reach the saddle of Gatescarth Pass with Longsleddale falling away before you. Turn right on a secondary path which climbs hard around the back of Harter Fell and which, within half a mile, brings you to the summit ridge above the crags.

The path runs north-west towards the summit cairn: the cliffs fall away at your feet, and the views to the north and west are staggering in their immensity. Most of the visitors will still be down at the car-park, and look like ants from this lofty perch. Up here you are alone with the wind and the racing clouds.

The track now descends rapidly through substantial crags and turns back towards the Mardale Valley above the lovely mountain tarn of Small Water. From here the descent through the great corrie is straightforward.

This is a real fell walk of 4 miles (6½km), much of it very hard going. It can be dangerous in bad weather.

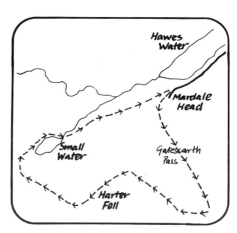

The North York Moors National Park

As one approaches from the south through the arable fields of the Vale of York and the Wolds, a high table-land comes into view. This is the North York Moors National Park, designated in 1952 and extending to 553 square miles (1,431sq km).

Man first appeared up here some 5,000 years ago, and his early efforts at clearing the forest were largely responsible for the open heather moorland.

The main visitor centre is at Danby Lodge, near Castleton in Eskdale, while Sutton Bank Information Centre is open from Easter to October.

Wildlife Walk: The White Horse of Kilburn and Gormire Lake

This is a five-mile (8km) round walk along the ridge of the Hambledon Hills and down the scarp to Gormire Lake, best in early summer for its wealth of limestone flowers and insects.

Take the A170 from Thirsk eastwards, climbing the steep western scarp of the Hambledon Hills at Sutton Bank; park at the information centre and obtain nature-trail leaflets – the view back westwards is quite stunning, with the Vale of York 400 feet (122m) below, stretching to the shadowy blue-grey hills of the distant Pennines. Follow the footpath south along the limestone ridge, part of the Cleveland Way long-distance footpath. A steep, partially forested scarp drops away to the right and, after about a mile, the Yorkshire Gliding Club field is on the left. Stand on the edge of Ivy Scar at the end of the glider field and you will feel the strong up-currents of air rising rapidly up the slopes. Along these steep limestone crags in company with the gliders, float squadrons of jackdaws, rooks and the occasional kestrel, peregrine or sparrowhawk.

One feature of the landscape is the White Horse, a large open chalk patch, which lies on the steep southern edge below Low Town Brow carved by a group of nineteenth-century schoolboys and their teacher. The conical, wooded Hood Hill to the west marks the previous scarp edge which is being slowly eroded away by undercutting and collapse.

The limestone woodlands hold a superb calciole flora with many rare plants: lily of the valley, herb Paris, baneberry, columbine, bird's-nest orchid, green hellebore, greater butterfly and small white orchids all being found in the district. There is just an outside chance of finding the nearly extinct ladies' slipper orchid in these limestone hills, too.

The limestone grasslands, especially in the disused quarries along the scarp slope, also have an excellent flora, orchids in particular being abundant in some years: fly and bee orchid, frog orchid, fragrant and green-veined orchid can all be found, as also can bloody cranesbill, rockrose, field gentian and felwort. Limestone butterflies are particularly prominent with four species of blue, and Dark Green Fritillary in late June.

Return along the scarp and cross the main road to the Sutton Bank viewpoint, checking the open grassland for orchids and limestone flowers. Follow the path north along Sutton Brow and descend the nature trail through Garbutt Wood Nature Reserve. The 70 foot (21m) cliff of Whitestone Crag towers above and clearly demonstrates the thickness of the limestone bed lying on the more easily eroded layer of shale.

Gormire Lake itself has a wealth of flowers, with tufted loosestrife, bird's-eye primrose, marsh cinquefoil and bogbean; and Little Gormire nearby has extensive growths of bogbean and water violet covering most of the water surface.

Return along the nature trail to the Sutton Bank car-park.

Address of Site/Warden

North York Moors
N.P. Committee
The Old Vicarage,
Bondgate, Helmsley,
York YO6 5BP

Highlights and Features

England's largest expanse of heather moorland. Fine range of moorland flowers and birds. Southern sector of the park based on limestone dales, with many rare limestone flowers. Farndale noted for millions wild – and carefully protected – daffodils in spring.

Facilities

Information centre at Sutton Bank.
Well-known tourist area with many facilities.

Photo Tips

Flowers are most likely source of pictures. Use wide-angle zoom lens.

The kestrel is the most numerous of Britain's birds of prey, here hovering on the wind to watch for insects or rodents in the grass below

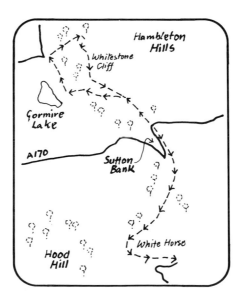

Upper Teesdale
CO DURHAM

Address of Site/Warden

Upper Teesdale National
Nature Reserve
Warden:
Hunt Hall,
Forest in Teesdale,
Barnard Castle,
Co Durham
Bowlees Visitor Centre,
Newbiggin in Teesdale,
Barnard Castle,
Co Durham

Highlights and Features

Vast area of moorland, parts
of which are on limestone
rock. Probably untouched by
last Ice Age so many arctic-
alpine plants survive. Good
for moorland birds.

Facilities

Visitor centre at Bowlees
open daily from 1000–1700

Photo Tips

Plants are speciality here but
it is important to keep to the
path, therefore both wide-
angle and medium telephoto
lenses are worthwhile.

*High Force is a
magnificent waterfall
where the River Tees
crashes over the hard
edge of the Great Whin
Sill*

The landscape and flora of the Upper
Teesdale National Nature Reserve are
relicts from the last Ice Age. This is not
apparent to the visitor driving across its
wide fells in summer, and yet it possesses
one of the most fascinating plant communities in Britain.

The current theory on the amazing
assemblage of plants surviving here is that
the area has remained largely untouched
since the ice retreated 10,000 years ago.
The underlying rock is a friable 'sugar'
limestone, formed when the hot magma
of the Great Whin Sill, which runs for 70
miles (112km) across northern England,
baked the surrounding limestone into
marble; this gives thin, easily eroded,
freely draining soils, and in consequence
these arctic Ice Age plants survive in large
numbers.

Their survival is aided by a notably cold
winter climate. The presence of more
southerly species such as hoary rockrose
and horseshoe vetch – this is their most
northerly location in Europe – is explained
by the extent to which the climate has
warmed to its present summer levels.

In the 1960s great controversy was
caused by the decision to dam the River
Tees above Cauldron Snout waterfall
which would drown a large area of the
best limestone flora. The conservation
lobby lost this particular battle, but it
helped to bring the need for environ-
mental protection to a wider public awareness. In any case, the growing population
and industry of Teesside did need the
water supply, so the argument was strong
for both causes. The reservoir was com-
pleted in 1970.

This is a subtle place which needs
information and investigation by the
visitor to obtain the best from his day.
Without information, the area at first sight
appears to be little more than sheep walks
and peat moorland.

Do first visit the Bowlees Visitor Centre,
housed in the old Methodist chapel, just
off the main road. An excellent information display produced by the Durham
Conservation Trust is laid out here and
provides a good introduction to the wildlife of Upper Teesdale. Nearby is a picnic
site established in an old quarry, and there
are good local walks to Low Force and
High Force waterfalls, all worthwhile.
High Force in particular is a spectacular
moorland waterfall, quite majestic by any
standards, where the River Tees crashes
70 feet over the hard edge of the Great
Whin Sill. It is easily reached from the car-
park by the High Force Hotel, along a
wooded path and attracts over 100,000
visitors annually.

In Upper Teesdale one walk is described which follows the nature trail of
Widdybank Fell, and then goes for a short
distance south along the Pennine Way.
You are 1,650 feet (503m) up on the fells
here: take an anorak and wear walking
boots to tackle the Pennine Way at
Cauldron Snout.

You *must* keep to the path to avoid
damaging the precious flora. No removal
of any plant or specimen is either allowed
or warranted. Teachers with parties of
students are sometimes guilty of this, as
indeed are amateur botanists, and it is
quite unforgivable.

Wildlife Walk: Cow Green Reservoir and Cauldron Snout

Turn off the B6277 main road west at
Langdon Beck, to Cow Green Reservoir,
signposted after 3 miles (4.8km). This is a
high road across wide open country, and
the fells full of hardy Swaledale sheep
which are themselves an important factor
in the management of the unique
sequence of vegetation. Soon the great
sheet of water which forms the reservoir –
770 acres (315ha) – fills the valley before
you. A large car-park is the access point at
Wheelhead Sike and you can obtain a
leaflet from the dispenser, though first
examine the car-park display of information. The nature trail runs along the tarred
road south around the reservoir for a mile
to the Cow Green Dam. This part of the
walk is on fairly level ground, and accessible to the disabled.

Wild, open hillsides roll away in gentle
slopes in all directions – Cross Fell to the
west is the highest part of the Pennine
Way. Curlew 'bubble' around you. Here
and there golden plover and dunlin nest
on the open undisturbed moorland, and
short-eared owl and merlin also breed in
small numbers, the owl living on voles
while the merlin hunts the abundant
meadow pipit. Red grouse are also
numerous.

Two hundred yards down the gravel
path the track passes through a kissing-

gate; on the left you will see a small limestone exposure which has many plants including spring sandwort and rock rose. Where the departing glaciers left a layer of boulder clay over the rocks, peat developed in the waterlogged soils; this difference in foundation matter is why there is such a contrast between the peat bog covering large areas and characterised by cottongrass, bog moss and heather, and the areas where it is limestone soils that are exposed.

Some of the limestone soils a little way down the track from the gate have been untouched by the magma intrusion of the whinstone. Here, blue moor grass dominates, with thyme, tormentil, heath bedstraw, dog violet and mountain pansies, which are of the rarer purple form; the Teesdale violet, an individual and rare plant, also grows in the area. A small cliff of 'sugar' limestone occurs near Stop 5 on the trail with a lime-rich stream below where spring sandwort, harebell, thyme and rock rose are common.

Two hundred yards (183m) beyond, near Stop 7, is a broad strip of limestone turf. Growing close to the track are many of the specialities including spring gentian, alpine bistort, hair sedge, moonwort, lesser clubmoss and sea-plantain; autumn gentian flowers later in August.

The path descends beyond the Meteorological Station towards the dam, crossing areas of sugar limestone and two small streams.

A small fenced area by the track clearly demonstrates how much the flowers increase if sheep are excluded. However, if the area were not grazed regularly the grass sward would eventually become dominated by coarse grasses which in fact would overwhelm all the rare plants.

In the stream 'flushes', bird's-eye primrose, butterwort, rare Scottish asphodel, yellow mountain saxifrage and alpine meadow-rue all flower abundantly. Just before the dam the track crosses the flat top of the Whin Sill, forming a natural shallow bay in the reservoir. Lapwing, snipe and redshank may be found here. The vegetation of the Whin Sill plateau is dominated by bog-mosses and it is clear that the area is blanket peat bog.

Below the dam the water of the Tees, now tamed, splashes down a series of rapids for 100 yards (91m), before vanishing over the edge of the Sill at Cauldron Snout. This is Britain's highest waterfall at 200 feet (61m), and a spectacular sight at maximum flood. Clamber down the path of the Pennine Way which picks its way carefully to the foot of the fall beneath the cliffs of Falcon Clints. Ring ouzels and wheatears are found on the rock faces, while common sandpipers nest along the river bank. The unremitting thunder of the

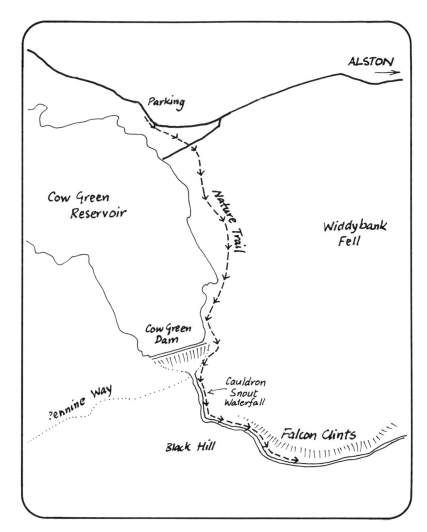

falls cannot fail to leave an indelible impression of Upper Teesdale on your mind.

Provided you have kept to the roadway and taken nothing but photographs, you will have left these rare arctic plants safe in their fragile environment for future generations of visitors to enjoy.

A rare flower of the mountains, the spring gentian is a speciality of Upper Teesdale

61

The Galloway Forest Park
DUMFRIES AND GALLOWAY

Address of Site/Warden

Forestry Commission,
231 Corstorphine Road,
Edinburgh EH12 7AT

Highlights and Features

Huge area forests mostly
planted by Forestry
Commission some 40 years
ago. Above the forests large
area mountainous country
with few roads. Good for roe
deer, red squirrel, pine-forest
birds. Occasional golden
eagle, hen harrier.

Facilities

Information centre at the
Deer Museum on A712 at
Clatteringshaws Loch, open
daily April–September
1000–1800.

Photo Tips

Some birds may be tame
where used to tourists. Deer
and wild goats in enclosures
at Clatteringshaws Loch.
Use medium telephoto
lenses.

*Roe deer are numerous in
many parts of forested
Britain*

Rugged granite mountains, white torrents of waterfalls, vast expanses of peat bog and huge conifer forests give a real 'wilderness' feel about the Galloway Forest Park. The scenery is quite magnificent, and yet so many southern tourists rush past it on their way to the Highlands.

The hills in the main are softer and more rounded than those of the far north but they are still high, and in places like Glen Trool, possess huge glaciated corries and great crags. The climate, warmed a fraction by the Gulf Stream, is a little more equable than in the Highlands, so the wildlife is very rich with some mountain species occurring in good numbers. The conifer forests, which cover wide areas, had a dramatic effect on the wildlife when they were first planted over thirty years ago.

One wildlife walk and a tour are described. The mountain sections are strenuous and demand full walking equipment; most of the animals and birds may be seen at lower levels and the walks are best tackled in the spring through to autumn.

Wildlife Walk: Rhinns of Kells

These hills are the backbone of Galloway, running north–south for 10 miles (16km) through its heart.

On the A713 4 miles (6km) north of New Galloway take the minor narrow road signposted 'Forrest Road' at Polharrow Bridge, through a wide valley full of damp pastures with open oak, alder and birch wood along the Polharrow Burn. The sheep walks which mount the hills are unfenced, so beware the numerous sheep and Highland cattle which lie actually *in* the road.

Wheatear and stonechat are numerous in the rocks, and buzzard and sparrowhawk haunt the lower wooded hills. After 4 miles (6km) the hills in front of you are covered by conifer plantations; park in the tiny car-park provided by the Forrest Estate. A hundred yards further on, turn left through light, mixed woodland – ignore the first 'hillwalkers' notice and proceed through a latch-gate past the white cottage of Forebush.

Polharrow Burn has dipper and grey wagtail while many redpolls, siskin, tree pipit and willow warblers are present in the light birch-woods. A path climbs the

open hill to the right of the cottage and provides the more open, scenic route but you have to ford a rushing torrent. If you prefer not to tackle this, climb the stile on the left of the cottage and walk the main track through the conifers. This emerges in half a mile on the hills above Loch Harrow.

The long ridge of the Rhinns of Kells stands above you, filling the skyline. These are no dramatic crags but huge boulder-strewn shoulders rising to the summit of Corserine at nearly 2,660 feet (810m). This is eagle country: scan the hillsides and the skyline. Three or four pairs breed in these hill fortresses, although recently with little success.

All around, new plantations have sprung up and new hill tracks clearly indicate the likelihood of trees over all these slopes. While the trees are small, hen harriers and short-eared owls breed in their cover – watch the moorland for both, gliding low. However, once the trees reach 6–8 feet high (2m) they close in too much, and the harriers and owls have to leave. A long ribbon of white shows Folk Burn tumbling down the side of Corserine; here, it rushes past in a dredged channel which drains the peat bog for the new trees. Roe deer are numerous and easily seen in these young plantations.

Follow the track up Folk Burn towards the hills, signposted 'stile over deer fence'; the fence is 7 feet high (2m), the plantation comes to an end and the open hills tower above you. Watch prominent objects, as large boulders and fence posts are used as look-outs by peregrine and merlin, both rare but possible here. Corserine summit is gained by a rough, boulder-strewn climb through knee-high heather, up the ridge to the left to North Gairy Top. Allow two hours from the deer fence. The ridge-walk north is long and arduous, and it is better to return by the way you have ascended. Only the meadow pipit is present in force. Scan the skies for golden eagles.

Wildlife Tour: Galloway Forest

The tour runs from New Galloway via Newton Stewart to the head of Glen Trool. The A712 from New Galloway runs through the middle of the Forest Park with its great forests, albeit 1950s plantations, and the lovely Clatteringshaws Loch. The

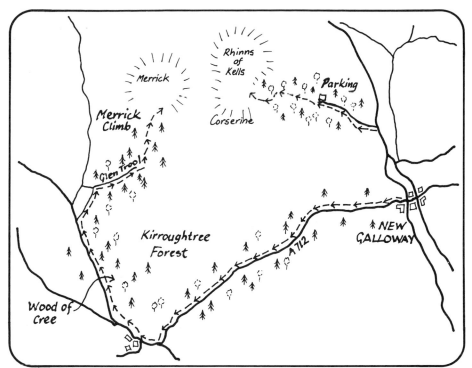

Deer Museum by the loch is a good source of information on the park. West of the loch is the Deer Range, two square miles (5sq km) of Brochlach Hill where red deer are easy to see because they are enclosed within its fences.

Murray's Monument is a good vantage point to watch for birds of prey: golden eagles sometimes pass over, goshawk is a possibility and peregrines are often to be seen soaring around the towering crags of the 150-acre (60ha) Wild Goat Park. The wild goats are usually along the fence by the road waiting for hand-outs.

Four miles (6km) north of Newton Stewart on a minor road through Minni-gaff lies the RSPB Wood of Cree. There is a grassy parking spot by the large informa-tion notice, with a one-mile long forest walk through this old coppiced oak and birch woodland. The road overlooks the marshy meadows and stream of the Water of Cree, which is noted for its salmon; its regular inhabitants are dippers, grey wag-tails and goosander which are numerous on the stream water, and the marsh is a riot of colour in summer, with purple loosestrife, yellow flag, meadowsweet and marsh bedstraw; there are always plenty of damsel- and dragonflies.

Buzzard, sparrowhawk, woodcock, tree pipit, redstart, pied flycatcher and some 40 pairs of wood warblers breed in the wood; and at dusk, barn owls regularly hunt the marsh fields. The roads are lined with bluebells, broom, gorse, hawthorn and rowan, all out together in a blaze of colour in June.

Continue on the minor road north, turning right through extensive forests into Glen Trool in 4 miles (6km) by the large car-park at Stroan Bridge. The Water of Minnoch rushes south here in a tumbling torrent, and dippers can be seen by the bridge. The road continues into Glen Trool, through lovely oak, birch and conifer woods; the tree-cover gets less as you climb the glen, and so more birds breed up here than in the dark forests further down – the woods around Loch Trool have many redstarts, wood warblers and pied flycatchers, with siskin and cross-bill common in the pines.

This is a really scenic spot. Park in the very last car-park, from where you can appreciate the open mountain views which are superb. Mulldunnoch Hill on the opposite shore of the loch often has wild goats on its ledges. This car-park is the start of the Merrick climb, which is quite a hard one! Merrick summit, at 843 metres (2,768ft), lies four miles and four hours to the north. The first two miles are very wet underfoot because the path has small streams running down it, subsidiary to the crashing waters of Buchan Burn. It then runs through conifers for half a mile before climbing steeply up the long southern ridge of the mountain which rises slowly to the summit with superb views. Mountain hare and hen harrier are found on the peat moorland, with peregrine and golden eagle on the high crags. All these birds may be visible from the car-park; watch the skyline.

With a lot of luck you may see an otter in the waters, or a pine marten in the forests – pine martens were extinct but have been re-introduced in the last few years.

Not exactly wild animals, and yet the shaggy Highland cattle are very much a part of the Scottish countryside

62

The Queen Elizabeth Forest Park

ARGYLL

Address of Site/Warden

Forestry Commission
David Marshall Lodge,
Aberfoyle,
Argyll

Highlights and Features

Large area of mountainous country including the Trossachs, the forest being across the Highland Boundary Fault. Many mountain birds and animals associated with the Highlands. Forests have many typical highland species such as crossbill, black grouse. Arctic-alpine plants on Ben Lomond.

Facilities

David Marshall Lodge – excellent information centre open 0930–1800 daily April–October. Area is of open access at all times.

Photo Tips

Animals and birds may be sometimes approachable where they are used to tourists, such as at the Lodge, along Loch Lomondside. Use medium telephoto lenses. Try wide-angle shots from Ben Lomond.

The globe flower is an uncommon mountain plant of the north and west

Loch Lomond and the Trossachs are for many people the epitome of Highland scenery, and the Queen Elizabeth Forest Park is a mecca for tourists from all over the world and in particular for 'day trippers' out from Scotland's central industrial region.

Main information point is the David Marshall Lodge just north of Aberfoyle on the A821, set in beautiful, open countryside surrounded by hills and woods, with its own reed-fringed lochans and nature trails. Loch Lomond is the largest freshwater lake in Britain, famous for the beauty of its wooded shores and islands. 1,040 acres (420ha) in the south-eastern corner, including five of the islands, is a national nature reserve. The loch is famed as a fishing spot for salmon, sea and brown trout.

Dozens of walks exist in the area around Loch Lomond and the Forest Park to the east, and despite the hordes of summer tourists the wildlife of the area is still good. A good time to visit is late spring when you can best see the wildlife before the roads are jammed with tourist cars. Two walks are described. One is a straightforward forest and lochside walk; the second is the ascent of Ben Lomond, looking at the birds and flowers en route.

Wildlife Walk 1: Loch Ard

This is a six-mile (9.6km) round walk on fairly level ground. From Aberfoyle drive one mile west on the B829 to the car-park on the left at Milton. A well marked forest track runs along the southern shore of Loch Ard, with good views looking north to the rugged mountains of the Trossachs. The sudden and dramatic change of scenery here is the result of a great geological divide known as the Highland Boundary Fault – south are the softer farmland hills of sedimentary sandstones, but to the north the mountains are hard metamorphic schists, slate and gritstone.

The narrow wooded neck of Loch Ard is a good place to look for waterside birds: dipper, grey wagtail and common sandpiper are all frequent; mallard, teal and tufted duck all breed here and, with the regular provision of large nest-boxes by the Forestry Commission, the lovely goldeneye is also sometimes encouraged to breed. This is a recent arrival from Scandinavia, only in the last few years and

starting with a few pairs in the Spey Valley – 800 nest-boxes have been erected by the RSPB and the Commission in central and southern Scotland. Goosanders breed here too, and may use the nest-boxes.

The path runs through lovely mixed oak, birch and conifer woodland, a mixture of natural and planted forests, and the bird population of this damp lochside woodland is very rich. In May, breeding birds include many wood warblers, redstarts, woodcock, tawny and long-eared owls, siskin, redpoll and crossbill. It is worthwhile to look out for red squirrels along the track, too.

After two miles the track turns right round Couligartan Farm, with steep wooded slopes rising to the west. Buzzards are seen frequently, circling the hill of Coire Eirigh, while roe deer emerge to feed in lochside fields at dawn and dusk. The track joins the road at Kinlochard and it is a three-mile (4.8km) lochside walk back to the Milton car-park.

Wildlife Walk 2: Ben Lomond

Hundreds of hikers troop up Ben Lomond in summer, but try the walk in late spring. This is a real mountain walk and needs full mountain equipment, boots, wet gear and so on – Ben Lomond summit is 3,192 feet (972m) and it can snow hard even in May. This a four-hour climb, and an hour-and-a-half return trip.

Access is easiest from the car-park 100 yards (91m) north of the Rowardennan Hotel right by the loch shore. The path starts uphill to the left of the little toilet block, initially through sallow and birch woodland. Lots of woodland birds can be found here with willow and wood warbler, redstart and tree pipit. The path climbs suddenly and steeply, eroded and worn in places, up a rocky track through the conifer plantation of Rowardennan Forest – volunteers have been working constantly on the track here, fitting boulders firmly into place to help prevent erosion. One twenty-foot section involves a little mild scrambling with the aid of some 'stepping stones'. The forest thins out quite quickly several hundred feet above the loch and suddenly, there is your goal: the green summit of Ben Lomond. It looks so easy from here, just over the next hill! Do not be fooled – you still have three hours' climbing to do.

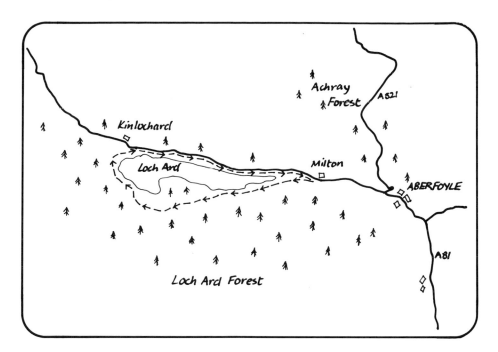

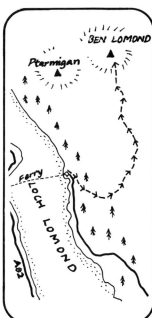

The forest edge, a long deer fence along the dense mass of conifers, is a good place for a stop. Light birch scrub borders a tumbling hill burn and birds are good, with the species typical of a mountain woodland, wood and willow warbler, redstart, woodcock and sparrowhawk along the wood edge.

Go through the kissing-gate and start climbing the track up open, tussocky moorland, the forest receding to become an unbroken line of trees below you. The views of Loch Lomond are sublime, if the weather is kind. The track winds upwards, steeply, over an enormous sweep of hillside towards the high shoulder of Sron Aonaich. Here you are likely to be alone with the wind and the sheep.

Mountain plants are impressive on Ben Lomond and are best sought in places inaccessible to sheep, along the rocky edges of the burns. Cailness Burn on the north-western flank and along the Bealach Buidhe Burn are good sites, but any stream is worth examining. There are also a number along the track; alpine plants include alpine ladies' mantle, globeflower, starry, mossy, purple and yellow saxifrages, fairy flax, cyphel and many mountain species of fern.

This area of lower moorland will almost certainly have breeding curlew. If you are lucky you may see a merlin or a hen harrier, although buzzard and raven are more likely; a few ptarmigan may be found on the least disturbed areas of the high tops.

The path climbs a little rocky gully, good for flowers, to the first main shoulder. Stop for a gaze at the ever-widening ranks of mountains, and a breather. Pass through a second kissing-

gate and then climb a long steep pull onto the south-eastern ridge of the mountain. The views eastward, previously obscured, begin to open out. The first of a line of stone cairns, with wheatears nesting in the holes, marks the path along this high, broad ridge and the going is a little easier for a while. You may see red deer and mountain hare may be on the mountain if there are not too many other walkers, and also wild goats, especially on the crags of the Ptarmigan.

Over the final shoulder and there is the summit, still apparently miles above you. The path rises gently on springy peat turf before you tackle the final steep, short section to the summit ridge. The path actually runs through a line of crags, not at all the green summit you saw from far below, which was only thin grass among the rocks. A small col in the middle of these crags gives superb views down the huge cliffs of the eastern, hidden face of the mountain and if you are lucky, drifting buzzard, eagle and peregrine may be encountered. A few more yards and you are on the top with the survey triangulation point, and a feeling of airy elation. The crags fall away on all sides. Rank upon rank of mountains stand all round you, while far below the twenty-seven square miles (70sq km) of the loch look surprisingly far away.

Loch Lomond from 'the Ben', a view back down the Lomond path

63 Ben Lawers

PERTHSHIRE

Address of Site/Warden

Ben Lawers National Trust for Scotland Reserve, Warden: Mountain Visitor Centre, Ben Lawers, Killin, Perthshire FK21 8SH

Highlights and Features

Widely regarded as best site in Britain for arctic-alpine flowers. Ben Lawers range of mountains lies on lime-rich soils providing tremendous range of plants. Also good for mountain birds with golden eagle as occasional visitor.

Facilities

Superb interpretative mountain centre on lower slopes. Area open at all times. Visitor centre open Easter–May and September 1100–1600, June to August 1000–1700

Photo Tips

Many alpine flowers. Use wide-angle zoom lens and tripod. Try some shots to show the mountain scenery behind the flower.

Red deer are numerous in the Scottish hills

High above the northern shore of Loch Tay towers the mighty mountain of Ben Lawers, at 3,984 feet (1,213m) one of the highest in Britain. The Ben Lawers range includes six separate mountains and two other tops, all over 3,000 feet (914m).

This range of mountains has a unique arctic-alpine flora due to the formation of its underlying rock; so spectacular is the range and quantity of alpine plants that the mountain is internationally famous as a 'mecca' for botanists. Some 8,000 acres (3,237ha) of the southern part of the range belongs to the National Trust for Scotland, acquired to protect this wonderful alpine flora which is under heavy and increasing pressure from visitors, many of whom may be unaware of the special importance of the area.

In 1975 the whole area was declared a national nature reserve and the Nature Conservancy Council now assists the Trust with grants towards conservation management projects. A visitor centre, carefully designed to blend with the mountain, is sited on the road from Loch Tay to Glen Lyon. A large car-park exists here and is used most by walkers seeking to 'bag' Ben Lawers; as a direct result of the considerable increase in the use of the path (300 people per day in summer) to the summit, the slopes are becoming badly eroded. The centre provides a superb interpretative display of the geology and wildlife of the area, together with many guides and leaflets and is essential visiting before setting out on the mountain. A ranger/naturalist of considerable standing is employed to manage the reserve and provide guided tours of the nature trail in the peak visitor months of July and August.

Quite apart from its flowers, Ben Lawers also has a fine variety of mountain birds and mammals. One wildlife walk around the nature trail is described, together with a tour along the northern side of the range through Glen Lyon.

Anyone attempting the summit climb is reminded that this is a strenuous mountain walk of some six hours up and down, and requires full mountain equipment. Snow is possible on the summit even as late as June. Visiting for flowers is best from May to August.

Wildlife Walk: Ben Lawers Nature Trail

Buy a leaflet from the visitor centre – the nature trail is signposted and forks right, away from the main summit trail. A boardwalk runs across the first 200 yards (183m) of boggy ground which is acid, peaty, nutrient-poor soil in total contrast to much of the rest of the mountain. Growing here among the sedges and rushes are bogmoss (sphagnum), bog-bean, bog cotton (cotton grass) and bog asphodel. Sundews and butterwort are also found, adding to their nitrogen requirements by catching insects on their sticky leaves. The bog pools support dragonflies, frogs and palmate newts.

Curlew breed on the moors, their haunting call following you as you descend to the footbridge over the Endramucky Burn. Here the geology of the mountain is made more apparent in the exposed rocks: Ben Lawers is composed largely of metamorphosed (ie changed by heat and pressure in the earth's crust) lime shales which are now lime-filled mica-schists. It is because of this particular rock formation that the flora is so superb, and the few other areas of Central Scotland made of the same material are all nearly as rich in alpine flowers. Ben Lawers is unique because its climate has allowed a larger number of species to be present.

Hard by the footbridge, along the burn edge and especially where afforded protection by the rocks, are many mountain plants: purple saxifrage flowers in April, while yellow mountain saxifrage flowers in July; pink cushions of moss campion grow on rocky ledges, flowering best in late May; alpine ladies' mantle is abundant down the watercourse. The trail climbs steadily up the eastern side of the burn with all these flowers just a few feet away.

Birds are few, with meadow pipit and skylark most numerous. Wheatears nest among the rocks, while dippers use the burn; red grouse are present in the heather areas which are burnt off in spring – away from the Trust estate – to maintain the population for shooting. There is no shooting on the Trust's property.

When the estate was purchased, many local farms retained the right to graze sheep on the hills. Man removed the trees centuries before and now the sheep graze any new seedlings to ground level so

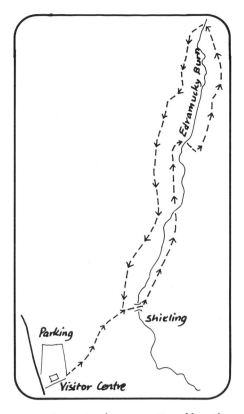

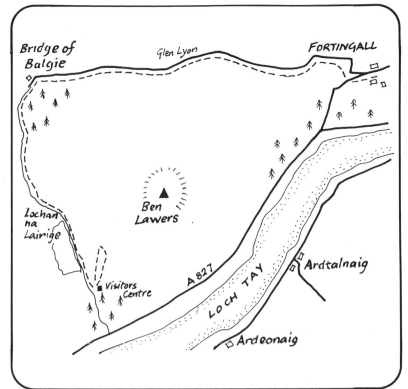

preventing natural regeneration. Near the top of the trail are just two small trees, a rowan and a birch protected from the sheep by the ravine.

The gorge itself is full of plants; wood anemone, primrose and male fern grow here too, indicating that even shade-loving woodland plants can survive at this level. Many mountain flowers can be seen to advantage with large clumps of saxifrages and moss campion.

Above the gorge, the trail crosses the burn below a small dam – wheatears and ring ouzels may appear on the rocky slopes, and there are tadpoles by the hundred in burnside pools. There are many alpine plants growing here, including alpine and stags-horn clubmoss; tormentil and alpine ladies' mantle which are common; while mountain pansies are found in the grassland of this upper section. In rock crevices there are maidenhair and green spleenwort ferns, but the dominant plant with striking fountains of bright green leaves is the mountain fern.

Wildlife Tour: Northern Ben Lawers and Glen Lyon

On leaving the visitor centre, turn right along a narrow single-track road with many sheep. After one mile, a large dam blocks Lochan na Lairige; the huge crags of Meall nan Tarmachan tower over the western side of the loch, and this is really high open mountain country. Scan the crags for raven, frequent in this area and watch the hilltops for gliding golden

eagles – this road into Glen Lyon is a good spot to see them. Buzzards are frequent.

Around the dam, huge stretches of grassland are filled with alpine flowers, alpine ladies' mantle being abundant. The road is very narrow and hugs the mountainside, and as it turns onto the northern slopes the vegetation changes to brown heather moorland. Here the climate is cooler.

Red deer are regular on the Ben Lawers range and may often be seen by the Mhuilinn Burn which flows north into Glen Lyon; mountain hares are frequent along this road. Wheatears and ring ouzels inhabit the rocks, the former being very numerous.

Light birch woodland, backed by conifer plantations, runs alongside the road for a mile into Glen Lyon at the Bridge of Balgie – look out for roe deer in the open fields along the river bank; upper Glen Lyon to the left is scenically superb. The road ends in 10 miles (16km) at a dam at Loch Lyon.

Downstream the road runs for 14 miles (22km) along delightful, partially wooded riverside slopes to Fortingall. Dipper, grey wagtail, goosander, common sandpiper and even goldeneye may all be seen from the various well-sited picnic spots. Buzzards are frequent and often sit on telegraph poles, golden eagles sometimes drift over from their high top range and ospreys visit the river. A lucky visitor may even glimpse a Scottish wild cat, known to be present in these lovely hills.

Moss campion is an arctic-alpine found on mountains in Scotland, the Lakes and in North Wales

64

The Cairngorms
HIGHLAND

Address of Site/Warden

NCC Head Warden,
Regional Office,
Achantoul,
Aviemore PH22 1QD.
RSPB Warden,
Insh Marshes,
Ivy Cottage,
Insh,
Kingussie,
Highland PH21 1NT

Highlights and Features

Highest continuous
mountain block in Britain.
Alpine-arctic conditions most
of year. Northern corries
disturbed by skiing but rest
of area little used.
Eagles, dotterel, snow
bunting, ptarmigan on tops.
Osprey, crested tit,
capercaillie etc in valleys.
Best all round mountain area
in UK with greatest variety of
species.
Many mammals – with red
deer numerous on the hills
and roe deer common in
valley woods, along with red
squirrel. Otters in the Insh
Marshes.

Facilities

Many tourist facilities
including ski lift to near top
of Cairngorm at 4,000 feet.
RSPB reserve at Insh
Marshes with hides.
Trout Farm at Aviemore.

Photo Tips

Snow persists here much of
the year so learn to
compensate for extra light
from snow landscapes. Long
telephoto lenses in the
valleys will provide pictures
of red and roe deer.

Stand on the summit of Cairngorm and below is a breathtaking view covering 100 square miles (259sq km) of mountain country.

These mountains form the most extensive area higher than 3,000ft (914m) in Britain. This is the land of red deer, wild cat and golden eagle. Only the toughest plants survive among the pink granite boulders on the exposed summit plateaux, and there are no trees – the tree line is left far behind at 2,000ft (609m) in the more sheltered valleys. Ice Age glaciers gouged out these high mountain valleys and the great 'corries'; the mountain sides are covered in heather and the valleys are peat 'mosses' of some depth.

For those who are fit and know about mountains, anywhere in the Cairngorms can be rewarding, in particular the famous Lairig Ghru pass from Speyside to Deeside which crosses right through the middle of the mountain block. This is a severe walk of 25 miles (40km). Two wildlife walks are described, one in lowland forest and marsh, and the other on the high tops which involves a steep hill climb to make your heart really pound. Go prepared – any walk in these mountains needs good protective clothing, walking boots, spare jumpers and food, maps and a compass.

Wildlife Walk: The Hill Top, Carn Ban Mhor (3,443ft (1,047m))

From Aviemore take the B970 to Feshiebridge and then the tiny back road on the left to Achlean and Glen Feshie. Travel 2 miles (3km) past the glider field until the cliffs of a rock spur, Creag Ghiuthsachan, rise above on the left. Park here briefly. Scan the crag for golden eagles, though beware of identity problems with smaller buzzards; in Glen Feshie you may see both together, with raven thrown in for comparison.

Park after another mile, off the narrow road; a gate bars the way and Achlean Farm is still a mile further south. Walk towards Achlean with the rushing Feshie river on your right – dipper, grey wagtail, goosander and merganser may all be seen up and down its waters. The sparse conifer plantations hold willow and wood warbler in summer and hundreds of redwings in autumn; roe deer are numerous.

Just before the farm, take the footpath

left across rough ground and climb the six-foot (2m) 'stepped' stile over the deer fence. Before you are the western slopes of the Cairngorms stretching northwards to Aviemore: to the south are the mountain ramparts of Glenfeshie Forest and Blair Atholl.

The path, through dense heather, dips to a footbridge in the midst of a scattered copse of Scots pine with a rushing torrent running through it; crossbills and siskins are frequent here. It then climbs steadily up the hillside through heather and tussock grass. You may climb right to the top and see little wildlife, but excitement will certainly follow your every step. Scan the skies for eagles and peregrine. Eagles are frequent over the hilltops here, hunting ptarmigan, grouse and mountain hare. Red deer are always present, but the autumn rut is exceptional and brings hundreds into the southern end of Glen Feshie so that the hills echo with the roaring of the stags. Access here is controlled in late autumn because of the deer cull – check with the Glen Feshie Estate (telephone on Kingussie 453).

The Carn Ban Mhor summit, a flat, broad top with a cairn, is reached in two hours of uphill walking. In May the snow recedes only slowly, but on the moorland all around will be 'piping' golden plover and the sound of 'bubbling' curlew – scan the tussocks carefully for dotterel, too.

The views from the top are stunning. Westwards, mile upon mile of Monadliath peaks fill the horizon, while to the east the great snow-filled corries of Braeriach fall to Loch Einich in the valley. North are the great cliffs of the Sgoran. There is just a chance of seeing a snowy owl – one appears on these remote Cairngorms tops most years. Return by the same path, watching for eagles all the way down.

Wildlife Tour: Forests, Lochs and Marshes

This takes in the three main habitats of the Spey valley as it runs between the mountains. Start at the small car-park at Loch-An-Eilein, two miles south of Aviemore on the B980 – the loch is very picturesque, with a ruined castle on an island and the snow-covered Cairngorm foothills rising above; the forest is ancient Scots pine with birch-scrub and juniper. Follow the obvious path to the right of the loch with

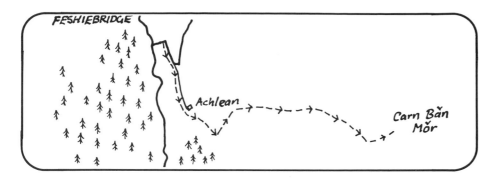

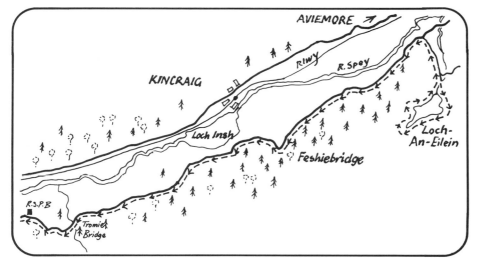

the steep Ord Ban behind you – in summer this is a favourite picnic site. In May it is usually quieter and the forests hold all the birds one could hope for: crossbill, crested tit, siskin, redstart, wood warbler and singing willow warblers.

At the far end of Loch-An-Eilein the track continues to the smaller Loch Gamhna, and the forest gives way to more open moorland. Goosander and golden-eye often breed round these lochs and may be seen from time to time.

The track runs back along the forest edge behind both lochs, and offers the best chance of seeing black grouse; roe and red deer may appear here too, while in the foothills to the east is the only herd of reindeer existent in Britain. Piles of eaten pine-cones indicate that red squirrels are about, and as at Loch Garten with its many visitors, they may become fairly tame in midsummer, waiting for hand-outs. The track finishes the two mile circuit in the car-park.

Four miles (6km) further south one comes to Loch Insh, used for sailing. This is the start of five miles (8km) of loch and fresh-water marsh, much of which forms the RSPB Insh Reserve. Loch Insh itself is an excellent place for watching ospreys in summer: park by the roadside at the sailing club, or buy a drink at the bar and sit on the verandah. Ospreys regularly fish the shallows of Loch Insh – and this is

bird-watching in comfort!

Four miles further south still towards Kingussie along the B970 the road crosses the River Tromie at Tromie Bridge. Stop here and walk round the rough track along the edge of the Scots pine woods, because it is an excellent spot to see red squirrels and crossbills. The river has dipper by the bridge.

A mile further on the tiny RSPB car-park is on the right; access to the reserve is usually limited to two hides and their entrance tracks to avoid disturbance. The great flood plain of the Spey with its extensive sedge fen and reed-beds is the heart of the area, and the views from the hides are magnificent – so, too, are the birds, with an extensive list of rarities.

Autumn and winter bring an extra six feet (2m) of water and three hundred whooper swans, and grey-lag geese pass through in thousands on migration. Teal, wigeon, tufted duck, goldeneye, goosander, merganser, mallard and shoveler all breed here in spring, and an enormous black-headed gull colony occupies much of the marsh in summer.

Although only buzzard and possibly sparrowhawk breed, hen and marsh harriers, ospreys, peregrines and merlins together with the occasional eagle or goshawk may all be seen over the reserve. Even a gyr falcon has been seen in recent years.

The high tops support little life, but the ptarmigan, a high altitude grouse, is specially adapted to deal with the cold climate

The Central Glens

AFFRIC AND CANNICH

HIGHLAND

Spring brings fountains of bright green mountain male ferns to many damp flushes in the highlands

The Central Glens which penetrate deeply into the Highlands from east to west are regarded by many as among the loveliest places in all Scotland.

All these glens, of which Glen Affric and Glen Cannich are splendid representatives, were once clothed by the old Caledonian forest of Scots pine and birch, and the flat river-sides of the lower straths covered with impenetrable thickets of alder and willow. Hills, lochs, rivers, waterfalls and woodland combine in these glens to create a glorious scenic tapestry at all seasons of the year. Here, Bonnie Prince Charlie found refuge in a cave after Culloden, high above Badger Falls; while a century or more later Landseer painted his 'Monarchs of the Glen'.

Two wildlife walks are described, and each of the glens described is subtly different in character one from the other, although both display a rich Highland flora and fauna. Information on side walks is also given. Best time to visit is May–July, but autumn is beautiful.

Wildlife Walk 1: Glen Affric

Access from Loch Ness is from the main A82 west on the A831 at the 'Official Loch Ness Monster Exhibition Centre'. This road leads through Glen Urquhart, which serves as a gentle introduction to the high hill country to come – Loch Meiklie and the small lochs around Milton have Slavonian grebe as regular summer visitors. In Cannich, take the minor road south to Glen Affric, turning right at the Fasnakyle Power Station.

This is the best known of the central glens, much of it run by the Forestry Commission. Facilities for the visitor are provided, whereas Glen Cannich and Strathfarrar to the north are private estates still largely devoted to farming and deer stalking. Despite the number of visitors its wildlife is still superb, especially for those prepared to walk a little.

Badger Falls, and the Bonnie Prince's cave, are passed just inside the entrance to the glen, the whole of the lower half of which is filled with graceful woods of birch, alder and oak, brilliant green in early summer and filled with primroses, bluebells and bird-song. Wood and willow warbler, redstart, redpoll and spotted fly-catcher join the many other common woodland birds. In autumn the woods are

silent, but the glen shimmers with great fountains of tremulous gold.

One mile beyond Badger Falls come Dog Falls. Here there is a car-park with a forest-walks indicator. Two footbridges over Dog Fall gorge allow access to the stands of old Caledonian pine forest, the River Affric hurtling past below. Two walks of some 4 miles each (6km) are possible, as well as a 7-mile (11km) walk to Affric Lodge.

Capercaillie, black grouse, crossbills, crested tit, siskin, buzzard, sparrowhawk and woodcock are all numerous in these woods. Red squirrels are frequent, and towards the end of the tourist season may come to picnic sites for food; roe deer are common in the forests, in fact so much so, that strong measures have had to be taken by the Forestry Commission to control deer to allow regeneration of the natural woodland.

These wet, native pine-woods are noted for the hundreds of species of lichens, mosses, ferns and liverworts which clothe all the twigs and branches and make this a botanist's paradise.

Beyond Dog Falls the road runs along the north shore of Loch Beinn a Mheadhoin, also called Benevean, for 4 miles (16.4km). Two well spaced car-parks allow access to the whole of the loch. There are several wooded islets. Black-throated and red-throated diver are present all summer although the latter only visits to feed; goosander, goldeneye and red-breasted merganser all breed in the area, and the Forestry Commission has erected nest-boxes to encourage the expansion of the goldeneye. Ospreys regularly fish the loch.

The road crosses a bridge over the tumbling waters of Fiadh burn – by this time the glen has opened out with high hills all around. A track rises high across the hills here to Glen Cannich in 13 miles (21km), the last six having no track at all and for experienced hill-walkers only.

Oystercatcher, common sandpiper and dipper are found by the bridge. Beyond, the road becomes a gravel track to the Affric river car-park in a mile, with wide views to majestic mountain peaks. Many walks are possible from this spot, varying in severity from short strolls along the several paths, to long-distance mountain walks involving full expedition prepara-

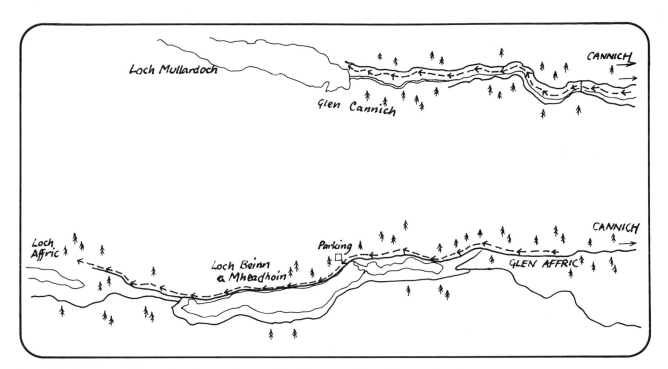

tions. The longest of these heads west along the north shore of Loch Affric for 21 miles (34km) to Kintail on Scotland's west coast.

A good idea is to walk a mile or two along this path beside Loch Affric, past Affric Lodge, with wide mountain views. Golden eagle and peregrine are often seen.

Wildlife Walk 2: Glen Cannich

The entrance to Glen Cannich lies directly west from Cannich village up a steep hill next to the Glen Affric Hotel – the road is single track with passing places. After two miles, you will see tiny Loch Craskie on the right, fringed with sedge and partly hidden by woodland, which holds breeding teal and wigeon; herons fish the shallows.

For three miles (4.8km) the glen sides are filled with birch and oak woodland, as in all these glens, the climate being marginally warmer on the east- and south-facing slopes. The glen suddenly opens out after a further mile, with the whisky-coloured River Cannich rushing past to join the River Glass at Cannich village.

The open moorland comes right down to the road, and this is an excellent spot to see wild red deer outside the stalking season. Notices in the glen warn of deer-stalking on the hills from August to January, but in early summer the deer have not been shot at for six months and may be seen on the valley floor, in the small fields and grassy 'lawns', feeding with the sheep.

The road crosses a wooden bridge and passes Mullardoch House, with a wonderful backdrop of snow-topped mountains, the snow lying here into mid-June. These are lovely craggy hills with open heather moorland, dotted with Scots pine. Birds are similar to Glen Affric, with peregrine and buzzard frequent over the hill-tops and redstarts, wood warblers and siskins in the forests.

Deer are far more plentiful here than in Glen Affric and may be seen along the road right up to Loch Mullardoch and its great dam. Mammals are the stars of the area, although difficult to see apart from the deer. Red squirrels are frequent in the woods with pine marten and wild cat both relatively common. Mountain hares occur on the hills, while hill-top birds include red grouse and a few ptarmigan on the highest tops. Wheatears, whinchats and ring ouzels occupy the rocky slopes above the dam, while far above between the snowy peaks flies the golden eagle.

Still rare, but increasing its range, the wildcat is a true native Scotsman, living in undisturbed hill country

139

66

Strathfarrar

HIGHLAND

Address of Site/Warden

Strathfarrar National
Nature Reserve
c/o NW Scotland Regional
Office
Nature Conservancy Council
Fraser Darling House,
9 Culduthel Road,
Inverness IV2 4AG

Highlights and Features

Large remnant of the old
Forest of Caledon. Most of
the typical highland birds
and mammals with
numerous red squirrel, pine
marten, wild cat, red and roe
deer, golden eagle and other
typical mountain birds in the
higher parts of the glen.

Facilities

None.

Photo Tips

Scenics only during a day
trip. Access at all times on
foot, but limited to
0900–1800 by car at
Leishmore gate.

*Above the forests
Strathfarrar is a land of
rugged mountains and
wild water. A land where
eagles fly*

Strathfarrar is Scottish Highland scenery at its most magnificent. Huge forests of native Scots pine hug the deep gorges of the river bank, their very inaccessibility having saved them from destruction in the past. Higher up the glen the woods were cleared, and the combination of open mountain, deer moorland and the Ancient Forest of Caledon is Scotland at its wildest.

Since deer-stalking and sheep-farming became important parts of the Highland economy, Strathfarrar has really been overgrazed because of its comparatively sheltered wintering grounds, especially for deer from the hills; this means that over the last 150 years very few seedlings have survived. The lower part of the glen is therefore now a national nature reserve by agreement with the private estates of Culligran and Struy, and a fenced 'forest regeneration' programme has been started to try and prevent the ancient forest from disappearing simply of old age!

One wildlife tour through the Glen is described. This is a long day's walk of some 15 miles (24km) but access by car is possible at Leishmore – up to thirty cars may obtain a permit from the gatekeeper from 9am to 6pm. Walkers and cyclists have access at all times. Entry is at Struy village, by Struy bridge. Turn west on the signposted road, and obtain your entry from the gatekeeper.

Two hundred yards beyond the gate, open fields on the right often hold wild red deer outside the stalking season, which is 12 August to 20 October. Notices at various points ask walkers to keep off the hills or travel at their own risk – which is high! During the stalking season the deer will be very wary, but by early summer can often be seen easily. At this time they will be growing new antlers, still covered in velvet.

The River Strathfarrar runs in full spate along the left of the road; for the first mile the glen is filled with bright green birch and alderwoods in early summer. A further wide 'lawn' on the right occurs after half a mile, with good chances of wild red and roe deer near to the road.

Three miles (4.8km) into the glen, the massive and impressive native pine forests rise above the river's southern bank on the steep slopes of Coille Gharbh. The huge old trees are impressive, but can be reached only by locating the tiny wooden footbridge across the torrent of the river – the key to exploring these wonderful forests. The car can be safely pulled off the road nearby. If you reach the first small hydro-electric dam on the river, you have passed the bridge by half a mile.

Across the bridge the path is very steep and very boggy, and anything less than strong boots will be soaked in seconds. A few birch trees mix with the Scots pine, with juniper near the river banks. The steeper slopes have a dense shrub layer of bilberry, cowberry and heather, mixed with vast quantities of mosses and beneath the bushes the humus/litter layer may be several inches deep. The trees are hung with ferns and lichens, whose purpose seems to be to transform this into a 'cloud forest', and indeed it is – it can be very wet in Strathfarrar.

The path continues to climb steadily, passing a white post after some twenty minutes – ignore this and continue climbing. Ten more minutes and a tumbling peaty burn is reached. On a fine day the wildlife of these woods is revealed in all its splendour: crested tits, coal tits and crossbills, both common and Scottish species, are numerous; willow and wood warblers fill the wood with birdsong, while tree pipit, redstart and spotted flycatcher are all present. Capercaillie and black grouse are common, although the latter is more readily found at the higher tree-line on the moorland edge.

Mammals are a great attraction, with red squirrel and roe deer plentiful; pine martens are quite common, but because they are mainly nocturnal they are less likely to be seen – try really early, or at dusk, and sit quietly near a rocky outcrop in the forests: you may be one of the very lucky few to see a wild pine marten.

At first sight flowers seem few, but among the heather grow two special pine-wood orchids, creeping ladies' tresses and lesser twayblade. Single-flowered and intermediate wintergreens are also present.

The path climbs past a storming waterfall and then, 400 yards (365m) beyond, dips to a little wooden plank bridge over the burn; beyond, the tree-line and the open moor are soon reached. Return by the same route, a very rough two-mile walk.

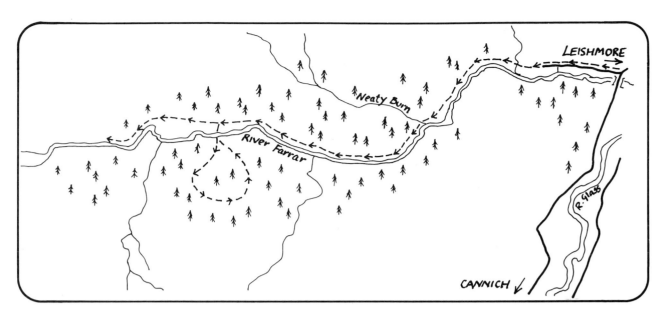

Further up the glen the road passes a small hydro-electric dam and the views beyond the forest begin to open out to show dramatic crags and huge snow-capped peaks. The nature reserve western boundary is reached at Deanies Lodge, a white-painted cottage on the right of the road. Two small lochans by the roadside hold a colony of black-headed gulls; goosander and red-breasted merganser may appear here, breeding in the glen. Dippers are found on the burn.

Beyond Deanies Lodge the glen is half-a-mile wide, with the mile-long Loch Beannacharan filling the valley floor. Ospreys sometimes fish the loch, and oystercatcher and common sandpiper breed around its edge, besides elsewhere along the glen.

Beyond the first loch there is a small underground power station buried deep in the hillside. Creag a Bhruie above has substantial cliffs. Beyond the power station the hills sweep right down to the road, while a stalkers' track climbs to the right towards the peak of Sgurr na Ruaidhe, along a rushing stream.

Loch a Mhullidh is the next small loch, a mile in length with wooded islets. Black-throated divers visit it, while goosander, merganser and goldeneye may all breed nearby. This is superb wilderness country and good for golden eagles – scan the hilltop skyline. Beyond the second loch the glen is wide, nearly a mile in places, with extensive mountain views. The road rises above the valley floor, with peat bog stretching half a mile to the river. Many small lochans here shelter breeding curlew, and goosander families. Red deer can be numerous with herds of 100 or more feeding on the plain.

Braulen Lodge is passed on the left; it was quite ruined, but in 1987 it was being restored. A bridge, and then a wide track off to the right climbs past the waterfalls of the Allt Toll a Mhuic burn. This track runs for three miles (4.8km) into the remote hill country to the north, and allows access to the high tops for experienced mountain walkers. The spectacular crags and peaks all around are good for golden eagle, so watch the skies!

The road climbs hard towards the head of the glen with wheatear, ring ouzel and common sandpiper along the roadside. The great dam at Monar Loch seems almost a sacrilege in such lovely untamed country, but hydro-electric power is essential in the Highlands. Common gulls have colonised an island in the loch beyond the dam, and divers, goosander and sometimes common scoter are sometimes to be seen on its waters, but the roadway is now private.

Strathfarrar penetrates some of the most remote fastnesses of the Highlands.

The pine-woods of the lower reaches of Strathfarrar are now a national nature reserve, and part of the ancient Forest of Caledon

67

Beinn Eighe and Torridon
HIGHLAND

Address of Site/Warden

Beinn Eighe National
Nature Reserve,
Warden:
Aultroy Visitor Centre,
Kinlochewe,
Ross-shire
Torridon – National Trust
for Scotland,
5 Charlotte Square,
Edinburgh EH2 4DU

Highlights and Features

Magnificent mountain
scenery with lochs, sea-lochs
and pine forest. Wild cat,
pine marten, red deer, otter,
golden eagle, divers, waders.
Arctic-alpine plants.

Facilities

Information centre in
Kinlochewe and National
Trust Centre at junction of
A896 and Diabaig road. Area
open at all times. Real
mountain country away from
the roads.

Photo Tips

Scenics. Any wildlife
photography requires time
and an 'expedition'
approach.

*The true monarch of the
glen, the golden eagle just
holds its own at some 350
pairs throughout the
Highlands*

This is a land of loch and mountain splendour unsurpassed in all of Britain – great peaks divided by long sea-lochs create real fjord country.

Much of the area is owned by either the National Trust for Scotland or the Nature Conservancy Council. The two principal mountains of the Torridon group, Liathach and Beinn Eighe, are quite outstanding for the grandeur of their corries, crags and soaring ridges. Beinn Alligin and Beinn Dearg, although lower, are also steep and craggy.

Beinn Eighe was the first national nature reserve to be declared in Britain, in 1951, and its lower nature trails are a good introduction to the area.

Three walks are described, one around the nature trail of Beinn Eighe, the second around Loch Clair and the third a real mountain walk through the pass between Liathach and Beinn Eighe. None of these walks reaches up to the summits, and anyone who is considering climbing to the heights of Liathach or Beinn Eighe is reminded that conditions change rapidly and can be very severe. The area is best visited from May to July.

Wildlife Walk 1: Beinn Eighe
Stop at the Aultroy Visitor Centre, a little white-painted cottage one mile west through Kinlochewe by Loch Maree. The trail's car-park is on the bank of the loch a further mile along the road.

In these mountains the best wildlife areas tend to be on lower ground – the high tops of the Beinn Eighe ridge, although so magnificently scenic have just two species of breeding birds: ptarmigan and, very rarely, snow bunting.

From the car-park, walk out onto the loch shore and scan its waters. Black-throated diver and wild grey-lag geese breed and are usually present. Red-throated divers breed on many small lochans and often feed on Loch Maree, together with goosander and red-breasted merganser.

The huge mountain massif on the far shore is Slioch and its undisturbed corries are home to nesting golden eagles; this car-park is one of the best sites in Scotland to see a golden eagle. Keep scanning the hilltops – birds often drift out over the loch or across from one range to the next.

The nature trail, just over a mile long,

has its entrance through a tunnel under the road, and starts to climb past the Allt na h-Airidhe burn over a footbridge; it quickly gains height through light birch and gorse, and then into tall heather and an extensive area of ancient native Scots pine woodland. This band of open pine forest runs for some way along the lowest slopes, with the tree-line visible some 300 feet (91m) above.

A 'Mountain Trail' of some four miles (6.4km) rises well above the tree-line to 1,750 feet (532m), but erosion damage has caused frequent closure. A pony-trail behind the visitor centre provides good access to the higher ground.

The birds and animals of this pine forest include pine marten and wild cat which are the main attractions. They are largely nocturnal hunters and seeing one is a matter of great good fortune – tall heather, bilberry and cowberry among abundant moss means that animals can easily slip by unseen. Red and roe deer are both numerous, using the woodlands for food and shelter.

Birds are few but include many willow warblers, wood warbler, redstart, siskin and redpoll; both common and Scottish crossbills are present. Woodcock and sparrowhawk breed, the latter often hunting the roadside for small birds. Red grouse are common in the heather.

The views from the top of the trail are superb with the heights of Slioch facing you across the loch. Peregrine, buzzard and merlin are all likely, especially where the steep valley of Gleann Bianasdail cuts north under Slioch. An open-fronted 'conservation cabin', made of logs and roofed with turf and heather, is at the top of the trail and is a marvellous place to sit and watch for eagles. The trail descends to the car-park through the pine-woods.

Wildlife Walk 2: Loch Clair
Two miles south of Kinlochewe towards Torridon on A896 a small car pull-off allows access to the track south round Loch Clair. This is a four-mile (6.4km) round walk on level ground, muddy on the last section. Follow the track past a notice 'Coulin Estate – Footpath Only'.

This is a tarmac drive to Coulin Lodge. A tiny lochan on the left is fed by a rushing burn under a wooden access bridge 400 yards (365m) from Loch Clair. Dipper,

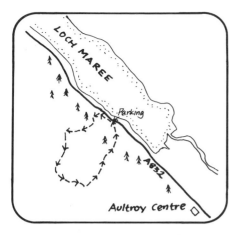

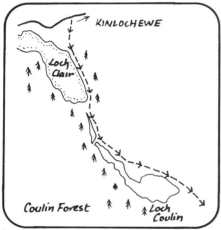

common sandpiper and oystercatcher may appear along the banks and hundreds of heath spotted orchids and butterwort grow in the grass, with waving cotton grass on boggy ground.

Half a mile brings you to Loch Clair, with the classic view of Liathach towering to the south, and Sgurr Dubh and its formidable craggy shoulders directly above the loch shore. Scan the waters of Loch Clair for black-throated divers, regular here.

The estate now has a fish farm at the loch's southern end.

The road runs under steep crags covered in light birch woods full of purple rhododendrons in June. Bluebells and primroses line the path, still in flower in June even so far north.

Kestrel and peregrine are frequent round the crags, and scan the dark slopes of Sgurr Dubh for cruising golden eagles.

Substantial pine woodland divides Loch Clair from Loch Coulin, a mile-long lochan farther south down the Coulin river valley.

Birds are good with redstart, wood-warbler, siskin, redpoll and crossbills.

The brown, clear, peaty burn connecting the two lochs is full of trout but you must not touch or off to the Sheriff you will go.

Fish farm cages are suspended in the first part of Loch Coulin, but the rest is a superb, highly vegetated loch with extensive areas of emergent water plants including bogbean and marsh horsetail. Mallard, teal and wigeon all breed here, while greenshank feed along the shallow margins. The greenshank do sometimes breed on higher ground but are unpredictable.

The last section of the path is rather rough and muddy along the lochside but gives superb wild country views. Return by the same route.

Wildlife Walk 3: Liathach – Beinn Eighe Pass

This is a nine-mile (14km) five-hour, one-way rough walk with minor hill sections, which takes you right into the heart of the Torridon mountains.

Park at the stone bridge car-park three miles (4.8km) west of Torridon on the Diabaig road above the Torridon sea-loch. Catch the post-bus which passes here at about 10.15 am (not Sundays), alighting at Coire Dubh by the Ling mountain hut – this cuts out the five-mile (8km) roadwalk to regain your car. The huge bulk of Liathach rises above, dominating the landscape: its tiered parallel precipices of Torridon sandstone look like a giant's wedding cake, made from pastel bands of maroon and terracotta.

The path climbs easily along the western side of the burn, deep into the mountains beneath Liathach on one side and the huge west face of Beinn Eighe on the other. After nearly three miles (4.8km) the stream is forded and the path crosses the watershed above some small lochans – red-throated diver are often on these small pools, with curlew and golden plover on the moorland.

The track, a little indistinct across the boggy ground, continues westwards for four miles (6.4km) to a wooden footbridge over Coire Mhic Mobuil, whence an easy mile descends to the stone bridge car-park.

Loch Maree, the 'enchanted loch', is a good spot for eagles drifting out from Slioch mountain to the north

143

68

Inverpolly
HIGHLAND

Address of Site/Warden

Inverpolly National
Nature Reserve,
NW Scotland Regional
Office,
Nature Conservancy Council,
9 Culduthel Road,
Inverness IV2 4AG

Highlights and Features

Huge area of mountains,
moorland, peat bogs, lochs.
Very wild country difficult of
access.
Eagles, deer, otters, wild
cat and many more highland
birds and animals.

Facilities

Information centre at
Knockan Cliff open
Monday–Friday 1000–1800
May to September.

Photo Tips

Very wild area – needs full
walking gear. Close
encounters with area's
wildlife unlikely due to open
moorland aspect. Wild
country provides many
opportunities for landscape
pictures.

*The crumbling ridges of
Stac Pollaidh stand
sentinel over the wild
country of the 'far
north-west'*

North of the great mountains of Torridon; north of Ullapool, perched dazzling white on the shore of Loch Broom; gradually the landscape undergoes a subtle change. Gone are the huge steep-sided mountains piled rank upon rank, and instead the hills have more space with great open moorlands, full of shining lochs spread between.

Inverpolly is the start of this transition from a mountain realm to the great seascapes of the far north coast. It has wonderful coastal scenery with, inland, the largest wilderness area in Britain ever designated as a national nature reserve.

Access to Inverpolly is largely unrestricted but the Nature Conservancy Council would rather you kept to the few paths to avoid disturbance of the wildlife. In any case, walking away from footpaths is likely to involve impassable bogs, unfordable streams and unexpected cliffs.

Two walks are described followed by a tour around the peripheral roads. One of the walks is the popular ascent of Stac Pollaidh, giving an overview of the area's geology. Best time to visit is from April to July.

Wildlife Walk 1: Loch Sionascaig
Ten miles (16km) north of Ullapool on the A835 turn left on a minor road signposted to Achiltibuie. This runs through magnificent country along the south side of the national nature reserve for 15 miles (24km) to the coast. After three miles it is possible to park by the roadside, just before the only visible building for miles, a tiny bungalow surrounded by trees.

A track to the right climbs steeply through a copse of Scots pine, quite unmistakable as there are no other trees hereabouts. The track is rough and very boggy in places.

After half a mile the steep climb ceases, the track levelling off past a small lochan on the left. High to the right are the crags of Cul Beag, while before you lies the great bulk of Cul Mor, like a sleeping giant, with Suilven in similar repose to the rear.

The path runs forward for perhaps another half-mile over very boggy ground with superb views of wide lochscapes, with Loch an Doire Dhuibh and Loch Sionascaig shining silver-white beneath Cul Mor. A remnant light birch woodland

runs along the shore of Loch an Doire Dhuibh, and the path runs through it to end under the great cliffs of Cul Mor within yards.

This is wonderful wild country, and yet you may come across nothing apart from the odd meadow pipit. If you are lucky you might see golden eagle, buzzard, peregrine, merlin, short-eared owl, greenshank, curlew, golden plover and raven as you cross the moor. In the birch woods the trees are very stunted, rarely exceeding ten feet (3m) in height, but they usually hold willow and wood warbler, and spotted flycatcher. Black- and red-throated divers may be seen on the lochs.

Return by the same route, and as you go, check all boulder tops and fence-posts for birds of prey which use them as 'lookout' points.

Wildlife Walk 2: Stac Pollaidh
One mile further west round Loch Lurgainn a car-park is found on the lochside. The great scree slopes and crenellated ridge of Stac Pollaidh tower immediately above. The distance to the summit and back is three miles (4.8km), the walk takes four hours.

The track climbs out onto the moor opposite the car-park. Because of the mountain's popularity this track has become a broad black scar across the peat – try not to widen it any further.

Although there is a path which climbs hard up the facing scree, the better route forks right along a narrow cairned track which rises under the buttresses of the eastern summit. The golden eagles that once lived here have long been driven out by disturbance.

The path is steep to the shoulder and then levels out round the north side of the mountain. It then rises in zig-zags up the rough scree slopes to the lowest point of the summit ridge. Only confident climbers should attempt the highest point on the western end. This entails some twenty feet (6m) of rock-climbing on good holds, but one slip would mean a death! The sandy summit ridge-path wanders for 300 yards (274m) through huge bluffs and pinnacles of weathered sandstone.

The view north and east covers the magnificent hinterland of the reserve: glaciers carved the mountains into their present forms and cut the valleys, scoop-

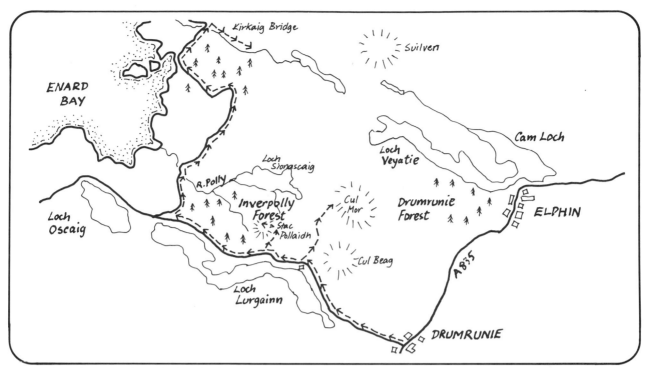

ing out deep basins to form the hundreds of lochs and lochans flung like jewels across the landscape. Weathering has fashioned Stac Pollaidh, consisting of soft red Torridon Sandstone, into its fantastic shape – the impressive cliffs of Cul Mor and Suilven are made of the same rock but they are capped by a hard quartzite, preventing erosion. The whole is based on a bedrock of Lewisian Gneiss, which, at 3,000 million years, is the oldest type of British rock and forms a characteristic scenery of rugged knolls.

Wildlife Tour: Inverpolly Periphery

As you turn off the A835 towards Achiltibuie the impressive, isolated Stac Pollaidh dominates the western skyline. Like so many places in the Highlands the best wildlife is found lower down in the more sheltered valleys – only the hardy ptarmigan and the rare snow bunting are regularly found on the highest tops.

Masses of yellow gorse line the first mile of the Achiltibuie road. Watch the gorse tops for stonechat and redwing – breeding redwings are a possibility throughout north-west Scotland.

Several small lochans on the left hold breeding wigeon with curlew, golden plover and greenshank on the boggy moorland.

Loch Lurgainn and Loch Bad a'Ghaill, joined by two tiny gaps, run for several miles along the roadside. Black- and red-throated divers may be seen here, and goosander, red-breasted merganser and grey-lag goose all breed. Birds of prey are frequent and may appear anywhere, as can herds of roving red deer.

Turn right at the first junction after some 8 miles (12.8km) signposted to Lochinver and Inverkirkaig. One mile along this road a lay-by allows an extensive view across a loch-strewn land dominated by the soaring west faces of Stac Pollaidh, Cul Mor and Suilven from right to left. This is a land of mountain, peat bog, waving cotton grass and silent staring sheep. Glimpses of a startling blue sea appear in hidden bays to the west.

The bogs and lochs along this road are very productive, with both divers, greenshank, golden plover and birds of prey frequent. Watch out for rarer breeding waders; wood and green sandpipers have bred in north-west Scotland.

The road runs through extensive light birch woods with much gorse, past beautiful sea-lochs with a rocky coastline. Suddenly the sea holds sway over the mountains. Summering great northern divers are frequent in these bays, with small colonies of Arctic tern, fulmar, shag, black guillemot and eider.

At Kirkaig Bridge you have crossed the border into Sutherland. A footpath runs east along the Kirkaig river for two miles (3km) as far as some dramatic waterfalls, passing through woodland of stunted birch and hazel which shelters many moor and woodland birds: willow and wood warbler, spotted flycatcher, twite, redwing, ring ouzel and woodcock are all found in this glen.

Half-way along the path, a mass of heath spotted and small white orchids grow in the heather.

Otters may be seen on the stream, and are regular on the sea-lochs.

Red deer, once forest animals, roam the open country of the north, now long cleared of true old forests

69

The Sutherland Flowes
HIGHLAND

Address of Site/Warden

None.

Highlights and Features

Vast expanses of open moorland with hundreds of lochs of all shapes and sizes. Various rather isolated mountains. Vast monoculture forests. Stronghold of many breeding waders, divers and other highland species in Britain. Otter and red deer.

Facilities

Picnic site at Borgie Forest – otherwise none. Difficult area to work other than round the edges. Needs full walking equipment.

Photo Tips

Needs an 'expedition' atmosphere with plenty of time to be successful. Wide open spaces mean close approach to birds or mammals unlikely.

The whimbrel is a rare breeding wader mainly confined to Shetland, with a few pairs on the mainland bogs

As one crosses the boggy land of the Mhoine peninsula between Loch Eriboll and the Kyle of Tongue a frontier, hardly noticed, is passed. To the south is the great peak of Ben Hope with its huge western escarpment, and a little to the east, the multiple rocky summits of Ben Loyal which rise distinctively above a broad, gently undulating landscape.

This is the beginning of a vast tract of blanket bog and lochans which until recently, stretched without interruption right across north-east Sutherland and much of Caithness. This is by far the largest area of peat moorland in Britain, and is generally regarded as its last great wilderness.

On its western side the mountains rise steeply to give a certain assurance to the view but to the east the walker, picking his way carefully around sinister-looking bogs, could be forgiven for a feeling of loneliness in a terrain akin to arctic tundra.

This impenetrable wilderness is the stronghold of many of Britain's rare and common breeding waders and moorland birds, and the whole area is under severe threat from afforestation. Huge areas have been covered with monocultured conifer plantations. Ditches are dug to drain the moors which are then ploughed up.

It is worth exploring the area not just to see its wealth of rare breeding birds but also to witness at first hand an object lesson in the destruction of wilderness for a 'quick buck'.

Needless to say, the easiest access is now that provided by the forestry tracks. Two wildlife walks are described, one of which passes along the edge of the new forests to view the open moor. An ascent of Ben Loyal is given, together with a short two-mile (3km) walk at Loch Craggie.

Best time to visit is late May to mid July. The Flowes resound to the crash of the gun after 12 August and you should keep off the open moor. However, by then most of the birds will have flown!

Wildlife Walk 1: Borgie Forest

This is a Forestry Commission 'new' woodland with good access off the A836 about 7 miles (11km) east of Tongue village. Most of the small lochans along this road have breeding red-throated divers, which can be easily observed without even leaving one's car.

Turn south onto a gravel track with Borgie Forest well signposted, just west of Borgie bridge. A car-park is situated half a mile along the track with picnic tables around a clearing in the trees.

These forests are largely a mono- or duo-culture of Sitka and Norway spruce, with the main mass already two decades or more old. It is the vast tract of new, tiny trees which threaten the existence of the Flowes.

There is a forest walk here but ignore it, and walk directly to the River Borgie, 100 yards (91m) east through the trees, and turn south along its riverbank. Open moorland stretches away to the east, providing three habitat 'edges' – the river, the moor and the forest.

Otters are possible on this river, so learn to look for clues to their passing, probably all you will see. The riverbank glows with gorse and broom in mid-June, and there is always a wide variety of birds to be seen here: dipper, grey wagtail, common sandpiper, goosander and merganser all live along the fast-flowing river; wheatears and stonechat are on the moorland, with numerous red grouse. Siskin and redpoll are common along the forest edge, and buzzard, sparrowhawk and merlin can all be seen.

Continue along the bank, fording a side burn by using the four stepping stones, and past a deer-fenced clearing to a strong weir. Here the main mass of Borgie Forest is lined up in dense ranks from the far bank over the low horizon. A deer-fence blocks the way, even hanging over the river to keep the deer out.

Redwing may breed in the scattered birch and gorse, and small forest birds are fairly numerous, with many coal tits and goldcrests.

Climb the stile, four steps each side, over the deer fence on the right, and walk 100 yards through the dark, lifeless interior of the forest to regain the main gravel track.

Return in half a mile north to the car-park.

Collect the car and drive south down the gravel track for 3 miles (4.8km) to emerge at the southern end of the forest. The huge eastern block of conifers stretches on south for three more miles. To the south and west however, the moor

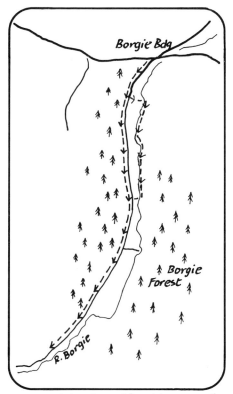

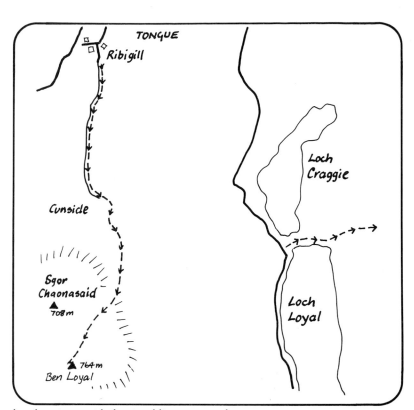

opens out to give wide vistas over the rolling Sutherland Flowes.

The track crosses a cattle grid and becomes very bumpy, but continue for a further half mile; there are spaces to park just three cars with a little turning room. To the west, Ben Loyal raises its many peaks beyond Loch Craggie.

Moorland birds are all around you here. The wonderful calls of many curlew, a clatter of red grouse from the heather, snipe drumming over marshy bogs, and if you are lucky a hunting hen harrier or short-eared owl may skim the hillsides.

Wildlife Walk 2: Ben Loyal and Loch Loyal Moorland

From Tongue village take the A836 south, towards Lairg. After one mile the road is out on wide moorland with the magnificent fish-tailed peaks of Ben Loyal high to the south. Two small lochans on the left of the road are fringed with sedges and bogbean, and wigeon and teal probably both breed here.

Loch Craggie, separated from Loch Loyal by a tiny isthmus of land, presents a wild and lonely face. Red-throated divers, goosander and merganser are found on Loch Craggie, with black-throated divers occasionally on this and other lochs in the district.

An ascent of Ben Loyal is possible from here, but the best route is to go in from the north, leaving the car one mile south of Tongue near Ribigill Farm. Take a track past a shepherd's cottage at Cunside and then strike slightly east up the grass and

heather to avoid the tumbling crags of Sgor Chaonasaid. It is a very steep, three-hour pull to the top, but on a fine day the view of northern Scotland is unbelievable: Ben Hope, Foinaven and Arkle lie to the west with a silver lochan-speckled moor to the east; north lie the lochs, bays and cliffs of Britain's north coast right to the huge cliffs of Hoy in Orkney far to the northeast. This ascent is only for experienced, well equipped mountain walkers.

A wonderful compensation for the exertion is the frequent passage of golden eagles, which soar around the inaccessible cliffs of the Ben. These may also be seen from the road at Loch Craggie!

Park in the lay-by overlooking Loch Loyal, and walk across the isthmus between the lochs on a rough track which runs east. Take your time here, particularly as otters are just possible on the lochs. A few grey-lag geese breed and pass to and fro across the moor. Curlew, golden plover, snipe, lapwing, dunlin and oystercatcher all breed on the moors nearby or near the lochans, and one or two pairs of merlin hunt the moors for larks and pipits.

The track passes a long birch wood at the head of the loch where siskin and redpoll are common and redwing occasional in summer.

The tiny lochans further out, anywhere on the moors, may hold a pair of red-necked phalaropes, wood sandpiper, common scoter, whimbrel or nothing. This is the land for new discoveries in Britain.

Destruction of the Flow country – this is Borgie Forest, an old-established monoculture of alien conifers. Wildlife is threatened by the new forests

BIRD ISLANDS AND SEA CLIFFS

This chapter describes some of the most magnificent wildlife spectacles to be seen in Britain: the great sea-bird colonies on the cliffs and islands of the north and west. These colonies are amongst our richest wildlife assets and are of major international importance, representing as they do a large proportion of the North Atlantic sea-bird population and the largest concentration in Europe.

The west and north coasts are dotted with many offshore islands because the rock which forms them is old and hard, whereas the east- and south-coast rocks, being predominantly soft, weather easily and do not remain as islands for long. It is not until one travels as far north as the Whin Sill rocks of the Farne Islands that the east coast rock hardens. Towards the far west the rocks of Land's End are made of granites, as are the offshore Isles of Scilly. Orkney at the other end of Britain is built mainly from the Old Red Sandstone of Caithness and Shetland, even more remote, lies on a bed of older metamorphosed gneiss.

The cliff coastline of England and Wales runs to approximately 2,700 miles (4,345km) in length – in Scotland the coastline of Shetland alone, much of it cliffs, amounts to nearly 1,000 miles (1,609km).

Along the Channel coast hardly any sea-birds other than gulls are found. The Needles off the Isle of Wight, the Purbeck cliffs, Portland Bill cliffs (fenced in by the Navy) in Dorset, Prawle Point and Berry Head in Devon, hold small colonies of auks.

Not until we reach the Isles of Scilly and Lundy do we meet larger colonies. Lundy has hundreds of breeding guillemots, razorbills and kittiwakes with about a hundred pairs of puffins mainly found at Battery Point. Manx shearwaters and storm petrels breed, arriving late in the evening to their burrows.

Steep Holm, further north in the Bristol Channel, houses a huge colony of herring gulls and also, rather strangely, a small colony of introduced muntjac deer – and lots of hedgehogs.

Moving north up the east coast, kittiwakes breed at Dover and at South Pier, Lowestoft, using old buildings in place of cliffs. A few fulmars are found along the low cliffs of Norfolk around Sheringham and Hunstanton. The first and quite the largest colony in England is found on the huge chalk cliffs at Bempton and Flamborough Head in Yorkshire. From Bempton on the east and Lundy on the west, the cliffs hold more frequent colonies, culminating in the huge numbers found on northern islands like St Kilda, Foula, and the isolated cliffs of Clo Mor.

Some species such as guillemots and razorbills require cliffs that are sheer because their young jump into the water before being fully able to fly. Guillemot colonies in particular are the most crowded, birds standing shoulder to shoulder on the ledges.

The single guillemot egg is a masterpiece of adaption, being large, four inches long (10cm) and tapered like a pear. If kicked about – as often happens – it rolls in a tight circle on the ledge, and so the number falling off is minimised.

Razorbills, which have more rounded eggs, nest in crevices in the rocks, while kittiwakes stick their nests of seaweed and mud to the tiniest of rock projections forming vast colonies on seemingly impossible cliffs.

Britain possesses 70 per cent of the world's population of razorbills, while the number of kittiwakes is rising quickly and in some places they have taken to nesting on buildings. These lovely little birds are quite the most oceanic of all our gulls, spending July until the following April far out in the Atlantic.

Fulmars compete a little with kittiwakes for ledge space, although they need the larger, grassier ledges not used by the kittiwakes and auks, forming well spread-out groups rather than dense colonies. Their numbers have expanded dramatically in the past 40 years, so that in Orkney and Shetland they nest on ruined crofts, in old stone walls and sometimes on ledges in grassy banks. Fulmars may now be seen prospecting the low shale cliffs of Reculver in Kent, and even nest on the window-sills of the south-east nuclear power stations.

Gannets are the most spectacular and the largest of our sea-birds, with a wing-span of six feet (2m). They usually breed in dense but carefully spaced colonies, each bird a bill thrust away from the next, on remote islands. The two colonies most easily studied are the growing group at Bempton, now over 600 pairs, and the large colony several thousand strong at Hermaness on Unst in Shetland. The Noup of Noss also carries several thousand pairs and is easily accessible from Lerwick.

Britain now supports 70 per cent of the world's gannets with the largest colony on St Kilda, where the island of Boreray and its gigantic stacks hold 100,000 pairs. Other large gannetries which can be visited – or at least circumnavigated – by boat are on the Bass Rock in the Firth of Forth, Ailsa Craig off the Ayrshire coast and Grassholm off the Pembroke coast of Wales. Sula Sgeir in the Hebrides and Sule Stack in Orkney are both more difficult of access, but hold thousands of pairs of gannets, along with many other sea-birds.

Most people's sea-bird favourite is the auk, the northern hemisphere's equivalent of the southern penguin, and especially the puffin, with its human-esque posture and its Charlie Chaplin walk.

Puffins have declined in the northern Atlantic, sometimes drastically. 'Operation Seafarer', organised by the 'Sea-bird Group' in 1969 to count Britain's breeding sea-birds, came up with the total for the whole of Britain of half-a-million pairs, less than the size of the single St Kilda colony of thirty years before. Despite much research, the reasons have not become apparent.

Black guillemots are rarer and more solitary birds nesting in scattered groups in boulder beaches and low cliffs around much of the Scottish coastline.

Good-sized auk colonies exist in many places in the outer islands, but on the mainland of Britain the least disturbed and most isolated cliffs are most likely: Clo Mor, the huge 900ft (274m) cliffs east of Cape Wrath, Dunnet Head in Caithness, Helmsdale and Bullers of Buchan cliffs on the Scottish east coast – all these support good numbers. South of the border, St Bees Head in Cumbria is an RSPB reserve holding several thousand guillemots and razorbills, though with fewer puffins. Peregrines and raven haunt the cliffs with many kittiwakes and fulmars. A few black guillemots here are the only English colony.

South Stack cliffs on Anglesey comprise another RSPB reserve, with many fulmar, kittiwake, shag, guillemot and razorbill, and a few puffins. Peregrine, raven and chough can be found on the cliffs, the choughs sometimes even appearing in the car-park! Worms Head on the Gower peninsula in South Wales has small colonies, but access is restricted to prevent disturbance.

Shearwaters and petrels, being nocturnal, have been little studied and even their colonies are not fully known. Numbers may be very high, as on Rhum where 130,000 pairs of Manx shearwaters live in burrows on the mountain tops; Skokholm off the Pembroke coast supports 35,000 pairs, while nearby Skomer has 100,000 pairs. Storm petrels and Leach's petrels often occupy tiny uninhabited islands, although storm petrels do breed on Lundy, Fetlar, and on Skomer. Some colonies are thought to be very large, but estimates have proved very difficult.

Arctic terns breed in huge colonies on open moorland, especially in Orkney and Shetland. Papa Westray's North Hill holds 6,000 pairs while Fetlar has nearly as many. Terneries exist on many of the outer islands with 500 pairs on Coquet Island, 300 on Samphrey in Yell Sound and a similar number at Balranald in the Hebrides.

Accompanying the terns in the north are the predatory skuas – great skuas have recovered from their last ditch stand on Hermaness and are now found on many Shetland and Orkney islands. A few pairs seem to be colonising the moors of Caithness. Arctic skuas, more agile but more easily disturbed, have fared less well and some colonies have even decreased.

Coastal mammals are naturally restricted, but all Britain's grey seal breeding sites are on offshore islands except two, at Loch Eriboll, and a few in some isolated coves in South Wales. Tiny inaccessible coves, sea-caves and beaches are used to avoid being disturbed. Common seals may use offshore islands especially in Shetland, Orkney and on the east coast.

With the near-extinction of the otter on Britain's rivers, the outer islands and the wild sea-coasts of the north and the west are now the main stronghold for the animal in this country. Visitors to quiet sea-lochs from Solway to Shetland may be rewarded by the sight of a tumbling group of otter cubs playing over the rocks, splashing through the kelp beds, and leaving their webbed footprints in the wet sand.

There have been Soay sheep in the St Kilda group for a thousand years, directly related to the Stone Age stock of early domestication. Small flocks of Soay sheep are also found on Ailsa Craig, Lundy, and on Cardigan Island. Feral goats too are found on a number of islands, brought over and managed, as were rabbits over the centuries, by farmers as a profitable enterprise. However, goats cause ecological disaster if allowed to roam wild, and are capable of turning a green paradise into an empty desert. Lundy, Mull and Islay, all have feral goat populations.

From these great cliff headlands and isolated islands the other most noticeable mammals are porpoises, dolphins and whales. Sometimes quite large schools may come close inshore after shoals of mackerel or mullet, although all you will usually see is a grey back and a dorsal fin rolling slowly back into the depths.

It is difficult to walk the sea cliffs of Britain in summer without being struck by the brilliant splashes of colourful flowers. As the sea-cliff year begins in March with the birds returning to their ledges, so the first flower-show appears, often as carpets of blue spring squill on the cliff tops. Sea spray affects the variety of plants and only those tolerant of salt survive. Pink thrift, white sea campion, yellow bird's-foot trefoil and white plantain provide a mass of colour which admirably sets off the birds throughout the summer.

Suddenly the sea-bird cliffs are quiet, and by early August all will have departed. The biggest threat to sea-bird colonies is oil pollution, especially with the oil-fields of the North Sea and the terminals so close to the best colonies and their feeding grounds. Extra-special vigilance is needed to ensure the survival of our wealth of sea-birds for future generations.

The Isles of Scilly

Highlights and Features

Picturesque islands 28 miles (44km) west of Land's End. Many breeding sea-birds. Superb islands for migrant birds in spring and autumn. Good for grey seals.

Facilities

Well-known tourist islands with access by British Airways, boat from Isle of Scilly Steamship Co and others.

Photo Tips

Telephoto lenses needed. Birds and seals likely to be at a distance.

A colourful migrant from southern Europe, the hoopoe is regular on the Scillies in the spring

Just over the horizon from Land's End and situated some 30 miles (48km) out into the great Atlantic, lie the Isles of Scilly, strewn like pebbles from a giant's hand across ten miles of sea. Six of the islands are inhabited and the largest, St Mary's, is a pleasant 10-mile (16km) ramble in circumference.

Islands – small, secure and self-contained – seem to exert some sort of power over the mind of man, and in good weather the Scillies are quite the most blessed of all the kingdom's islands, basking in a Mediterranean climate which allows the blossoming of its two major industries, tourism and flower-farming – most of the farmland grows flowers, especially bulbs.

The Scillies are nowhere much higher than a hundred feet (30m), and when an Atlantic storm thunders out of the west, one wonders why the little houses of Hugh Town, just ten feet (3m) above the shore line, are not swept into the sea. However, the islands seem to protect each other since the hundreds of rocky islets and barely submerged ridges and reefs all lie in great circles round the central lagoon.

Access is by sea or air from Cornwall, usually Penzance, arriving at the Hugh Town quay or dropping into the small airport nearby. British Airways use a helicopter, but Brymon Airways use eight-seat Islanders from Plymouth, Exeter or Newquay. The sea crossing is usually marvellous for sea-birds and you are almost bound to see storm petrels, Manx and sooty shearwaters, but it can be very rough and takes nearly three hours.

The Scillies are famous for rare bird migrants, straggling in to make a landfall from all corners of the compass. Any time of year can be productive although spring and autumn are best. October in particular always produces rare birds, often blown in from the American coast. It also produces an invasion of birders of all creeds, colours and cults, viewed with some apprehension by those islanders seeking solitude.

Breeding birds tend to be limited in number and variety as there are very few wooded areas and all these are small. A morning's walk round each of the three main islands, St Mary's, St Agnes and Tresco is described.

Wildlife Walk 1: St Mary's

Leave Hugh Town westwards, past Tregarthen's Hotel and up a steep hill onto 'The Garrison'. A small stand of pines near the playing field, and rows of elms along the lower walk at Sally Port, often hold migrants. A walk of under a mile will bring you back to Porthcressa Beach, past the birders' café and nightly gathering roost. Little Porth in the bay's south-west corner often holds waders, including sanderling, purple sandpiper, greenshank and oyster-catcher. Look carefully at the piles of storm-tossed seaweed for migrants feeding on the insects; black redstarts and white wagtails are frequent visitors and great northern divers often appear in the bay, too.

Take the path to Peninnis Head, scanning the gorse for stonechat and migrants. A little further on the headland has short, springy turf which attracts ring ouzels, wheatears, hoopoes and pipits; the top of the headland is a good spot for sea-watching with auks, gannets, skuas and shearwaters passing to and fro.

The path drops down to Old Town Church where the elm trees always hold migrants – the scrub on the left just before the church is also a good stopover for passing warblers, including many black-caps and wood warblers. Walk round Old Town Bay towards the airport. Almost everywhere along the edge of the beaches grow dense clumps of mesembryanthemums or hottentot figs, imported into Britain by sailing ships from Africa and also into the whole Mediterranean area. The Scilly Island shrew, the tiny white-toothed shrew, is often found hunting along the shore.

Check the airfield thoroughly, without trespassing. Many rare birds have been seen here, but regular waders include golden plover, curlew, whimbrel, and even dotterel. Large parties of wheatears, ring ouzels and sometimes rare pipits appear on the short turf, especially in April and October.

Continue north along the coastal path to Porthellick Bay, checking the beach for waders as you go, and turn left through a wooden gate down the nature trail to Porthellick Pool hide. Waders usually gather in the top left corner away from the hide, together with various sandpipers including ruff, spotted redshank and water

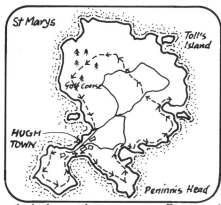

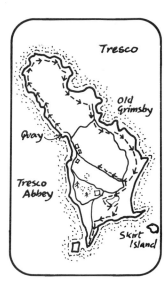

rail which are often numerous. Egrets and purple herons may sometimes appear in the reeds, and passerine migrants, especially firecrests, are found in the sallows.

Cross the road and use the path through sallows and brambles into an area of tall elms and dense undergrowth. This is called Holy Vale, and often has rare birds and many bird-watchers! The trail runs half a mile past Holy Vale Farm to the main road.

Return along the main road by way of the golf course edges on the west of the island where dotterel, golden plover and buntings occur regularly, and sometimes the rarer pipits.

Just before Hugh Town, by the golf course road at Rose Hill, lies the Lower Moors Nature Trail with a short walk through marshy reeds to a small wader scrape overlooked by a hide – the dense sallow bushes here nearly always hold migrants. Return to Hugh Town after a round walk of some six miles (9km).

Wildlife Walk 2: St Agnes

St Agnes is the most westerly island, facing the turbulent Atlantic, and only a mile in length; Gugh is joined to it by a sand-bar at low tide. Leave the boat at New Quay by Black Point and turn right away from the jetty through a gate. Cross the field to Porth Killier Bay which is a good spot for waders, especially ruff, redshank and purple sandpiper – do not forget to check the drifts of seaweed for birds. Grey seals are numerous round Scilly and appear in this bay and many others at high tide.

Cross behind Big Pool to Perigilis Bay, checking the bushes for warblers and firecrests; the bay often holds seals and waders, too. Return to the left of the brown-painted church by the shore, aiming at the old (1680) gleaming white lighthouse and the nearby Parsonage Garden; the latter is superb for rare and commoner thrushes, warblers and fly-catchers – you can go through the gate into the garden but *not* into the orchard, which is private. Continue on past the shop and turn right down Barnaby Lane, a tree-lined road well favoured by thrushes,

warblers and others, for 500 yards (456m) to the open heather and gorse of Wingle-tang Down. Golden plover, ring ouzel, woodcock and short-eared owl are regular, with occasional birds of prey including merlin and peregrine. Return from the bay along the coastal path, having covered some three miles (4.8km) and look carefully at the offshore skerries for pairs of great black-backed gulls.

Wildlife Walk 3: Tresco

Tresco, especially at its heart, is a beautiful, lush, nearly sub-tropical island with an amazing mixture of trees and plants, nearly all imported by the owners, the Dorrien-Smith family, for well over a century. The north however, is bleak, a flat heather moor on gritty granite soil. Boats land at New Grimsby and a landing charge is payable – although private, the whole island is accessible by road and path, and in any case is only 2 by 1 miles.

From the quay, walk north along the coast to Cromwell and King Charles Castles and then on to Gun Hill, the most northerly point with good sea-watching, where gannets, auks, fulmars, and shear-waters pass, often close along the shore. Continue round the coast to Gimble Porth with great northern divers on the sea, and wheatear and ring ouzel on the moorland.

Walk south past the luxurious Island Hotel and round Old Grimsby Bay, checking the fields and hedges of Borough Farm for migrants; follow the northern edge of Great Pool, full of reeds and only partially visible where egrets, water rail and crakes may occur, and rarer American wildfowl appear with some frequency. Keep an eye open for small birds in the sallow bushes and then continue past the east end to Abbey Pool, much smaller and sandy-edged and good for waders. Beyond Abbey Pool a roped-off area holds a colony of common terns with a few pairs of roseate terns in summer, while the nearby Abbey Gardens have wandering golden pheasants.

Half a mile beyond the Abbey is the jetty of Carn Near and the return boat trip to St Mary's.

Great black-backed gulls breed on isolated rocks all round the rocky coastline of the north and west

71

The Pembroke Coast National Park

DYFED

Address of Site/Warden

West Wales Trust for
Nature Conservation
7 Market Street,
Haverfordwest,
Dyfed SA61 1NF

Highlights and Features

Flat plateau with cliffs between 200–450 feet (61–136m). Long-distance footpath round coast. Many good sites – breeding birds especially sea-birds, ravens, choughs. Good cliff-top flowers and many butterflies. Grey seals offshore all year. Sea-bird migration in autumn after westerly gales.

Facilities

Well-known tourist area with many holiday facilities. Lockley Lodge Information Centre at Martin's Haven.

Photo Tips

Area large enough for lengthy holiday. Long lenses for breeding sea-birds, and grey seals. Wide-angle zoom for flowers.

Thrift, or sea-pink, provides a blaze of colour on sea-cliffs and coastlines in early summer

The sea, shaping the long peninsula of the Pembroke coast and playing such a major part in its history, has made this wild and rocky shore a haven for wildlife. The 200-foot (61m) high rolling plateau was forced into tortured folds by violent earth movements and then planed smooth by the ice.

The Normans divided Wales into north and south and made Pembroke almost English, with several English place-names and a system of castle defences against the Celts. Until the advent of the railways in the late nineteenth century, Pembroke's links with the outside world were all by sea.

Now its coast is a national park with some of the finest coastal scenery in Britain, spectacular sea-cliffs, good beaches, picturesque little villages and round it, for 167 miles (267km), runs one of the best long-distance footpaths in the country. Four individual walks are described, all fairly approachable by car, and walking boots are a good idea for all of them.

Wildlife Walk 1: Dinas Island

Access is off the A487, 3 miles (4.8km) north of Fishguard, down a very steep little hill to the car-park by the beach at Pwll Gwaelod, next to the Sailors Safety Inn. Wildlife interest is best from spring to autumn when gales can bring rare sea-birds into the coast. May and June provide the best variety with many breeding birds, flowers and insects. This is a hilly three-mile (4.8km) round walk.

Take the path out of the car-park over the stile uphill and onto the headland cliffs. Flowers in spring include white scurvygrass, lots of blue spring squill and later kidney vetch, thrift, agrimony and sheepsbit. The path climbs steeply up the bracken-covered hillside and some thirty steps, with Green Hairstreak butterflies among the gorse and sea campion. At the top, the cliffs are 100 feet (30m) high and the path runs out towards the higher headland. Bell heather, gorse and burnet rose, with English stonecrop on the rocks give bright colours all summer. Below, oystercatchers 'pipe' on the rocky shore while scores of rooks and jackdaws forage on the grazed fields.

The path swings up and inland following the fence. Watch the posts for migrant wheatears or a watchful kestrel, and in spring, look carefully at the bramble and gorse scrub which has breeding stonechat, linnet and meadow pipit. Toadflax, golden rod and foxgloves grow among the bracken.

The final slopes, more rocky out towards the head, give wonderful cliff views. The rock is tilted from the 450 foot (137m) Dinas Head back to sea-level at the car-park, and the 'dip' of the rock bands is clear in the cliffs here; cormorants nest on the crags below the head. Buzzard, herring and great black-backed gulls drift along these heights, up to the trig point, and it really is an excellent place to watch autumn sea-birds, especially on a strong westerly gale.

Turn inland, with lovely views of the Pembroke coast, and walk along the eastern cliffs towards Needle Rock. The path is steep, muddy, and in one place takes you above a sheer 100-foot (30m) drop so take care. In spring fulmars, together with two hundred or so pairs of guillemots, and razorbills, nest on the cliffs of the Rock. Shags nest on ledges lower down, and peregrines can be seen regularly, hunting the gulls and pigeons while the lovely aerobatic chough plays on the cliff air-currents with the larger ravens, also nesting on the rock. Watch out for the bobbing heads of grey seals offshore.

The path dips under a wind-pruned hawthorn tree and descends rapidly across an area of dry grass slopes, with common lizard and the occasional adder on warm days.

An area of blackthorn and hawthorn scrub, covered in ivy, is much used by woodland birds, the most noticeable being willow warbler and whitethroat, while thrushes come and feed on the berries in autumn. Orange-tip, Peacock, Small Tortoiseshell, Red Admiral and Painted Lady butterflies all appear here, with Speckled Wood under the bushes; Graylings, and both Small and Large Skippers haunt the cliffs in midsummer.

Follow the path to the Sailors Safety Inn along the back of the boat-park and past the caravans, through an old iron gate in the corner. This path then runs for ¾ mile along the marshy valley of Cwm Dewi, with dense thickets of willow, reed, sedges, bog asphodel, marsh marigold and yellow flag. Many warblers, including the more elusive grasshopper warbler,

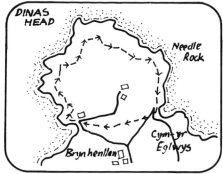

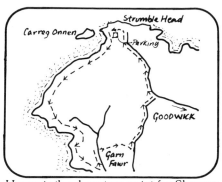

inhabit these thickets, and there are always common frogs and grass snakes in the marsh. The rare Marsh Fritillary butterfly may be seen in June – and all the while overhead, buzzards soar out from the woodland.

Wildlife Walk 2: Strumble Head

Strumble Head, the main headland west of Fishguard, has two car-parks by the smart white lighthouse and on quiet early mornings, choughs may be seen wandering about picking up scraps along the edge. The walk is about 4 miles (6km) and takes you along the cliff path round to Pwllderi and back again. Besides the choughs, the other birds which breed and live along the cliffs include ravens, kestrel, buzzard, stonechat and wheatear, while hunting peregrines are frequent.

Strumble Head is a superb place to watch migrating seabirds in spring and autumn provided that a strong westerly wind, preferably a gale, is blowing. Then, birds moving through the Irish Sea will be pushed inshore, with thousands of Manx shearwaters, kittiwakes, gannets, skuas, duck, divers, auks and terns passing the head. Rarer birds, such as sooty shearwaters and Leach's petrel appear in gale conditions.

Follow the Pembroke coast path from the lighthouse along the switchback cliff path for 2 miles (3km) through gorse, bracken and heather. The next headland is good for spring squill and has masses of thrift and sea campion among the rocks; it is topped by a red-brick wartime bunker.

The path follows a drystone wall for nearly a mile to the magnificent 400 foot (121m) Pwllderi cliffs, below the little grey stone Youth Hostel. Choughs and peregrine are frequent here, and you can use the seats by the viewpoint at the end of the road to watch for them. A footpath runs back over the rocky hillside above Tal-y-Gaer Farm to rejoin the road to Strumble Head. Wheatears breed in the rocks while buzzards circle the patchwork fields on wide wings.

Wildlife Walk 3: Martin's Haven

From the National Trust car-park a mile beyond Marloes, the little cove of Martin's Haven is the departure point for Skomer; the Lockley Lodge Centre provides wildlife information. The promontory beyond, called the Deer Park, has a 1½-mile (2.7km) walk of stunning beauty. The path runs steeply uphill through a wide expanse of gorse, bramble and bracken to the coastguard's white emergency lookout on the hill-top. Wooltack Point, the rocky headland 300 yards (274m) beyond, looks directly across the choppy waters of Jack Sound to the cliffs of Skomer. All these coves and beaches are a splendid spot for grey seals, where the tiny white pups are born in October. Seals can be seen offshore all the year round, so watch for their bobbing heads and listen for their eerie wailing.

Sea-birds pass up and down Jack Sound in large numbers in early summer, Manx shearwaters in particular gathering offshore each evening in huge rafts, before flying to their burrows on Skomer. Gannets fish the waters from the huge colony on Grassholm, just visible ten miles (16km) or so to the west. Choughs, ravens and buzzards haunt the cliffs all year while wheatears, whinchats and stonechats breed on the headland in summer.

Wildlife Walk 4: St Ann's Head

St Ann's Head is on the southern tip of the Marloes Peninsula and is reached down the B4320, but you have to park in the large National Trust car-park one mile short of the lighthouse. The best route is across the fields to the Pembroke Coast Path only 200 yards away (183m) and then left along the cliff edge. These are cliffs of Old Red Sandstone, with a 'dip' in the layers of 80 degrees due to the vast forces unleashed in the rocks 300 million years ago. The fretted, jagged cliffs are crumbly and dangerous, so keep to the path. Choughs, ravens, buzzards, kestrels and offshore sea-birds are frequent.

The grassy headland is approached through the main gates of the lighthouse and then a green wicket gate on the left. Superb views of the long inlet of Milford Haven with its oil terminals and other scars are compensated for by the gannets diving offshore, at present in a clean and carefully guarded sea.

Auks, like guillemots, are on the decline, but the lovely little kittiwake has spread widely

72

The Pembroke Islands
DYFED

Address of Site/Warden

West Wales Trust for
Nature Conservation
7 Market Street,
Haverfordwest,
Dyfed SA61 1NF

Highlights and Features

Skomer is main island.
Superb sea-bird colonies
with many other species
breeding. Good for choughs.
Grey seals breed. Superb
sea-cliff flora.

Facilities

Day tips to Skomer from
Martin's Haven; allow 5
hours on island. Residential
accommodation on both
Skomer and Skokholm for
weeks at a time via the
WWTNC. First boat usually
1000.

Photo Tips

In view of boat trip and
4 mile (6km) walk one wide-
angle zoom and one long
telephoto recommended for
flowers and sea-birds.
Camera gear in polythene
bags for protection.

*Cormorants are scattered
in small colonies around
the cliff coastline. A small
number live on the
Skomer cliffs*

When you stand on the headland at Martin's Haven and look across the waters of Jack Sound you will see, it seems almost within touching distance, the lovely island of Skomer, green but still with a touch of the austere imposed by the cliff-girt shore. Turn a little to the left and there is Skokholm, rather flatter, tucked into Broad Sound between the Pembroke headlands. And further out still, some 10 miles distant but visible on good days, lies the tiny hump of Grassholm; viewed through binoculars from the shore, you can see quite clearly the white swathe across one side of the island – the huge colony of gannets, over 28,000 pairs, the second largest colony in British waters.

Skomer is easily visited for a day trip and up to 100 visitors are allowed; Skokholm is run as a bird observatory and is a place for the real enthusiast to stay; and Grassholm can be visited by arrangement with the RSPB. The walk described is the 4-mile (6km) nature trail round Skomer.

Wildlife Walk: Skomer

Skomer is the best of the islands for its variety of wildlife, and a truly magnificent spectacle in early summer when its cliffs are thronged with sea-birds. Access is by boat from Martin's Haven, and the crossing, often choppy, takes perhaps 20 minutes; the fare and landing fee is £5 (1987). There are no toilets or facilities on the island although simple accommodation is available for naturalists staying a week or more.

The warden usually meets the little blue boat at the tiny jetty in North Haven. A new concrete path with good handrails helps you to clamber up to the flat plateau of Skomer's surface, which covers 720 acres (291ha).

Skomer is basically a mass of volcanic Silurian rock, fretted into huge 200-foot (61m) dark grey cliffs made colourful by bands of orange lichens.

From North Haven a well-marked nature trail runs round most of the island, and the five hours ashore allow plenty of time to walk the whole of it.

The slopes all around the landing place are riddled with burrows of breeding puffins and Manx shearwaters; there are 7,000 pairs of puffins nesting on the island, but this is a sad decline from a former peak of 50,000 pairs. The shearwater population is huge, with about 100,000 pairs, and their burrows can be found all over the island – surprisingly they are not often seen, being quite nocturnal. If you are only on a day trip the best way to see them is to sit on the cliffs at Martin's Haven at dusk, when thousands collect in Jack Sound. At night Skomer is filled with their mournful wails as they flit ghost-like through the dark sky. The warden's modern prefabricated house stands just above North Haven by one of the main colonies.

The view above the landing place is startling. A large chunk of Skomer, the Neck, is joined to the rest by a narrow causeway just 12 feet wide (3.6m) – in a few years' time erosion by the sea will turn this into a separate island. Look down at the caves and coves of South Haven, a favourite spot for the grey seals which haul themselves out to produce their pups in autumn.

In May and June the island is covered in carpets of flowers – millions of bluebells, followed by red campion with thrift and sea campion covering the cliff tops. Continue for 400 yards (365m) and you will come to South Stream valley, marshy, sheltered and full of wetland flowers, purple loosestrife and water mint being particularly obvious. Dense growths of bramble provide resting places for tired migrants in spring and autumn.

The cliffs of South Haven are visible for the whole length of the path and from March till July are filled with birds, a dense colony of kittiwakes low down on the rocks, with razorbills and guillemots higher up. On the flat plateau as you approach the High Cliff are parts of the huge gullery, largely lesser black-backed gulls, but some herring gulls too. It is possible to approach really closely and there are 15,000 pairs on the island – the damage to the vegetation is obvious.

The huge stack on the southern corner is called the Mew Stone, where some twenty pairs of cormorants nest. The path swings round and beneath your feet the magnificent cliffs of the Wick appear, jammed with seabirds: guillemots, razorbills, kittiwakes, and the upper slopes are lined with hordes of puffins.

The rock ridges on the right of the path usually have several nesting pairs of great black-backed gulls. Keep an eye open for the pied flash of wheatear, nesting in the rocks and old walls.

Beyond the little stream the scree slope is a breeding site of many storm petrels which, like the shearwaters, are largely nocturnal.

A further 400 yards (365m) rounds Skomer Head, full of great drifts of thrift in May and June; Grassholm is clearly visible 7 miles away (11km) and some of its gannets fish just off the Skomer cliffs, plunge-diving from 50 feet (15m). A fenced area here shows how dramatic the change in the vegetation would be if the thousands of rabbits seen all over the island were kept out.

Pigstone Bay, some 300 yards (274m) further on, always has a few grey seals loafing about, while the next hollow at Bull Hole has a good number of small birds, whitethroats, wrens and surprisingly the much larger wood-pigeons, nesting in the brambles.

At the northern tip of the island the offshore rock called the Garland Stone is another favourite grey seal spot, and the surrounding cliffs often have ravens and usually some choughs.

The path returns down a stream-bed full of yellow flag to the ruined farmhouse in the island's centre; a small pond nearby is full of frog and toad spawn in early spring. The farm is of historical interest and the

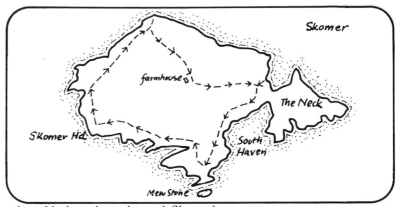

solitary black poplar in the yard, Skomer's only tree, may be lined with redstarts, warblers and flycatchers during an overnight 'fall' of migrants. A pair of short-eared owls regularly hunt the stream valley, looking for Skomer voles, a larger sub-species of the bank-vole.

Stonechats and reed buntings sit on tops of bushes down the stream valley into the farmyard. Curlew, lapwing and oyster-catcher breed in the fields around the stream and North Pond, which is the largest pond on the island.

The path returns directly through bracken-covered fields much loved by hunting buzzards looking for a vole, to the large monolith called the Harold Stone. The little blue boat will be waiting below to take you back to the mainland.

The Pembroke islands are a haven for wildlife. Skomer, largest and most varied, teems with sea-birds

73

Bempton Cliffs
and Flamborough Head
YORKSHIRE

Address of Site/Warden

Bempton Cliffs RSPB
Reserve
Summer Warden from April
to August
c/o The Post Office,
Bempton,
nr Bridlington,
Humberside

Highlights and Features

Bempton – Huge chalk cliffs
with large colony breeding
sea-birds, with over 200,000
birds at peak times. Only
mainland colony of gannets
with 650 pairs (1987).
Flamborough Head – Superb
migration watchpoint, spring
and autumn. Thousands of
sea-birds, waders and
wildfowl offshore. Small bird
migrants in bushes. Many
rare birds. Good for dolphins
and porpoise.

Facilities

Small information hut at
Bempton. Area open at all
times.

Photo Tips

Breeding sea-birds easy to
photograph along cliffs.
Many very close near cliff
top. These cliffs very
dangerous.
Use lenses from 200mm and
larger.

*Part of the gannetry at
Bempton RSPB reserve.
In 1987 the colony had
reached 650 pairs*

South of Filey Bay on the Yorkshire coast, the low clay cliffs give way to a rising ridge of chalk downland. Like chalk hills reaching the sea elsewhere in Britain, the rock has been 'planed' by the winds and waves over millions of years into sheer cliffs – between Filey and Flamborough they rise to 445 feet (135m), lashed by the grey North Sea and battered by easterly winter gales.

Erosion of the soft rock provides cracks and narrow ledges for breeding sea-birds in huge numbers at Bempton Cliffs. The area has been an RSPB reserve since 1970 and constitutes the largest sea-bird colony in England, as well as being the most southerly and the only large colony on chalk.

Flamborough Head juts out into the North Sea precisely in the middle of the east coast arrival area for huge numbers of bird migrants from the Continent.

Two wildlife walks are described although they can easily be put together by walking south from Bempton along the switchback cliff path all the way to the Head.

Wildlife Walk 1: Bempton Cliffs

Bempton Cliffs RSPB reserve runs for five miles (8km) south from Speeton. In most places the reserve is only a few yards wide, running the length of the cliff top; the landward side has intensively cultivated arable fields and there is hardly a tree to be seen, except the occasional stunted hawthorn.

The breeding sea-birds are present from April to July.

The reserve is best approached by driving into Bempton village and turning east up Cliff Lane by the White Horse Inn. Drive for nearly two miles (3km) to the end of the road at the little reserve car-park, where there is also an information hut.

Walk towards the cliff top between cereal fields and short stretches of hedge. Corn buntings and linnets are virtually the only summer birds, though skylarks and meadow pipits breed in the early crops. The old low buildings on the left are part of a disused RAF station.

A signpost on the cliff-edge points south to Thornwick Bay in 2½ miles (3.8km) – ignore it and turn north. The cliffs fall in a huge white precipice straight into the thunderous sea far below the path.

Quite rightly the RSPB has put up 'DANGER' notices; chalk cliffs are notoriously bad, especially when wet. The society has also erected sturdy green-painted railings on two or three of the headland bluffs to provide safe observation platforms.

As you walk the cliff path birds zoom past in hundreds, guillemots, puffins, kittiwakes and occasionally a large black-and-white gannet – the noise from the bird colonies is deafening, and out to sea a constant procession moves to and from the feeding grounds.

The first observation platform is only 100 yards (91m) along the cliff path. A large and noisy colony of kittiwakes inhabits the cliff face to the north just at your feet, while lower down hundreds of guillemots seem stuck to the vertical chalk rock; only thirty feet away puffins pop in and out of holes near the cliff top.

Continue north along the path. Many chalk flowers grow on this narrow strip of uncultivated land, with 220 species already recorded. Most striking in summer are the massed clumps of red campion which vie with hawkbits, trefoils and vetches to produce a brilliant splash of colour, filled throughout the summer with scores of butterflies, Common Blue, Small Copper, Skippers and Browns. Just 300 yards (274m) further on is the next set of low railings – the view back shows ranks of huge and dazzling cliffs marching south the 4 miles (6km) to Flamborough Head.

Northwards again, and there is a large colony of guillemots, smaller numbers of kittiwake and the start of the gannetry. Bempton is the only place on the British mainland where gannets breed, and the only English colony; only a handful of pairs were present till the early 1970s but now there are over 600 pairs and the colony is increasing every year.

Wind buffets these cliffs constantly and the birds, especially kittiwakes, perform an aerial ballet on winnowing wings, hanging on the updraughts before you.

The last main observation point is a further 400 yards (365m) north, through a kissing-gate and opposite the RAF huts. Puffins and kittiwakes are very close here while a hundred pairs of gannets are visible farther down the cliff.

The totals at Bempton are very large:

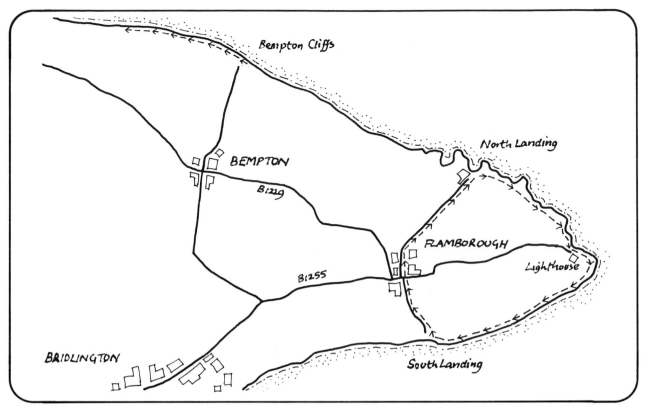

80,000 pairs of kittiwake on the whole cliff complex, 6,000 of guillemots, 3,000 razorbills and 3,000 of puffins, 1,000 herring gulls, 800 pairs of fulmars but only a very few shags.

Rock dove, jackdaw, starling, rock pipit and house martin nest in the cliffs and peregrines are now regular visitors.

Wildlife Walk 2: Flamborough Head

Flamborough Head is the best sea-watching site on Britain's east coast, and only St Ives in Cornwall produces a similar spectacle of numbers and variety of migrating sea-birds. Its prominent position jutting out into the North Sea also means that many of the night migrant passerines and several rare birds have been seen.

It must be stressed that most of the area is private farmland and hordes of trespassers are very unpopular, so please stay on the areas of public access.

Leave Bempton travelling south-east on the B1229, or Bridlington on the B1255, crossing Danes Dyke after a mile. Turn north out of Flamborough village and park at North Landing, in a car-park by the lifeboat station. The path runs south along the cliffs for a mile and a half to the lighthouse near the Head; the areas of thorn scrub are worth checking for passerines. The B1209 from Flamborough ends here, cutting out the north cliff walk if desired.

In strong northerly weather this section is well worth the walk. A track leads down from the lighthouse 200 yards to the foghorn and most birders sea-watch from the grassy ledges below it. This is not to be recommended in poor visibility! The alternative is ear-plugs.

Wind-pruned hedges anywhere on the Head are worth checking for migrants. A public path runs south from the old lighthouse along Old Fall Hedge and past the plantation – the hedge holds migrants but the plantation is strictly out of bounds!

The cliff path continues right round to South Landing and Danes Dyke, both with car-parks and lots of bushes. This southerly sector is best for tired migrants, offering more shelter and food.

Sea-birds can be seen offshore at all times, and the Head is a good place to watch porpoises and dolphins passing along the North Sea coast.

Late spring and autumn herald huge movements of sea-birds: divers, duck, geese and waders of many species, and wildfowl join in too.

Arctic and great skuas pass in scores on most days, with thousands of fulmars, kittiwakes and Manx shearwaters; sooty shearwaters may reach 500 and little gulls 100 on good days; a handful of pomarine and long-tailed skuas are regular and Sabine's gull, a notable rarity, sometimes with as many as 20 in a year. Black terns are occasionally numerous in autumn.

Passerine migrants include 'falls' of redstart, pied flycatcher, wheatear and whinchat with common warblers. Rare birds are regular, especially the tiny yellow-browed warblers, in late autumn.

Bempton cliffs march down the Yorkshire coast to Flamborough Head. Made of chalk they hold a huge sea-bird colony in spring

74

The Farne Islands
NORTHUMBERLAND

Address of Site/Warden

National Trust
Warden:
8 St Aidans,
Seahouses,
Northumberland NE68 7SR

Highlights and Features

Isolated islands a few miles
off the coast. Full of sea-birds
and grey seals. Lots of eider
ducks. Good for sea-bird
migration.

Facilities

Access by boat from
Seahouses. National Trust
Information Centre at
16 Main Street, Seahouses.

Photo Tips

Very good for pictures with
birds very close. Medium
telephoto lenses from
200mm to 300mm should
suffice.

*Large numbers of grey
seals use the Farne Islands
to breed. Over 60%
of the world population
lives in British waters*

Birds have been protected on the Farne Islands since the seventh century, when St Cuthbert lived on Inner Farne and laid down rules for the protection of nesting eider ducks, still known locally as 'Cuddy's Duck'. The islands are now in the care of the National Trust, and there is a full-time warden to look after 'Cuddy's Duck' and the rest of the wildlife.

At low tide there are twenty-eight islands while at high tide there are usually only fifteen and they lie a few miles offshore from the Northumberland coastal village of Seahouses, in two main groups separated by the waters of Staple Sound, a mile wide. The islands are the eastern tip of the Great Whin Sill, the huge 70-mile (112km) long igneous rock intrusion which crosses northern England in a great arc. Elsewhere in this book we meet the Whin Sill on the hard edges of Teesdale (see pp 128–9). On the Farnes this hard columnar rock, split by so many vertical faults, provides innumerable ledges for nesting sea-birds. The Farnes are a sea-bird paradise.

There are two islands usually accessible; boats operate from Seahouses and several ply to and fro, although the islands are only open for specific periods; tickets must be obtained from the local boatmen. The large National Trust Information Centre is at the roundabout in Main Street.

It should be noted that a heavy sea swell may well prevent landing. A wildlife walk is described around both islands, and visiting is best from April to July.

Wildlife Walk 1: Staple Island
Staple Island is the first island of the outer group: it is open from 1030 to 1330 between 15 May and 15 July, and outside this period, from Good Friday to the end of September, from 1000 till 1800. It is not always easy to alight as there are no jetties; landing is usually attempted on the west cliff or the south-east hole. A nature trail exists and you must keep to the track to avoid disturbing nesting birds.

The island next to the landing site is the Brownsman, while beyond, the red and white lighthouse on Longstone surveys the view. This was the setting for the heroism of Grace Darling and her father in rescuing survivors from the SS *Forfarshire*, which struck the rocks in a storm in September 1838.

Walk south across the Whin Sill rocks towards the Pinnacles at the southern end of the island. The fissures and scratches in the rock surface were left by the retreating ice of the last Ice Age which also deposited a layer of boulder clay several feet thick across the hollowed top of the island. A peaty soil has developed on the surface providing a foothold for nearly all the island's vegetation.

Many puffins nest in burrows in the peat and there are good views to enjoy on this first section of the track.

After some 300 yards (274m) the off-shore stacks of the Pinnacles rise 50 feet (15m) from the sea in front of you, crammed to the brim with about 1,000 pairs of guillemots. There are three stacks, and at low tide the broken remains of a fourth which was destroyed by storms in the 1780s. The ledges of the columnar rock are occupied by shags and kittiwakes.

Walk beyond the squat, ruined beacon tower to Kittiwake Gully, a huge fissure in the Whin Sill rock where hundreds of kittiwakes may be viewed closely.

Beyond Kittiwake Gully is a ridge that once housed hundreds of puffins, but their burrows eventually fell in, and they were forced to move elsewhere. Large colonies of shags live on the surrounding ledges.

Turn back north across the centre of the island which is filled with a carpet of sea campion in summer. The top of the island gives a good view across the whole of the outer group: the nearest is Brownsman which often houses large colonies of terns, especially Sandwich terns with up to 3,000 pairs. However, some years they move en masse and breed on Inner Farne.

The path to the West Face crosses the island for 300 yards (274m). Hundreds of puffins nest in burrows with the predatory herring and lesser black-backed gulls nesting in the vegetation.

From the West Face there is a good view of the inner islands across Staple Sound. Grey seals may be seen hauled out on rocks, or around the islands throughout the summer, although the main breeding season is in November, when most of the pups are born. In 1970 the colony numbered nearly 9,000 and was severely overpopulated. A controversial 'seal cull' was organised, to prevent destruction of the island's vegetation and damage to the bird colonies, and to

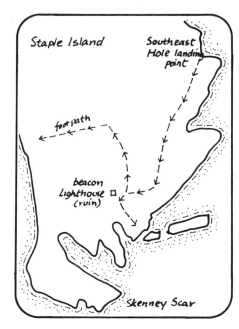

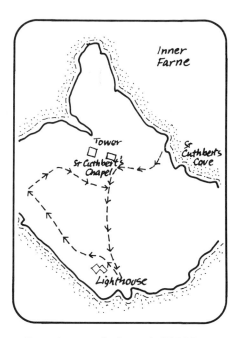

prevent starvation of the pups which had reached 45%. The population is now on a good level, so no culling is carried out at present.

From Staple Island it is possible to cross to Inner Farne.

Wildlife Walk 2: Inner Farne

The island opens at 1330 as Staple Island closes and shuts at 1700.

Walk up from the landing place to St Cuthbert's Chapel only a few yards away. The stone font outside was 'rescued' from Gateshead parish church in about 1850, and the tiny chapel dates from about 1370 although it was partially restored in the 1850s.

Eider breed throughout the islands and are found sitting on nests in many strange spots; some 1,500 pairs breed, making this the second largest British colony after the Sands of Forvie.

Cross the island southwards along a grassy path to the lighthouse. Thousands of terns nest amongst the grass and sea campion, with Arctic terns, at 2,000 pairs, being the most numerous – sometimes all the Sandwich terns from Brownsman breed here too; common terns number several hundred and there are usually a few pairs of the rare roseate tern.

Some 700 to 1,000 eider breed in the vegetation of Inner Farne.

The cliffs and the great stack by the white lighthouse hold large colonies of kittiwakes and guillemot, with a few razor-bills. Shags and fulmars are not plentiful and only a few hundred pairs of each breed throughout the islands. Most of the 250 pairs of cormorants nest on two inaccessible islands in the outer group. The 4,000 pairs of kittiwake and 6,000 of guillemots are overshadowed by the huge puffin colonies which total 15,000 pairs for the islands altogether.

As you walk through the thrift and sea campion along the island's west coast, you pass a large colony of puffins.

At the south-west tip of the island is a large storm 'blow-hole', the Churn Pool, which in summer is much favoured by eiders and their ducklings. Winter storms, however, force sea-water into the Churn, projecting a column of water as high as 90 feet (27m) into the air.

Walk back along the lower northern shore towards the chapel. Ringed plover and oystercatchers nest on the low rocks while late summer brings the first migrant dunlin, turnstone and purple sandpiper.

Descend the final few yards beside the garden wall to St Cuthbert's Cove – be careful not to disturb the eiders which always nest in the shelter of the wall. A few rock pipits and starlings breed among the rocks – the only land-birds nesting regularly on the Farnes.

The Farne Islands lie just off the Northumberland coast and hold huge colonies of sea-birds and grey seals

75

South Scottish Cliffs

ST ABB'S HEAD BORDERS

Address of Site/Warden

St Abb's Head
National Trust for Scotland
Reserve
Warden:
Rangers Cottage,
Northfield,
St Abbs,
Berwickshire TD14 5QF

Highlights and Features

Huge sea-bird cliffs with very large colonies. Good for migrant birds in spring and autumn.

Facilities

Information hut with leaflets at main car-park.

Photo Tips

Medium and long telephoto lenses will give good shots of breeding sea-birds.

Prime predators of young sea-birds, along the cliffs, herring gulls breed in open cliff sites all round the coast

As the huge estuary of the Forth runs south its flat, industrial coastline, lined with docks, power-stations and industrial estates, gives way to cliffs which rise beyond the town of North Berwick and stride towards the English border. The crown of this line of cliffs is St Abb's Head a few miles north of the border, a reserve of the National Trust for Scotland and a superb, easily accessible sea-bird colony.

Walk: St Abb's Head

Access is from Coldingham; make your way through its tiny, narrow streets along the B6438, and then fork left into the nature reserve approach road (the right fork continues to St Abbs village). The reserve car-park is just down the track at Northfield Farm where there is an information hut. It is possible to drive right up to the lighthouse, the very narrow road winding uphill for nearly two miles (3km).

In order to see the whole headland it is better to walk from the main car-park east along the footpath for 300 yards (274m) to the cliffs of Starney Bay.

The geology of the area is complex and the steep cliff path at Starney Bay rises up a hillside with short turf, bracken, cowslips, purple milk-vetch and early purple orchids in spring.

The huge cliff called the White Heugh rises sheer in front of you as you mount the path, and has a large colony of guillemots jammed onto the impossibly sheer cliff face. Many herring gulls breed on the cliff tops, and the tops of the offshore stacks.

Down on the shoreline eider bring ducklings into Starney Bay while turnstone, purple sandpiper and rock pipit are found throughout the year picking insects from the rocks.

The path falls back from the top of White Heugh down towards the sea in the next bay, Horsecastle Bay. The short, crisp, grassy sward is rich in plants here with thyme, thrift, sea campion and purple milk-vetch a blaze of colour in early summer. Butterflies are good in the more sheltered spots with Grayling particularly noticeable later in the summer.

The path swings away from the cliffs to mount the final slopes towards the squat white lighthouse perched on the top of the cliffs at Harelaw Hill.

The huge and deeply indented cliffs of the headland, 300 feet (91m) high, provide nesting sites for 60,000 sea-birds, mainly kittiwakes (15,000 pairs) and guillemots (about 12,000 pairs). Far fewer razorbills at 1,500 pairs and only 50 pairs of puffins are regularly found. Like all sea-bird colonies the noise and bustle provides a constantly exciting spectacle, while the waves that batter the great offshore stacks of red rock add to the feeling of exhilaration.

From the little car-park by the lighthouse the short turf makes easy walking around the cliff edges with wonderful views of all the sea-birds, although the outermost buttress has been fenced off to avoid too much disturbance.

Offshore gannets pass in file to and from the Bass Rock to the north, while spring and autumn bring good sea-bird passage with great and Arctic skuas, Manx shearwaters and occasional pomarine and long-tailed skuas and sooty shearwaters.

Follow the cliffs round through drifts of thrift, trefoil, thyme and sea campion in early summer, down towards the deep bay of Pettico Wick. There is a small car-park here for divers' use only. The headland area is scoured clean by underwater currents with clear unpolluted water, and has become a voluntary marine reserve.

The pink cliffs hold large colonies of kittiwakes which form a constant stream as they go to bathe in the fresh water of Mire Loch in the dip under the headland. Dabchick, mallard, tufted duck and mute swan breed in the reeds of this narrow strip of water, while many migrants use the stunted hawthorn and sycamore scrub in spring and autumn, especially following an easterly wind across the North Sea.

East Scottish Cliffs
FOWLESHEUGH GRAMPIAN

Eastern Scotland is blessed with a wide variety of wildlife habitats, from sand-dunes as at Forvie, through wide estuaries like the Beauly and Dornoch Firths to sheer cliffs hundreds of feet high.

Consequently it has a far richer fauna than the west coast fjord country, restricted as this is to a somewhat specialised bird community of eider, shag, oyster-catcher and merganser as its principal inhabitants.

A sample of the east-coast estuaries are described elsewhere (see pp 74–114). The sea-bird cliffs, although lower in the east than in the far north-west, still hold huge sea-bird colonies where they are undisturbed. Many smaller colonies exist on rocky headlands and the largest, Fowlesheugh, is described.

The cliffs are sheer rock faces for the most part, and are very dangerous. Take sensible precautions, don't stand on the edge, and you will be quite safe. People who have not heeded this advice in the past have sometimes lived to regret it, but not always! Breeding sea-birds are present from April till July.

Wildlife Walk: Fowlesheugh

Fowlesheugh is an RSPB reserve, purchased with donations raised by the Young Ornithologists' Club and situated some 4 miles (6km) south of Stonehaven. The reserve consists of nearly two miles of cliffs running north towards the town.

From the A92, turn east on a minor road signposted to Crawton. The road is a 'dead-end', running through a mile of flat arable farmland with no hint of what is to come.

The reserve car-park is near the shore, with spaces for twenty cars. There is no warden and an RSPB information board provides all you need to know, including a 'dangerous cliff' warning.

Go through the kissing-gate onto the cliff-top, which runs above a cutting penetrating the line of the cliffs here, with hundreds of kittiwakes and fulmars nesting on the ledges; many herring gulls nest on the broken cliff-tops.

The path descends twenty-five wooden steps to a footbridge over a little burn; you will find the RSPB information board down here.

As you emerge on the gentle slope beyond, the full force of discovery hits you. Fowlesheugh is a fantastic sea-bird city, quite one of the largest in the country with upwards of 150,000 birds crammed into two miles (3km) of cliffs, only 200 feet high (61m).

Outside the breeding season, from April till July, the cliffs are quite empty.

The noise at the cliff edge is deafening. Kittiwakes are most numerous near the entrance – a thousand or more off-duty birds rest on some flattened rocks and take it in turn to bathe in the waters of the little burn where it tumbles over the cliff.

All you have to do here is to walk north along the track which follows the cliff edge. In June the cliff-top is a mass of colour from common flowers, thrift, bird's-foot trefoil, clovers and stonecrop. The path is springy grass, easy to walk.

52,000 pairs of guillemots, 5,000 of razorbills and 22,000 of kittiwakes are the main inhabitants, with 300 pairs of fulmar, 300 of herring gulls and a few shags and eider duck.

Puffins are certainly present, near the cliff top some ¾ mile north of the entrance, but there are only about 100 pairs; they are easy to see, however, because of their position.

Fowlesheugh is a truly wonderful spectacle, the cliffs vibrant with life.

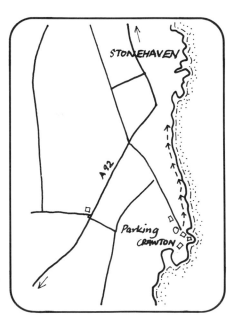

Address of Site/Warden

Fowlesheugh – no warden
RSPB Scottish Office
17 Regent Terrace,
Edinburgh EH7 5BN

Highlights and Features

Large sea-cliffs with huge breeding seabird colonies.

Facilities

None.

Photo Tips

Medium and long telephoto lenses will give good pictures. The cliffs are dangerous.

A considerable decline in puffin numbers over the past 40 years may be attributable to sea-pollution

Islay
HEBRIDES STRATHCLYDE

Address of Site/Warden

Loch Gruinart
RSPB Reserve
Warden:
Bushmill,
Gruinart,
Isle of Islay,
Argyllshire PA44 7PW

Highlights and Features

Lovely Hebridean island with over 100 species of breeding birds. Good for chough. Seals, otter, red deer. Superb in winter for barnacle geese with up to 20,000. Many birds of prey. 5,000 Greenland whitefronted geese.

Facilities

Normal tourist facilities.

Photo Tips

Wide ranging variety of wildlife means lenses from wide angle to long telephoto. Best shots will be of masses of geese in winter. Good site to photograph hares.

Far less numerous than the other auks, black guillemots breed in rocky crevices around the north and west of Scotland

Islay, the Queen of the Hebrides, is a supremely beautiful island some 26 miles long by 15 wide (43 × 24km), and two hours' sailing time from Kennacraig, Kintyre, by the bustling little Macbraynes car-ferries.

Islay is protected a little from the full force of the Atlantic gales by the bulk of Ireland, and is a greener isle of softer outlines than many of its neighbours. It is a remnant, as indeed are all the surrounding islands, of the great lava flows and ash-beds of past volcanoes. Here the Ice Ages left an everlasting impression, especially in the raised beach system produced when the huge weight of ice melted at two stages, which raised the land by twenty-two and then by eight metres respectively. The water-front of Port Ascaig shows the eight-metre mark very clearly.

Islay, because of its variety of habitats, is a wildlife paradise at all times of the year – in winter great flocks of geese feed on its fields, while in summer its hills and cliffs hold a wonderful variety of birds. The weather, however, can sometimes be less than kind.

One wildlife tour is described by car and on foot round the northern shores of the island. This tour takes in the new RSPB reserve at Gruinart, but there is much to see away from the reserve. Over a hundred bird species breed here. Probably the best time for a visit is early spring in late March or early April when the goose flocks have built up to their largest numbers just before they leave for their Arctic breeding grounds.

Accommodation, and the ferry, need booking well in advance.

Wildlife Tour

As the ferry runs into Port Ascaig, the Sound of Islay will have many black guillemot breeding on the low eastern cliffs. The sheltered waters of the Sound often hold numbers of duck and divers including merganser, scoter and long-tailed duck, and great northern and black-throated divers moving north in spring.

The single road 8 miles (12.8km) from Port Ascaig to Bridgend runs into oak and birch woodland around Islay House and then north along the shore of Loch Indaal. Look for dippers by the bridge over the River Sern. Roe deer are frequent here, often feeding out on the grassy 'lawns' of the machair. Red deer, of which there are a number in the hills, are best seen along the road from Ballygrant southwards towards Beinn Bheigeir, the highest point of the island and open moorland at 1,609 feet (490m). Black and red grouse are found on these moors.

Take the B8017 north towards Gruinart – there will probably be barnacle geese on the fields and grassy banks at the turn-off. After two miles the lovely shining inlet of Loch Gruinart comes into view.

In winter and until the end of March, hen harriers roost in the rough, marshy ground which can be seen to the west of the B8017 at this point; up to a dozen may appear at dusk. If disturbed the birds may roost just north of Laggan Bridge, on the B8016.

A tiny side-road signposted to Killin-allan runs down the eastern side of Loch Gruinart. Grassland fields rise gently behind Craigens Farm, and before you are the open wet meadows of the RSPB reserve and the mudflats of the loch. From October until early April there are bar-nacle geese in thousands here – they often congregate on the fields above Craigens Farm at dusk and then fly down to roost on the loch, and 20,000 geese in clamorous flight filling the sky in the sunset quite defies description. Barnacle geese will be all around you throughout your visit up until mid-April when they head for the Arctic. Occasional wild snow geese join the great flocks in winter.

Continue on down the track alongside the loch towards Killinallan; superb water-side views are with you all the way. In spring as the tide recedes, the flats are used by many waders migrating to their breeding grounds. Flocks of bar-tailed godwit, curlew, grey plover, redshank and the occasional party of greenshank and whimbrel may all be seen. Sanderling dash about the sandy beaches while purple sandpipers and turnstones gather on the rockier parts to turn the seaweed for hidden food.

Curlew, golden plover and dunlin breed on the hills, especially the wide, lonely stretches of moorland from Craigens back towards Port Ascaig. Ringed plover and oystercatcher breed on the beaches all round the loch, especially on the sandy Killinallan Point; snipe, redshank and lap-wing all prefer the wet roadside meadows.

Scan the low-tide channel, or the water's edge on a rising tide – sea-duck are often numerous in the bay: several breeding pairs of eider, common scoter which also occasionally breed, long-tailed duck especially in spring and large groups of red-breasted mergansers diving for fish. Divers may use the bay for shelter and there are rare gulls sometimes which come in with the substantial numbers of common gulls always present. Watch for 'white-winged' glaucous and Iceland gulls especially in spring. Whooper swans may be seen throughout the winter, and pass on migration through the area right into April.

The track from the road-end at Killinallan may be followed as a walk and goes for miles along the low cliffs of Sgairail to Rhuvaal lighthouse at the northern tip of the island. It is a round 15-mile (24km) walk.

Returning to the B8017, through fields full of geese and dashing hares, take the next road out past the RSPB reserve headquarters at Gruinart Farm towards Ardnave Point. This appears to be a repeat of the road you have just traversed on the other side of the loch, but it can produce some extra wildlife surprises. You will enjoy close views of large flocks of geese. The road ends at Ardnave Loch on the left where red-throated divers are often to be seen, together with tufted duck and wigeon.

Arctic terns and little terns frequent the sand and hillocks of Ardnave Point. Machair flowers here are superb in midsummer.

Views across the loch here at low tide will usually reveal fifty or more common seals hauled out to bask on the sandbanks.

Walk the mile from your car to one of the several lochs to the west of the road. This will take you across low moorland with golden plover and curlew for company; red-throated divers may be on any of these lochs in spring, wheatears, twite, stonechat and whinchat are frequent on the moors after their spring arrival and occasional pairs of redwing breed in the woodlands.

Continue on the B8017 to Loch Gorm, best overlooked from the narrow minor road to Kilchoman. This area is a favourite with the 5,000 Greenland whitefronted geese, large dark-grey geese which prefer these higher, rougher pastures – substantial flocks form here in March. Loch Gorm itself has islets with breeding tern and duck in some variety and substantial wintering groups of mergansers and goldeneye. Parties of up to fifty whooper swans are regular.

Take the little by-road to Kilchoman Church and park in the tiny car-park. Scan

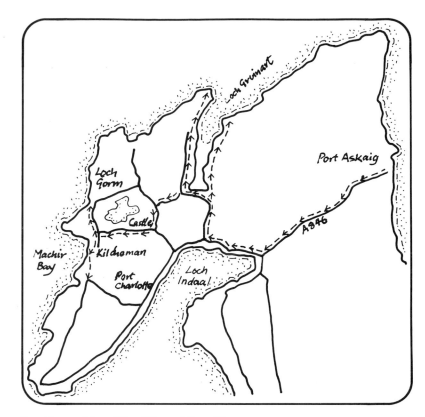

the skies and the cliffs of Creag Mhor. The sea at Machir Bay lies below you to the west and round about there will be hundreds of jackdaws 'chack-chacking' away; with them there may be forty or fifty choughs, curved red bills, wide rounded wings and distinctive 'pew' call picking them out as they roll and tumble through the skies like aerial acrobats. The cliffs of Islay hold one of the best colonies of this rare bird in Britain.

These cliffs are predator country. You can walk them two miles (3km) south to Kilchiaran, or take the road north two miles to Saligo Bay. Kittiwakes, fulmars and auks are found along them; so too are peregrine, buzzard and golden eagle.

Islay holds some 20,000 Greenland barnacle geese, and 5,000 Greenland whitefronts during the winter months

78

Mull
HEBRIDES STRATHCLYDE

Address of Site/Warden

None

Highlights and Features

Lovely green island large enough for long exploration. Wide variety of birds, seals, otters, red deer, eagles.

Facilities

Well-known tourist island.

Photo Tips

A wide range of equipment needed for scenics, flowers. Birds likely to be distant.

Kestrels haunt the cliffs and plantations of the Hebridean islands

The island of Mull is one of those rare places where sea, sky, hill, loch, forest and town seem to mingle magically to make a whole landscape. Nothing seems out of step.

Even Tobermory, the island's main holiday centre, nestles nicely under the Mishnish Hills. Its harbour front, little fishing boats, row of colourful shops, visiting yachts and the red and black Macbraynes Ferry all seem right in their setting.

The harbour is good for glaucous and Iceland gulls. In the world of fable, Mull is famous for the Tobermory Galleon, one of the Armada allegedly full of gold and wrecked somewhere offshore, the treasure still waiting to be found.

In the world of hard reality, Mull is a tertiary basalt overlain with lava-flow terraces and compressed beds of ash. The variety of habitat is such that a wide range of montane and coastal birds, animals and plants are found. One wildlife tour is described through this lovely green island that merits a long holiday to explore properly. Access is by MacBraynes Ferry from Oban.

Wildlife Tour: Mull

The tour starts and finishes in Tobermory, although there are other places to stay. Best time to visit is in summer when the breeding birds are present. However, winter has its attractions because of the large numbers of winter wildfowl.

Check the rocky shores of the Tobermory bay for purple sandpiper; grey seals appear regularly in the harbour.

From Tobermory take the B8073 west towards Dervaig. After only a mile a string of three interconnected small lochs, known locally as the Mishnish Lochs, can be seen near the road on the left. Open woodland with low conifer plantations extends uphill behind the lochs.

Red-throated divers breed here, and there are usually two or three pairs present. The moorland is the breeding site for hen harrier and short-eared owl, but you will have to examine the hillsides closely for these low-flying birds as they blend so well with the background. Red grouse wander along the roadside.

At the western end of the lochs a hill track runs north for three miles (4.8km) to Glen Gorm Castle. Steep moorland hills rise to the right, while a long boggy valley is overlooked by the path. Both Loch Frisa and Loch an Tor may hold black-throated diver.

The evocative moorland cry of curlew and the mournful pipe of golden plover follow you along this track, and it is a good place for golden eagles which patrol these hills ready to snatch a rabbit or a grouse.

Continue through Dervaig for 4 miles (6.4km) nearly to Calgary, and turn right on a minor road to Caliach Point. The cliffs and coastal scenery here are rugged. Watch the sea for razorbills, shags and black guillemots, which all have their nests in the broken, rocky cliffs. Ravens and fulmars can be seen frequently on this hilly Mornish Peninsula, while gannets and Manx shearwaters pass offshore.

Return towards Dervaig and take the road right by the church and the new chalets towards Salen. This is a lonely, narrow road which runs for nearly ten miles (16km) through wild country.

The wide valley of the little River Bellart is full of rushy wet meadows filled with fen flowers in midsummer, and a few corncrakes still appear in these each spring: do they breed? Listen along the quietest stretches for their quite unmistakable 'crex-crex' callnote.

Kestrel and peregrine hunt from the rocky spurs along this valley and sparrowhawk from the conifer forest encountered after two miles. Crossbill and siskin are found in these woods.

Examine the marshy meadows for breeding waders: curlew, redshank, lapwing, snipe and oystercatcher, even an occasional dunlin might appear. This is a lovely spot and very scenic – golden eagles regularly glide down the valley, usually to be challenged by the fury of the resident pair of tiny kestrels.

Red deer may sometimes be seen in the fields bordering the river, having come down from the moorland heights towards Loch Tuath, and also otters on the headwaters inland but these are most often seen on the sea-lochs.

From Salen and the Sound of Mull drive south on the B8035 in just two miles (3km) to the head of Loch Na Keal. This is a five-mile (8km) long sea-loch and nearly two miles (3km) wide in places.

The seaweed-covered rocky coast together with the tiny marshy estuary of

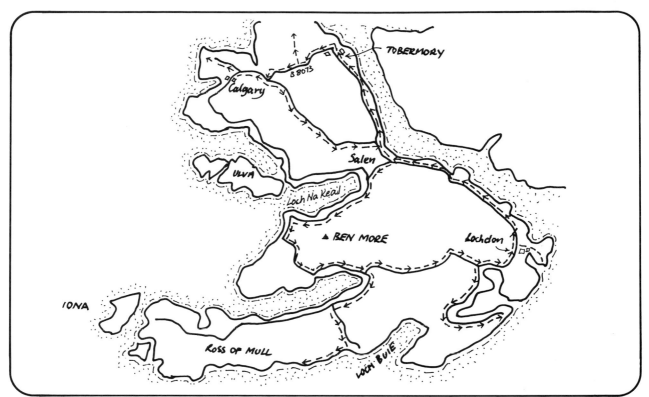

the River Bà, have their own special birds and animals. Otters are a possibility here – watch the water's edge. Herons wade among the rock pools. Eider and red-breasted merganser breed on the shore or nearby, and may be numerous in the bay and in spring and autumn, migrant parties of great northern and black-throated divers and Slavonian grebes come to shelter and fish in the loch.

The road runs along the southern shore under the great basalt dome of Ben More, at 3,171 feet (966m) one of the highest mountains in the Hebrides.

Its huge, brooding, mysterious cliffs tower hundreds of feet above the road at the Gribun. There are frequent rock-falls so hurry by, find a safe spot and then watch the cliffs. Golden eagles have eyries and are frequently seen, as are buzzard and peregrine.

Just offshore the island of Inch Kenneth with its many skerries was used as a burial place for Scottish chiefs when the passage to Iona was stormy. Both grey and common seals haul out on the rocks here, although the grey is more numerous.

Take the road south under the great cliffs and make for the Ross of Mull round the head of Loch Scridain. Here too, watch for otters in the quieter bays. At the western end lies Iona, called the 'Cradle of Christianity' – originally this was a place of pilgrimage, the last resting place of dozens of Scottish kings and chiefs and the home of St Columba; the island is now full of tourists, so visit off-season.

Just round the head of Loch Scridain

turn left off the A849 to Carsaig. Great cliffs form the shoreline four miles each side of Carsaig Bay.

One of Britain's most memorable cliff walks starts from Carsaig Bay and heads west along the shore – walking gear is needed as the way is rough and sometimes steep. This is a round, seven-mile (11km) walk to Malcolm's Point beneath cliffs which in places are 700 feet high (213m). Their geology is striking and displayed in most spectacular fashion at Carsaig Arches, huge piles of columnar basalt reminiscent of Fingal's Cave. Sea-birds seen at Carsaig Bay breed on the cliffs here, with shag, razorbill, guillemot all numerous. Golden eagles and wild goats may be seen along these huge cliffs.

The A849 runs eastwards through wild hill country to Loch Spelve, a sheltered sea-loch on the island's east coast. A side-road south at Strathcoil will take you all round Loch Spelve's southern arm and down to the head of Loch Buie.

Red deer are common on the hills here, as are many of the island's birds of prey, hunting grouse and rabbits.

Whooper swans favour these waters in winter and come in large herds to enjoy their shelter.

Loch Don, a little further north, is full of mud and rushes and a superb habitat for migrant waders, with greenshank, spotted redshank and many more in spring and autumn.

The road, now the island's main route, returns north along the coast to Tobermory.

All of the auks, like this razorbill, spend much time on the sea, fishing, and are most in danger from pollution

Isle of Rhum
HEBRIDES HIGHLAND

Address of Site/Warden

Rhum National Nature
Reserve
Warden:
The White House,
Isle of Rhum,
Scotland

Highlights and Features

One of the Small Isles of the
Hebrides. Mountainous
island and cliff and sea-loch
shore. Famous site for
reintroduction of white-tailed
sea eagle. Many highland
birds, flowers and animals.
Good site to see red deer
and otter. Resident golden
eagles. Huge colony of
130,000 pairs Manx
shearwaters in summer.

Facilities

Day trips from Mallaig and
Arisaig.
Residential accommodation
at the Castle.

Photo Tips

Birds, mammals, flowers,
insects . . . all are possible so
go with at least a wide-angle
zoom for the smaller
creatures and scenics. One
300mm lens may give some
good bird pictures. Trails are
rocky and steep – remember
you have to carry everything.

*Green Hairstreak
butterflies are found
throughout Britain, often
living on gorse bushes*

High above the battlements of Kinloch Castle a huge eagle soars on wide wings, its broad white tail gleaming in the sunlight. This is an adult sea eagle and the castle is on Rhum, one of the Small Isles of the Hebrides. Rhum is the setting for the Nature Conservancy's most famous project, the reintroduction of the sea eagle to its rightful home on the cliffs and lochs of the Scottish coast.

Rhum was declared a national nature reserve in 1957 and, with the exception of the school-teacher, the population are all NCC employees and their families.

Rhum is the site of an ancient and long-extinct volcano which deposited material over even older layers of Red Sandstone, visible in the north of the island.

The cliffs and ridges of the spectacular hills of Askival and Hallival in the south are what remains of the base of the old volcano, but the corries, lochs and glens have been carved by the last Ice Age. The island has a total area of 26,400 acres (10,683ha).

Access used to be very restricted but is now much easier. Day trips by Macbraynes Ferry are possible from Mallaig and the boat sails on Monday, Wednesday, Thursday and Saturday (1987); it returns the same day, allowing 3–4 hours on the island, which gives time to walk the nature trails around the castle. The castle itself is now open as a hotel, providing good food and luxuriantly faded Edwardian elegance. The best time to visit is from April to June, when some limited camping is also possible, since from July onwards midges make things particularly uncomfortable.

A tour around the main sites of the island is described but day visitors will have time only for the nature trails. The walks are wet and rough and full walking gear is needed.

The boat trip, which takes 3–4 hours each way, is superb for sea-birds: Arctic terns, gannets, auks, three species of diver, storm petrels, Manx and sooty shearwaters are all usually encountered on the way. The return evening trip is especially good for the more crepuscular petrels and shearwaters.

As you approach the landing stage in Loch Scresort the view is dominated by the high hills of the southern mountains and the fantastic purple-red sandstone castle built by the past owner, Sir George Bullough in 1900–2. If you are coming to stay, you are in for some elegant surprises.

Loch Scresort is surrounded by high, bare, rain-soaked hills, but in their shelter, around the shore and along the valleys, considerable planting with native trees has been carried out, especially in the last twenty years.

Much of the woodland in the castle area is a mature mixture of Corsican pine, rowan, alder and Scots pine, all planted early in the century.

Take the Kinloch Glen nature trail which is a four-mile (6.4km) round walk west towards the hills. The starting point is the old lime kiln which is covered in unusual ferns, maidenhair fern, black spleenwort and the commoner polypody.

Good views of the bay from the road will show eider and red-breasted mergansers in family groups, while red-throated divers are usually to be seen fishing in the sheltered waters. They breed on several of the island's lochans. Oystercatchers are numerous on the shoreline, with a few curlew and common sandpiper; while herons, which now have a breeding colony, wade in the shallows looking for anything edible. The hooded crow is probably the most obvious tide-line scavenger, collecting cockles and mussels and dropping them from fifty feet (15m) onto rocky boulders to get at their contents.

The woodlands at the head of the bay are full of birds, many of which have colonised since the trees were planted, and the process will continue in view of the more recent plantings by the NCC. Wood and willow warbler, blue, great and coal tits, goldcrest and treecreeper may all be seen or heard, while some of the robins and chaffinches will take food from the hand. Even Speckled Wood butterflies have colonised the woodlands.

The old Post Office, still in use for cards, drawings and small quantities of food, stands near the head of the bay and is backed by a high beech and sycamore wood which dates from 1830. Woodcock and long-eared owl breed in the woodlands in small numbers, and one or two pairs of sparrowhawk hunt the bay area. A further scan of the bay before turning inland may produce sightings of grey and common seals hunting for fish.

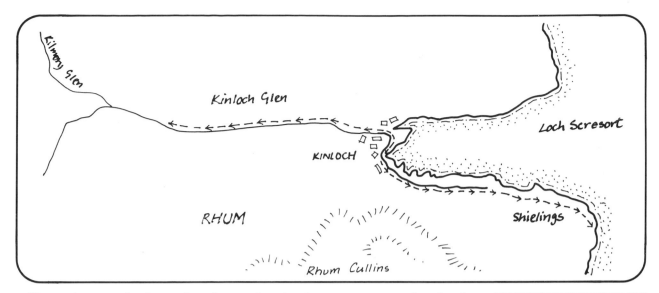

The track turns inland past the white gates of the tree nursery, and rises to provide a good view of the small area of farmland around Kinloch village. Rhum ponies are an ancient breed and although living on the hills, they often drift into the farmland to graze. Corncrakes may occasionally breed in the small farm fields, while a pair or two of dippers inhabit the Kinlock river running alongside the path.

The path rises, giving clearer views of the surrounding hills, with Hallival and Askival rising to 2,500 feet (760m) on the left, and the Barkeval ridge nearer and most prominent. These mountains, called the Rhum Cuillins, are terraced peaks of the old volcano and are home to 130,000 pairs of Manx shearwaters, probably the largest single bird colony in Britain. They are rarely visible by day, living in their honeycombed burrow city high on the slopes.

These rugged hills are accessible from a track running south from near the castle, but a permit, and a reason for hiking and camping, are required. Golden eagles regularly hunt through the glens and along the shearwater terraces. Here, too, the few sea eagles remaining on Rhum are likely to be seen. Some eighty-two birds have been released as juveniles from chicks brought from Norway, and most have ranged among the neighbouring islands of Skye, Eigg, Muck and Mull.

The hills hold a wide range of arctic–alpine flowers, especially on the upper levels, with moss campion, cyphel, purple, mossy, starry and alpine saxifrages, parsley fern, globe flower and roseroot. They also support an intensively studied population of red deer, often seen in summer from the top of the path.

Near the trail-head an extensive area of some 1,450 acres (587ha) has been deer-fenced and planted with a variety of native trees and shrubs. Short-eared owls may breed in the most open areas, but already the trees have gained wood and willow warbler.

The roadside flowers vary from bog-soil plants such as bog asphodel, to heather on dry ground, to dog violet on limestone soils. Butterflies are numerous in summer with Small Pearl-bordered and Dark Green Fritillaries, Green Hairstreaks, Large Heaths and Graylings. Emperor and Fox Moths breed in the heathers.

The South Side Trail is a three-mile (4.8km) round walk above the shore of Loch Scresort and is usually very wet. It begins at the slipway near the jetty, and runs through extensive areas of woodland, as well as some of the older trees planted by the Bullough family. The little bay next to the slipway is regularly used by eider families.

The ground is very boggy and the vegetation comprises typical flowers such as bog asphodel and all three species of British sundews, also common and pale butterwort. A mile through the woodland brings you to open moorland. The coast line, rough and rocky with many skerries, is a favourite otter haunt; they may appear at any time but early morning is most likely.

The path continues over heather and purple moor grass hummocks to the tiny ruined village of Port nan Caranean, deserted in 1861.

Common and lesser black-backed gulls nest with eider ducks among the ruins, while herring gulls, oystercatchers and common sandpipers nest on the shore. Here and there great black-backs breed on isolated skerries.

Late evening brings huge rafts of Manx shearwaters onto the sea, the birds flying in at dusk to their burrows on the upper slopes of Hallival, clearly visible from here, along with hunting eagles always on the look-out for a quick meal.

A few herons, now resident on Rhum, check the shallows for food

80

Handa
HIGHLAND

Address of Site/Warden

RSPB Scottish Office,
17 Regent Terrace,
Edinburgh EH7 5BN
Summer Warden:
c/o Mrs A. Munro,
Tarbet,
Foindle,
Lairg,
Sutherland IV27 4SS

Highlights and Features

Small offshore island just
over 1 square mile.
Moorland and huge sea-
cliffs. Very large sea-bird
colonies. Breeding great and
Arctic skuas, red-throated
divers.

Facilities

Small bothy for RSPB
members to stay overnight.
Access from Tarbet by boat
from 1000. Island shut on
Sunday.

Photo Tips

Medium and long telephoto
lenses will provide superb
pictures of sea-birds and
skuas.

*A kittiwake tends its eggs
and chick at its nest
cemented to the vertical
cliff face*

Tell a group of birders that you have been
to Handa and there will be a moment's
envious silence. Handa has a breeding
sea-bird population of international importance, it is a place of unique isolation, and
yet it lies only a few hundred yards
offshore. It is an RSPB reserve.

The road to Handa is long, winding
through the narrow, one-track roads of
Wester Ross, around the vast emptiness of
Inverpolly and into Sutherland.

Seven families lived on the island until
1848, and the remains of their fields, crofts
and a little graveyard can still be seen.
Since 1962 the RSPB has leased the 766
acres (310ha), and a summer warden is
resident from 1 April to 10 September
when the island is open.

Access is from Tarbet reached from
Scourie and a minor road off the A894 in
three miles (4.8km). The local boatman is
at Tarbet and the first little boat leaves at
10am; the island is shut on Sundays.

One wildlife walk is described round the
whole island. The walk is three miles
(4.8km), can be very muddy and needs
walking boots. It takes about three hours
but you will probably want to stay all day.

Wildlife Walk: Handa

The boat leaves Tarbet jetty and is quickly
out among the oceanic world of the
seabirds, which positively throng this
narrow stretch of water between the island
and the mainland – gulls, terns, auks,
ducks and divers. Look in particular for
black-throated and great northern divers
in the sheltered channel, and even the
occasional red-throated diver may appear,
giving a good chance of all three British
species together. However, red-throated
divers prefer to feed on the fresh-water
lochs inland.

The boat lands in a few short minutes at
a low, sandy bay with rocky skerries.
Oystercatcher, ringed plover, rock pipit
and common tern all nest on these islets,
and Arctic terns are frequent in the sound
from colonies elsewhere.

Eider ducks bring families of ducklings
to this sheltered bay in summer, while
black guillemots also appear on the sea.

Once on shore there is a little shelter
and an information display by the quay;
the warden or one of his assistants usually
meets each boat and the numbers of
visitors are limited daily.

The path climbs fairly gently up close-
cropped, peaty turf. Rabbits are the
island's only common mammal, with an
estimated population of 3,000 – visitors
on quiet days may wonder if they all live
around this one spot. Interbreeding often
produces colour variations, and there are
a number of black rabbits.

The machair flowers above the sheltered southern shore rarely survive above
'nibble' height. Several pairs of wheatears
breed in the old holes here.

The path climbs onto the open peat
moorland, passing ruined crofts on the
left. Wheatears sometimes nest in the
stones. Boardwalks have been placed
along the wettest sections of the bog path
which runs for just over a mile across the
island, but it is still very muddy at times.
You must stay on the path here to avoid
disturbance of the breeding birds. Snipe
and golden plover may nest, but the moor
is fairly quiet until you meet the skuas:
both great and Arctic skuas breed on this
moorland and are increasing, and cur-
rently there are fifty pairs of great skuas
and a dozen or so pairs of the lighter,
more agile Arctics. You will be dive-
bombed by any pairs with territory near
the path – keep your eyes peeled and
throw up your fist at the last moment.
Although lighter, Arctic skuas are quicker,
more agile and work well as a pair.

A sharp clip round the ear from an
unseen bird descending from the rear is
quite a possibility, but you will come to no
harm. Dodging the skuas is good sport –
keep to the footpath.

Red-throated divers breed on the tiny
hill lochans.

The path rises steadily to the cliff top
and as you walk the last few yards a
sudden rush of noise bursts upon you.
Handa's northern cliffs spring up at you
from far below where crashing surf sprays
white spume across the rocks.

The path runs to the left for a few yards
and then the Great Stack, separated a few
yards from the island, comes into view.
Thousands of sea-birds wheel and dive
around these huge cliffs and every ledge is
crammed with birds.

The island is a chunk of Torridon
Sandstone whose horizontal layers have
weathered unevenly, forming ideal breeding sites for over 100,000 assorted sea-
birds.

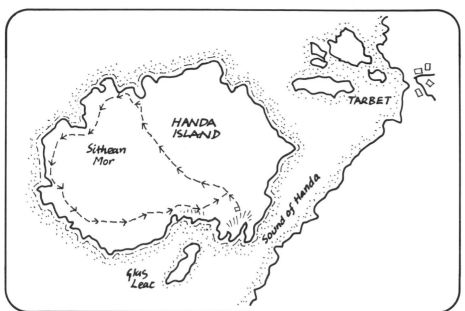

The short turf of the cliff tops, among clumps of pink thrift and white sea campion, makes a good seat to study these huge multi-storey bird cities. Great Stack itself, smothered in some 12–15,000 birds holds the largest single colony.

Puffin Bay, the first point of arrival at the cliffs, actually holds very few puffins but it does have large colonies of fulmars and many of the 300 pairs of herring gulls which breed on the island. A few guillemots and razorbills have colonised the small, needle-shaped rock. Grey seals can usually be seen in the bay.

Great Stack shows exactly how a large sea-bird colony divides itself up, like a high-rise block of bird-flats: kittiwakes plaster their nests to every rocky projection; guillemots use horizontal ledges on the open cliff face; razorbills are found in holes in the more broken rocks near the top; finally on the grassy summit puffins nest in burrows and any available holes. Competition for nest space is therefore neatly avoided.

Follow the cliff path towards the western end of the island – the noise and fish smell of the colonies, combined with the swirling masses of birds along these huge cliffs, makes this a dramatic place.

The cliffs at Poll Ghlup rise to over 400 feet (122m). A huge razorbill colony can be found here while shags nest on the lower cliffs in many places; a little further on more large colonies of guillemots occur. Estimated totals of breeding pairs of sea-birds are: 30,000 guillemots; 13,000 kittiwakes; 9,000 razorbills; 3,500 fulmars; 300 puffins; 250 shags.

Peregrines used to breed on these cliffs, and are now noted with increasing frequency. A lucky visitor may find a sea eagle drifting by on huge wings, as birds from the introduction scheme on Rhum

are seen in many parts of the north-west coast; buzzards and golden eagles occasionally visit from the mainland. Ravens breed regularly on the westernmost cliffs with great black-back gulls on rock stacks.

The western cliffs are good for sea-watching. Gannets and shearwaters pass offshore while a regular passage of pomarine skuas occurs in early May.

From these cliffs the next land west is Labrador so they are also a good spot for whale-watching. Whales, especially porpoise, common dolphin and killer whale, may sometimes be seen 'coasting' along the Atlantic's eastern seaboard.

Follow the track around the south of the island, leaving the noise of the cliffs behind. Otters are worth looking for at all times in the quieter and more sheltered bays.

The path returns across the waters of Hill Burn to join up with the outward path by the old crofts. The warden's bothy with its tiny plantation of Lodgepole pines and alders attracts one pair of robins to add a touch of home.

The north and west hold huge colonies of guillemots on undisturbed cliffs

81

The Far North-west

CAPE WRATH
AND FARAID HEAD
HIGHLAND

Address of Site/Warden

None

Highlights and Features

Cape Wrath – Wild moorland backing highest mainland cliffs in Britain. Difficult access. Huge colonies breeding sea-birds in summer with golden eagles and peregrines along the cliffs.
Faraid Head – Lower and more accessible but still with formidable cliffs backed by dunes. Many breeding sea-birds.
Good site for sea-bird and whale migration in spring and autumn.

Facilities

None

Photo Tips

Medium and long telephoto lenses will give pictures of sea-birds. Long walks involved here, so watch weight of rucksack.

Large colonies of puffins occupy the cliff-tops at Cape Wrath and Faraid Head

Pounded by the fearsome North Atlantic, lashed by gales and virtually uninhabited, the far north-west coast of Britain presents a challenge to everybody interested in wildlife. It is the most difficult part of the whole of the mainland to reach, with some planning needed to explore and see everything that this magnificent coastline has to offer. From Kinlochbervie on the west coast, north to Cape Wrath and east to Durness, this wild, remote country offers some of the most rewarding cliff-walking in Britain with truly spectacular scenery.

The whole area except Durness is based on solid, ancient Lewisian Gneiss, and the inland scenery is typical of the Sutherland hinterland, heather moorland and peat bog with many small lochans.

The shoreline has stupendous cliffs, skerries and islets which toss the waves high into columns of thunderous spray, wide sandy bays and myriads of sea-birds.

Two wildlife walks are described. The first deals with the more accessible Faraid Head, the second describes the Cape Wrath–Clo Mor cliffs. Summer is the best time to see the wildlife, though winter can be quite dramatic.

Wildlife Walk 1: Faraid Head

Durness is an attractive straggle of white-painted houses looking out across the cold waters of the North Minch. The setting is lush and green for here the rock is limestone, forced up over the bedrock of gneiss as at Knocken Cliff in Inverpolly further south.

Drive west through the village away from the main road, and follow the little roadway round to Balnakeil Bay. There is a tiny car-park and some toilets here. The lime-filled rock supports a far richer flora than the surrounding hills of peat and heather. A burn, filled with golden marsh marigolds in June, is a blaze of colour – these flowers bloom two months later here than in the southern counties.

Before you stretches the wide white sand of Balnakeil Bay – at low tide the firm sands, rippled by the waves, allow a walk to the offshore skerries of A'chleit. High tide lines the part-submerged rocks with shags and nesting gulls and Arctic terns flicker over the wide beauty of the bay's blue water.

The walk round Faraid Head is straight-forward providing no attempt is made to clamber on the cliffs. You should avoid disturbing the nesting birds.

Walk the mile-long stretch of dazzling beach. The sand is firmest at the high-tide line where ringed plover, rock pipits and twite gather tit-bits from the seaweed flotsam. As you near the headland a concrete track runs up into the huge dunes, some of which are 200 feet high (61m). Walk up the track for 200 yards (183m) and then strike east across the marram-covered dune ridges.

Hundreds of herring gulls and a scattering of lesser and great black-backed gulls haunt the dunes, waiting to pounce on chicks, eggs, or even a luckless baby rabbit. There are thousands of rabbits, easy to watch by sitting quietly in the marram grass.

Three hundred yards brings you suddenly to sheer cliffs, 150 feet high (45m), on the eastern side of the isthmus. Several rocky bluffs allow close views of the bays and hundreds of birds breed here, with fulmar in particularly high numbers. Guillemots, razorbills and puffins may be seen flying in and out of the lower cliffs, and black guillemots and shags abound on the skerries.

Walk north towards the invisible headland along the cliff edge. Large gulls and fulmars by the score will hang on the breeze above you.

The cliffs rise steadily, the path climbing upwards on short turf filled with thrift and campion. The sheltered rocky bays below are good for grey seals; Loch Eriboll five miles east (2km) is one of only two mainland breeding sites for grey seals, an indication of the wildness of this coast.

The scenery is quite breathtaking: look back at the long, rugged north coast of Scotland, with Loch Eriboll, Whiten Head, the Mhoine, Strathy Point and Dunnett Head far to the east.

After half a mile, huge sea-stacks rise offshore. Enormous numbers of kittiwakes splash white down the cliffs, while guillemots jostle for position with shags and a few razorbills.

Large colonies of puffins live in the very steep dune headlands. These cliffs are quite unsafe but excellent views may be had from the cliff path – this rises quite sharply, reaches a wire fence and crosses the brow of a hill. There, suddenly, one

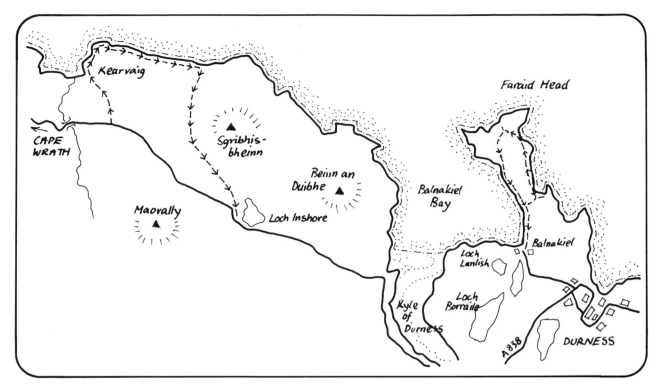

comes face to face with modern warfare: a radar-tracking station, with army tents and huts behind a chain-link fence, which prevents you from reaching the true headland. What a terrible intrusion in such a wild and lovely place!

Skirt the fence to the 300-foot (91m) northern cliffs. Lots of puffins and hundreds of fulmars nest among the thrift-covered ledges; an occasional great or Arctic skua harries the terns and kittiwakes, while gannets fish offshore.

The white lighthouse of Cape Wrath beckons on the western horizon.

The return is easy back to the sands of Balnakeil Bay, down under the 50-foot (15m) western cliffs. A few alpine flowers grow in damp crevices at sea level, with clumps of roseroot and starry saxifrage obviously thriving.

Wildlife Walk 2: Clo Mor and Cape Wrath

Two miles south of Durness on the A838 a signpost leads you the last few yards to Keoldale and the Kyle of Durness ferry. Apart from very long approach walks, this is the only way to reach the Cape Wrath headlands. From the other side, a minibus runs the nine miles (14km) to Cape Wrath – the fare is £3 (1987) and the bus runs several times daily in summer.

To see the Clo Mor cliffs, alight by request at the Kervaig track, and ask to be collected either at the same point, or – as long as you are prepared for a very rough five-mile (8km) walk – at Inshore, a building and loch by the roadside back towards Durness. Full walking equipment

and food are absolutely essential.

Walk the mile down the track to lovely Kervaig Bay, turn east crossing the burn, and climb steadily up the steep cliff slopes. The walking is straightforward for three miles (4.8km) on peaty turf along the top of Clo Mor.

These are the highest and most spectacular cliffs on the mainland, rising to nearly 900 feet (274m). Huge colonies of fulmar, gulls and auks occur, with many thousands of puffins; gannets, Manx and sooty shearwaters are usually offshore. The cliffs hold two or three pairs of golden eagles and peregrine, spectacular birds in a spectacular setting.

After nearly three miles (4.8km) turn south, following a low ridge running inland. There are no tracks and this is a two-mile (3km) walk round the thousand foot (305m) hill of Scribhn Bheinn. Ptarmigan, red grouse and greenshank are present. Meet the bus at Inshore.

Like most names on this coast, the name 'Cape Wrath' is derived from the Norse, in this case from 'Hvarf', 'a turning point'. It is most easily reached by continuing on the minibus service which runs right to the lighthouse.

Autumn and spring migrations can be spectacular with thousands of sea-birds turning this corner of Britain on their long flight.

Whale-watching can be rewarding too, with several species frequent, including common dolphin and porpoise, pilot and killer whales.

From here there is no more land until the North Pole.

Whales of various species pass to and fro on migration round the north coast. Pilot whales may occur in large schools

82

The Uists
WESTERN ISLES

Address of Site/Warden

Balranald RSPB Reserve
Summer Warden:
Visitors Cottage,
Goular,
nr Hougharry,
Lochmaddy,
North Uist,
Outer Hebrides
Loch Druidibeg National
Nature Reserve
Warden:
Stilligarry,
South Uist,
Outer Hebrides

Highlights and Features

Long dazzling sandy
beaches, machair grassland,
and inland a mosaic of lochs,
marshes, rock, moorland
and mountain.
Very high density of breeding
waders on the machair.
Many other highland
specialities. Golden eagles.
Red-necked phalaropes,
corncrakes. Good for otter,
seals, whales.
Special machair dune flora.

Facilities

Observation tower at Loch
Druidibeg. Many inhabitants
follow a strict regime on
Sundays, so check normal
meals are available. Access
at all times to reserves.

Photo Tips

Islands for long holidays of
exploration, so take all the
gear you feel you can carry
and may need.

The Western Isles are islands where time seems to have sauntered quietly onto the edge of the modern world. In the Outer Hebrides you can drive for miles and see nothing but moorland, loch and sea. Lewis and Harris in the north are in fact one landmass and not two separate islands, while North Uist, Benbecula and South Uist are joined by causeways and known collectively as 'the Uists'.

Distances are deceiving in these islands. Lewis and Harris are over 80 miles (129km) long, while the Uists are nearly the same. They are all that remain of an ancient eroded platform of Lewisian Gneiss, 3,000 million years old, where hills have been scoured by the glaciers and covered in glacial drift and then in peat, which may be 15 feet (4m) deep in places.

These islands are among the wildest and most attractive parts of Britain. Trees are rare, only found where small copses have been planted for shelter, and the islands are a veritable maze of lochs, dubh lochans and peat bog. The Atlantic coast has long, dazzling, sandy beaches, the land slowly rising through the crofting areas towards the eastern hills, peaking at 2,033 feet (620m) on Beinn Mhor in South Uist, but only 1,139 feet (347m) at Eaval in the low-lying and lochan-riddled North Uist. The eastern seaboard facing the mainland is a mass of cliffs and deeply indented sea-lochs. There are few roads and accommodation is sparse, while at weekends, and especially on Sundays, some of the population follow a strictly religious way of life. You should check your situation in advance with regard to accommodation and meals.

There are two superb reserves, Balranald RSPB Reserve on North Uist and Loch Druidibeg National Nature Reserve on South Uist, but access to each is fairly limited and they should be seen as part of a wider tour, which is described below, the whole of the Uists being regarded as one vast nature reserve.

Access is by Caledonian Macbrayne car ferry from Uig (Skye) to Loch Maddy (North Uist) in two hours, or Oban to Loch Boisdale (South Uist) in six to eight hours. LoganAir fly from Glasgow to Barra and Benbecula while British Airways fly daily into Benbecula. Wildlife interest is exceptional all the year round, but May to June are best for flowers and breeding birds.

Wildlife Tour
This description assumes an arrival at Loch Maddy by boat from Skye. The boat-trip itself provides some excellent wildlife viewing with many seabirds. Black guillemots are particularly noticeable in the water near the coasts, but further out watch for storm and Leach's petrel, Manx and sooty shearwaters. Great northern divers are frequent on the sea in mid-summer. Whales, dolphins – especially common and bottle-nosed dolphin – and porpoises frequent the waters of the Minch.

Loch Maddy harbour and the many offshore islands are worth scanning for gulls, and in particular glaucous and Iceland gull, black guillemots, purple sandpiper, Arctic and little terns. The 600 foot (183m) hills of the Lees to the south hold golden eagles, often visible from the harbour jetty.

Turn left just out of Loch Maddy along the A867, which runs for five miles (8km) to Clachan on the island's west coast. The land on either side is flat, marshy and filled with lochs. Loch Skealter, just after the left turn, is good for divers, especially black-throated, which form in little flocks by late summer. Loch Scadavay a mile further west is also excellent for divers, although any loch or lochan may hold a pair, the red-throated diver preferring smaller waters. In summer red-throats are quite numerous, but autumn and winter bring great northern divers and this species then outnumbers the others. Arctic skuas breed nearby on the moorland.

Breeding waders in the marshes along this road include oystercatcher, lapwing and redshank. Dunlin, golden plover and greenshank are also present but in small numbers.

The small hill of Ben Langass on the right has a conifer plantation which sometimes houses a long-eared owl. Two miles (3km) beyond, turn right on the A865 to Balranald. The wide, white sands of the bays are backed by machair grassland, particularly well developed at Balranald, some five miles (8km) north up the road.

The RSPB reserve covers some 1,625 acres (657ha) and visitors must report to the reserve cottage on arrival. This is two miles (3km) north of Bayhead, signposted to Houghany on the left, forking left again to the cottage at Goular. Visitors must keep to the paths which allow good views. The area is a mix of marsh, crofting land, machair and coastal dunes, and includes the rocky headland of Aird an Runair, the most westerly point of the Hebrides.

A walk to the headland passes through wet grazing land where the ditches are filled with dense stands of sedges, rushes, reeds and flag iris, alongside small fields full of flowers. These ditches are the favoured haunt of the corncrake, with perhaps ten pairs on Balranald. Inland from the dunes lies the machair, a mix of peaty soil and lime-rich sand blown from the shell beaches. Flowers and birds are incredible in their abundance in this rich land. Machair supports the densest population of breeding waders in Britain, with 300 pairs of lapwing, 100 pairs each of redshank, dunlin, ringed plover and oystercatcher, and occasional phalaropes at Balranald alone.

Machair flowers are one of the glories of the Hebrides, and the fields are full of them: yellow bird's-foot trefoil, kidney vetch, silverweed, hawkbit, blue harebells, milkwort, speedwell, purple tufted vetch and self-heal, white chickweed, clover, purging flax, and red thyme, clover, bartsia and storksbill. In damp places, ragged robin, marsh marigold and Hebridean marsh orchid cover huge areas.

Mallard, teal, wigeon, gadwall, shoveler, coot and mute swan all breed in high numbers in the marshland; the drier areas of machair are ploughed for winter crops, and therefore provide food and cover for larks, pipits, twite, buntings and wheatear. Little and Arctic terns often nest in these dry fields. The whole abundant collection is predated by buzzard, kestrel, peregrine and short-eared owl.

The most exciting mammal is the otter which can be encountered anywhere, although it is most likely to be seen on the sea-lochs, along with grey seals.

The Runair headland, only a mile from the reserve cottage, provides magnificent sea-watching with gannets, petrels, auks, fulmars, terns, gulls and skuas. Manx shearwaters may reach a thousand per hour and gannets five hundred in spring and autumn, with sooty shearwaters frequent. In late May large numbers of pomarine and long-tailed skuas pass up the coast on any westerly wind.

South from Balranald and across the causeway, down the A865, lies Benbecula with excellent views of wide sandy bays with curlew, whimbrel, godwits, sanderling and plovers.

Five miles (8km) – with much Army traffic from the nearby rocket range – brings you across Benbecula to South

Uist, and Loch Bee with its 600 mute swans. Here a few whooper swans stay all summer; otherwise they form large gatherings from their autumn arrival right through the winter until they leave in April.

Two miles south of Loch Bee, turn left on the B890 along the northern edge of Loch Druidibeg reserve. Access is limited but much can be seen from the road and the wooden tower. Wild grey-lag geese breed here, with about 80 pairs present most years. About a dozen hen harrier nests can usually be located, with lesser numbers of merlin, kestrel, buzzard and short-eared owl. Golden eagles hunt from the heights of Hecla down towards the road at Loch Skipport, while sea eagles wandering from Rhum are quite likely along the higher, rocky east-coast cliffs.

Along the B890 just west of Loch Skipport is a grove of firs, Chilean pine and rhododendrons; this often shelters migrants, as well as breeding goldcrest and long-eared owl. Scan the heights of Hecla for eagles from here. The road ends at a jetty from which in 1746 Bonnie Prince Charlie was rowed to meet Flora Macdonald.

Five miles (8km) south of Druidibeg, a road to the left travels two miles to Locheynort, with golden eagles on the heights of Beinn Mhor to the north. A similar road to the right, a mile further down the main road, goes to the headland of Rubha Ardvule, another fine sea-watching spot between long sandy beaches. The road runs south down the crofted machair west coast, with hen harriers and short-eared owls frequent along the roadside hunting voles, Loch Hallan near Daliburgh being particularly good for both species.

The road ends at the Sound of Barra, across which ferries ply to the island four miles (6.4km) away, watched by the seals and otters of the southern Uist shore. You can watch these from the door of the Polochar Inn, which is wonderfully situated right at the tip of the Uists.

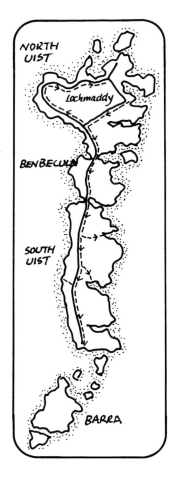

Restricted as a breeding bird to the far north-west, the black-throated diver has declined considerably in recent years

173

83

Orkney

Address of Site/Warden

RSPB Orkney Officer,
Smyril,
Stenness,
Stromness,
Orkney KW16 3JX

Highlights and Features

67 islands mostly just north of Caithness mainland. Greener and more easily farmed than Shetland. Huge sea-cliffs and wide moorlands. Vast colonies of sea-birds. Stronghold of hen harrier. Many other moorland birds. Otters. Seals. Whales.

Facilities

Numerous RSPB reserves, many with hides to view marsh and moorland birds. Cliff reserves usually are of open access while moorland reserves have access at selected points to avoid disturbance.

Photo Tips

Islands for long holidays. Sea-birds are the speciality so medium or long telephoto lenses are essential.

The main stronghold of the Arctic skua is in Orkney and Shetland

Where Atlantic Ocean and North Sea meet across the windswept waters of the Pentland Firth lies Orkney, a mosaic of sea and islands filled with an abundance of wildlife quite unique in Europe. Sea and land, man and wildlife mix in Orkney in a softly curving patchwork of farms and moors, lochs and cliffs, fens and ditches.

Orkney is nearer to the Arctic Circle than it is to London and yet the Gulf Stream warms the waters which bathe the islands so that severe cold is rare. In summer the sun is visible for twenty hours a day and birds flock here to reap the benefits of the continuous day to rear their young.

Orkney consists of sixty-seven islands, and there are nature reserves on many of them. The best way to get around is by car, but many small islands have no facilities for car ferries. One wildlife tour of the main sites is described.

Mainland

Access is by P&O car ferry from Scrabster to Stromness and the voyage takes two hours. Alternatively fly to Kirkwall and hire a car.

From Stromness head north on the A967 for nine miles (14.5km) to the A986 and then turn left on a minor road 400 yards beyond the junction. On the left is a lovely loch-filled, marshy RSPB reserve, The Loons. Access is *only* allowed to the hide, one mile west along the minor road. Breeding birds include many waders at high density, including 50 pairs lapwing, 35 pairs curlew, 20 pairs redshank, 15 pairs snipe and about 10 each of oyster-catcher, ringed plover and dunlin. Red-throated diver and even corncrake occur. Eight species of duck breed, with wigeon and pintail as specialities. Arctic tern, black-headed and common gull all have good colonies.

One mile only further west down a 'dead-end' road is Marwick Bay; an easy path rises to the cliff edge over peaty turf and pink thrift, blue spring squill, and white clumps of sea campion line the cliff-top.

As at all sea-bird colonies, the non-stop noise and strong fish odour hit you in successive waves. The path runs for a mile round fretted cliffs of Old Red Sandstone rising to 280 feet (85m). 80,000 birds cram the ledges, with 35,000 guillemots and

20,000 kittiwakes. Thousands of fulmars breed here, with smaller numbers of razor-bills. Puffins are few. Raven, rock dove and peregrine are found on the cliffs with twite and wheatear on the cliff-top around the monument to Lord Kitchener of Khartoum. A peregrine sometimes uses this as a perch. Great and Arctic skuas haunt the colonies for chance meals.

Otters appear from time to time in Marwick Bay, and even on the Loons marshes; grey and common seals are numerous along all coasts and appear in Marwick Bay daily.

Marwick is also good for whale-watching when these mammals pass between the Atlantic and the North Sea. Schools of porpoise and common dolphin are frequent, while Risso's and white-beaked dolphins, pilot and killer whales are all regularly seen. Some of the rarer large whales have been noted.

Ten miles (16km) east of Marwick Head along the north coast road, the A966, is the huge 5,700 acre (2,306ha) RSPB reserve of Birsay and Cottasgarth. Parts of this wonderful moorland area can be viewed from the B9057 between Geurth and Dounby but the two main access points are hides at Lowries Water just north of Geurth at the A966/B9057 junction, and four miles (6.4km) south down the A966. Here, take a minor road west and then turn right after half a mile to the hide at Lower Cottasgarth.

This is a heather and peat moorland which always offers outstanding views of breeding hen harrier, short-eared owl, merlin, kestrel, great and Arctic skuas, eight species of wader including hundreds of curlew and many golden plover, red-throated diver on many lochans, and teal, wigeon, and red-breasted merganser among eight species of ducks.

Do not walk on the moors, otherwise the disturbance may cause these rare birds to lose their eggs to marauding hooded crows, gulls and skuas.

From Birsay, head south to Hobbister, five miles (8km) west of Kirkwall. Access to yet another RSPB reserve is only allowed between the A964 and the sea, although 1,875 acres (778.4ha) are leased from the Highland Distillers Co. Hobbister is primarily heather moorland with the Swartaback Burn draining the northern sector. Waulkmill Bay has 100 foot (30m) cliffs and a good-sized car-park.

The bay is good for seals and the occasional otter. Black guillemots breed on the cliffs, with raven and rock doves.

Winter sea-watching into Scapa Flow is always good with many divers, 2,000 long-tailed ducks and many grebes and diving ducks generally.

The moor is very rich with several pairs of hen harriers, short-eared owls and merlins. Nearly 100 pairs of curlew breed along with many heather birds, such as twite, red grouse, wheatear and stonechat.

Hoy

Access for vehicles from the mainland is by the Orkney Islands Shipping Co ferry from Houton to Lyness.

Hoy is the most rugged island in Orkney, more reminiscent of the Sutherland hills, and is largely peat moorland. The northern cliffs are quite spectacular, the stretch from St Johns Head to the Kame of Hoy rising to over 1,000 feet (304m) in places. Two miles south is the 450 foot (137m) sea-stack 'The Old Man of Hoy' famed as a severe test of rock climbing skill.

The RSPB 9,700 acre (3,925ha) reserve of North Hoy includes cliffs which hold large concentrations of breeding sea-birds, especially fulmars. Manx shearwaters and storm petrels also probably breed.

The Orkney vole which feeds the birds of prey on Mainland is absent from Hoy, and correspondingly fewer numbers of hen harriers and owls are found. Peregrines, not dependent on the vole, are more numerous on the great cliffs, and merlins are still present in the heather. Buzzards breed and golden eagles visit from nearby Caithness, sometimes appearing over Ward Hill, which is the island's highest point. Mountain hares are numerous and act as prey species for the larger birds.

Shearwaters and petrels often gather offshore at Rackwick on the west coast in the evening.

Inland, huge numbers of great skuas (1,500 pairs) and Arctic skuas (400 pairs) breed on the moorland.

Best access to the whole reserve is from the minor road between Orgil and Rackwick, or the footpath which runs for three miles (4.8km) to Rackwick, between Ward Hill and the Cuilags.

North Islands: Westray and Papa Westray

Nearly all of Britain's seabirds breed on these tiny islands at the north of the group. LoganAir flies from Kirkwall into both. The RSPB Noup Head reserve on Westray is a four-mile (6.4km) walk from the airfield, although it is possible to arrange a car. The cliffs from Noup Head

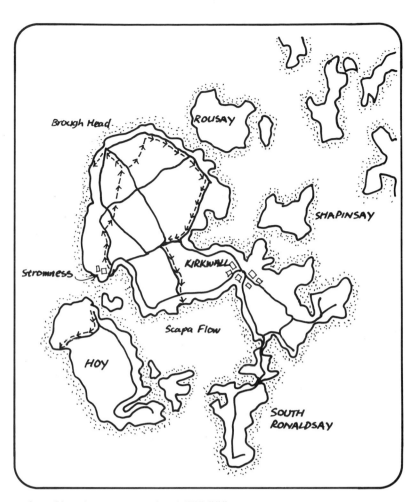

to Inga Ness house upwards of 200,000 birds with 60,000 pairs of kittiwake and 30,000 pairs of guillemot. Peregrines are frequent along these cliffs. Inland 2,000 pairs of Arctic tern breed on the nearby heathland with many Arctic skuas.

A short hop of *two minutes* by LoganAir to land at Papa Westray is next. North Hill has huge colonies, 6,000 pairs of Arctic terns just fifteen minutes' walk from the strip of grass that acts as the airfield, while 100 pairs of Arctic skuas hunt the terns.

Killer whales are surprisingly frequent off the coasts of the northern isles

Shetland

Address of Site/Warden

RSPB Shetland Officer,
'Seaview',
Sandwick,
Shetland ZE2 9HP
NCC Shetland,
1 Albert Buildings,
Alexandra Wharf,
Lerwick,
Scotland

Highlights and Features

Over 100 islands, many uninhabited. Just short of the Arctic Circle. Peat-covered hills, voes, lochs, marshes, cliffs and rock. Many thousands of breeding sea-birds, many rare waders. Divers, skuas, snowy owls. Otters, seals, whales.

Facilities

Usual tourist facilities. None otherwise.

Photo Tips

Medium and long telephoto lenses will provide good shots of sea-birds and some waders. Skuas in flight. Remember to compensate for the bright sky when taking pictures of 'attacking' skuas. Try a head-on view.

Red-throated divers are most numerous on lochs in Orkney and Shetland, but are rare elsewhere

Far to the north, scattered over 70 miles (112km) of sea are the hundred or so islands of Shetland. Muckle Flugga – the northernmost tip of Britain – is farther north than parts of Alaska. Shetland has that really 'wild' feel – isolated, windswept and set in a silver sea. Access is either by P&O ferry from Aberdeen, thirteen hours overnight; or – easier but much more expensive – British Airways from Aberdeen, or LoganAir from Edinburgh. It is possible to be in Shetland only four hours from London. LoganAir fly inter-island services but travel round the main islands is very easy by the frequent and cheap (£1) little ferries, though try to book in advance by telephone Burravoe 259. Accommodation is sparse, especially on the outer islands. A few 'self-catering' cottages are available but are often very primitive – if you can take your own accommodation, tent, caravan, motorhome, so much the better.

The weather can be fickle even in summer, with icy blasts and sleet whilst the rest of Britain is bathed in sunshine, so go prepared. Midsummer nights are never dark, the sun dipping below the horizon for only an hour or two around midnight – bird photography is still quite possible at 10pm. Winter however, with its short semi-arctic days, can be fierce, though it brings, nonetheless, high arctic birds for shelter. Many great northern divers and the occasional white-billed diver are found together with glaucous and Iceland gulls. Ivory gull and Ross's gull sometimes occur.

Several summer nature walks are described.

Mainland, Sumburgh Head

This is the southernmost tip of Mainland. The road goes straight across the airport runway so beware of taxiing aircraft. A small quarry just beyond the runway holds a number of breeding fulmar at 'touch' level, and the nearby beaches hold Arctic tern colonies. Sumburgh cliffs, although sheer in places, are broken in others and are negotiable with care. Thousands of breeding seabirds are here, with kittiwake, shag, guillemot, razorbill and puffin; five species of gull nest on the headland, and the bay on the northern flank has very accessible black guillemots on low rocks. Great rafts of eider and long-tailed duck

use these bays for shelter in bad weather.

Fitful Head to the north has great and Arctic skua and the 600 foot (183m) cliffs have peregrine.

Noss

A tiny island but very accessible from Lerwick via Bressay. Hail the boatman who will row you across the short intervening gap. This is one of the largest sea-bird colonies with over 50,000 nesting pairs of all the usual species plus a huge 6,000 pair gannetry. The Noup of Noss rises to nearly 600 feet (183m) and serried ranks of birds line its ledges. Both skuas breed in the moorland with eider in the heather. One of the best places for photography.

Unst, Hermaness

Access from Mainland is via two ferries, but return the same day is well-nigh impossible. The whole of Unst is a naturalist's paradise but for Hermaness take the only road north past the last telephone box in Britain, and park 300 yards (274m) uphill overlooking Burrafirth.

There are corncrakes in the little marsh in the dip. Fresh-water Loch of Cliff is used by kittiwakes and skuas for bathing and is excellent for photographs; fulmars and kittiwakes line the Burrafirth cliffs.

From the tiny car-park take the footpath uphill. This is skua territory, and you will be dive-bombed all the way up, some 2–3 miles. Wear a bobble hat, keep an eye on the sky and one in the back of your head, and stick a fist in the air at the last moment. You will come to no harm! Try some spectacular eyeball to eyeball photographs.

Half an hour's trudge uphill will bring you in sight of some tiny hill lochans on the left. These hold breeding red-throated diver and should not be disturbed; the divers fish on the Loch of Cliff. The moorland has breeding golden plover, dunlin and whimbrel.

Heather gives way to springy sward near the top where there is a hut and a visitors' book! From here branch out westwards down the slopes. Bird noise increases and suddenly you are there – on the cliff edge amid a bird-city filled with wings. This is one of the most dramatic spots in Britain. The cliffs are very steep, quite sheer in some places, but negotiable

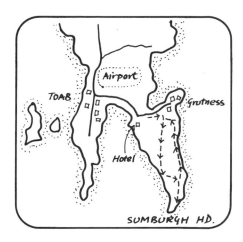

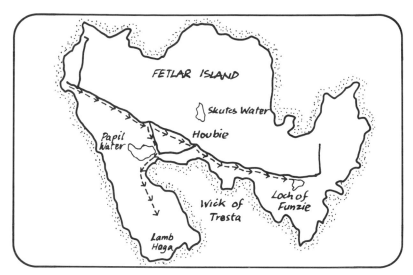

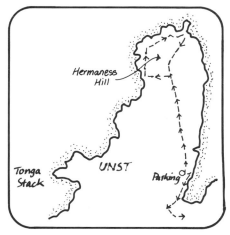

along sheep paths in others. However, only the surefooted and fit should consider them.

Close-encounter photographic opportunities abound. Puffins can be seen all along the cliff top. Thousands of sea-birds throng the cliffs and stacks, with an 8,000 pair gannetry as the centre-piece. Peregrines are frequent.

It is an hour's stroll along the cliff-top right round the headland and an hour back, but you may want to spend days here.

Fetlar
A small island, only 5 miles by 4 (8 × 6km) but with far too many exciting birds for a day-trip. There are only one or two cottages with accommodation, so be prepared! A road runs from the landing west to east, and north of it is an RSPB reserve with breeding red-necked phalarope, whimbrel and many sea-birds. There is an enormous Arctic tern colony on the moorland. Loch of Funzie is the easiest place to see phalaropes, right by the roadside! Red-throated divers breed at this loch and Arctic terns feed over it all day.

A late evening walk along the cliffs at Lambhoga will show you thousands of Manx shearwaters and storm petrels all of which have breeding sites here. Check all

of the little bays for otters and seals.

Away from the reserves, birds, animals and flowers are found all over the islands. Shetland ponies in small, wandering groups, foal alongside mother, are irresistibly photogenic, with most on Unst. Otters are more numerous here than in almost any other part of Britain, and pop up among the seaweed in the bays from time to time. Grey and common seals are found on most suitable haul-out areas.

Flowers are something special in Shetland where the tiny meadows are rarely touched by chemicals. Acres of buttercups, spring squill, thrift, red campion and kidney vetch colour the landscape in summer. Cliffs and roadside cuttings are true rock-gardens, glowing with wild thyme and scores of other semi-alpine plants. The Keen of Hamar on Unst, a belt of serpentine rock, is notable for its display of rare alpines at low altitude.

May to July are the best months to visit the islands but many birds have left for the open ocean by the end of July.

A large colony of gannets occupies the cliffs of Hermaness on Unst at the northern tip of Britain

BIRD OBSERVATORIES

There are a few places in Europe where bird migration is so obvious that no one can fail to notice the birds as they pass to and fro. The narrow waters of the Bosphorus at Istanbul, or the Straits of Gibraltar are places where thousands of large birds, storks, raptors and millions of small birds make the crossing en route between Europe, Asia and Africa.

The first proper observatory was founded by Heinrich Gatke on the island of Heligoland on the North Sea coast of Germany in the latter half of the nineteenth century.

In Britain Ronald Lockley founded the first observatory on the Welsh island of Skokholm in 1933. Since that time some have come and gone, but there are a dozen or more sited round the coastline at the present time.

Some are on isolated islands, primarily because these offer landfall to tired migrants on their long sea-crossings, thereby concentrating a wave of birds at that point. Islands often have lighthouses, which attract night-flying migrants in poor weather, and next day birds are easy to count on small isolated spots in the middle of the sea.

Every day during the migration season, which runs from March to November with just a short mid-summer lull, the observatory area is checked with great care to note what birds are present, and a daily log is written up, noting directions of migration and the numbers and species involved. Patterns of bird movement, often associated with particular weather conditions, become apparent after years of collecting such records and notes.

It is now generally known from studies with high-powered radar that birds migrate at considerable heights often on a broad front, especially at night. Birds navigate by the stars and moon at night, the sun during the day, and also apparently use the earth's magnetic field.

Natural geographical features play a part in migration by channelling birds along obvious routes during the day time, hence observatories placed on exposed headlands such as Dungeness receive birds funnelled along the coast. Birds also learn by experience to use geographical features such as coastlines, hills and river valleys which lie along their main route.

Localities like Dungeness must seem like home to exhausted migrants arriving over the waves, and needing to make a landfall. Some birds may lose all their energy just short of the beach, and in sudden poor weather small birds such as pipits and larks may be seen to flop into the sea and drown.

Migration is a risk undertaken by a species to provide optimum conditions for the survival of the greatest number, which is why many of our birds migrate to Africa during our cold winter. Similarly in late autumn birds arrive in Britain escaping from the rigours of the high Arctic and the extremes of northern European winters. Fieldfares and redwings from Scandinavia, blackbirds, song thrushes and starlings from Russia, geese from Greenland, Lapland and Iceland, waders from the whole northern tundra flock to these islands, still warm by comparison.

The bird-ringer places a tiny aluminium ring numbered for identification purposes around the bird's leg. Also on the ring is a return address, in Britain, the National History Museum, London. This fixes two points in the bird's life; the place and date that it was originally marked and the locality and date at which it was subsequently found.

It stands to reason that in many parts of the world, especially in Africa, few people who find a dead ringed bird are likely to be in a position to write and return the ring, although one man in the Cameroons who shot a ringed cuckoo walked 185 miles (300km) to a mission station to do precisely that. The recovery rate of many small birds, such as swallow, is under one per cent, so ringing is a long-term study with results measured over many years.

Most observatories use one or more Heligoland traps, originally designed by Gatke in the nineteenth century and consisting of a long funnel-shaped tube of wire netting over a line of bushes, tapering to a 'catching box' after ten or fifteen yards (9–13m).

More portable are mist nets, fine nylon nets limited to about seven feet (2m) in height and made of horizontal panels. Placed in gaps in hedges and scrub at observatories the nets catch birds flitting across the gaps. The birds fall into a loose pocket of netting, from which they are quickly extracted. Most birds are released within two or three minutes, when they quickly re-locate and return to their migration route.

Large 'falls' of migrants can be very exciting as one walks round the 'trapping area' at dawn to see what the winds have brought to the observatory.

Ringers undergo a long and extensive training during their spare time at bird observatories before being allowed a national licence to catch and ring birds alone. Recoveries are normally notified to the individual ringer who will derive intense satisfaction from learning that 'his' or 'her' starling or swallow has turned up in Moscow or in Cape Town.

Dungeness
Bird Observatory
KENT

Stones dumped by the sea make Dungeness the largest shingle ridge in Europe, at present extending to nearly 9,000 acres (3,642ha).

Its prominent position on the south-east Channel coast, means its forte is migration; and not only bird migration, as insects migrate through Dungeness, sometimes in huge quantity. For the botanist it is an intriguing place with many shingle plants found nowhere else in Britain.

Butterflies pass inland, in huge numbers in good years, Red Admirals, Peacocks, Painted Ladies and Clouded Yellows – Silver-Y Moths appear later in the autumn.

'Dunge' as it is known to its many 'afficionados' is not a pretty place. Unusual, almost freakish in its landscape certainly, but not pretty, and man, as usual, has actively contributed to its desecration. It now boasts many shingle extraction units, the old lighthouse and a modern, slim-line version, dozens of shacks, chalets and derelict huts and to crown them all, a huge nuclear-power station. Despite all this it is a wonderful place to get the 'feel' of a dramatic bird movement in full swing.

The bird observatory is at one end of the coastguards' cottages behind the old lighthouse. The RSPB has a separate reserve of 1,962 acres (792ha) south of the Lydd road, past the ARC Pits on the left, and the entrance to the RSPB reserve is on the right. The latter has gravel pits too, and the 'Open Pits' – the only known natural lakes on shingle in the world. Large colonies of common and Sandwich terns and black-headed gulls nest on islands in the pits in summer, together with a few pairs of common and herring gulls. Roseate terns and Mediterranean gulls sometimes nest in the colonies but are difficult to pick out.

The observatory is surrounded by a moated area full of bushes and Heligoland traps are sited here to catch migrant passerines moving up from the coast.

Access is largely unrestricted and it is a simple matter to walk around the trapping area and north-west for a mile to the RSPB reserve.

Spring migration starts in mid-March and continues to mid-May and good days are those with south-east winds and a drizzly start to the morning, when hundreds of small birds will be flitting up from the beach, from bush to bush, frantically searching for food. Spring produces all the common warblers, chats and flycatchers, along with regular ring ouzels and firecrests. Rarer wrynecks, icterine warblers, shrikes and hoopoes sometimes put in an appearance.

Many birds use the power station fence as a perch, and several pairs of black redstarts actually breed in the power station.

Sea-bird and wildfowl passage in spring involves countless birds: thousands of common and velvet scoter flying east in long lines low over the sea. Large numbers of waders, especially godwits, also moving east; brent geese, divers, ducks, and substantial numbers of gulls, terns and skuas; and a concentrated easterly movement of pomarine skuas in early May.

The best place for sea-watching is half a mile west along the shore overlooking the warm-water outfall of the power station known as 'The Patch'. This attracts many unusual seabirds, with little gull, black tern, roseate terns and Mediterranean gulls frequent.

Little terns breed on the coastal shingle.

Autumn passage is impressive, with steady movements of many species of land-birds south out of Britain and sea-birds coasting west. By October large numbers of diurnal migrants will be arriving each morning from Europe for the winter: skylarks, pipits, starlings, finches, robins, thrushes, crows and even blue tits will pass inland over the huge shingle ridge. All the pits hold *flocks* of diving duck in winter, including smew, completing the year's pattern of migration.

Address of Site/Warden

Bird Observatory Warden:
Dungeness Bird Observatory,
Romney Marsh,
Kent TN29 9NA
RSPB Reserve
Warden:
Boulderwall Farm,
Dungeness Road,
Lydd,
Kent TN29 9NP

Highlights and Features

Huge area shingle. Many flooded gravel-pits. Large breeding colonies of terns on the pits. Large numbers of wildfowl in winter. Intense migration spring and autumn. Many rare birds. Superb shingle flora. Excellent for migrant insects.

Facilities

Full residential Bird Observatory which welcomes day-visitors. RSPB reserve has four hides overlooking pits. RSPB area open 0900–2100 or sunset if earlier, all days except Tuesday. Rest of area of open access.

Photo Tips

Summer provides good views of breeding terns and gulls.
Use long telephoto lenses from the hides.
Migrant birds may be photographed in the hand with standard lens and small flashgun at the Observatory, provided they are not in the middle of a 'rush' of migrants.

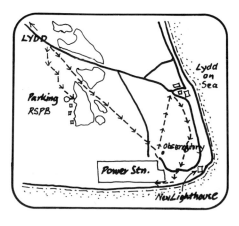

Sandwich Bay Bird Observatory

KENT

Address of Site/Warden

Hon Warden:
2 Old Downs Farm,
Guildford Road,
Sandwich Bay,
Kent CT13 9PF

Highlights and Features

Large area dunes and fresh marshland at mouth of the River Stour. Good for birds all year with many migrants, especially in autumn. Many waders and ducks in winter when good for birds of prey. Superb dune flora but whole area is private. Some flowers can be photographed from the paths.

Facilities

Hostel type accommodation at observatory. Otherwise access at all times to area.

Photo Tips

Wide-angle zoom lens for flowers in summer. Birds in hand at observatory using small flashgun and close up lenses.

The little tern is one of our rarest breeding sea-birds with small colonies on beaches, particularly vulnerable to disturbance

The quiet, ancient Cinque Port of Sandwich, now hemmed in a little by power stations, hoverports and industrial estates, nonetheless retains its open aspect to the sea where the coast is dominated by a series of sand-dune ridges. Golf courses run the length of these, with famous clubs such as the Royal St George's and Prince's. Behind the dunes are fresh marshlands, while out on the foreshore and looking a little out of place, is the Sandwich Bay Estate.

The marshlands have built up along the estuary of the River Stour which runs through Sandwich and into the sea at Pegwell Bay, where the sea retreats for a mile at low tide and races in as fast as a walking man when the tide begins to flow.

To get to the observatory, drive along Sandown Road through an expensive toll-gate (£2 – 1987) to the coast road, or walk the mile from Sandwich. The observatory is housed in Old Downs Farm on the right, a hundred yards (91m) beyond the toll-gate.

Sandwich is good for birds throughout the year and also has a superb dune flora and a great variety of insects; because it is so close to the Continent many birds and insects are migrants making their first landfall in Britain. It is worth looking carefully along hedges around farm fields and along the coastal strip around the estate for migrants. There are three Heligoland traps with bushes near the observatory, but a lot of the ringing is carried out with mist nets.

The road turns north around the estate and continues to Prince's Golf Club. Examine the foreshore for waders at low tide and seabirds as the tide returns – seabirds are not really prominent because of the bay's sheltered position, but many terns pass through, and thirty pairs of little terns breed locally. Kittiwakes pass up and down the shore regularly from their breeding cliffs at Dover.

Continue north along the beach past the pines which are also worth checking for migrants, and on to Shellness at the mouth of the Stour. This is a good spot for waders in winter, with large flocks of curlew, godwits, dunlin and redshank which roost on the farm fields at high tide, so the best time to arrive is on a rising tide which will push them off the flats and give good views.

Autumn wader passage is much heavier than in the spring and a good variety of species pass through, including fresh-marsh species such as wood sandpiper. Winter can be bleak on the foreshore but usually produces snow buntings and twite, with short-eared owl and hen harrier hunting the marshland.

The same walk in summer is a botanist's paradise, famous for its rare flowers, so much so that full time protection is provided to prevent collection by the unscrupulous. Star attraction is the lizard orchid which flowers in July in some numbers on the golf-course dunes; there are usually a few near the road. Several other orchids are found in the shell-rich dune slacks including green-veined, bee, man, pyramidal and many marsh orchids and marsh helleborines.

Clove-scented broomrape is a nationally rare, but here widespread flower, and this is also found in the dunes; sea-holly grows in less disturbed dune areas.

Good butterfly years bring thousands of Red Admirals, Painted Ladies, Clouded Yellows and many migrant hawk moths.

As the summer declines to late autumn the largest bird movements of the year take place, with enormous numbers of inbound thrushes, starlings, robins, goldcrests, larks, finches, lapwings and wood-pigeons all escaping the Continental winter; cool, misty October mornings mean hedges at Sandwich Bay alive with birds.

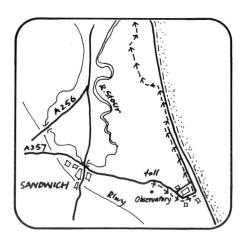

Portland
Bird Observatory
DORSET

The Isle of Portland juts out some six miles (9km) into the English Channel with the observatory at the southern tip, boasting mass migrations of common species and enviable lists of rare migrants.

Portland is not actually an island because it is connected to the mainland by the continuation of the Chesil Beach, a massive 18-mile (29km) shingle bank built up over centuries by the longshore drift current down-Channel.

Enclosed by Chesil Beach is a long brackish lake, The Fleet, which is often excellent for birds including waders, terns and wintering brent geese. Portland Harbour on the eastern side has a wide variety of winter wildfowl including Slavonian and black-necked grebes.

Wildlife Walk

That first sight of Portland, approaching down the A354 from Weymouth across the narrow shingle ridge joining the Isle to the mainland, makes you wonder, just a little, if you might not have made a mistake!

Drive past the naval base, HMS *Achilles*, on past the prison and the Borstal, through Fortuneswell and down past some enormous limestone quarries. Apart from a few bronchitic sparrows where is the wildlife, one wonders? Keep going. Two miles further on at Southwell the landscape changes to more rural farm fields, and anywhere south of the village may hold migrants at peak times.

The road continues past the bird observatory which is the 'Old Lighthouse' painted white.

Portland Bill is not terribly picturesque. Behind the observatory are about a hundred rather motley beach huts; there is a pub – The Pulpit – and a large car-park, two or three beach-style cafés and the new red-and-white painted lighthouse; the MOD has a naval shore battery.

March to May and August to November are the best times here. The Bill's position right out in the Channel means that sea-watching can be very good, with large-scale movements on many days past the point. Walk up from the car-park to the obelisk in front of the lighthouse and watch from there. Alternatively there are huge limestone boulders filled with fossils, from old quarrying activities, which provide shelter.

Divers, gannets and duck, especially scoter, move east in March, followed by Manx shearwaters, terns and skuas, especially pomarine skuas, right into May. The return movement in autumn contains a wider variety but is less predictable.

Walk a hundred yards west to the MOD fence to see the small colony of guillemots, razorbills and a few puffins fly in and out of their ledges on the west cliffs (the ledges themselves are not visible). Fulmars also breed, and kittiwakes – thousands of which pass through on migration.

Return to the bird observatory and look in the bushes in its garden for migrants, then walk back up the road some 200 yards (183m) and carefully scrutinise a two-acre clump of bramble, elder and blackthorn on the left. Stretching back for half a mile behind this is a criss-cross pattern of drystone walls with thick thorn hedges. All these bushes in a treeless landscape are good for migrants.

Good days produce hundreds of warblers, flycatchers, chats, wagtails and many rare stragglers.

From early October huge movements of diurnal migrants such as skylark, chaffinch and starling occur daily.

Portland is superb for watching migration – but try and ignore the scenery.

Address of Site/Warden

Warden:
Portland Bird Observatory,
Old Lower Light,
Portland Bill,
Dorset DT5 2JT

Highlights and Features

Rather barren limestone headland with cliffs for small colonies breeding sea-birds, and hedgerows full of migrants in spring and autumn. Very good sea-watching site.

Facilities

Comfortable self-catering bird observatory. Day visitors welcome.

Photo Tips

Most birds too distant. Birds in the hand at observatory with close up lenses and small flashgun.

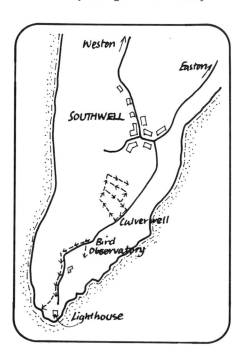

Bird observatories catch birds, and ring them, for migration studies. Here a blue tit is being extracted from a mist net

Bardsey Island Bird Observatory

GWYNEDD

Address of Site/Warden

Bookings Secretary,
Mrs H. Bond,
21a Gestridge Road,
Kingsteignton,
Newton Abbot,
Devon

Highlights and Features

Small island just off the
Lleyn Peninsula in
North Wales.
Small sea-bird colonies plus
about 3,000 pairs Manx
shearwaters.
Excellent spring and autumn
migration site with
thousands of birds attracted
to the lighthouse. Good for
sea-watching with birds
passing down the Irish Sea.
Breeding chough.

Facilities

Full residential bird
observatory, mainly self-
catering. Bookings on weekly
basis only. Two sea-watching
hides.

Photo Tips

In spring long telephoto
lenses will provide pictures
of breeding sea-birds.
Migrants trapped during the
ringing programme may be
photographed in the hand.
Use a small flashgun. This
also useful for night
expeditions to catch Manx
shearwaters as they return
to their burrows. Don't forget
a strong torch.

Bardsey lies off the tip of the Lleyn Peninsula in North Wales. The *Mary K* leaves from the little port of Pwllheli, starting at 0830 on Saturday – this is often delayed by the weather conditions because the tide runs through the narrow Bardsey Sound at a rate of nine knots. The journey may take three hours. Accommodation on the island is self-catering, on a weekly basis, Saturday to Saturday. Bardsey is not a day trip, and may be cut off by bad weather.

The island is now owned by the Observatory Trust and is some 444 acres (180ha) in extent. It splits into two distinct areas, with the larger northern sector being separated from the lighthouse headland by 'The Narrows'. It is quite possible to walk round the island in a morning, having covered perhaps four miles (6.4km) in all, and there are two sea-watching hides provided at the northern and southern tips of the island. Bardsey is but a little hump of rock from the mainland, hidden behind its huge eastern cliffs; beyond lies a patchwork of tiny banked meadows sloping westwards to the sea.

The roadway from the harbour leads the 600 yards (548m) to the observatory at Cristin, with its old grey farmhouses now renovated for visitors. Dominating the northern quarter is the rock- and bracken-covered 'Mountain' rising to 550 feet (167m), under the north-west corner of which lie the ruined tower and buildings of the Augustinian Abbey of St Mary, which is at least 700 years old.

Best times to visit are April to June for spring migrants and breeding birds, while August through to November can bring big falls of night-flying migrants. Grey seals are numerous and may be seen offshore at all times – on summer nights their wails and groans mingle with the eerie cries of Manx shearwaters flying to their colonies on the rocky slopes; some 3–4,000 pairs of shearwaters are thought to breed.

The eastern cliffs support small colonies of fulmar, shag, razorbill, guillemot and a few kittiwakes. Razorbills nest mainly among the boulder piles along the shore below the Mountain, which is best scaled from the western road. The rocky summit area is used every year by ravens and a pair of kestrels for nesting, while on the eastern side large rock screes have built

up inhabited by wheatears, rock and meadow pipits, jackdaws and many shearwaters. Two or three pairs of little owls may sometimes be seen hunting here.

The steep eastern side of the Mountain is dangerous and any scrambling must be done with care.

The star breeding bird is the chough, and there are six or seven pairs. They are a delight to watch 'tumbling' on the up-currents of air over the eastern hills.

Bird migration is one of the main attractions of Bardsey, although night-time expeditions to catch and ring incoming shearwaters high on the Mountain must compete closely for excitement.

Bardsey Light on the southern tip of the island attracts migrants on the west-coast flyway, and was for many years the scourge of tired birds which, confused by the powerful lamp in the dark, crashed to their deaths in hundreds. A 'false light' has now been built nearby and many birds simply rest in the floodlit bushes.

On nights of full cloud cover and mist the Bardsey Light can certainly become an 'attraction', when thousands of warblers, chats, thrushes and even waders may fly round in dizzying circles.

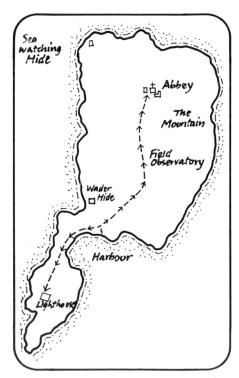

Gibraltar Point
Bird Observatory
LINCOLNSHIRE

South of the bustling resort of Skegness lies Gibraltar Point, a national nature reserve of 1,063 acres (430ha) with the bird observatory as its focus. Here the coast, turns abruptly west into the Wash – this whole coastline is relatively unspoiled. Access is from Skegness sea-front south on a minor road.

Gibraltar Point is continually gaining land because the drift current erodes the coastal strip to the north and deposits the sand and soil material on the point.

From the Field Station, walk eastwards on the track across the old marsh along the nature trail. Looking back towards Skegness, the two ancient major sand-dune ridges – East and West Dunes – are strikingly obvious.

From here the entire coastline may be viewed, to the far-off chalk cliffs of Hunstanton in Norfolk, 15 miles (24km) away.

The dunes are stable and lime-rich, and the vegetation is correspondingly varied, with carpets of colourful flowers all summer: bird's-foot trefoil, viper's bug-loss, cowslip and ladies' bedstraw com-pete with various orchids for attention.

Sea-buckthorn is now the dominant shrub over large areas of the reserve, which is unfortunate as it stifles a proper dune sward. However, it provides shelter for the migrant birds which flood through Gibraltar Point in huge numbers.

After crossing the old marsh, turn north along the East Dune track for half a mile; Mill Hill observation platform is to the right on a high point and provides views over most of the area. A path runs west across the dune ridges for a mile to the Mere and an observation hide. A substantial fresh-marsh around the Mere brings many extra birds and animals. The Centre is one mile south of the Mere along West Dune path.

Summer breeding birds are typical of dune and marsh areas and include a large colony of little terns at the Spit, which is therefore out of bounds in summer so as to avoid disturbance.

The Spit is used from August to April by waders roosting at high tide.

Fresh-water waders occur around the Mere with wood sandpiper, greenshank and spotted redshank frequent.

Sea-watching is best outside the breed-ing season from near the Spit. Apart from the many waders and wildfowl 'coasting'

along the shore, scores of skuas, terns, gannets and kittiwakes pass through. Autumn brings high numbers when a north-east wind is blowing and sooty shearwaters and pomarine skuas often occur.

Night-flying passerine migrants occur in large 'falls' when cloud and rain combine with an east wind. Hundreds of warblers, chats, flycatchers and rarer species such as firecrest, barred warbler, bluethroat and icterine warbler may arrive.

By October enormous numbers of winter birds begin to arrive: huge flocks of blackbirds, and fieldfares feeding on the buckthorn berries; goldcrests, finches, tits, pipits, larks and starlings pass through in some numbers; great grey shrikes appear in ones and twos in November.

Winter brings large flocks of common waders on the Wash with brent geese and a few Bewick's swans. Predators, includ-ing hen harrier, merlin and short-eared owl frequently hunt the bird flocks. The beach and dune slacks gather large groups of snow buntings, larks, twite and pipits searching for food.

Rabbits are present in large numbers on the dunes and inevitably attract fox and stoat as predators. Common seals can usually be seen offshore from the large colonies of the Wash.

Address of Site/Warden

Warden:
Gibraltar Point Field Station,
Skegness,
Lincolnshire PE24 4SU

Highlights and Features

Headland at mouth of Wash – dunes and marshland. Large concentrations of migrant birds. Excellent dune flora.

Facilities

Basic self-catering accommodation. Visitor centre open daily May to October and weekends in winter. One public hide. Access at all times to area.

Photo Tips

Dune flora photographed with wide-angle zoom 28–80 lens. Birds in hand at observatory with small flashgun.

The dunlin is our commonest shore-line wader, although only a few pairs nest on our northern moorlands

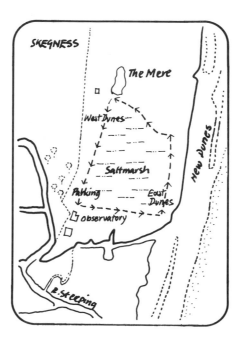

Spurn Point Bird Observatory

YORKSHIRE

Address of Site/Warden

Warden:
Spurn Nature Reserve,
Kilnsea,
Patrington,
Hull,
Humberside HE12 0UG
(please send sae)

Highlights and Features

Narrow sand and shingle spit projecting some 3 miles (4.8km) into the Humber estuary. Superb migration watch point, at all seasons. Excellent for winter estuarine birds.

Facilities

Full bird observatory including basic self-catering accommodation. Information centre and sea-watching hide for residents. Access to area at all times.

Photo Tips

Birds in the hand at the observatory – use small flashgun and close-up lenses.

A major success story is the rise in gull populations. Gulls adapt well to man, and herring gulls now breed all round the coast

Spurn Bird Observatory was the first to be established on mainland Britain, in 1946. It is the premier site on the Humber estuary; it is also a superb place for a constant traffic of bird migration. The nature reserve belongs to the Yorkshire Wildlife Trust.

Spurn is a narrow shingle and sand spit projecting some three miles (4.8km) into the Humber estuary. Access is from the B1445 at Easington. A car-park, the bird observatory and the information centre are a mile past the Crown and Anchor Inn at Kilnsea. A charge is made for use of the road to the Point, where there is another car-park.

Beacon Lane Pond and Easington Lagoons north of Kilnsea are good for waders throughout the year but especially at migration periods; walk north along Beacon Lane – spotted redshank, little stint and curlew sandpiper are regular.

The hedges around Kilnsea are easiest to work for migrants, although most birds shelter in the dense thickets of sea buckthorn which is found along much of the spit. The spit itself really starts at the observatory, and runs in a curve south-west on the longshore drift – at the Narrow Neck a mile south along the shore it is just 40 yards (36m) wide. Halfway towards the Point is Chalk Bank, where chalk was laid down to stem a tide breakthrough in the nineteenth century; a small salt-marsh exists here. South of Chalk Bank concrete blocks and a 'tank ditch' are relics of wartime fears.

The Point itself is scenically a bit of a mess, with dilapidated military buildings scattered about. The lifeboat and its cottages make up a small community, the lifeboat having the only full-time crew in Britain, such are the problems of dense boat traffic in the shifting sands of the Humber. Point Camp is closed to the public, but is used by members of the observatory for bird-ringing among the dense vegetation of bramble, elder and sea buckthorn.

Many day-trippers come in crowds in summer, somewhat of a problem for birders when trying to locate rare birds among the picnickers – the power-cable poles along the road give good perching sites for birds of prey.

Summer breeding birds are few, with common species such as linnet, white-throat, willow warbler and sedge warbler in the scrub.

Spring passage starts in March with winter flocks moving out to the Continent. Lapwings, starlings, chaffinches and many others pass south or south-east. East winds bring falls of migrants in April and May with chats, flycatchers and warblers; wryneck, bluethroat and the occasional shrike occur most years.

Large tern movements, including black terns in full summer plumage also occur in spring.

Return passage starts in July, but late August onwards sees a peak with waves of birds arriving in good migration conditions. Easterly winds seem to produce most passerines, while sea-birds arrive on more northerly breezes.

Sooty shearwaters, pomarine and long-tailed skuas regularly pass among the more common species, with up to a hundred little gulls in a day. Little auks appear late in the autumn.

Passerines occur in large numbers from late August with many rare birds caught up in the rush. By October large flocks of redwing and fieldfare appear, feeding on the sea buckthorn berries, while long-eared owls can often be flushed from the thickets. Great grey shrikes arrive at the same time, with four or five often visible.

Harriers, merlin and short-eared owl hunt the winter wader roosts, especially at Chalk Bank, while large flocks of snow and lapland buntings are found on the shore. Red-throated divers occur in some numbers throughout the winter.

Spurn provides a lifetime's work for anyone interested in bird migration.

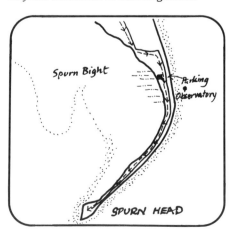

South Walney
Bird Observatory
CUMBRIA

Walney Island is the largest of a group of seven islands at the tip of the Furness Peninsula. The Cumbria Trust for Nature Conservation has owned a 230-acre (93ha) reserve at the southern tip since 1963.

South Walney has been one of Britain's bird observatories since 1965, projecting into the western end of Morecambe Bay and sharing the bay's large population of winter waders and wildfowl.

Throughout the breeding season from late April till late July the reserve is taken over by the gulls. Huge colonies of herring and lesser black-backed gulls have built up over the years until (1987) some 40,000 pairs occurred, roughly split between the species. Wherever you walk in South Walney, you cannot escape the attentions of the adults as they raise and protect their families.

Spring and autumn see many passerine migrants moving along the coast. Large numbers of warblers, especially willow warblers, with goldcrests, redstarts and flycatchers, work their way from bush to bush, whilst overhead meadow pipits, wagtails and wheatears go by on most days.

Rare birds are often caught up in the rush of the commoner species. Sea-bird and wader migration can be spectacular, especially after westerly gales.

Wildlife Walk

To reach Walney is complicated. Take the bridge onto Walney Island, through the Barrow dockyards, turn left at the traffic lights; bear right down Ocean Road, and left beyond a small area of marsh between two housing estates after half a mile. Drive on through Biggar village for four miles (6.4km), across 'fresh' marshland with the shore on the left. At the 'South End Caravan Park only' sign, take the right-hand pot-holed track to the reserve car-park which you should reach in 1½ miles.

Walk the few yards to the brick-built observation hide on a large sand-dune. The view from here extends for half a mile over the grassy dunes. In summer, thousands of herring and lesser black-backed gulls with scurrying chicks of all sizes are right in front of the hide.

Leave the hide and take the 'red post' trail along the inner shoreline track. Some sort of old hat is a good idea, as you will be dive-bombed by the gulls. They will break away before 'clipping you round the ear' – unlike Shetland skuas – but they have other ways of venting their displeasure upon you. Fluffy gull chicks will trot beside you down the road.

Eider ducks, with their tiny chicks clustered tightly round them, can be seen closely on the shore. These protective measures save them from the gulls, which take the chicks of most other birds on the reserve including any unguarded chicks and the eggs of their own species. Eiders have flourished here; up to a thousand pairs breed regularly.

The trail continues past old flooded gravel pits, where great black-backed gulls breed on the shingle ridges.

The disturbed gravel near the inner point has a fine selection of flowers in late summer, attracting thousands of migrant butterflies, including Small Tortoiseshell, Painted Lady and Red Admiral.

Pier Hide at the inner point overlooks the spit with colonies of common, Arctic, Sandwich and little terns in summer.

Autumn and winter high tides force thousands of waders onto the spit to roost.

Walk south from Pier Hide, round behind the lighthouse for some 400 yards (365m) to Groyne Hide. This, and Sea Hide, a full mile west along the beach, are excellent places to watch sea-birds.

From Sea Hide the car-park lies just two hundred yards over the dunes – follow the blue tipped posts.

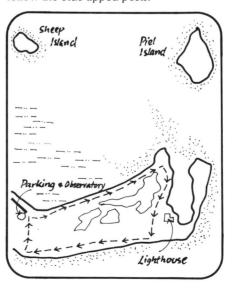

91

Address of Site/Warden

Warden,
South Walney Nature Reserve,
Coastguard Cottages,
Barrow-in-Furness,
Cumbria LA14 3YQ

Highlights and Features

Large area of dunes at tip Walney Island projecting into Morecambe Bay. Huge mixed gullery of herring and lesser black-backed gulls. Many waders in winter. Large colony eiders. Good for migrants spring and autumn.

Facilities

Day visitors require permit obtainable from hut at reserve. Information centre. Residential accommodation available. Several hides and nature trail. Open 1000–1700 daily except Mondays. September–April till 1600.

Photo Tips

During summer the gulls may be photographed easily using a 200mm lens. Eider and ducklings in the same way. Birds in the hand at the observatory – bring small flashgun and close-up lenses.

At South Walney some 40,000 pairs of mixed herring and lesser black-backed gulls raise their chicks

Fair Isle
Bird Observatory

SHETLAND

Address of Site/Warden

Fair Isle Lodge and
Bird Observatory,
Fair Isle,
Shetland ZE2 9JU

Highlights and Features

Isolated rocky island famous
for rare bird migrants in
spring and autumn. Good
sea-bird colonies in summer
with new gannetry. Good for
seals and whales offshore.

Facilities

Full residential bird
observatory. Not a day trip.
Access by LoganAir or boat.

Photo Tips

Good sea-bird pictures in
summer. Use 200mm or
300mm lens.
Birds in hand at observatory.
Small flashgun useful and
close-up lenses.

*Like the gulls, the fulmar
has expanded
dramatically this century,
and is now found on all
coastlines*

Midway between Orkney and Shetland, lies the tiny island of Fair Isle. Just three miles long (4.8km) and some 1,890 acres (765ha) in extent, it boasts a magnificent coastline with cliffs of Old Red Sandstone rising to 500 feet (152m) on the north and west sides.

The island is cut in two by Hill Dyke, with the northern half rising to Ward Hill at 712 feet (217m). This is mainly heather moorland, with peat and stony hillsides, though south of the Dyke the soil is better and well cultivated. It is here that the present island people live, in a small crofting community surrounded by sheep pasture and small fields of crops.

The bird observatory was established in 1948, and the island handed over to the National Trust for Scotland in 1954.

Its prime wildlife attraction is its birds, although grey seals breed in a number of the more secluded coves.

Fair Isle's unique position in the path of wind-drifted bird migrants was first recognised by Eagle Clark in the early years of the century. In addition to its migrants, exceptional colonies of sea-birds occur in summer.

Boats to Fair Isle leave twice a week from Grutness in Shetland, from May to September; and then Tuesdays only for the rest of the year – the cost (1987) is 40p. This trip is not for poor sailors! Quicker and more expensive are the LoganAir flights from Tingwall, which operate three times weekly from May to October, and twice weekly thereafter. Fair Isle is not a day trip. Accommodation is available at the bird observatory and, by observatory standards, is positively luxurious. It is sited at South Haven, on the eastern side of the island and dominated by Sheep Rock which lies like an enormous arm-chair to the south across the bay.

It is possible to walk round the island in a morning. In summer the breeding sea-birds are well spread round the cliffs with large auk and kittiwake colonies on the western side; puffins, guillemots, kittiwakes and fulmars all exceed 10,000 birds, with smaller numbers of razorbills. Shags and black guillemots breed on the lower rocks and there is a new colony of nearly 300 pairs of gannets, with similar small colonies of storm petrels.

The northern moorland has nearly 100 pairs of both great and Arctic skuas. Significantly, long-tailed skuas sometimes spend weeks in the colonies in summer – perhaps they may breed one day, too.

Only a few other species nest, including wheatear, oystercatcher, ringed plover and snipe.

Migration and rare 'overshoots' are the seasonal attractions which draw people up to Fair Isle. May is the best spring month, while September to November is best for autumn rarities.

Migrants arrive on Fair Isle if pushed off their normal track (overshoot) by strong winds – westerly winds from the Atlantic may mean no birds at all, but any type of easterly wind produces great excitement. Scour the island then, looking carefully through every ditch, clump of bracken, and all the tiny inlets (geos) on the coast.

Large numbers of common migrants arrive, especially in autumn – huge flocks of fieldfare, redwing, chats and warblers, and even woodcock.

The list of rare birds which turn up annually, is mouth-watering to the enthusiast – Siberian rubythroat, citrine wagtail and pechora pipits are examples.

Sea-watching is often neglected in the search for rare Russian passerines, but can be most rewarding, with large numbers of shearwaters, including sooty, passing offshore.

Whale-watching may produce porpoise and common dolphin, but larger species are more often seen from the LoganAir plane as it skims the waters from Shetland.

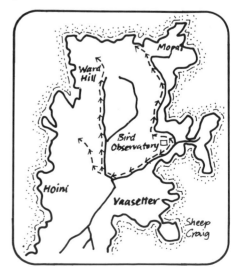

BIBLIOGRAPHY

It is clear that a book such as this draws upon many sources of information, including many other specialist reference books. The author would like to acknowledge the use of the following books which were consulted during the preparation of this book.

AA Guide Discovering Britain
(Drive Publications)

ALLABY, M.
O/S Outdoor Handbook (Macmillan)

ANGEL, H.
The Natural History of Britain and Ireland
(Michael Joseph)

BUTTERFIELD, I.
The High Mountains of Britain and Ireland
(Diadem Press)

CONDRY, W.
Snowdonia (David & Charles)

CRAMP, S., BOURNE, W., SAUNDERS, D.
The Seabirds of Britain and Ireland
(Collins)

CRAWFORD, P.
The Living Isles (BBC Publications)

DARLING, F., BOYD, W.
The Highlands and Islands (Collins)

DOUGALL, R., AXELL, H.
Birdwatch Round Britain (Collins/Harvill)

DURMAN, R. (ed)
Bird Observatories in Britain and Ireland
(T. & A. D. Poyser)

GOODERS, J.
Where to Watch Birds (André Deutsch)

The New Where to Watch Birds
(André Deutsch)

A Day in the Country (André Deutsch)

HAMMOND, N. (ed)
RSPB Nature Reserves (RSPB)

HEWER, H.
British Seals (Collins)

HOLLIDAY, F. (ed)
Wildlife of Scotland (Macmillan)

HOLM, J.
Squirrels (Whittet Books)

HYWEL-DAVIES, J., THOM, V.
Macmillan's Guide to Britain's Nature Reserves (Macmillan)

LLOYD, C.
Birdwatching on Estuaries, Coast and Sea
(Severn House)

LOCKLEY, R. M.
Grey Seal, Common Seal
(André Deutsch)

MANNING, S. A.
Nature in East Anglia
(World's Work Ltd, The Windmill Press)

McNALLY, L.
Wild Highlands (J. M. Dent)

MILES, D.
The Pembrokeshire Coast National Park
(David & Charles)

MILES, H.
The Track of the Wild Otter
(Hamish Hamilton)

MORRIS, P. (ed)
Natural History of the British Isles
(Country Life Books)

NETHERSOLE-THOMPSON, D.
Highland Birds
(Highlands & Islands Development Board)

NORMAN, D., TUCKER, V.
Where to Watch Birds in Devon and Cornwall (Croom Helm)

OGILVIE, M. A.
Wild Geese (T. & A. D. Poyser)

PARSLOW, J. (ed)
Birdwatchers' Britain (Pan Books/OS)

PRATER, A. J.
Estuary Birds of Britain and Ireland
(T. & A. D. Poyser)

RACKHAM, O.
The History of the Countryside
(J. M. Dent)

RATCLIFFE, D. (ed)
A Nature Conservation Review (NCC)

Highland Flora
(Highlands & Islands Development Board)

READER'S DIGEST
Havens of the Wild
(Reader's Digest Association)

REDMAN, N., HARRAP, S.
Birdwatching in Britain. A Site by Site Guide
(Christopher Helm)

RICHMOND, K.
A Regional Guide to the Birds of Scotland
(Constable)

SUMMERHAYES, V. S.
Wild Orchids of Britain (Collins)

TATE, P.
East Anglia and its Birds (Witherby)

THOM, V.
Birds in Scotland (T. & A. D. Poyser)

TUBBS, C. R.
The New Forest. A Natural History
(Collins)

WHITEHEAD, G. K.
The Deer of Great Britain and Ireland
(Routledge and Kegan Paul)

WILSON, K., GILBERT, R.
Classic Walks (Diadem Press)

The Big Walks (Diadem Press)

And many other leaflets and local guides published by the National Trust, The National Trust for Scotland, Tourist Boards, The Countryside Commission, The Forestry Commission, the National Parks, the Nature Conservancy Council, the County Naturalist and Wildlife Trusts, the Nature Conservancy Council and the local authorities.

USEFUL ADDRESSES

Addresses of individual sites, where an address exists, are given in the main text. Addresses below are of the main national organisations. Local county trust addresses are not given but may be obtained easily from the RSNC or your local library.

British Trust for Nature Conservation
36 St Mary's Street
Wallingford
Oxfordshire OX10 0EU

Council for Protection of Rural England
4 Hobart Place
London SW1 0HY

Country Landowners Association
16 Belgrave Square
London SW1X 8PQ

Countryside Commission
John Dower House
Crescent Place
Cheltenham
Gloucester GL50 3RA

The Field Studies Council
9 Devereux Court
The Strand
London WC2R 3JR
(*runs nine residential centres and one day centre.*)

Forestry Commission Headquarters
231 Corstorphine Road
Edinburgh EH12 7AT

Her Majesty's Stationery Office
49 High Holborn
London WC1Y 6HB

National Trust (Headquarters)
42 Queen Anne's Gate
London SW1H 9AS
(*there are 15 Regional Offices, details from Headquarters.*)

National Trust for Scotland (Headquarters)
Chief Ranger
'Suntrap'
43 Gogarbank
Edinburgh EH12 9BY
(*there are 3 Regional Offices.*)

Nature Conservancy Council (Headquarters)
Northminster House
Peterborough PE1 1UA
(*there are 15 Regional Offices.*)

Ramblers Association
1/5 Wandsworth Road
London SW8 2LJ

Royal Society for Nature Conservation
The Green
Nettleham
Lincolnshire LN2 2NR
(*RSNC co-ordinates County Wildlife Trusts.*)

Royal Society for the Protection of Birds
The Lodge
Sandy
Bedfordshire SG19 2DL
(*there are 10 Regional Offices.*)

Scottish Wildlife Trust
25 Johnston Terrace
Edinburgh EH1 2NH

Wildfowl Trust
Slimbridge
Gloucester GL2 7BT

Woodland Trust
Westgate
Grantham
Lincolnshire NG31 6LL

Youth Hostels Association
Trevelyan House
St Albans
Hertfordshire AL1 2DY

INDEX OF PLACES

This index is of localities described in detail in the text. All other place names in the text, of which there are many, are for direction and location.

INDEX OF SPECIES

189